KANT'S METAPHYSICAL EXPOSITION OF THE CONCEPT OF SPACE

An Exegetical and Critical Study

KANT'S METAPHYSICAL EXPOSITION OF THE CONCEPT OF SPACE

An Exegetical and Critical Study

by

Kumudranjan Goswami

MAHA BODHI BOOK AGENCY
4A, Bankim Chatterjee Street
Kolkata - 700 073, INDIA

KANT'S METAPHYSICAL EXPOSITION OF THE CONCEPT OF SPACE

An Exegetical and Critical Study

By

Kumudranjan Goswami

First Published : 2017

Published by :
D.L.S. Jayawardana
MAHA BODHI BOOK AGENCY
4-A, Bankim Chatterjee Street
Kolkata-700 073 (India)
Phone : 9831077368
Email : mahabodhibookagency@hotmail.com

Printed by :
Sagarika Press, Kolkata-700 009

ISBN : 978-93-84721-94-7

Price : ₹ 1,450.00

Dedicated

to the memory of my mother,
Menakasundari Goswami

TABLE OF CONTENTS

PREFACE

Kant's view that space is a pure intuition is generally regarded nowadays as untenable. The arguments for this view are re-arranged, in the second edition of his first *Critique*, under two Expositions. The present work, as its name suggests, is concerned only with the four arguments pertaining to his Metaphysical Exposition of the Concept of Space. Its primary objective is to show that these arguments, and with them the view that space is a pure intuition, are eminently susceptible of defence.

Many of the objections to the arguments in question are based on interpretations that do not survive examination, as will be seen. The arguments are indeed brief, so much so that some are led to doubt whether they are arguments at all. (Cf. J. E. Wilkerson, *Kant's Critique of Pure Reason*, Oxford University Press, 1976, Part II, 2, *passim.*) Yet these arguments have made the Transcendental Aesthetic famous, and have not altogether lost their appeal. So it is necessary to study them in depth. I have accordingly engaged in a good deal of exegetical analysis. Care has been taken of course to maintain readability and clarity of line throughout. As regards the strictly philosophical issues raised by Kant's arguments, these have been sorted out and discussed, within the framework of an ordered exposition, as far as possible with reference to contemporary controversies.

The general course of our inquiry may be described as follows :

In the First Chapter, which is Introductory, it is argued that Kant's view that space is a pure intuition, as expounded in the Metaphysical Exposition, is not itself a transcendental-idealist view, but is rather an austerely interpretable one about how space is originally apprehended. As such the view concerns the nature and status of the idea of space. The chapter explains the importance of this view, examines the two dichotomies of 'a priori and empirical', and 'intuition and concept', which are presupposed in the Kantian formulation of this view, and indicates the distinctive features of the present Study.

In the Second Chapter, Kant's first argument on space, which is concerned mainly with the apriority of the idea of space, is taken up for discussion. Some objections to this argument hinge on the interpretation according to which the idea of space is for Kant a priori in the sense that it exists in the mind in conscious form temporally prior to experience and even sensation. The chapter examines this interpretation in detail and discards it.

In Chapter Three a logical interpretation of Kant's first argument is presented, and some further objections to the argument are assessed. It is shown, by way of meeting the objections, that the argument, although it refers to sensations, does not depend *essentially* on a particular theory of sensation, and that it is not at all trivial. Its historico-philosophical perspective is examined and re-examined, and it becomes amply clear that it embodies an attempt to expose the circularity involved in the sort of space-empiricism that goes with the reductionist-cum-relational analysis of the idea of space. Kant's rejection of such analysis serves to highlight the unique status in experience of the idea of space, a status in virtue of which the idea has a strong claim to be regarded as 'a priori'.

Chapter Four is an excursus demanded by the discussion that precedes. The problem considered here is whether sensible objects are individuated necessarily and sufficiently by their qualitative differences or by their spatio-temporal locations. It is argued that the Kantian stance in this regard, which consists in the adoption of the second alternative, is justified. It then becomes clear that Kant's first argument on space has a great deal of inherent strength.

In the Fifth Chapter Kant's first argument is critically appraised in the light of some contemporary criticisms and views. Concluding comments on the argument are added.

In Chapter Six Kant's second argument on space comes up for discussion. This argument has the same aim as its predecessor ; but it is explicitly an argument from necessity. Some put upon it an interpretation on the basis of which they complain that its conclusion is a glaring *non secuitur*. The interpretation is examined and rejected, and the case for a detailed study of the argument is established. The structure of the argument is then analysed.

In Chapter Seven the first part of Kant's proof in the second argument (that is, the first clause of the sentence containing 'Kant's Proof' in this argument, as Kemp Smith calls it) comes under scrutiny. It is argued that this part of the proof is, as it stands, elliptical, and that when the relevant additional words are inserted, it comes to express the relative necessity of the idea of space, that is, its necessity relatively to the possibility of objective experience. The chapter thus provides an occasion for a critical comparison of Kant's view with the views of some contemporary philosophers on the issue of whether non-spatial objective experience is conceivable.

The Eighth Chapter is devoted to an examination of the second part of Kant's proof in the second argument. Its *prima facie* difficulties are stated clearly, and an attempt is made to find a way out of them. The heart of this chapter is an elucidation of the oft-ignored Kantian view regarding the role of the idea of empty space in experience.

In Chapter Nine Kant's third argument on space is up for discussion. It is intended to establish that space (or rather, the original idea of space) is not a discursive concept, but a (pure) intuition. A common objection to it is that the whole space is in fact not an object of intuition. The objection owes its plausibility to a misunderstanding as to the Kantian notion of intuition. A discussion is made to show that there are indeed good reasons to believe that the idea of the whole space is originally intuitive in the sense of being a conceptually non-mediated representation of an individual. The question then arises whether or not there is a sense in which Kant admits a general concept of spaces (or spatiality). Some contend that Kant neither does nor can admit such a concept. It is shown that the contention cannot be upheld. A not unrelated contention is that, on the Kantian view of the pure intuition of space, the parts of space are only the products of conceptual distortion of the prior given whole. The contention is rejected after due examination.

In Chapter Ten the difficulties besetting the view of the unity of space—a view that finds expression in Kant's third argument—are examined. Some of the difficulties are answered, and it is argued that if the others persist, Kant's view that the idea of space is primarily intuitive is not in jeopardy.

The Eleventh Chapter contains a discussion of some miscellaneous points of interest concerning Kant's third argument.

Kant's fourth argument on space is discussed in Chapters Twelve and Thirteen. This argument, too, is intended to establish that the original idea of space is an intuition. Kant's observation in the argument that space is represented as an 'infinite *given*' whole has been criticized sometimes on the ground that an infinite whole cannot be given, and sometimes on the ground that space is in fact not infinite. I argue that the former criticism is largely due to a misunderstanding of Kant's view and that the latter criticism is based on a cosmological theory that is in fact not accepted by all scientists.

In the Final Chapter some post-Kantian alternatives to the Kantian view that the idea of space is originally an a priori intuition are examined, and the examination reveals that they are all vitiated by circularity. This serves to provide some additional confirmation of Kant's critique of space-empiricism. A contemporary criticism of Kant's theory of pure intuition from an evolutionary point of view (or more specifically, from the point of view of linguistic relativity) is also considered, and it is found that its basis is weak. The chapter ends with a concluding note on the present Study.

A note on references will now be in order.

Immanuel Kant : Samtliche Werke, hg. v. O. Buek, P. Gedan, W. Kinkel, J. H. v. Kirchmann, K. Vorlander, F. M. Schiele, Th. Valentiner [Felix Meiner, Leipzig] is the only edition of Kant's collected works that I could constantly keep beside myself. The *Kritik der reinen Vernunft* is cited from Band I, 1922, of this edition. All quotations in English from the *Critique of Pure Reason* are, unless otherwise noted, from the Kemp Smith translation, Macmillan, London, 1963. These titles are abbreviated as *Kritik* and *Critique* respectively. References to the first and the second edition of the work in question are, as usual, indicated by 'A . . .' and 'B . . .' .

As the word 'a priori' has to be used every now and again, it is not underlined except where an emphasis is required or in quotations from others in whose writings it originally appears in italic type.

For convenience of cross-reference, a particular numerical system is used in presenting the divisions of chapters. Thus '1.1' signifies the first section in the first chapter, '1.2' signifies the second section in the first chapter, and so on. Then, again, e.g. '4.1.1' signifies the first subsection under the first section in the fourth chapter, '4.1.2' signifies the second sub-section under the first section in the fourth chapter, and so on. '4.1.2.1', for example, signifies a still further sub-division under '4.1.2'.

* * * *

This work was submitted as my Ph.D. dissertation. The thesis was prepared under the supervision of the Late Professor Sibajiban Bhattacharya. The work was written about forty years ago, and only very slight revisions are made to make the manuscript ready for publication.

I am greatly indebted to Dr J. N. Mohanty under whose inspiring guidance I began my study of the Kantian philosophy of space. He was on the staff of the department of philosophy of Calcutta University. He was then Acharyya B. N. Seal Professor of Philosophy at Calcutta University. He read parts of my thesis in manuscript and made many a valuable suggestions, which I subsequently followed.

Dr Herbert Herring, a noted Kantion scholar, Kindly helped me to some useful information and sent me relevant extracts from certain books not easily available in India.

I am thankful to Sri Arun Kumar Mukherjee of Jadavpur University for placing at my disposal more than a dozen of books when I most needed then.

My obligations to previous writers are many and have been acknowledged as far as possible in the proper places. If I have dared to criticise my superiors, it is because I believe criticism of this sort is an indirect way of paying homage.

I am thankful to my wife, Smt. Rina Mukhopadhyay, for her marvelous help of various kinds towards the publication of this book. I assign the copyright of the book to her.

Finally I am grateful to D.L.S. Jayawardana, Maha Bodhi Book Agency for his interest in the publication of this book.

Kumudranjan Goswami

Merlin Daffodil
10/7, Jyangra Ghosh Para
Flat No. 1A
Kolkata-700 059
August 30, 2017

CHAPTER ONE

INTRODUCTORY

1.1 Kant's Problem in the Metaphysical Exposition of the Concept of Space

In § 2 of the Transcendental Aesthetic, 'Metaphysical Exposition of this Concept' [the Concept of Space], Kant's problem is not metaphysical in the sense of being ontological; it is rather epistemological. His object here is to determine not what space ultimately is, but how it is originally represented, that is, apprehended. He concludes this Exposition by saying, 'Consequently, the original representation of space is an *a priori* intuition . . .[1] Clearly, this has an epistemological sense.

Gottfried Martin, however, denies that Kant has anything to do in the Aesthetic with the problems of how space is represented.[2] He calls attention to Kant's own formulation of his problem in the introductory paragraph of the Metaphysical Exposition under consideration. Kant there writes :

> What then, are space and time ? Are they real beings ? Or are they only determinations or relations of real things, but yet such as would belong to things in themselves even if they were not intuited, or again such as only attach to the form of intuition and hence to the subjective nature of our mind, apart from which these predicates could not be ascribed to anything whatsoever ?[3]

After quoting this passage, Martin observes :

> The question that Kant is asking is not how we can know space and time, but quite simply what space and time are. This question has an ontological sense, and there is a close connection between the way it is asked and the methods of

> ontological enquiry that had been worked out in the course of history . . .[4]

Doubtless the question that Kant is asking in the passage quoted by Martin 'has an ontological sense' ; but it is strange that Martin has failed to see that this is not the only question with which Kant is concerned in the Aesthetic and that this is not the question at all with which he is concerned in the Metaphysical Exposition under examination. The sentence in Kant's *Critique* occurring immediately after those quoted by Martin is in this connexion crucially important. It runs : 'In order to obtain light upon these questions, let us first give an exposition of the concept of space.' (B 38) Analysis of this sentence brings out in full relief the following facts :

(1) Kant proposes to proceed step by step and to begin with space.

(2) He thinks that the general question of what space is, of which the specific forms are those that he calls 'these questions', is such that light upon it cannot be obtained until after 'an exposition of the concept of space'.

(3) Accordingly he thinks that he should 'first give' an exposition of this concept.

(4) It is clear from (2) and (3) that, prior to the question of what space is, there is for Kant the question of what the concept of space is. If, in order to ascertain what the concept of space is, an 'exposition' is required, this indicates surely that even here Kant finds a problem. It is the problem of making clear the exact nature and status of the concept (representation or idea)[5] of space. This problem is undeniably epistemological, not ontological.

Pace Martin, then, it has to be said, as D. P. Dryer puts it, that 'Kant's primary concern is not to answer the question, What is space ? In discussing space, he is primarily concerned to find how we are conscious of space.'[6]

In the second edition of the *Critique* Kant distinguishes clearly between the Expositions of the Concept of Space and the 'Conclusions' from those Expositions.[7] In the Expositions he investigates the nature of the representation of space, and in the Conclusions he addresses himself to the question of what space is, offering answers to those specific 'questions' into which he, in the passage quoted by Martin, has subdivided that general question. This affords re-enforcing evidence for the view that the ontological question or questions referred to by Martin are not for Kant primary in that the answer or answers thereto have to await the answer to the epistemological question of how space is represented, or as Martin puts it, 'how we can know space'.

Martin seems to have been influenced by the fact that the passage quoted by him occurs in the introductory paragraph of Kant's Metaphysical Exposition of the Concept of Space. This fact raises the presumption that Kant's real problem even in this Exposition is what space is, and not how it is represented. But the subheading 'Metaphysical Exposition of this Concept' is inserted by Kant in the second edition and in a place where it is liable to be, and has been, misleading : it would be better placed a little lower down, that is, after the sentence examined above, namely, 'In order to obtain light upon these questions, let us first give an exposition of the concept of space.'

It may be objected that a rigid demarcation is not feasible between a treatment of the problem of how space is represented and a treatment of the problem of what space is. This objection may hold if the latter problem is construed in a very broad sense. But in the present context this problem is to be construed in the narrower sense of the problem whether space is a real thing or a determination of real things or a subjective form of human sensibility, that is, whether it is absolutely real or ultimately ideal. It is this narrower, more specific, ontological problem regarding space that, according to Kant, depends for its consideration on an antecedent discussion of the epistemological problem of how space is originally represented.

In his early writings on space till 1768, Kant was mainly preoccupied with the ontological side of the problem of space.[8] In his famous essay of 1768 entitled 'On the First Ground of the Distinction of the Regions in Space' Kant, although he is still concerned with ontological issues, comes to reflect no less remarkably also on the nature and status of the concept of space.[9] Garnett, however, observes : 'Now, in 1769, he [Kant] faced squarely for the first time the problem, how is space apprehended ? Euler raised this question for him.'[10] Whether or not this view of Garnett's, which is admittedly conjectural,[11] is accepted, one can hardly afford to miss the fact that in 1770, in Kant's *Inaugural Dissertation,* his method of approach towards the problem of space officially takes a new and decisive turn : this method consists in proceeding from reflections on how space is originally represented to those on what space ultimately is.[12]

In the Metaphysical Exposition of the Concept of Space Kant seeks to establish that the original representation of space is a priori and intuitive. The Transcendental Exposition of this Concept has also the same aim, the difference between the two Expositions being mainly procedural in that the first is direct and the second indirect : it is argued in the second that unless the representation of space is an a priori intuition the synthetic a priori propositions about space contained in geometry cannot be explained. The reason why the first Exposition is selected for study in this work is the belief that it is the more important of the two. This belief now needs to be justified.

1.2 Importance of the Metaphysical Exposition

The special importance of the Metaphysical Exposition lies in the fact that it contains the *basic* arguments for Kant's view that the representation of space is originally a pure intuition. The argument for the same view contained in the Transcendental Exposition cannot be regarded as basic for the following reasons :

The Transcendental Exposition claims to provide a justification for the view that the representation of space is a pure intuition by reference to the possibility (i.e. possibility of explanation)[13] of the synthetic a priori judgments of geometry. But later on Kant himself implicitly claims to have provided an explanation of the very possibility of such synthetic a priori judgments by reference to his theory that the representation of space is a pure intuition.[14] So there seems to be a vicious circle. As Lovejoy says : '. . . since the supposed fact that Space is a *reine Anschauung* is inferred from the fact that geometrical theorems are necessary *a priori*, the necessity and apriority of those theorems cannot in turn depend upon a proof that Space is a *reine Anschauung*.'[15] This difficulty can be resolved, but only by resorting to an appeal to the Metaphysical Exposition. Kant's general problem in the *Critique* is :

How are synthetic judgments a priori pessible ? A special form of this problem is how synthetic judgments are a priori possible in geometry. Since Kant's solution to this problem is in terms of his theory of the pure intuition of space, it is necessary that an independent justification of this theory should be given that does not refer at all to geometrical judgments. This independent or antecedent justification is in fact provided by Kant in the Metaphysical Exposition. The Transcendental Exposition can have an appropriate place in the *Critique*–appropriate in the sense of not generating a circle–if its role is reinterpreted in the light of its relation to the Metaphysical Exposition. This reinterpretation is offered by Paton by saying : '. . . the Transcendental Exposition shows that the theory [of the a priori intuition of space] thus independently established [in the Metaphysical Expesition] is alone able to account for the possibility of geometrical science.'[16] It is in this sense indeed that the Metaphysical Exposition is *basic.*

It should not be supposed that Kant has devised the Metaphysical Exposition from the motive of providing a basis for subsequent explanation of the possibility of the synthetic a priori propositions of geometry. Such a supposition is operative indeed behind the view that has nowadays become a commonplace, namely, that if the propositions of geometry be not synthetic a priori, Kant's theory of the pure intuition of space is devoid of significance and that, as modern research has shown, the propositions of geometry, whether pure or applied, are not synthetic a priori. Now leaving aside the question of the actual status of geometrical propositions–since consideration of this does not fall within the purview of this work–, it must be pointed out that there is nothing in the psychological-biographical history of Kant to license the inference that his theory of pure intuition of space was propounded with the ulterior motive of justifying the supposedly synthetic a priori status of geometrical propositions. Garnett has persuasively argued that Kant's discovery that the representation of space is a pure intuition antedates his discovery that geometrical propositions are synthetic a priori, and Garnett's arguments need not be repeated.[17] Moreover, the theory of the pure intuition of space has an importance not only for the Kantian investigation concerning the foundation of geometry, but also for Kant's metaphysics of experience that is developed through the *Critique.*

There can be no doubt, then, that the Metaphysical Exposition of the Concept of Space has considerable importance.

What falls to be considered next is whether the two distinctions in terms of which Kant's arguments in the Metaphysical Exposition are presented are clear, these being the distinction between a priori and empirical, and that between intuition and concept. He seeks to establish first that the representation (idea) of space is not an empirical concept and, secondly, that this idea is not a discursive concept ; and thus he concludes that it is an a priori intuition. So what needs to be considered first is his distinction between an a priori and an empirical concept. It is worth pointing out here that the Kantian expression 'the concept of space' may be taken in the wide sense of 'the representation or idea of space' ; but even if the word 'concept' in it is taken in the narrower sense of a discursive concept, no real conflict occurs with the view that the idea of space is originally an intuition ; for it will be explained in the proper contexts[18] that the *general* concept of spaces, to which Kant has referred in the Aesthetic, or the singular concept of space, to which he has referred in the *Inaugural Dissertation*, is ultimately derivative upon the pure intuition of space.

1.3 The Distinction between an A Priori and an Empirical Concept

The word 'a priori', which is primarily an adverb, may secondarily be used as an adjective, although Kant himself prefers the word 'pure' for the adjectival use. The adjectival use of 'a priori' is nowadays common, so much so that little will be gained by demurring to it.

'A priori' is defined by Kant in terms of independence of experience.[19] So an a priori concept is for him one that is non-empirical.[20] When he maintains, with regard to a concept, that it is a priori, he means that an 'empirical deduction' of it is not germane. 'For in view of . . . [its] subsequent employment, which has to be entirely independent of experience, . . . [it] must be in a position to show a certificate of birth quite other than that of descent from experiences.'[21] This is to say that it is not open to the standard empirical explanation.

The standard empirical explanation of a concept is only too well known. Briefly, the method consists in reducing a given concept, if it is complex, to simple concepts, and then explaining the simple concepts in terms of comparison, reflection, and abstraction exercized upon items of a certain sort presented in experience. Sensible items of a certain sort are compared with one another ; their common features are reflected on ; and their differing features are abstracted from ;[22] and in this way a simple empirical concept is obtained.[23] So an empirical account of a concept is in the main reductionist and/or analytic. In so far as it is analytic, it presupposes that items of a certain sort are presented in experience as numerically different from one another ; for otherwise an analysis of what they have and what they have not in common would not be possible.

Now, for Kant, the reductionist-cum-analytic method of empirical explanation cannot be applied to the concept of space. According to one of his arguments to be considered later,[24] an attempted reduction of this concept to that of an order of externality and adjacency, or even an order of coexistence, among objects of experience is ultimately vitiated by circularity.

The circularity objection is Kant's patent objection to any attempted empirical deduction (explanation) of what he regards as an a priori concept.[25] An a priori concept is for him non-empirical in the precise sense that it cannot be 'deduced' from (that is, explained in terms of) experience without circularity.[26] One test of the validity of Kant's claim that the idea of space is a priori is, then, to see whether the available major empiricist accounts of this idea are all vitiated by circularity. This is indeed one of the important tasks to be accomplished in this work.

For Kant, an a priori concept can be distinguished from an empirical one by another test also, namely, the test of necessity. A necessary concept is defined by him as one that yields an 'objective ground of the possibility of experience'.[27] A scheme of objective experience in which such a concept has not work to do is not possible, that is, capable of being rendered intelligible to ourselves. Any empirical concept like that of redness is eliminable in the sense that objective experience in which such a concept has not work to do is still possible, that is, intelligible. The concept of space is necessary in the sense that the scheme of a non-spatial objective experience is not possible, that is, intelligible. That this is Kant's actual view will become clear later on.[28] [The expression 'objective experience' will also be defined, and it will, moreover, be explained that in addition to logical possibility or impossibility consisting in consistency or inconsistency, Kant recognizes another dimension of possibility or impossibility according to which a logically possible state of affairs is impossible if it cannot be rendered intelligible to ourselves.[29]]

It has sometimes been argued that the necessary-contingent distinction throws no light whatever on Kant's a priori-empirical distinction of concepts. Thus George Schrader argues that Kant's necessary a priori concepts are also contingent; 'The categories are contingent though necessary, or put less confusingly, they are contingently necessary. They are necessary as conditions of the possibility of experience and contingent in that they are valid only for possible experience'.[30] What is said here of the categories might also be said of the concept of space. That Schrader's contention is based on a misunderstanding of Kant has been shown in detail by J. J. Economos.[31] For the present purpose, the following criticism of Schrader may suffice.

Schrader fails to distinguish between the origin and the use, or better, between the status and the application, of a concept. That certain concepts yield conditions of the possibility of experience is a matter that concerns their *status,* whereas that they are valid only for possible experience is a matter that concerns their *application.* The distinction between status and application is Kantian and is important. It ' is Kantian', because the pre-Kantian rationalists and empiricists did not recognize this distinction; for them, application or use is determined automatically by status or origin. The rationalists who were convinced of the a priori origin of certain concepts, thought themselves thereby justified in applying them transcendentally (i.e. beyond the limits of possible experience), whereas the empiricists, who were convinced of the empirical origin of concepts, thought themselves justified in denying their transcendental application. For Kant, however, the question whether a concept is empirical or a priori is not equivalent to the question whether its application is only empirical or can be transcendental.[32] The distinction between status and application 'is important', because the necessary-contingent distinction has, for Kant, a relevance only to the determination of status, and not to the determination of sphere of application. Not all concepts applicable to objects of experience have for Kant the same status. Of concepts applicable to objects of experience and so not distinguishable in respect of status by their application, some differ from the others in respect of their status by the necessity-contingency mark : those are to be called a priori which have to be recognized as necessary, and those are to be called empirical which have to be recognized as contingent. In this investigation, contingency is not to be recognized, as Schrader suggests, from the fact of application within experience ; it is rather to be decided by the test of dispensability without nullifying the whole conception of objective experience. Of concepts having application within experience, those are to be recognized as necessary which cannot be dispensed with, and those as contingent which can be dispensed with, without nullifying the conception of objective experience. So Schrader's criticism that necessary a priori concepts are also contingent is misdirected.

Before leaving this topic of the Kantian meaning of the word 'a priori', a note on the ambiguity that has come to attach to this word in the Kantian usage will be of some importance. A distinction may be made, after Strawson, between the 'relatively austere interpretation' or sense and 'the transcendental idealist interpretation' or sense of 'a priori' in the Kantian usage.[33] Upon the former interpretation, 'a priori' means 'absolutely independent of experience', that is, non-empirical, while upon the latter interpretation 'a priori' (or its variant 'pure') is connected with 'in us'.[34] Kant usually expresses his view, in the case of space, by saying that space is a priori. This statement is ambiguous ; for it may mean either that the idea of space is a priori (i.e. non-empirical) or that space itself is a priori (i.e. transcendentally ideal). A similar ambiguity is involved in the phrase sometimes used to describe the Kantian view, namely, 'the apriority of space'. It may mean either the apriority (i.e. non-empiricality) of the idea of space or the apriority (i.e. transcendental ideality) of space itself. Now it has to be explained why it is important to see the ambiguity pointed out above. In the Metaphysical Exposition of the Concept of Space, Kant is concerned with the apriority of space only in the austere sense of the non-empiricality of the idea of space and not in the transcendental idealist sense of the formality-cum-ideality (or 'subjectivity', as it is sometimes called) of space. [Kant is concerned with the latter in his 'Conclusions'.[35]] Much confusion can be avoided by constantly keeping in view this distinction throughout this work.

For a great many of the criticisms actually urged against Kant are vitiated by neglect of this distinction.[36] Even Strawson virtually dismisses Kant's arguments in the Metaphysical Exposition on the ground that they fail to establish the a priori character of space in the sense of the transcendental idealist interpretation of 'a priori'.[37] After what has already been said above, it need hardly be stated that this and similar criticisms of Kant are quite beside the point.

1.4 The Distinction between Intuition and Concept

Before considering the Kantian distinction between intuition and concept, some preliminary observations will be in order. Intuition for Kant is a mode of representation, and so when he sometimes speaks of space as an intuition, he really means that it is an object of intuition (that is, as Broad prefers to call it, an intuitum[38]). It is not quite correct to suppose, as some do,[39] that Kant does not distinguish between an intuition *representing* something and that something *being* an intuition itself. Although Kant often speaks of space itself as being an intuition, he, when careful, says that 'the . . . representation of space is an . . . intuition',[40] where clearly an intuition is a *representing*. Similarly, when he denies that space is originally a concept, he means that it is not originally a conceptum, that is, as he himself otherwise puts it, that it is 'never . . . known through mere concepts'.[41] The word 'concept' is ambiguous between conceiving and conceptum, and it would be well if 'conception' could be reserved for the former and 'concept' for the latter. Since, however, this is not actually done–for Kemp Smith in his translation uses 'concept' indifferently for both and Meiklejohn does the same with 'conception'[42] –there is ultimately no choice between 'concept' and 'conception' as a term for conceptual representation : the risk of ambiguity is there in either case.

To come now to the Kantian distinction between an intuition and a concept. Some commentators–notably Paton and Hintikka–rely mainly on Kant's *Logic* in holding that for Kant an intuition is 'a singular representation', whereas a concept is 'a general representation'.[43] According to this view, a concept is a representation of what is common to several things, that is, of a general character (or universal),[44] whereas an intuition is a singular or non-general representation in the sense of a representation of an individual (or, as it is sometimes called, a particular). Evidently, an intuition and a concept are here distinguished by reference to their objects, and not by reference to their cognitive relations to objects. In the *Critique*, however, Kant usually distinguishes between them by reference not to their objects, but to the way in which they are related to objects.[45] Thus at A 320 = B 377 he says that an intuition 'relates immediately to the object', whereas a concept 'refers to it mediately by means of a feature which several things may have in common'. It is clear here that for Kant a concept and an intuition may relate to *the same object*, the distinction between them lying in the way in which they relate to it : a concept relates to it mediately, and an intuition immediately. And there can be no doubt that 'the object' here means an *individual* (or a particular); for a concept is mediately related not to a common character (i.e. a universal), but to an individual. Moreover, at A 656-57 = B 683-84 Kant says : '. . . a concept, containing only what is common to different things, . . . cannot . . . be directly related to an individual [*ein Individuum*]' The word 'individual' here shows that the object to which a concept cannot relate directly (immediately), and so relates only mediately by means of common marks, is an individual.

In case of a conflict between Kant's *Logic* and his *Critique*, greater importance is to be attached to the latter surely, since the *Logic* 'was, after all, compiled not by Kant himself but by Jäsche, from a lot of Kant's scribbled notes'.[46] If what Kant says in the *Critique* is kept in view, then not every singular representation– that is, not every representation of an individual–can be regarded as an intuition, but only an immediate representation of an individual can be so regarded. At this point the dispute that has arisen between Hintikka and Parsons over the characterization of what the former calls 'the Kantian intuition' may be taken up for consideration. The point at issue here is whether any representation of an individual or an immediate representation thereof is an intuition in the Kantian sense.

Hintikka opts for the first interpretation, maintaining that any singular (i.e. individual or particular) representation is an intuition in the Kantian sense. He expresses this in a more contemporary way by saying that

> Kant's notion of intuition is not very far from what we would call a singular term. An intuition is for Kant a 'representation' – we would perhaps rather say a symbol– which refers to an individual object or which is used *as if* it would refer to one.[47]

This view–that any singular term is a linguistic analogue for a Kantian intuition–is certainly not acceptable. A definite description is a singular term that refers, or purports to refer, to an individual object ; but there are reasons to believe that such a term is not the linguistic expression of a Kantian intuition, but of a concept. These reasons are clearly and succinctly stated by Robert Howell as follows :

> Contrary to Hintikka, I think it reasonably clear that definite descriptions are for Kant concepts, not intuitions. To apply a definite description surely is to subsume an object under a concept, and Kant says at B 67 and elsewhere that intuitions occur independently of any act of thinking (subsuming individuals under concepts). In the Transcendental Ideal (A 571 = B 599ff ; . . .) the description 'the highest reality' is said to give a *concept* of reason. (See also A 178/B 221, where Kant seems to claim that grounds for supposing a priori that the x such that Fx exists do not give an intuition of the object.) Finally, Kant in a letter speaks of the description 'the black man' as giving a concept which involves the synthetic unity usual to such concepts. (Kant to Beck, 3 July 1792, and Beck to Kant, 31 May 1792, . . . both translated in Zweig . . .)[48]

The thought of an individual on the basis of a definite description is surely a conceptual representation of an individual, and such a representation, simply because it purports to refer to an individual, cannot be construed as a Kantian intuition. Intuitions for Kant, Wilfrid Sellars says,

> differ from other conceptual representations of individuals by

not being mediated by general concepts in the way in which, for example,

> the individual which is perfectly round is mediated by the general concept of being perfectly round. A more positive clue is provided by Kant's reference to intuitions as 'in immediate relation to an object' (A 68 ; B 93).[49]

The above discussion makes it plain that Parsons[50] is right in emphasizing, against Hintikka, the immediacy of a Kantian intuition over and above its individuality (or singularity). Kant himself does this at A 320 = B 376-77 of the *Critique*, where he says that an intuition 'relates immediately to the object and is single'.

The question, however, arises : What does the *immediacy* of an intuition mean for Kant ? This question has bearing on the dispute between Hintikka and Parsons. Hintikka is led to interpret the immediacy of an intuition in what he calls the 'minimal sense' in which it consists in not being mediated by the representation of a general character, and he maintains that in this sense (a negative sense) immediacy is just 'a corollary of singularity'.[51] Parsons, however, takes the view that the immediacy of an intuition 'means that the object of an intuition is in some way directly present to the mind, as in perception . . .'[52] In other words, it consists, according to him, in the sensible givenness of the object of intuition. We think, however, that Hintikka is right in his account of the meaning of 'immediacy', although he is wrong in supposing that on this account immediacy is just a corollary of singularity.

The following are the main reasons for thinking that Hintikka's account of the meaning of 'immediacy' is correct, while Parsons' is not :

(i) Hintikka's account is borne out by certain passages in the *Critique*. At A 320 = B 376-77 and A 656-57 = B 683-84 Kant takes the mediacy of a concept to consist in its being mediated by the representation of what is common to several things. This suggests by implication that the immediacy of an intuition consists in its not being mediated by the representation of a common feature or general character.

(ii) At B 146 Kant observes : '. . . as the Aesthetic has shown, the only intuition possible to us is sensible'. This shows that Parsons' account of immediacy in terms of sensible givenness presupposes the results of the Transcendental Aesthetic. As G. Brittan puts it : 'On Parsons' interpretation, that (human) intuition is sensible follows as a trivial consequence of the definition and should not require the extended argument of the Aesthetic'.[53] It may be pointed out in this connexion that when at A 19 Kant himself interprets the immediacy of a human intuition in terms of the givenness of its object and the latter in terms of sensible affection, he does this in anticipation of the results to be established by arguments in the Aesthetic.

(iii) Although Kant denies the possibility of intellectual intuition for man, he does not regard the notion of such an intuition as self-contradictory. Now intellectual intuition *qua* intuition is of course immediate, and its immediacy certainly does not consist in the sensible givenness of the object, or, in other words, in the sensible passivity-cum-receptivity of the representation. It just consists in not being *mediated* by the representation of a general character.

The all-important question to be considered now is whether the immediacy of an intuition, which consists in not being mediated by the representation of a general character, is just a corollary of its singularity. Hintikka thinks that it is, but his view is untenable, as can be shown in two steps :

Step (I) : 'This is a singular representation' means the same as 'This is the representation of an individual'.

Step (II) : 'This is the representation of an individual' does not imply 'This representation is not mediated by that of a general character'.

To obviate misunderstanding, some explanatory words on these two steps are necessary. As regards Step (I), Hintikka himself, and many others including Paton, do interpret the phrase 'singular representation' in the sense of 'representation of an individual', and this interpretation can be supported by reference to, e.g. A 713-14 = B 741-42 of the *Critique*, where the singularity of an intuition is said by implication to consist in its individuality.[54] As regards Step (II), it may be said that since a definite description is a singular term and a singular term is a linguistic expression of an individual representation (that is, representation of at least and at most one object), the representation on the basis of a definite description is surely an individual representation which is nevertheless mediate, that is, not immediate in Hintikka's minimal sense of not being mediated by the representation of a general character or characters.

So although Hintikka's interpretation of the meaning of 'immediacy' is accurate, his view that immediacy is just a corollary of singularity (individuality) is not.

Of course, if the expression 'singular representation' be construed in a broad enough sense, the situation alters. In a broad sense 'general representation' may be construed so as to mean what is meant by 'representation of a general character, or representation mediated by that of a general character', and correspondingly 'singular representation' may be construed so as to mean what is meant by 'representation which is neither that of a general character nor mediated by that of a general character'. In this broad sense of 'singular representation', the immediate representation of an individual is of course just a singular representation, so that immediacy turns out to be a corollary of singularity. But, as has been pointed out above, Hintikka and many others construe 'singularity', not in this broad sense, but in the narrower sense of mere individuality, and singularity *qua* individuality does not imply immediacy.

For the sake of clarity, and to obviate misunderstanding, it will, then, be better to characterise the Kantian intuition, in conformity to what Kant himself sometimes does, as an immediate representation of an individual (construing the immediacy of it in the minimal sense explained above).

As regards the representation of space, Kant's contention that it is an intuition and not a concept rests on the claim that it is an immediate representation of an individual. Appreciation of this point requires some understanding of the meaning of the word 'space' (*spatium, der Raum*) in Kant's contemporary usage. Ivor Leclere, in his article 'The Meaning of "Space" in Kant', shows that

> . . . in the seventeenth century the term *spatium* meant *locus*, place . . .
>
> It was this meaning of the word *spatium* which was accepted by Leibniz and right through to the pre-critical Kant. This was also the meaning current in England, . . .
>
> . . . Kant understood 'space', *der Raum*, as meaning the totality of the order of places–the late seventeenth century meaning of the word, as it had been made clear by Leibniz.[55]

'Space', then, primarily means for Kant the totality of places, or as he says, the whole of spaces. The question is whether space in this sense is just a class of spaces or an individual whole of them, and whether or not it is represented mediately through the general concept of spaces. Kant's contention is, as will be clear in the proper contexts,[56] that space is not a class *under* which spaces are subsumed, but rather an individual *in* which these are contained, and that the idea of it is not mediated by 'the general concept of spaces', because this concept, along with the intuitions of spaces from which it presumably derives, presupposes the idea of space (i.e. of the whole unlimited space). The implication of the contention is that the primary representation of space, in the sense in question, is singular (that is, of an individual) and immediate (that is, non-mediated), and so is an intuition. This raises a number of issues, which will of course be brought under discussion in this work.

1.5 Relation of This Study to Previous Researches

Although much has already been written before by eminent scholars on Kant's Metaphysical Exposition of the Concept of Space, it has by no means become an exhausted topic of research. In older commentaries (such as those written by Vaihinger, Prichard, and Kemp Smith)[57] the Kantian doctrine of the apriority of the idea of space has been interpreted in a psychological-temporal sense. Paton has taken great pains to show that this interpretation is mistaken; but the interpretation holds its sway despite his criticism. Thus Garnett, through a critique of Paton's view, has sought to re-establish the interpretation. Since Garnett's is the fullest study in English of the Kantian doctrine that space is a pure intuition,[58] an examination of his arguments in some detail is necessary, but, as far as is known, has not been attempted yet. It is attempted in the present work.

Paton has questioned the desirability of expounding the Kantian view 'in the terms of current philosophical controversy',[59] and he sometimes goes so far as to observe : 'For the purpose of understanding Kant we must place ourselves at the point of view of the eighteenth century'.[60] This attitude is both good and bad : 'good' in so far as it encourages us to put the Kantian view into its proper historico-philosophical perspectives and judge it accordingly, and 'bad' in so far as it suggests that Kant has become frozen in time and is no longer capable of speaking to the moderns. In the present work attention has of course been given to the historico-philosophical perspectives of Kant's major arguments on the idea of space; but an attempt has also been made to judge the value of his arguments in the light of contemporary controversy on relevant issues. Recent expositors like Strawson, Bennett, and Walker do not agree with one another in their appraisals of the Kantian view in the contemporary context; and so a review of their appraisals is necessary, and has been made in this Study.

The problem of the nature and status of the idea of space has been brought into prominence for the first time by Kant, and the post-Kantian views on this topic–e.g. those advocated by Mill, James and Russell–may be said to embody several reactions to the Kantian view. An examination of these later views which claim to supersede the Kantian one cannot be avoided in a critical work like this. What is attempted in this regard in this work is such an examination of them as proceeds according to a single principle that is derived from Kant himself.

1.6 The Adopted System of Reference to Kant's Arguments in the Metaphysical Exposition of the Concept of Space

As has already been pointed out, the sub-title 'Metaphysical Exposition of this Concept' (i.e. the Concept of Space) has been inserted by Kant in the second edition of the *Critique*. In the first edition there were five arguments under the relevant sub-section. In the second edition the third of them, which belongs properly to the Transcendental Exposition, is removed, and the fourth and fifth arguments are renumbered. But the renumbered third argument of the second edition, which is a mere reproduction of the fourth argument of the first edition, should have been shorn of its last sentence, which also belongs properly to the Transcendental Exposition. In the present work that sentence will therefore be ignored. The fourth argument of the second edition is not, however, a mere reproduction of the fifth argument of the first edition, but a considerably modified version thereof, and this modification is made not because the expunged sentences of the corresponding argument of the first edition belong properly to the Transcendental Exposition. Accordingly, in the present work both the first and the second edition version of this argument will be considered.

The system adopted by Kemp Smith for referring to Kant's arguments on space in the Metaphysical Exposition is misleading. Thus in the body of his *Commentary* he refers to Kant's third argument in the second edition as 'Fourth (in second edition, Third) Argument', while referring to the same argument, on the top of the pages concerned, simply as 'FOURTH ARGUMENT ON SPACE'. This latter mode of reference by an implicit allusion to the first edition is misleading, because it suggests as if the third argument of the first edition were retained in the Metaphysical Exposition; and the former mode of reference is partly open to the same objection and is therefore only seemingly accurate.

The system adopted in this work for referring to Kant's arguments in question is, after Garnett, based on an implicit allusion to the second edition. Thus they are referred to as 'Kant's First Space Argument', and so on up to 'Kant's Fourth Space Argument'. Under the last heading, two arguments are considered under the subheadings of 'The First-edition Version of This Argument' and 'The Second-edition Version of This Argument'. It may be objected that the argument indicated by the first of these subheadings is not in the mentioned first edition the fourth argument, but the fifth, and that the *explicit* allusion to the second edition embodied in the second of these subheadings is not *strictly* in accordance with the principle of an *implicit* allusion to that edition followed for the headings for Kant's arguments in question. This objection can be avoided by noting, *with regard to the first subheading*, that it may well be construed as being short for 'Kant's argument in the first edition corresponding to his fourth space argument in the second edition', and, *with regard to the second subheading*, that it is particularly apt, because the argument indicated by it, unlike the others in the second edition, is peculiar to this edition, being not a reproduction from the first edition, but rather an innovation.

NOTES :

1. *Critique*, B 40.
2. Gottfried Martin, *Kant's Metaphysics and Theory of Science,* trans. P. G. Lucas, Manchester University Press, 1955, p. 11.
3. *Critique*, A 23 = B 37-38 (in Lucas's translation).
4. Martin, *loc. cit.*
5. Cf. H. J. Paton, *Kant's Metaphysic of Experience,* George Allen and Unwin, London, 1951, vol. I., p. 108 n. 1; also see below, 1.2, last paragraph.
6. D. P. Dryer, *Kant's Solution for Verification in Metaphysics*, George Allen and Unwin, London, 1966, p. 173.
7. By adding subheadings to the Expositions in the second edition (viz. at B 37 and at B 40), Kant distinguishes them clearly from the Conclusions that he begins to draw at A 26 = B 42.
8. We say 'mainly', because in his Prize Essay entitled 'Enquiry Concerning the Clarity of the Principles of Natural Theology and Morals' (written in 1762, but first published in 1764, although Walford refers to it as 'Kant's 1763 *Enquiry*') there is an anticipation of Kant's epistemological view that space is an intuition, not a concept; cf. his Prize Essay trans. by G. B. Kerferd and D. E. Walford in *Kant : Selected Pre-Critical Writings and Correspondence with Beck*, Manchester University Press, 1968, p. 12 [AK. II, 281], or trans. by L. W. Beck in *Kant's Critique of Practical Reason and Other Writings in Moral Philosophy*, University of Chicago Press, 1949, p. 267, along with L. W. Beck's observations in his *Early German Philosophy : Kant and His Predecessors*, Belknap, Cambridge, Mass., 1969, p. 448. But although in the Prize Essay Kant seems to maintain that space is an intuition, the question is whether he means thereby that it is an a priori intuition ; cf. C.B. Garnett, Jr., *The Kantian Philosophy of Space*, Columbia University Press, New York, 1939, pp. 108-109.

For an account of Kant's earlier views on space, see L. W. Beck, *Early German Philosophy,* pp. 446-451.

9. Kant's essay of 1768 is discussed below in 4.1.2.2.
10. Garnett, Jr., *op. cit.,* p. 123. On the importance of the year 1769 for Kant, cf. his Reflexion No. 4, in B. Erdmann, ed., *Reflexionen Kants zur Kritischen Philosophie*, Bd. II, Leipzig, 1884, p. 4.
11. Cf. Garnett's remark, 'If this account of Kant's original formulation of his leading doctrine of space is correct, . . .' *ibid.,* p. 126.
12. From 'A', 'B' and 'C' under § 15 of the *Dissertation*, where Kant reflects on how space is apprehended, he proceeds to 'D', where he begins to consider what the ultimate nature of space is.
13. N. K. Smith, following Vaihinger, distinguishes several meanings of 'possibility' : N. K. Smith, *A Commentary to Kant's 'Critique of Pure Reason',* Macmillan, London, 1918, pp. 43, 50-52, Here what is in question is possibility of explanation.
14. Cf. *Critique*, B 73.
15. Arthur O. Lovejoy, 'Kant's Antithesis of Dogmatism and Criticism', in Moltke S. Gram., ed., *Kant : Disputed Questions*, Quadrangle, Chicago, 1967, p. 128.
16. Paton, *op. cit.,* p. 130.
17. Garnett, *op. cit.,* pp. 120, 130-133.
18. In 9.4 and 10.3.
19. *Critique*, B 2, A 2.
20. B 5-6.
21. A 86-87 = B 119.
22. For this use of 'abstract from', see *Kant's Inaugural Dissertation and Early Writings on Space*, trans. John Handyside, Open Court, Chicago, 1929, p. 47. See also Immanuel Kant, *Logic*, trans. R. S. Hartman and W. Schwarz, Bobbs-Merrill, Indianapolis, 1974, § 6., Note 2., pp. 100-101.
23. Cf. Kant's *Logic*, § 6; Hartman and Schwarz trans., p. 100. Cf. also Paton, 'The Key to Kant's Deduction of the Categories', in M. S. Gram, ed. *op. cit.,* p. 254.
24. In Chapter 3.
25. Cf. Kant, *Inaugural Dissertation*, § 14, 1, and § 15, D; Handyside trans., pp. 54, 62.

26. Of Course, such a concept can be rendered 'clear' through experience; Kant says : '. . . pure a *priori* representations–for instance, space and time. We can extract clear concepts of them from experience, only because we have put them into experience, and because experience is thus itself brought about only by their means'. (*Critique*, A 196 = B 241.).
27. *Critique*, B 126 = A 94.
28. Chapter 7.
29. See below, 7.4.
30. G. Schrader, 'Kant's Theory of Concepts', in R. P. Wolff, ed., *Kant : A Collection of Critical Essays*, Macmillan, London, 1968, p. 147.
31. John James Economos, 'Kant's Theory of Concepts. The A-Priori-Empirical Distinction Reconstituted', *Kant-Studien* 64 (1973), pp. 63-70.
32. Cf. *Critique*, B 81.
33. P. F. Strawson, *The Bounds of Sense*, Methuen, London, 1966, pp. 49, 51.
34. See *Critique*, e.g. A 373 (towards the end). Cf. also A 42.
35. That is, at A 26-30 = B 42-45.
36. See below, Chapter 6.
37. Strawson, *op. cit.*, p. 59 (first two paragraphs), pp. 64-65.
38. C. D. Broad, *Kant : An Introduction*, ed. by C. Lewy, Cambridge University Press, 1979, p. 31.
39. See, e.g. Jaakko Hintikka, 'On Kant's Notion of Intuition (Anschauung)', in Pennelhum and MacIntosh, eds., *The First Critique*, Wadsworth, Belmont, 1969, p. 43.
40. B 40; already quoted.
41. B 340 = A 284.
42. This will be clear from consultation of their translations.
43. See Kant's *Logic*, § 1 ; Hartman and Schwarz trans. p. 96. As for Paton, see *op. cit.*, pp. 94, 115, 194. As for Hintikka, see his article referred to above in Pennelhum and MacIntosh, eds., *op. cit.*, p. 42.
44. Perhaps the view of universals to be adopted in this connexion is not mere Conceptualism, but Conceptualism with some Realist feature; for a clarification and defence of such a view of universals (along the Kantian lines), see W. H. Walsh, *Reason and Experience*, Clarendon Press, Oxford, 1963, pp. 102-105.
45. For J. S. Beck's objection that an intuition as such does not *relate to*

objects, and for Kant's comment thereon, see A. Zweig, *Kant : Philosophical Correspondence* 1959-99, University of Chicago Press, 1967, pp. 180-81.

46. Ralph C. S. Walker, *Kant*, Routledge and Kegan Paul, London, 1978, p. 43.
47. Hintikka, *op. cit.*, p. 43. Cf. also his *Logic, Language-Games and Information*, Clarendon Press, Oxford, 1973, p. 44.
48. Robert Howell, 'Intuition, Synthesis, and Individuation in the *Critique of Pure Reason*', *Nous* 7 (1973), p. 210.
49. Wilfrid Sellars, *Science and Metaphysics : Variations on Kantian Themes,* Routledge and Kegan Paul, London, 1968, p. 3.
50. Charles Parsons, 'Kant's Philosophy of Arithmetic', in Morgenbesser, Suppes, and White, eds., *Philosophy, Science and Method : Essays in Honour of Ernest Nagel,* St. Martin's Press, New York, 1969, pp. 568-94 ; also in R.C.S. Walker, ed., *Kant on Pure Reason,* Oxford University Press, 1982, pp. 13-40.
51. J. Hintikka, 'Kantian Intuitions', *Inquiry* 15 (1972), p. 342 and p. 343; see also his article in Pennelhum and MacIntosh, *op. cit.*, p. 42 (last para).
52. See Parsons' article in Morgenbesser, et al., *op. cit.,* p. 569, or in Walker's edition, p. 14.
53. Gordon G. Brittan, Jr. *Kant's Theory of Science,* Princeton University Press, 1978, p. 50 n. 15 (in chap. ii).
54. In the passage referred to Kant compares the singularity of an intuition with the universality of a concept, and this shows that for him the singularity of the former consists in its individuality.
55. Lewis White Beck, ed., *Proceedings of the Third International Kant Congress,* D. Reidel Publishing Co., 1972, pp. 396, 399.
56. That is, while discussing Kant's third and fourth space arguments in the Metaphysical Exposition.
57. Their views are discussed below in Chapter 2.
58. L. W. Beck. *Early German Philosophy,* 1969, p. 448 n. 65 (in chap. xvii).
59. Paton, *op. cit.,* p. 17.
60. *Ibid.,* p. 163.

CHAPTER TWO

KANT'S FIRST SPACE ARGUMENT

2.1 Statement of the Argument and Preliminary Observations

Kant's first space argument runs :

> Der Raum ist kein empirischer Begriff, der von ausseren Er fahrungen abgezogen worden. Denn damit gewisse Empfindungen auf etwas ausser mir bezogen werden (d. i. auf etwas in einem anderen Orte des Raumes, als darinnen ich mich befinde), imgleichen damit ich sie als ausser und neben einander, mithin nicht bloss verschieden, sondern als in verschiedenen Orten vorstellen konne, dazu muss die Vorstellung des Raumes schon zum Grunde liegen. Demnach kann die Vorstellung des Raumes nicht aus den Verhaltnissen der ausseren Erscheinung durch Er fahrung erborgt sein, sondern diese aussere Er fahrung ist selbst nur durch gedachte Vorstellung allerest moglich. [*Kritik*, B. 38]

These words, in Kemp Smith's translation, are rendered as follows :

> Space is not an empirical concept which has been derived from outer experiences. For in order that certain sensations be referred to something outside me (that is, to something in another region of space from that in which I find myself), and similarly in order that I may be able to represent them as outside and alongside one another, and accordingly as not only different but as in different places, the representation of space must be presupposed. The representation of space cannot, therefore, be empirically obtained from the relations of outer appearance. On the contrary, this outer experience is itself possible at all only through that representation. [*Critique*, A 23 = B 38]

This argument, like the others in the Metaphysical Exposition, has received more than one interpretation from the commen-tators. According to what may be called the Vaihinger-Kemp Smith interpretation, the argument does not merely deny that the idea of space is empirical, but 'also yields a positive psychological explanation of its origin'.[1] It would not do to dismiss this interpretation off hand : not only that important names are associated with it, but even alternative interpretations by equally celebrated commentators[2] have failed to render it obsolete. Thus Garnett has tried all the more vigorously to re-establish it. It will, therefore, be appropriate to devote this entire chapter to an examination of this interpretation, as becomes its importance.

2.2 The Psychological-temporal Interpretation of the Argument

Upon the interpretation in question, which may also be called the psychological-temporal interpretation, the import of Kant's first space argument is that the original representation (idea) of space is psychologically and temporally prior to outer experience and so cannot be said to derive therefrom. Kemp Smith first refers to the word 'sensations' in Kant's proof (that is, the second sentence of the argument), and then maintains, with Vaihinger, that the argument is based on the unexpressed assumption that sensations are non-spatial, differing only in quality.[3] This assumption, he says, is already embodied in Kant's definition of the 'form' of sense at B 34 = A 20, but is nowhere (properly) justified. This being Kant's view of the nature of sensations, his proof in this argument can aptly be interpreted, Kemp Smith thinks, as follows : 'As sensations are non-spatial and differ only qualitatively, the representation of space must have been added to them. And not being supplied by the given sensations, it must, as the only alternative, have been contributed by the mind'.[4] The conclusion from this is plain that the representation of space is not derived from outer experience, but rather renders it possible.

This interpretation is sometimes set aside on the ground of unnaturalness.[5] But the air of unnaturalness about it can be removed through the following rendering of it.

In outer experience, Kant says, certain sensations are represented 'as not only different but as in different places', and so 'the representation of space must *schon zum Grunde liegen*', i.e. must already exist as a ground. Kant has not explained the point, but the explanation is this. In outer experience, sensations are represented as differing not only in quality, but also in spatial position.[6] Outer experience thus involves a spatial reference. This spatial reference is possible only if the representation of space already (*schon*) exists as a ground (*Grund*). It cannot be due to the sensations themselves, which are non-spatial and purely qualitative; and hence it must be due to a prior-existent idea of space. In other words, the idea of space is temporally and psychologically prior to outer experience, and makes outer experience possible (by being added to the given sensations).

This interpretation, whether or not it is ultimately tenable, is at any rate not artificial. If one stresses the word 'sensations' in Kant's argument and remembers his assumption that sensations are in themselves non-spatial, and looks for further explanation of the sentence containing his proof (which, as it stands, is hardly more than a plain assertion), one finds that the explanation given by this interpretation is far from being unnatural. Kemp Smith no doubt admits the possibility of an alternative interpretation of Kant's first space argument, namely, one in logical terms, and shows his awareness of the actual existence of such an interpretation. But he holds that if this argument is considered not in isolation, but in the light of 'the general trend of the *Aesthetic* as a whole', the greater reasonableness of his interpretation comes out.[7]

There is, however, an element of unclarity in the psychological interpretation as presented so far. It is not clear whether the alleged psychological-temporal priority of the representation of space is to be understood as its priority to sensation or to something occurring between sensation and outer experience, or to just the resulting outer experience. This unclarity is removed by Garnett, to whom it is necessary to turn for a better presentation of the interpretation in question.

2.2.1 Garnett's clarification of this interpretation

Garnett says that Kant's words in the first space argument can be taken to signify either

> that space is prior to all sensations, or that it is merely prior to any attempt on my part to give already existing sensations *a reference* to external things. In the former case, no sensing at all occurs prior to the representation of space. In the latter, sensing comes first, but cannot refer to anything outside me, or to one thing as outside another, except by means of a representation of space that is prior to such an act or process of reference.[8]

Thus Kant's argument can, Garnett thinks, be at first taken in one or other of two ways, according as the priority of space is understood in relation to sensations or in relation to the act or process of external reference. Now as regards the nature of this priority, this may be *prima facie* either temporal or logical, so that, ultimately, Garnett finds three alternative possibilities of interpretation of Kant's argument in question : (i) that space (that is, the representation of space) is temporally prior to sensations, and therefore also to the act or process of external reference; or (ii) that it is simultaneous with, or posterior to, sensation, but temporally prior to the act or process of external reference, or (iii) that it is logically prior to sensation, and therefore also to the act or process of external reference.[9] Of these three possible interpretations, Garnett prefers to accept the first by rejecting the other two.

There is, however, little in Kant's first space argument considered by itself to justify one's acceptance of the first interpretation by rejecting the second and the third. Of this Garnett is aware, and so he thinks fit to make a digression into the wider issue whether it is the logical or temporal priority of space that Kant has in mind in the Aesthetic. Garnett cites several passages from different parts of the Aesthetic, analyses them very minutely in favour of the temporal view and as against the theory of logical priority, and thus finally considers himself justified in having given to Kant's first space argument the above-mentioned first, temporal, interpretation as the only one possible for it consistently with the general trend of the Aesthetic as a whole. Thus he carries forward the Vaihinger-Kemp Smith interpretation of Kant's argument in question.

To avoid misunderstanding, two things may be noted here. First,

Garnett's phrase 'the priority of space' need not be objected to; it is more convenient, being shorter, than the phrase 'the priority of the representation of space'. Second, Garnett's appeal to such passages as are subsequent to Kant's first space argument, or otherwise presuppose the results of the Aesthetic,[10] is not meant to *justify* the apriority or priority as such of space, in which case it would doubtless be a begging of the issue, but is made only for the purpose of ascertaining what *meaning* Kant himself attaches to this priority.

Garnett's treatment of the aforementioned wider problem of the general trend of the Aesthetic is to be considered next. His treatment of the problem is sufficiently elaborate and more modern :[11] it includes a reply to Paton, whose critique of the temporal view of the priority of space is widely accepted. It is not feasible, however, to consider all of Garnett's arguments; but the chief ones at least must be examined.

As the proposed discussion of the general trend of the Aesthetic is an excursus, it may well be made in a separate section.

2.3 On the Nature of the Priority of the Kantian A Priori (A Study of the General Trend of the Aesthetic, with Reference to the Representation of Space)

Garnett first quotes from the introductory section of the Aesthetic. He says :

> At A 20 = B 34, We find that space, as the form of all appearances,
>
> . . . muss zu ihnen insgesamt im Gemüte a priori bereitliegen, und daher abgesondert von aller Empfindung konnen betrachtet werden.[12]

[The clauses quoted by Garnett are rendered in Kemp Smith's translation as : '. . . must lie ready for the sensations *a priori* in the mind, and so must allow of being considered apart from all sensation'. Kemp Smith has put 'the sensations' for the term *ihnen* (which means 'them'), and this is justifiable by the context. But the word *insgesamt* is ignored in this translation (as it is also ignored in Meiklejohn's and Max Müller's translations),[13] although the word matters much, as we shall see, in

Garnett's interpretation of Kant's first clause. Garnett translates the word as 'in its entirety', and construes it with 'space', and not with 'the sensations'. His treatment of the first clause suggests that he is for rendering it thus : '[Space, as the form of all appearances,]. . . must lie in its entirety in the mind *a priori* ready for the sensations.'[14] Whether this rendering is satisfactory will be considered later. With reference to the word *betrachtet* in Kant's second clause, Garnett says that it may be, though it need not be, translated as 'considered'. [The point will be clear in due course.]

Now with reference to the above passage, Garnett first of all points out what can be said in favour of the theory of logical priority. The following considerations, he thinks, mediate in favour of this theory. (1) The word *betrachtet* may be taken in the sense of 'considered', and then the view that space lies in the mind ready for the sensations a priori and so can be considered apart from all sensation suggests the logical priority of space in so far as it can be interpreted as follows : 'that the principles of its [space's] nature are not deducible from its sensuous contents but are worked out from within the mind on the occasion of sensation'.[15] (2) The expression 'apart from' (*abgesondert von*) may be interpreted by reference to the method of isolation adopted by Kant in a passage (at A 22 = B 36) which is two paragraphs later than the above extract. In that passage Kant chalks out his programme for the Aesthetic. He says that he will, first, isolate sensibility by taking away from knowledge all that the understanding thinks in regard to it, so that nothing else is left over than 'empirical intuition', and that, secondly, he will 'separate off' from empirical intuition all that belongs to sensation, so that nothing is left but 'pure intuition and the mere form of appearances' which alone sensibility can contribute a priori. All this indicates 'that Kant meant that space is separated out of empirical intuition in the same sense that empirical intuition is itself separated out of the wider whole of knowledge that includes understanding, and hence that space is merely logically prior to sensation'.[16] To explain : if space is separated out of empirical intuition which involves sensation also, then space (the represen-tation of space) and sensation are already there in empirical intuition and are there as actually combined,[17] i.e. at the same time. This suggests that neither space (the representation of space) nor sensation is temporally prior to empirical intuition[18] and that neither is temporally prior to the other. Hence the priority of space to sensation indicated by Kant's first clause *muss zu ihnen insgesamt im Gemüte a priori bereitliegen* has to be understood in a non-temporal, logical, sense.

Against these arguments for the logical view, Garnett now fixes upon Kant's first clause in question, and proceeds to show how almost every word in it speaks for temporal priority. He makes five points. The points are brief, but suggestive. These are : (1) ' "In its entirety" suggests more than a mere potential disposition.'[19] It rather suggests that space is fully 'displayed'. (2) 'If so, *im Gemüte* means that space is given in the mind.'[20] This being so, it can hardly be considered as merely separated out of empirical intuition, which is certainly not in the mind. (3) And 'if it is considered merely as separated out of empirical intuition and *then* given in the mind',[21] it lies *ready* not in the mind, but in empirical intuition. Yet Kant says explicitly that it lies ready (*bereitliegen*) in the mind. (4) The above considerations suffice to suggest temporal priority, no matter how the word *a priori* itself is taken. However, the significance of this word in Kant's clause remains to be determined. It might be supposed that the word signifies the logically necessary nature exhibited by space after it is given. But this supposition is possible 'only by distorting Kant's meaning'.[22] What should be noticed is that this word is placed 'in the midst of the other words'.[23] Instead of saying that space exhibits its *a priori* (i.e. logically necessary) nature after being separated out of empirical intuition, Kant rather says : 'It lies in its entirety in the mind *a priori* ready'. 'The meaning of the statement seems to link its *apriority* with the fact that it is in the mind, ready in the mind, and ready in the mind in its entirety.'[24] (5) There is another argument which, unlike the above ones, 'does not prove', but 'suggests the possibility' that for Kant 'space is temporally prior to sensation'. This concerns the interpretation of the word *betrachten* (in the next clause). It may mean 'to gaze at'. Although it is possible that Kant simply means 'that space is considered as separated from sensation', it is more than possible (i.e. it is probable) that he meant 'that space is gazed at, as separate from sensation'. Now if this interpretation is allowed, the temporal priority of space is strongly suggested : 'what is *betrachtet* would not be an innate tendency or disposition, for one does not gaze at a tendency, but at space'.[25]

These five points or arguments may now be examined.

(1) Garnett's first argument turns on the phrase 'in its entirety', which is his translation for Kant's word '*insgesamt*'. The use made of it by Garnett indicates that he construes it with 'space, as the form of all appearances', an expression interpolated by him as the subject-term for the Kantian clause concerned. It may be noted incidentally that Kant's actual term for the subject of the clause (or clauses) quoted by Garnett is not, as the latter says, 'space, as the form of all appearances', but simply (*die Form derselben,* which here signifies) 'the form of all appearance'. In the original paragraph, not fully quoted by Garnett, Kant is engaged in distinguishing, in a general way, between the *matter* and the *form* of all appearance, and is not specially concerned with space. Of course, his remarks apply to space, which is the *form* of all outer appearances. To come now to the question whether Garnett's translation, or rather, interpretation of the word *insgesamt* is satisfactory. The word occurs in Kant's clause concerned immediately after the word *ihnen*, which is here a pronoun for 'the sensations', and yet Garnett has construed it, not with 'the sensations', but with 'space'. The word commonly means 'all together' and is usually employed by Kant himself in relation to plural nouns or pronouns or the like to cover *all* the items denoted by them.[26] Accordingly in the present instance it will be more natural to construe the word with 'the sensations' and to translate it as 'all' : the phrase *zu ihnen insgesamt* will thus mean 'for them all', i.e., 'for all the sensations'. The sensations being many, there is indeed a point in urging that the spatial form lies ready for them *all* a priori. Just as at B2-3 Kant says of a priori knowledge that it is 'not knowledge independent of this or that experience, but knowledge absolutely independent of all experience', so also in the present context he may be taken to mean that the spatial form lies ready, not for this or that sensation, but absolutely for all sensations. This is a straight-forward interpretation, and Garnett in departing from it has given no reason for his departure.

In this connexion, the expression *aller Empfindung* ('all sensation') in the second of the two clauses quoted by Garnett is particularly noteworthy. It does something to confirm that in the first clause Kant, by the phrase *zu ihnen insgesamt*, means to refer to *all* sensations.

As regards Garnett's first argument, then, it may be said that the phrase 'in its entirety' on which it turns does not really occur in Kant's clause under consideration. What Kant in this clause says is not that space must lie ready *in its entirety* in the mind for the sensations a priori, but that space as the form of appearances must lie ready in the mind for *all* the sensations a priori. There is therefore no justification for Garnett's contention that for Kant space is *fully displayed* in the mind, i.e. that space is already there in the mind non-potentially as an object of representation[27] temporally prior to sensation.

At this point it may be well, for clarity's sake, to comment on a possible objection to Garnett's entire account. The objection is one on the score of inconsistency, and is as follows.

Garnett has later pointed to the distinction between space as the form of appearances and space as a pure intuition (i.e. a pure intuitum), and held that while the latter is for Kant temporally prior to all actual perceptions, the former is only 'logically prior' as a 'potential disposition'.[28] Space as the form of appearances, which is said to be originally in the mind, is space as the form of not-yet-experienced appearances, and is as such a potential disposition. With this later view Garnett's present argument is not consistent. The subject-term he has interpolated for Kant's clause at present under examination is, as already noted, 'space, as the form of all [outer] appearances'. In this clause, therefore, it is only space as the form of appearance that is under consideration. This being so, Garnett, for the sake of consistency, should have interpreted this clause as suggesting the *logical priority* of space to sensation. Actually, he has interpreted it as suggesting the *temporal priority* of space to sensation.

This inconsistency in Garnett's account is, however, apparent, not real. He for his part thinks that the phrase 'in its entirety' *is* a constituent of Kant's clause under examination, and it is his deliberate contention that this phrase 'suggests more than a mere potential disposition'. His line of reasoning may be set forth as follows. A potential disposition as such cannot be said to lie in the mind *in its entirety*. Space as the form said to lie in the mind in its entirety is, then, not mere form, but also a pure content, i.e. an actual object of pure, formal, intuition; and this pure intuition is in the nature of the case temporally prior to sensation.

The proper reply to Garnett here is that the above sort of reasoning is out of the question, because the phrase 'in its entirety' has to be removed, that is, altered, as has been explained already.

(2) To come now to Garnett's second argument. Clearly, this is a continuation of his first argument. He says that Kant's expression *im Gemüte* [taken along with 'in its entirety'][29] suggests that 'space is given in the mind', and he adds that this being so, space in its purity is not for Kant merely considered as separated out of empirical intuition. By taking Kant to mean that 'space is given in the mind', Garnett evidently takes him to mean that the spatial form is originally in the mind as an object of pure intuition.[30] The implication is left to be drawn that this original intuition is temporally prior to sensation.

But this argument of Garnett's is weak to the extent to which it implicitly relies upon his first argument, which has been set aside above. It is, however, true that, even without the backing of the phrase 'in its entirety', the locution '(lies) in the mind' is itself susceptible of being so interpreted as to mean the actual presence to the mind as an object in it.[31] It seems that Garnett is arguing here against Paton, who has said : 'On [Kant's] view space and time are potentially present in our sensibility even before experience begins. I do not think Kant believes that space and time are actually present to our minds before our experience begins'.[32] Against this (or this sort of) view presumably Garnett is arguing, by utilising the Kantian locution 'lies in the mind', that space for Kant is actually present in the mind as an a priori intuited pure form to be added to sensations to make experience itself possible. It remains to see whether this interpretation correctly represents Kant's view.

We may here refer to Kant's own interpretation of his view in the *Critique* as offered in his *On a Discovery.* He says : 'The *Critique* admits absolutely no . . . innate (*angeboren*) represen-tations'.[33] As to the form of intuition (i.e. the form of appearance), he distinguishes, for the sake of greater clarity, between the form itself and the ground of the form, which, he says, is also the ground of the possibility of pure intuition. This is to say that this ground itself is not an object of pure intuition. The ground is 'in the subject which makes it possible for these representations [of space and time] to originate . . .'.[34] 'It is the merely particular *receptivity* in the mind, whereby it receives representations in accordance with its subjective constitution, when affected by something (in sensation)'.[35] This implies (in the case of space) that when the mind with its innate liability to receive representations spatially is 'affected by something (in sensation)', there occurs an empirical intuition of an appearance having a sensed matter and a spatial form, the matter corresponding to sensation and the form corresponding to pure intuition; and this shows that pure intuition as a representation is not temporally prior to sensation. Kant says : 'Only this first formal ground, e.g. the possibility of a representation of space, is innate, not the spatial representation itself.[36] And he adds : 'No one can be in doubt concerning the meaning of the ground of the possibility of a pure sensible intuition, except he who roams through the *Critique* with the help of a dictionary, but does not think it through'.[37]

It is clear from the above that Kant does not mean to advocate in the *Critique* any such view as that a formal intuition of space lies in the mind temporally prior to sensation.[38] But it must be said, with due respect to Kant, that although this has been clear from his observations in *On a Discovery*, this really is not so clear from the *Critique* itself. In the *Critique*, the expression 'the form of appearance' is ambiguous between the form of yet-to-be-experienced appearances and the form of the concretely given appearances, i.e. between the subjective ground of the form (as also of formal intuition) and the form proper.[39] In the passage under consideration by Garnett, the expression 'the form of appearance' is used not without this ambiguity : it stands for the subjective ground of the form of appearance, in so far as Kant says that it lies in the mind ready for sensations, and it also stands for the form itself, in so far as he says both that it is a priori (which may suggest that it is represented a priori) and that it can be considered apart from all sensation (which suggests that it can be represented in its purity in isolation from sensations).

Since, however, Garnett's present concern is only to determine Kant's meaning, and since Kant himself says that he has not meant to advocate in the *Critique* any doctrine of the temporal priority of the spatial representation to sensation, Garnett's second argument, which purports to attribute to Kant this doctrine, is not acceptable.

[It has been argued by Kemp Smith, and accordingly it might be argued by Garnett too, that the view held by Kant 'in the 1790 reply to Eberhard' (i.e. in the work *On a Discovery*) is based on 'misrepresenting his own teaching in the *Critique*',[40] and that Kant's actual view as regards space in the *Critique*, particularly in the Aesthetic, is rather this : 'Space is no mere potential disposition. As a conscious representation it lies ready in the mind'.[41] But there is not a single line anywhere in the *Critique* in which Kant says that 'a conscious representation' of space lies ready in the mind. And to contend that Kant, although he does not expressly say this, at least means this at A 20 = B 34 would be to beg the issue against the other expositors. We are therefore led to attach greater importance to Kant's interpretation of his own teaching in the *Critique* (as offered in 1790) than to Kemp Smith's (or Garnett's) interpretation thereof.]

After all that has been said, a direct reply to Garnett's argument without any reference to Kant's *On a Discovery* will be in order. We may concede that there is a sense in which the expression 'lies in the mind' does not suit a mere potential disposition, because a mere disposition is strictly neither an existent nor an occurrent. Nevertheless it is a common enough practice (among philosophers who have work to do with the expression 'in the mind') to speak of a disposition as what is latent in the mind. What is more to the point, Kant does say quite clearly in the *Critique*, with regard to some dispositions, that they lie prepared in the mind. A passage to that effect will be quoted presently while examining Garnett's next argument.

(3) In his third argument, Garnett says that if space is given in the mind only after having been isolated from empirical intuition, then it lies *ready* not in the mind, but in empirical intuition, whereas Kant explicitly says that it lies ready (*bereitliegen*) in the mind. The subtle point of the argument seems to be that space (i.e. the spatial form) for Kant already exhibits itself in its purity to the mind temporally prior to sensation and does not wait for such exhibition till the adoption of the method of isolation from empirical intuition (which is a compound of the intuition of space and the sensation of matter).[42]

The emphasis of the argument is on the term *bereitliegen*. The implication is that what lies *ready* in the mind cannot exist in it *only potentially* : to be ready is to be full-blown (i.e. manifest).

But, misleading though Kant's way of speaking may be, he is wont to say, about something existing in the mind *only potentially,* that it *lies ready* in the mind. In confirmation of this, the following passage may be cited.

> We shall therefore follow up the pure concepts to their first seeds and dispositions in the human understanding, in which they lie prepared, till at last, on the occasion of experience, they are developed, and by the same understanding are exhibited in their purity, freed from the empirical conditions attaching to them. [A 66 = B 91]

Mark the expression 'lie prepared' (*vorbereitet liegen*). The a priori concepts *lie prepared* or *ready* in the mind *only potentially.*

It is true that in this passage Kant is dealing with the categories and not with space. But his remarks apply *mutatis mutandis* to space.

With regard to space as the form of appearance lying ready in the mind, we may, therefore, say with Riehl that this' "... bereitliegende" Form ist' for Kant 'nicht selbst eine fertige Vorstellung; sie ist der formale und subjektive Grund, ...'.[43]

(4) Garnett's fourth argument concerns the relation of the word 'a priori' to the other words in Kant's first clause under consideration. He suggests that this word occurs in that clause only by influence of the other words. The plausibility of this suggestion, which is apparently great, derives from the ambiguity of Kant's key term 'form [of appearance]'. This ambiguity, which is at the root of all troubles, has already been pointed out before (while discussing Garnett's second argument). Here it is incumbent on us to examine closely the original context of Kant's clause under consideration. Kant says : '... the matter of all appearance is given to us *a posteriori* only, its form must lie ready for [all] the sensations *a priori* in the mind ... '.[A 20 = B 34]. Clearly, Kant's primary contention here is that the form of appearance, as distinguished from its matter which is given *a posteriori*, is represented *a priori*. This is confirmed by his next clause 'must allow of being

considered apart from all sensation', in so far as it can be construed as 'must allow of being considered *independently of all sensation*'. So instead of saying, as Garnett does, that 'Kant puts "*a priori*" in the midst of the other words', we should rather say that his principal word '*a priori*' draws the other words (namely, 'lie ready in the mind') by attraction,[44] even although his key term 'form' is thereby rendered ambiguous between 'the form of the *given* appearances' and 'the form of to-be-given appearances'.

Since it is space as the form of given appearances (i.e. of appearances of which the matter is, as Kant says, 'given . . . *a posteriori*)' that is represented *a priori*, its apriority surely does not consist in temporal priority to sensation.

[We must not fail to note that corresponding to the ambiguity of the expression 'the form of appearance' in the present instance, there is the ambiguity of the word 'a priori' between its relatively austere and its transcendental-idealist sense : between the sense 'independently of experience' and the sense 'being in us independently of experience (i.e. originally)'.[45] The form of appearance, as the form of given appearances, is a priori in the sense of being represented independently of experience (and *a fortiori* of sensation), while the form of appearance, as the form of to-be-given appearances, is a priori in the sense of lying in us originally. In the latter case, 'lies ready in the mind a priori' is a pleonasm.

The complications raised by Kant's statement under examination could be avoided if, in line with his observations in *On a Discovery* cited above, it were reformulated somewhat as follows : 'The form of appearance is represented a priori and allows of being considered apart from all sensation, and being not given by sensation, must have its ground originally lying in the mind.']

(5) Garnett's fifth argument is admittedly not a strong one. One may translate *betrachtet* as 'gazed at' and then read into Kant's statement concerned the suggestion of the temporal priority of space, provided one thinks that there is an antecedent independent justification for that temporal priority. Garnett considers himself to be sufficiently provided with the required antecedent justification for the temporal priority of

space by means of his preceding arguments, and so he feels free to adopt the suggested translation of *betrachtet*. But since we have found his previous arguments to be wanting, we can no longer attach any importance to his fifth argument.

Some of Garnett's additional arguments for the theory of temporal priority fall to be considered next.

He again quotes several passages from the Aesthetic, which we put down here in Kemp Smith's translation. He says that these passages 'are important in reference to Kant's meaning in the first space argument'.[46] These are :

> [1] Further, this intuition must be *a priori*, that is, it must be found in us prior to any perception of an object, and must therefore be pure, not empirical, intuition. [B 41]
>
> [2] Since, then, the receptivity of the subject, its capacity to be affected by objects, must necessarily precede all intuitions of these objects, it can readily be understood how the form of all appearances can be given prior to all actual perceptions, and so exist in the mind *a priori* and how, as a pure intuition, in which all objects must be determined, it can contain, prior to all experience, principles which determine the relations of these objects. [A 26 = B 42]
>
> [3] [Space and time] alone can we know *a priori*, that is, prior to all actual perception; and such knowledge is therefore called pure intuition. [A 42 = B 60]

All these three passages concern space (though the last concerns time also). With reference to them, Garnett's contention is twofold : (a) that they afford clear evidence that Kant regards space as *temporally prior* to perceptions, and (b) that determination of the meaning of the term 'perceptions' in these passages is of crucial importance, if the argument of these passages is to be considered a carrying forward of Kant's first space argument where the word used is not 'perceptions', but 'sensations'.

(a) To begin with Garnett's first contention : He calls attention to what Kant repeatedly says in these passages. Kant says that space is found in us *prior* to any perception of an object, or given *prior* to all actual perceptions, or known *prior* to all actual perception. Garnett now observes that the word 'prior' (*vor*) is clearly indicative of temporal priority : '. . . the meaning of *vor* here is temporal'.[47] So he maintains that Kant here has in mind the temporal priority of space to all perceptions.[48]

Garnett does not deny that even here there are some *prima facie* reasons for supposing that Kant means only the logical priority of space to perceptions.[49] For example, it might be argued, particularly in the light of the second passage above, (1) that space like the receptivity of the subject is a potential disposition which is logically prior to its being 'affixed' by any object in perception, and (2) that Kant clearly says that space is given prior to actual perceptions as just the *form* of appearances. But Garnett contends that these reasons really do not annul the view that Kant has in mind the temporal priority of space. For (1) although the form like receptivity is only logically presupposed as a potential disposition, space for Kant 'is more than such a formal condition; it is also a pure intuition';[50] and (2) although Kant says that space as the form of appearances is prior to perceptions, 'there are not two different spaces. The space that is logically prior to all perceptions is also actual space. Space is given temporally prior to all perceptions as a pure intuition and, in addition, is logically prior to them as the form of the not-yet-experienced appearances'.[51] Garnett adds that while, in the second passage above, Kant says that space as the form of appearances is prior to all actual perceptions, in the first and third passages Kant clearly maintains that space is a *pure intuition* because we find it in us or know it prior to all actual perceptions. 'In all of these passages, Kant's words show unmistakably that he meant the temporal priority of space [as a pure intuition] to perception.'[52]

In criticism of Garnett, the following observations may be made.

First, it is not true that 'Kant's words show unmistakably' that he has in mind the temporal priority of space. Neither the word 'prior' nor even the whole phrase such as 'prior to all actual perception' provides *unmistakable* evidence of Kant's committal to temporal priority. Garnett asserts, but does not explain, that 'the meaning of *vor* here is temporal'. It is indeed true that 'prior' in its frequent ordinary uses has a temporal meaning; but it does not follow that, as used by Kant here, it has such a meaning. At this point, it will be as well to consider the following. In the third passage, Kant says that 'we know' space 'prior to all actual perception' and that 'such knowledge is therefore called pure intuition',[53] and towards the end of the second passage, he says, at least by implication, that 'pure intuition' is 'prior to all experience'. These, if combined, yield the statement that we know space prior to all experience, such knowledge being therefore called pure intuition. If now 'prior' be interpreted as 'temporally prior', this statement comes into flagrant contradiction with Kant's famous statement in so prominent a place as the first paragraph of his Introduction to the *Critique* : 'In the order of time, . . . we have no knowledge antecedent to [*vor*] experience, . . .'.[B 1]

Secondly, Kant in the second passage above applies the phrase 'prior to all perceptions' to the form of appearances, and in the first passage applies virtually the same phrase ('prior to any perception of an object') to the pure intuition. If now Garnett is to maintain that 'prior' means 'temporally prior', he should conclude that space both as the form of appearances and as a pure intuition is temporally prior to perceptions. But the conclusion actually drawn by him is that for Kant space as a pure intuition is temporally prior, while space as the form of appearances is logically prior, to perceptions. This amply shows that, unlike himself, Garnett also thinks that Kant's use of the word 'prior' (*vor*) does not by itself constitute conclusive evidence that Kant means thereby temporal priority.

Thirdly, only three sentences later than the second passage above there occurs a sentence which leaves us in no doubt as to Kant's actual meaning. It runs : 'The constant receptivity, which we term sensibility, is a necessary condition of all the relations in which objects can be intuited as outside us; and if we abstract [*abstrahirt*] from these objects, it is a pure intuition, and bears the name of space'. [B 43 = A 27] There is here not the least suggestion that the pure intuition of space precedes in time the outer intuitions of objects; on the contrary, there is here the clearest possible statement that it is by *abstraction* from outer intuitions of objects that we can arrive at the pure intuition of space.[54]

This sentence yields also a clue to Kant's meaning when he says that pure intuition is 'prior to', 'precedes', all perceptions. That is, 'prior to' here means 'independent of', not 'prior in time'.

So Garnett's contention that in the three passages quoted by him Kant holds the theory of the temporal priority of space as a pure intuition to perceptions is not acceptable.

(b) To come now to Garnett's second contention, which concerns the problem of the relation of Kant's argument in the three passages above to his first space argument. Garnett investigates whether the word 'perception' (*Wahrnehmung*) in these passages has a different meaning from 'sensation' (*Empfindung*).[55] His reason for making this investigation is that if grounds be found to conclude that Kant makes no distinction between perception and sensation in the Aesthetic, then Kant's 'defense' of the temporal priority of space to *perceptions* in the three passages above can also be taken as a defense of its temporal priority to *sensations*, and that all this has a bearing on the import of Kant's first space argument, where the word used is 'sensations';[56] for it can then be maintained that the view that the priority of space with which Kant is concerned in his first space argument is its temporal priority to *sensations* is quite in keeping with the general trend of the Aesthetic.

Now Garnett, in the course of his investigation, says that the distinction between perception and sensation is made by Kant 'later on', that is, in the Analytic.[57] For example in a note at A 120 (in the Analytic) Kant says that imagination is an ingredient in perception, and this means that the activity of the knowing mind contributes to perception. But Garnett finds no specific evidence to show that Kant has adopted such a view of perception in the Aesthetic also. Particularly in the context of the priority of space, there is, Garnett says, 'a marked similarity between those passages', which have been considered above, in which Kant holds that space is in the mind apart from all sensations and in the mind prior to all perceptions. This, in the absence of any 'greater specific evidence to the contrary', shows (Garnett says) that Kant has meant the same type of priority in those passages.[58] Garnett adds some other reasons to support his contention that 'in the *Aesthetic* Kant did not distinguish between sensation and perception'.[59] He then concludes that Kant's 'defense' of the temporal priority of space to perception in the three passages above 'must be' considered to be a carrying forward of the view– held in the first space argument–that space is temporally prior to sensation.

With regard to Garnett, it will suffice here to make only two observations.

First, it is not certain that Kant makes no distinction between perception and sensation in the Aesthetic. It is noteworthy that Kant is speaking of 'perception of an object'.[60] In the Aesthetic, an *object* is an appearance, which has both matter and form.[61] The matter corresponds to sensation and the form to pure intuition. So the perception of an object involves both sensation and pure intuition, which implies that it is more than sensation.[62] [Pure intuition is a constitutive formal condition of perception, and is for this reason both involved in and logically independent of perception.]

Secondly, the investigation made by Garnett about the meaning of the word 'perception' in the Aesthetic is prompted by his view that Kant in the three passages above does uphold the temporal priority of space to perceptions. But this view itself has already been found to be unacceptable. Accordingly, the results yielded by that investigation are after all of no significance.

So far Garnett's main arguments for ascribing to Kant the doctrine of the temporal priority of space (i.e. of the represen-tation or intuition of space) to sensation have been reviewed, and the review has shown them to be unacceptable. The question now arises whether the doctrine itself is acceptable; for if it is not, it can hardly be right to ascribe it to Kant, seeing that there already is an alternative way of interpreting him. The question is implicitly raised by Paton, who says that this doctrine is 'nonsense'.[63] Taking 'nonsense' as meaning 'untenable', we here cannot help agreeing with Paton. Garnett, however, by way of replying to Paton, maintains that this doctrine, although it is apparently untenable taken by itself, has nevertheless proved to be of some use to Kant. It remains to see how he tries to make good this point.

He maintains that only the doctrine of the temporal priority of the pure intuition of space enabled Kant to harmonize two other doctrines both of which he was compelled to accept without being able to reconcile them otherwise.[64] These are (as Garnett puts them) : (1) 'that space is not abstracted from objects of sense', and (2) 'that it is the product of the synthetic activity of the mind'.[65] Now since space is the product of the synthetic activity of the mind, such a synthesis must begin with some *given* materials. In view of the first doctrine, however, these given materials cannot be the objects of sense. Nor, again, can these be the parts of space *qua* parts; for, according to Kant's third space argument (to be considered later), the parts of space 'are themselves space', by which Garnett means that these parts are not the given features of intuition.[66] 'Therefore, the only thing with which it can begin is *space* as a whole. But if it begins with space, space is given temporally prior to it. And since it begins on the occasion of sense experience, space is temporally prior also to sense experience'.[67]

Without entering into details, it will suffice here to say only that the above argument is based on the mistake that for Kant the parts of space are *not* the given features of intuition. That this is a mistake will be shown while discussing Kant's third space argument. Here attention may be called to one important sentence in the *Critique* ; '. . . the synthesis of the manifold parts of space, by means of which we apprehend space, is successive . . .'. (A 412 = B 439). The sentence clearly says that the synthesis in question begins with 'the parts of space', and accordingly Garnett's interpretation becomes decisively refuted. It would not do, whether or not out of reverence for the Patchwork theory, to ignore this sentence on the ground that it does not occur in the Aesthetic; for then the view that space is the product of the synthetic activity of the mind is also one that is *not* to be found in the Aesthetic. (The doctrine of synthesis, of course, presents some difficulty for Kant's doctrine of pure intuition; but the difficulty will be considered later on in its proper place.)[68]

2.4 Back to Kant's First Space Argument

The general trend of the Aesthetic as a whole has been examined, but no justification has been found for ascribing to Kant the view that a conscious representation of space exists in our minds temporally prior to sensation. Returning to his first space argument, therefore, it can be said that the Vaihinger-Kemp Smith interpretation thereof, even after a vigorous defense of it by Garnett, should be set aside.

If that interpretation be adopted, Kant's argument must be rejected, and this, not because it would then be psychological, but because it would not be sound psychology. Hardly could any doctrine be more easily set aside on psychological grounds than the one which holds that a 'conscious representation'[69] of space exists in our minds temporally prior to sensation or even to outer experience. Prichard, in criticizing Kant's first space argument, says : 'We do not apprehend empty space before we apprehend individual spatial relations of individual bodies, . . .'.[70] This is an unexceptionable statement and constitutes a formidable objection to the doctrine, presumed to be Kant's, that a conscious representation of space temporally precedes our outer experiences of objects and their spatial relations.

The rejection of the psychological interpretation leads us to accept or attempt some logical interpretation of Kant's first space argument. It must be pointed out that there is not anything that might be called *the* logical interpretation of the argument. For the commentators who have preferred to interpret the argument in purely logical terms have not, in fact, all of them read the same meaning into it. In the next chapter we explain what we take to be the dominant significance of the argument.

NOTES :

1. Kemp Smith, *Commentary*, 1918, p. 102.
2. E.g. A. Riehl, *Der philosophische Kritizismus*, Leipzig, 1924, Bd. I, p. 462 (and *passim*) ; J. Watson, *The Philosophy of Kant Explained*, Glasgow, 1908, pp. 81-84; E. Caird, *The Critical Philosophy of Immanuel Kant*, Glasgow, 1909, vol. I, pp. 264-266; Paton, *Kant's Metaphysic of Experience*, 1951, vol. I, pp. 110-112.
3. Kemp Smith, *op. cit.*, p. 101.
4. *Ibidem.*
5. Cf. A. C. Ewing, *A Short Commentary on Kant's Critique of Pure Reason*, Methuen, London, 1938, p. 38.
6. The phrase 'as not only different but as in different places' is taken by Kemp Smith to mean 'as not only qualitatively different but as differing in spatial position also'.

7. Kemp Smith, *op. cit.*, pp. 101-102.
8. Garnett, *The Kantian Philosophy of Space*, 1939, p. 167.
9. *Ibidem.*
10. One of the passages (at A 20 = B 34) quoted by Garnett and to be discussed in the next section precedes Kant's first space argument and yet presupposes the results of the Aesthetic. Paton, *op. cit.*, I., 94 n. 1, explains this by saying that the passage should be taken as containing 'a statement of what is to be proved [in the Aesthetic]'.
11. For references to earlier discussions of the problem, see Garnett, *op. cit.*, p. 173 n. 13.
12. *Ibid.*, p. 167.
13. Meiklejohn's translation, Colonial Press, New York, 1900, pp. 21-22; F. Max Müller's translation, Macmillan, New York, 1902, p. 16.
14. Cf. Garnett, *op. cit.*, pp. 167, 169.
15. *Ibid.*, p. 167.
16. *Ibid.*, p. 168.
17. Cf. *ibid.*, p. 168 (1.10).
18. *Ibid.*, p. 168 (11. 18-19).
19. *Ibidem.*
20. *Ibidem.*
21. *Ibidem.*
22. *Ibid.*, p. 169.
23. *Ibidem.*
24. *Ibidem.*
25. *Ibidem.*
26. See, e.g. *Kritik,* B 11, B 14, A 15 = B 29, A 22 = B 37, B 41, A 31 = B 46, and so on.
27. It hardly needs pointing out that 'object of representation' here means what-is-represented, i.e. an objective or content of representation.
28. Garnett, *op. cit.*, p. 171.
29. The words 'If so' used in Garnett's second argument refer back to his first argument.
30. This is implied by Garnett's word 'given'. The word does not occur, however, in Kant's clause under consideration.

31. For the phrase '(lies) in the mind' allows of being interpreted as '(exists) in the mind', and it is possible to argue that what *exists* in the mind is something actual in it.

32. Paton, *op. cit.,* p. 102.

33. Trans. by H. E. Allison, in *The Kant-Eberhard Controversy,* Johns Hopkins University Press, Baltimore, 1973, p. 135, [AK. VIII, 221].

34. *Ibid.,* [AK. VIII, 221f.]

35. *Ibid.,* p. 136. [AK. VIII, 222].

36. *Ibidem,* Riehl, after quoting this passage in the original, concludes : 'Kant ist daher kein Nativist'. Riehl, *op. cit.,* p. 385. (The problem of the relation of the Kantian a priori to the innate is of some interest. H. Vaihinger discusses it in his *Kommentar zu Kants Kritik der reinen Vernunft,* Bd. II, Stuttgard, 1892, pp. 89ff. Riehl, whom we follow, discusses it in his work referred to, pp. 385-386. and *passim.*).

37. Kant, *On a Discovery,* Allison trans., p. 136. [AK. VIII, 223].

38. It need hardly be repeated that Kant's observations in *On a Discovery* are intended to explain his own teaching in the *Critique.*

    On 'formal intuition', by which Kant means 'pure intuition' (cf. Riehl, *op. cit.,* p. 450), Kant says in *On a Discovery* (Allison trans., p. 136) ; 'Thus the formal *intuition,* which is called space, emerges as an originally acquired representation . . ., the ground of which . . . is nevertheless innate . . .'. For an explanation of the notion of 'originally acquired representation', see *ibid.,* pp. 135-36 [AK. VIII, 221-23].

    For Kant's use of the expression 'formal intuition' in the *Critique,* see B 160a, and for commentary, see Felix Grayeff, *Kant's Theoretical Philosophy,* trans. D. Walford, Manchester University Press, 1970, p. 193 and n. 10; cf. also G. Buchdahl, 'The Conception of Lawlikeness in Kant's Philosophy of Science', in L. W. Beck, ed., *Proceedings of the Third International Kant Congress,* 1972, p. 165, and cf. also the book referred to by Buchdahl in note 29 to his paper.

39. The form proper is (as Paton, *op. cit.,* p. 103, says) 'the form of matter'. It may be noted, however, that some find no ambiguity in the Kantian expression 'form of intuition [or of appearance]' as used in the *Critique* ; thus Grayeff takes it to stand for just' [the form] as potentially determining' ; see Grayeff, *op. cit.,* p. 193, and cf. *ibid.,* p. 38. But the ambiguity of this expression as pointed out by us can hardly be ignored; it is clearly brought to light by Kant's own

observations in *On a Discovery*. In order to avoid this ambiguity, Paton proposes to reserve 'form of appearance' for the sense 'form of given appearances' and 'form of sensibility' for the sense 'the subjective form that is potentially determining'; cf. Paton, *op. cit.*, pp. 101-103, 102 n. 5, 103 n. 1.

40. Kemp Smith, *Commentary*, 1918, p. 93.
41. *Ibid.*, p. 92.
42. This is the sense in which the expression 'empirical intuition' is (as is admitted by Garnett also) used at A 22 = B 36.
43. Riehl, *op. cit.*, p. 449.
44. I.e., by virtue of his transcendental idealist position, Kant in his clause under consideration is speaking in *anticipation* of his final position; cf. Paton's observation quoted above in note 10 to this chapter.
45. Cf. 1.3 above.
46. Garnett, *op. cit.*, p. 169.
47. *Ibid.*, p. 170.
48. *Ibid.*, p. 171.
49. *Ibid.*, p. 170.
50. *Ibid.*, p. 171.
51. *Ibidem.*
52. *Ibidem.*
53. The difficulty attending the words 'know' and 'knowledge' here is at present of no concern; but it may be pointed out that unlike Kemp Smith some prefer to translate Kant's word *erkennen* generally as 'cognise', and not as 'know'; cf. G. Buchdahl, *Metaphysics and the Philosophy of Science : The Classical Origins : Descartes to Kant*, Blackwell, Oxford, 1969, pp. 507 n. 5, 473 n. 4.
54. It must be noted 'that the method of abstraction involved in such pure intuitions is different from the method of abstraction involved in conception'; see Paton, *op. cit.*, p. 126.
55. Garnett, *op. cit.*, p. 171.
56. *Ibid.*, pp. 171ff.
57. *Ibid.*, p. 172.
58. *Ibid.*, p. 173.
59. *Ibidem.*

60. See the first of the three passages in question (i.e. the one at B 41).

61. A 20 = B 34.

62. It may, then, be said that 'perception' in the Aesthetic means the same as 'empirical intuition' in its wider sense of sensible intuition that is made up of sensation and pure intuition. In this sense the latter expression is used at A 22 = B 36, where Kant speaks of isolating pure intuition from empirical intuition. And in this sense it is used in many other places in the *Critique* : e.g. A 21 = B 35, B 147, A 165 = B 206, and so on.

    Kant sometimes uses the expression, 'empirical intuition' in a narrower sense, however. In this sense empirical intuition does not contain, but is the same as, sensation. The clearest passage in this regard occurs in Kant's *Anthropology* (trans. Gregor, The Hague, 1974, p. 24. n.) : '. . . *sensation* will mean sense representations (emipirical intuitions), as distinguished both from concepts (thoughts) and from pure intuitions (ideas of space and time)'.

    That in the Transcendental Aesthetic 'perception' in 'perception of an object' means 'empirical intuition' in its wider sense, and not 'sensation', is confirmed by reference to an *analogous* passage in § 10 of the *Prolegomena*, where Kant says : '[Space and time] . . ., by their being pure intuitions *a priori*, . . . must precede all empirical intuition, that is, perception of actual objects, . . .'; Carus trans. revised by Beck, 1976, p. 31. Three things are noteworthy ; (1) Kant here equates 'empirical intuition' with 'perception of actual objects' (*Wahrnehmung wirklicher Gegenstände*) ; see Vorländer's edition of the *Prolegomena*, Leipzig, 1920, p. 37. (2) The expression 'empirical intuition' is used here in its wider sense; for the above passage is quoted from a context where Kant is engaged in isolating space and time from empirical intuitions. This shows that 'empirical intuition (with which 'perception' is equated) does not mean the same as 'sensation'. (3) In saying that pure intuitions 'precede all empirical intuition, that is, perception of actual objects' Kant is using the word 'precede' in a logical, not temporal, sense; for pure intuition, which surely is *involved in* empirical intuition (in the wider sense) from which it is isolated, can *precede* it only logically, i.e. in the sense of being logically independent of it.

63. Paton, *op. cit.*, p. 137 n. 1.

64. Garnett, *op. cit.*, p. 175.

65. *Ibidem.*

66. *Ibid.*, p. 186 : '. . . the parts [of space] are not the given features of intuition : only the whole is given'.

67. *Ibid.*, p. 175.

68. See below, 11.2.

69. 'Representation' in 'the representation of space must be presupposed' in Kant's first space argument is said by Kemp Smith (*Commentary*, p. 102) to be 'conscious representation' in order to emphasize that the priority of this representation is *psychological.*

70. H. A. Prichard, *Kant's Theory of Knowledge*, Clarendon Press, Oxford, 1909, p. 42.

CHAPTER THREE

KANT'S FIRST SPACE ARGUMENT (Continued)

3.1 A Logical Interpretation of Kant's First Space Argument

It has already been pointed out that Kant's argument is not psychological and that its proper interpretation is logical. But the exact interpretation will vary according as this or that sentence is emphasized. The first sentence, 'Space is not an empirical concept which has been derived from outer experiences', may suggest that the idea of space is not abstracted from outer experience as general empirical concepts (like redness etc.) are. And, indeed, Dryer has so interpreted the argument.[1] In so doing, he has no doubt brought to the fore an often neglected suggestion of the argument. But this suggestion does not seem to us to be the dominant one, even although there will be a need to hark back to it at a late stage of our inquiry.[2]

To begin with, it will be well to read between the lines of the argument. The first sentence read together with a later one, namely, 'the representation of space cannot, therefore, be empirically obtained from the relations of outer appearances', makes it seem likely that Kant has aimed an attack at the view that the idea of space derives empirically from our apprehension of the relations of outer objects (such relations as outside and beside). And the last sentence–.'. . . this outer experience is itself possible at all only through that representation'–induces us to think he argues that the idea of space is (logically) presupposed in such outer experiences as the apprehension of outer relations from which the other party has sought to derive it.

Supposing Kant has designed an attack on the view mentioned above, the question arises : To whom is this view to be ascribed ? This question may be reserved for a subsequent treatment for the sake of emphasizing at the very outset that Kant's argument has a certain polemical character,[3] being directed to show that an empirical deduction[4] of the idea of space from the representation of the outer relations of sensibles is vitiated by logical circularity. It is worth trying to see at first what advantages attach to this logical interpretation of Kant's argument. We submit that Kant's first space argument is really much deeper and more complex than the interpretation just now presented, or even anything said so far, can enable us to appreciate. The argument can unfold itself in its full inner strength only if it is put into its proper historico-philosophical perspective and then examined closely. The logical interpretation already presented can be itself relied upon to guide our steps to the vantage point at which we may start delving deeper into Kant's argument in review. So we shall proceed with that interpretation and see first, by way of exploring its advantages, how it enables us to answer certain objections to which Kant's argument has been subjected.

3.2 Reply to Kemp Smith's Charge that Kant's Argument is Vitiated by an Uncritical Assumption about the Nature of Sensations

Upon the logical interpretation under consideration, the word 'sensations' (*Empfindungen*) occurring in the proof (that is, in the second sentence) of Kant's argument seems to be not essential, but replaceable by some such expression as 'sensible objects', the latter expression meaning (or being taken to mean) 'sensibles, whether sensa or appearances or what might be called perceptual objects'.[5] According to Kemp Smith, Garnett, and others, the word 'sensations' plays a vital role in Kant's argument.[6] To be sure, they would not think of interpreting the argument in the way they did if they had not found this word particularly. Upon their psychological-temporal interpretation of this argument, the idea of space is presupposed in the experience of outer relations in the sense of being already existent in us temporally prior to such experience, because,–and this is for them an unexpressed, though essential, 'premiss' in this argument–, the spatial reference involved in such outer experience cannot come from *sensations* themselves, which are non-spatial. Kemp Smith, proceeding upon this interpretation, finds it easy enough to criticize the argument on the ground that it is vitiated by the 'unquestioned premiss'[7] that sensations are in themselves non-spatial. That this supposed 'premiss' is questionable he shows by saying that it is 'effectively called in question by William James' by his theory of the *extensity* of sensations.[8] This, however, is utterly irrelevant as a criticism of Kant's first space argument. There are reasons to believe that the argument is not based upon any assumption about the character of sensations or sensa : the word 'sensations' particularly is eliminable from its *proof* in favour of some less suggestive substitute. The following are the main considerations for our saying so :

(i) Kant's corresponding argument for time in the Aesthetic (B 46 = A 30) contains no reference to sensations or the impressions of sense, but, instead, to 'a number of things'.

It is true that in the *Dissertation* version of this argument for time, there is mention of 'the impressions of sense' in at least one sentence.[9] But the non-employment of the expression in the Aesthetic version is significant as showing that the argument does not turn on the special nature of sensa.

(ii) G. Martin,[10] who also says that the word 'sensations' is not essential to Kant's proof in the first space argument, refers us to the proof in the *Dissertation* version of the corresponding space argument, where Kant says : 'For I cannot conceive anything as located outside me unless I represent it as in a space from the space in which I myself am; nor can I conceive things as outside one another unless I arrange them in different parts of space'.[11] Instead of 'sensations' we find here 'anything' and 'things'. [Martin emphasizes the term 'conceive' (*concipere*), too, to establish the point that *sensation* is not meant.[12] But this is overshooting the mark; for (a) Kant could as well write 'perceive', as is suggested by his words 'outer perceptions' in the immediately next sentence (not quoted), and (b) he sometimes does use 'conceive' to mean *perceive*, as is suggested by his words 'conceivable by sense' in the footnote to § 14.5 of the *Dissertation*.]

In the *Dissertation* argument in question (not fully quoted) there is, no doubt, one reference to 'sensations' followed by two to 'the senses'; but the fact that 'sensations' is conspicuous by its absence from the (quoted) proof of the argument is itself indicative. It suggests that the special nature of sensa is of no concern to the proof.

We may now come back to Kemp Smith and put our point of view more clearly. There indeed is on the part of Kant, when he is considered in a larger context, the assumption that sensations in themselves are non-spatial, having 'intensive magnitude' only. But in his argument before us, as we have been trying to press, this assumption is not at work, not even implicitly, as a 'premiss'. Nor is the assumption unique to Kant; it is common property of a good many empiricists also. William James questions it for the first time, and obviously he comes out with a new form of space-empiricism, one to the effect that our idea of space is ultimately based on the hitherto unrecognized spatial quality of extensity of sensations. In an overall estimate of the Kantian apriorism with regard to the idea of space, due account must of course be taken of this form of space-empiricism; we propose to discuss it in an appropriate place.[13] At present it is necessary to emphasize that James's is a form of space-empiricism which is fundamentally different from the sort that Kant's argument under consideration is (we think) designed to combat. And the sort of space-empiricism it is designed to combat has already been pointed out. It is to the effect that the idea of space is obtained from the empirical representation of the outer relations (such as outside and beside) of certain sensibles. The question is whether any assumption regarding the nature of sensa is at all indispensably required by Kant to combat this sort of space-empiricism. The answer is, No. What Kant requires to maintain is simply that certain sensibles (whether sensa or appearances or phenomena) could not be represented as outside and beside one another without our already presupposing (logically) the idea of space. And this he does maintain indeed in his first space argument.

It has already been pointed out that Kant's argument, on the interpretation we are proceeding with, has a certain polemical character. We now add that blindness to this character can be the cause of much misunderstanding. Such blindness with the consequent misunderstanding is exemplified in Sidgwick's criticism to which we may now turn.

3.3 Reply to sidgwick's Charge of Triviality against Kant's Argument

Sidgwick maintains that Kant's contention in the first space argument is at best a truism and as such fails altogether to establish the intended conclusion. Referring to the word 'outside' in Kant's proof, he first points out its ambiguity, saying that it means either 'spatial externality' or 'otherness of existence' (i.e. 'distinct and independent existence'), and then observes that Kant has used it in the first sense.[14] 'This being so', he objects,

> the statement that I cannot apprehend things as being outside my body and outside each other, without apprehending them as occupying different parts of Space, is undeniable but insignificant; since material outsideness is a spatial notion, involved in and involving the notion of 'location in different parts of Space'. But the statement has no tendency to prove that the whole notion of Space and spatial externality is not empirical.[15]

Our reply to Sidgwick has already been hinted at (in advance) : his objection is based on a failure to see that Kant's argument in question has a certain polemical character. By virtue of this character, the statement in it which appears to be 'insignificant' is really not so. By calling the statement (that the representation of things as outside one another already involves that of their occupying different places) 'undeniable but insignificant', Sidgwick means to say, we suppose, that it is analytic and so uninformative. But he fails to appreciate that Kant in this argument is concerned not so much with giving us any positive information as with rejecting what he takes to be an error, namely, that the idea of space is derived empirically from the relations of outer appearances, such relations as being outside (external to) one another. The conclusion of the argument is accordingly negative : 'The representation of space cannot, therefore, be empirically obtained from the relations of outer appearances'.[16] For Kant, 'the task peculiar to negative judgments is that of *rejecting error*'.[17] It is a logical error (of the nature of circularity or *petitio principii*)–, such indeed is part of the import[18] of his present argument–, to base, or try to base, on the representation of things as external to one another an empirical deduction of the idea of space; for the idea of space is already involved, i.e. presupposed, in the said representation.[19] Had Sidgwick but an idea of the exact drift and motive of Kant's argument, he would not have mistaken the latter's implied charge of circularity against the space-empiricist for a mere triviality on his (Kant's) part.[20]

To preclude the suspicion that Kant's argument under discussion has demolished only an imaginary view, we hasten to point out that Wolff at least, despite the rationalism often read into his system, was enough of a space-empiricist to have been later a fit target of the Kantian argument which is being considered. Reference may be made here to his account of the idea of space contained in his *Vernünftige Gedanken von Gott*, etc., (§ 46) : this is partially quoted and translated by L. W. Beck as follows : 'Given a variety of things "external to one another" but simultaneous, there is an order among them, and "as soon as we represent this order we have an idea of space"[21] It is clear that Wolff has sought to derive the idea of space from the representation of a certain order of mutual externality among simultaneously given things; and it can be urged that Kant has criticized a view of this sort by contending, in the second sentence of his argument, that the representation of sensibles as external to one another ('outside . . . one another') already presupposes the idea of space.

Some evidence must be cited to show that Wolff was really an empiricist at least as regards the idea of space and that Kant's first space argument is consciously directed against him. We proceed to do this not, however, directly, but by way of a brief discussion of the general question that has been kept so long pending, namely, that of the targets of Kant's first space argument. Consideration of this general question is indeed necessary for a clear understanding of the historico-philosophical perspective of Kant's argument. It will be seen that in this argument he has more his German predecessors in mind than, as is often supposed, the English empiricists. And, moreover, an advance will thereby be made towards coming to see that there is under the surface of his argument a still deeper contention of considerable force against any relational and reductionist account of the idea of space.

3.4 Against Whom Is Kant's First Space Argument Directed ?

It is often supposed that Kant has his (English) empiricist predecessors in mind. Weldon, for example, says that the argument 'is directed primarily against the English form of empiricism'.[22] But the views on space held by Locke, Berkeley, and Hume are sufficiently various to forbid a summary putting of them into one identical form. May it, then, be said that Kant has ignored the distinctive aspects of their views for the sake of a compendious form of criticism ? Or, should it be said that he has criticized only one of them in particular rather than all of them together ?

It is sometimes said that Kant is here critical particularly of Hume.[23] Hume's account of the idea of space, however, occurs in his *Treatise*, but 'Hat Kant Hume's Treatise gelesen ?'[24]

Most Kantian scholars are of the opinion that Kant had no first-hand acquaintance with the *Treatise*,[25] and indeed there is no positive evidence that he had. Nevertheless Kant's ignorance of the original *Treatise* has not been conclusively established.[26] It is perhaps wisdom, therefore, to let drop the vexed question of Kant's perusal of the *Treatise*.

Those who deny the anti-Humean drift of Kant's present argument sometimes contend, however, that the argument would have probably taken a different shape had it been directed against Hume's reduction of the idea of space to a copy of impressions.[27] This contention exhibits, as we see, a simple misunderstanding of Hume's actual view in the *Treatise*. The idea of space is, for Hume, no direct *copy* of impressions, but is none the less empirical, being derived from the manner of appearance of certain kinds of impression.[28] Hume no doubt puts this view very variously, but the following might be taken as a fair enough summary of it : 'When certain sensations (namely, visible and/or tangible points)[29] are represented as disposed in a certain manner or order, we have the idea of space'. What the phrase 'disposed in a certain manner or order' means is not quite clear, and Hume-scholars have grumbled at this unclarity.[30] It might be supposed that the phrase means 'so disposed as to appear outside and alongside (i.e. contiguous to)[31] one another'; and this supposition is not without exegetical warrant. Thus in one passage Hume says of objects apprehended in space that their manner of appearance is such 'as to answer to our notions of contiguity or distance', and in the same passage he says that non-spatial objects do not appear in this manner : e.g. a 'moral reflection cannot be placed on the right or on the left hand of a passion'.[32] One is, then, within one's rights in paraphrasing Hume's view as follows : 'When certain sensations are presented in such a manner as to appear outside and contiguous to (i.e. alongside) one another, we have the idea of space'. The similarity of this view to the one criticised in the second sentence of Kant's first space argument can hardly be ignored.

Nevertheless, in the absence of any further evidence, it would remain a mere conjecture that Kant has really Hume in mind in the present argument. The evidence at our disposal suggests on the contrary that the argument is directed *primarily* against his own 'countrymen', particularly against Wolff.[33] That evidence we proceed now to furnish, aware also of the necessity of considering by the way whether Kant's attribution of space-empiricism to his countrymen under reference is after all justified.

In the Transcendental Aesthetic, Kant says that 'certain metaphysical students of nature' 'regard space and time as relations of appearances, alongside or in succession to one another–relations abstracted from experience, and in this isolation confusedly represented– . . .'; (A 40 = B 56-7). Now with reference to this passage, the following are the points to be noted :

(a) By 'certain metaphysical students of nature' Kant here means the followers of Leibniz. This can be confirmed by reference to the *Inaugural Dissertation* where, in an exactly similar context, Kant has stated the view that he states here and said that it is maintained by most of his countrymen, following Leibniz.[34]

It may be pointed out that when Kant speaks of the followers of Leibniz, he has usually and primarily Wolff in mind. [Even when he speaks of 'the Leibnizian-Wolffian system', his reference is not so much to Leibniz's own system as to that of *seine Nachfolger* (his followers), chief among them being Wolff, as is clear, e.g. from his observation in a quite different context : 'Although Herr von Leibniz did not announce the above proposition . . ., . . . *his successors* expressly incorporated it into *their Leibnizian-Wolffian system*'.][35]

(b) The view, which Kant states in the passage before us as being that of the Leibnizians, can be, in part at least, paraphrased by saying that the idea of space is empirically obtained from the relations of outer appearances.[36] So paraphrased, this view is *verbatim* identical with the view that Kant's first space argument rejects by saying : 'The representation of space cannot, therefore, be empirically obtained from the relations of outer appearance'.

(c) The expression 'confusedly represented' in the passage under consideration is doubly significant for our purposes. In the first place, it is strongly reminiscent of Wolff, an exposition of whose view in relevant respects will be given shortly. In the second place, it seems to provide some explanation of Kant's use of the term 'sensations' in his first space argument, supposing that the argument is directed against the Leibnizians.[37] The Leibnizians regard the so-called sensations as confused representations; they hold the view, as Kant puts it in the Aesthetic (B 60 = A 43), 'that our entire sensibility is nothing but a confused representation of things'. What is confusedly represented is on this view so represented through the interference of the senses.

To the above considerations the following may be added.

In the *Inaugural Dissertation* Kant has observed that in the account given by Leibniz's followers space is so defined as to give rise to a vicious 'circle'.[38] Now this is also the import of his criticism of the view against which his first space argument in the Aesthetic is directed. In this argument Kant contends that the idea of space is already *presupposed*[39] in the attempt to derive it from the relations of outer appearances, which is equivalent to saying that this sort of deduction of the idea of space lands us in a circle.

It might be objected that in the *Dissertation* passage just referred to Kant is critical of his countrymen's *definition of space*, whereas in the first space argument he is critical of a particular *derivation of the idea of space*, and that this difference of aims should be taken very seriously. To this several replies can be made, but the following will suffice. If one only cares to look at Kant's first argument for time in the *Dissertation*, one finds that, concerned as he is there with criticizing a particular *derivation of the idea of time*, he is none the less critical in that context of the implied *definition of time*. Thus a slight acquaintance with Kant's style of presentation suffices to put the objection in view out of court.

It is high time we took up the question whether Kant is justified in ascribing to Wolff the view of the empirical origin (status) of the idea of space. A detailed exposition of Wolff's theory of knowledge in general and of his theory of space in particular appears in L. W. Beck's *Early German Philosophy.*[40] What follows is only a brief statement containing one or two points relevant to our inquiry.

Wolff recognizes 'two ways of knowing truth' : by experience and by understanding. Understanding is the faculty that produces distinct representations, or concepts, on the basis of indistinct representations, or sensations, by a process of abstraction. Human understanding cannot work with concepts not abstracted from the senses; it is incapable, that is to say, of a quite pure employment. All knowledge and its principles arise from experience. Wolff thus 'sounds like a good empiricist', observes Beck, who hastens to point out that the philosopher has not been assiduous, however, in following out this all-important empiricist assumption.[41] Lest it should be supposed that the empiricist elements in the Wolffian philosophy are being over-stressed in this exposition, it might be pointed out that Wolff once demurred to the qualification 'Leibniz-Wolffian' applied to his philosophy, claiming that he was more indebted to the empiricist Aquinas than to Leibniz.[42] In actual fact, however, he is neither a consistent empiricist nor a consistent rationalist. Beck has clearly shown that the Wolffian philosophy is such a 'confused mixture' that it is 'impossible' to classify it as being either empiricistic or rationalistic.[43]

Anyway, our present concern is with Wolff's theory of concept-formation. As has already been pointed out, he holds the view that all our concepts are ultimately abstracted from sensations. It follows that the concept of space is similarly abstracted. When, however, he specially considers the concept of space, he makes use of his theory of confused representation. It is through confused representation of the *Ordnung der Dinge* ('order of things') that the idea of space is ultimately formed. His account of this idea as contained in his *Vernünftige Gedanken von Gott*, etc. has already been quoted before partially (in Beck's translation). It remains to add that when he says there that the idea of space is formed 'as soon as we represent' an order among mutually external things given at a time, the representation of which he speaks is a 'confused representation'; it is indeed natural that he should regard this representation as confused; for there is here a clear incidence of sense-interference, in so far as the represented order is an order among things presented by sense (the external sense of sight, say). There can be little question, then, that the deduction of the idea of space offered by Wolff is to all intents and purposes an *empirical* deduction.

The above discussion of the question as to the 'men' who might primarily have been in Kant's mind as targets of his first space argument is admittedly not exhaustive. Some further observations on this topic will have to be made in the next section. For our limited present purpose, however, the discussion of this section has been, we trust, sufficient. We now propose to give a second thought to Sidgwick's charge of triviality against Kant's first space argument and to ascertain how matters get complicated upon further reflection. In case complications arise, it may be easier to find an occasion for making a closer examination of Kant's argument under review to see what more may remain implicit in it than has been explored so far.

3.5 A Second Thought on Sidgwick's Charge of Triviality, and a Little More Study of the Historico-philosophical Perspective of Kant's First Space Argument

3.5.1 Sidgwick's charge of triviality revived

We have seen that Sidgwick's charge of triviality against Kant's first space argument is based on a failure to appreciate that this argument is implicitly polemical in character and is designed to expose the circularity of, for example, the Wolffian sort of empirical deduction of the idea of space. To this it may be objected that the Wolffian deduction is potentially free from the sort of circularity (which one might call 'obvious circularity')[44] that has been pointed out before and that therefore Sidgwick's charge of triviality against Kant's argument is after all not adequately met. To work out this objection it is of course necessary to study Wolff's account of the idea of space a little more minutely.

Following Kant's *Dissertation* strategy of examining his opponents' definitions, it may be well to consider Wolff's definition of space. Wolff has sometimes defined space in terms of an order of coexistence (in the sense of simultaneous existence) among sensible things rather than in terms of an order of mutual *externality* among those sensibles (in the sense of their being outside or beside one another). In his *Philosophia prima sive Ontologia*, we have his clearest possible definition of space, which runs as : 'Spatium est ordo simultaneorum, quatenus scilicet coexistunt.'[45] 'Coexist' here means 'exist at the same time', not 'exist in spatial contiguity' implying spatial externality.[46] In this respect, indeed, Wolff follows strictly in the footsteps of Leibniz. Leibniz, in defining as well as in accounting for the idea of space, speaks not in terms of externality at all, but only in terms of coexistence in the sense of existence at the same time. His view is worth quoting : '. . . I hold it [space] to be an order of coexistences as time is the order of successions. For space denotes, in terms of possibility,[47] an order of things which exist at the same time, considered as existing together, without inquiring into their particular manner of existing. And when many things are seen together one perceives that order of things among themselves'.[48] 'Together' in the last sentence obviously means 'at the same time'.[49]

The difficulty that now arises is this. If Wolff had based his deduction of the idea of space, closely following Leibniz as he sometimes does, on just the representation of the order of *coexistence* among sensible objects, instead of trying to base it as he also sometimes does on the representation of an order of mutual *externality* among simultaneously given sensible objects, then his deduction would be free, surely, from 'obvious circularity'; and since this is so, a follower of Sidgwick might all the more vigorously uphold the charge of triviality against Kant's first space argument either by maintaining that it would no longer do to circumvent the charge by converting it into an implicit Kantian charge of obvious circularity against Wolff, or by bringing it from a slightly different direction by saying that Kant's allegedly implicit charge of circularity against the Wolffian view had at least the triviality of being easily avoidable through a slight restatement of that view.

3.5.2 The need for delving deeper into Kant's first space argument to find a reply to the revived charge of triviality

The difficulty stated above can be overcome if it can be shown within the terms of Kant's first space argument that the Wolffian view, even after it is restated in the manner already indicated, does not altogether cease to be circular. If it ceases to be obviously circular, which indeed it does, there still remains the possibility that it is unobviously circular. The main task ahead of us is, then, that of delving deeper into Kant's first space argument in order to show, if we can, that for it any deduction of the idea of space by reference to the representation of any sort of *order* or *relation* at all, no matter whether such order or relation is described as that of externality or of coexistence, among sensible objects, is bound to fail because of the need to presuppose, on non-trivial grounds, the idea of space (and time) in such a deduction.

That task cannot be immediately undertaken, however; and the reason why a digression is necessary is this. It has been noticed that the restatement, or rather, the more guarded version, of Wolff's view of space turns it into a reiteration of Leibniz's, at least in the respect that is relevant to the present inquiry, and this at once makes it necessary that meanwhile something should be said in reply to each of these unavoidable queries : (1) whether Kant's first space argument is consciously directed against Leibniz also (as, e.g. Caird maintains[50]), and if so, (2) whether the ascription to him of what has been called 'space-empiricism' is exegetically supportable, seeing that Leibniz of all philosophers is most commonly believed to be a rationalist *malgre'lui*, according to whom all our ideas are innate.[51]

3.5.3 An unavoidable digression to consider whether Kant's first space argument is consciously, and justly, directed against Leibniz

Replies to the two questions formulated above follow.

(1) There is no strong internal evidence to show that Kant has Leibniz also in mind in his first space argument. We may recall the phrase 'certain metaphysical students of nature' in the previously quoted A 40 = B 56-57 passage of the *Critique*–a passage stating a view of which the affinity to the one criticized in Kant's first space argument was also remarked upon.[52] The philosophers denoted by that phrase are, in a comparable passage in the section 'On space' in Kant's *Inaugural Dissertation*, called (as we saw) 'following Leibniz, most of our countrymen', and in a parallel passage in the section 'On time' there, they are mentioned as 'Leibniz and his school.'[53] Since the emphasis

here is on the Leibnizian school, it may be said that although it is clear enough that Kant has Leibniz's successors in mind, it is not as clear that he has Leibniz also directly in mind.[54] That is to say, even if he has Leibniz also in mind, it is not quite clear that he is not considering that philosopher simply as he is represented by his followers.

Yet the precise question before us is whether Kant's first space argument is directed, among others, against the historical Leibniz. It is hoped that one may be allowed to answer this question in the affirmative if one can find reasons to believe that Kant for himself reckons Leibniz to be in a way a space-empiricist (that is, a philosopher whose account of the idea of space turns out to be empirical). For if that argument is already directed against the 'Leibnizians', which, as we have seen, it is, there is no reason why Kant, if he thinks Leibniz also to be a space-empiricist, should yet dissociate him from his followers while demonstrating against them the failure of space-empiricism. It will, then, be appropriate to consult some relevant material contained in Kant's exposition of Leibniz's account of space.

In an appendix to the *Critique* entitled 'Amphiboly of Concepts of Reflection', Kant, in the course of examining the intellectualist philosophy of Leibniz, considers what he calls 'Leibniz's famous doctrine of time and space',[55] and since in that examination he is sometimes careful enough to distinguish Leibniz's own position from that of his followers,[56] it is but fair to assume that when he speaks of Leibniz alone his reference is rather to the historical Leibniz. Now his exposition of Leibniz's doctrine of time and space remains diffused throughout the 'Amphiboly' section, and one has to piece together some two or three passages to reach what is wanted. He says : 'Leibniz conceived space as a certain order in the community of substances, and time as the dynamical sequence of their states. That which space and time seem to possess as proper to themselves . . . he ascribed to the *confusion* in their concepts . . .'.[57] Kant is here taking Leibniz to hold *inter alia* that our ideas of space and time are due to the confused representation of what are at bottom intellectual orders among intelligible substances and their states. All things for Leibniz are 'intelligibilia, i.e. objects of the pure understanding'; even the things that we regard as objects of the senses are on his intellectualist view intelligibilia represented only confusedly. 'Leibniz took the appearances for things-in-themselves, and so for intelligibilia, i.e. objects of the pure understanding (although, on account of the confused character of our representations of them, he still gave them the name of phenomena)'.[58] Now since for intellectualist philosophy matter is prior to form, inasmuch as unless something is first given there is nothing for the understanding to determine in a definite fashion,[59] Leibniz is led to regard 'the matter (or the things themselves that appear)'[60] as prior to spatio-temporal form, that is, he is led to reduce space and time to certain orders among the things themselves which appear. The error of this intellectualist-cum-reductionist account lies, for Kant, in the failure to see that 'space and time come before all appearances and before all data of experience', that they lie '*a priori* at the foundation of all perception', 'that so far is the matter (or the things themselves which appear) from serving as the foundation (as we should have to judge if we followed mere concepts) that on the contrary its own possibility presupposes a formal intuition (time and space) as antecedently given'.[61]

This criticism by Kant already presupposes his transcendental-idealist or subjective-formalist doctrine of space and time formulated in the Transcendental Aesthetic and is as such without relevance to the present inquiry. One thing, however, is quite clear, namely, that in Kant's judgement Leibniz should willy-nilly let himself be called a space-empiricist after all. The view that the idea of space as we have it is due to a confused representation of an intellectual order among confusedly represented intelligibilia amounts to the view that this idea derives empirically from a perceived order among sense-given things; for 'the despicable task' of yielding confused representations is, as Kant points out, assigned by Leibniz 'to the senses'.[62]

As we shall see, Kant's first space argument at its deepest serves to expose the subtle circularity involved in the reductionist account of the idea of space of the sort that is being described in the current excursus into Leibniz. Kant's doctrine of the apriority, in the austere sense, of the idea of space is that of an anti-reductionist.[63] Let us in the meantime speedily finish off what is still in arrears, namely, some consideration of the problem of historical justice of the Kantian ascription of space-empiricism to Leibniz.

(2) The fact remains that Leibniz has sometimes aseribed the origin

of our idea of space to some *sense*. In his 'Letter to Queen Sophia Charlotte of Prussia, 1702',[64] he distinguishes between 'the particular senses' and 'the common sense', and while ascribing our concepts of colours, sounds, smells, tastes, and tactual qualities to the particular senses, he ascribes to the common sense our concepts of 'figures' or 'shapes' and 'numbers'.[65] Further, Loemker has called attention to the fact that 'in the *New Essays* (II, 5)' also Leibniz ascribes our spatial concepts such as the concept of shapes '(called by Locke simple ideas which come from several senses) to the common sense (Aristotle *De anima* ii. 6) but identifies the common sense with "the mind itself, for they are ideas of the pure understanding, which relate to the external world and which we perceive through the senses".'[66] No doubt in this quoted passage of the *New Essays* Leibniz makes the idea of space both 'pure' and dependent on sense-perception; and this seems to be confusing. But the confusion can be got rid of by harking back to his 1702 Letter to Queen Sophia of Charlotte. There the ideas 'appertaining to' the common sense are called '*at once sensible and intelligible*', in distinction from 'those which are *sensible* only, which are produced by each sense in particular', and also from 'those which are *intelligible* only, which belong to the understanding'.[67] By calling an idea due to the common sense 'at once sensible and intelligible', Leibniz means that such an idea contains 'something which sense cannot furnish but which the understanding adds to it',[68] implying thereby that it does contain something which sense has furnished. This immediately raises the question how much of it is due to, and how much independent of, sense. But the answer to this we have not discovered in Leibniz. This is not to suggest, however, that we have failed to get rid of the confusion caused by the *New Essays* passage. One thing has been plain, namely, that the idea of space, as an idea of common sense, is not for Leibniz both *wholly* 'pure' and *wholly* due to sense-perception. There is, in other words, no self-contradiction in his assertion; it is thus that our confusion has come to an end. A dissatisfaction has, of course, begun; for we are yet in the dark as to the extent to which the idea in question is for him 'pure' and the extent to which it is impure. This obscurity notwithstanding, the fact that the idea in question is virtually admitted at all to be at least partly impure (i.e. due to sense) is enough to justify the ascription to Leibniz of some sort of space-empiricism.

Should it be objected that the actual term used by Leibniz is 'sensible', and not 'empirical', and that therefore even if the idea of space is for him partly *sensible*, it does not necessarily follow that it is for him partly *empirical*, the objection might be set aside on the ground of anachronism. For the equation 'sensible' = 'empirical' holds good for all philosophers except Kant or a Kantian. To deny this is to imply that the *history* of philosophy is a misnomer. The doctrine of the '*sensible a priori*' (i.e. of pure intuition) is peculiarly Kantian. The Aristotelian doctrine of *sensus communis*, which is here relied on by Leibniz, may be said, in its application to the idea of space, to anticipate the Kantian doctrine of pure intuition; but it would be wrong not to see the remote distance between the anticipating doctrine and the anticipated one.

As regards Leibniz, then, he is, we see, too big a philosopher for mere consistency. He may be credited with an unconscious (unapperceived) tendency towards the Kantian doctrine that the idea of space is at once *sensible* and *a priori*; but, to judge by his actual sentences, he remains a space-empiricist in not a few of them. When, in a passage already quoted before from 'The controversy between Leibniz and Clarke', he explains the idea of space by saying that 'when many things are seen together one perceives that order (i.e. the order of coexistence) of things among themselves',[69]–an order which for him constitutes space–, one cannot but take him to mean that the things in question are 'seen' by the external sense of sight and that the order which one 'perceives' is perceived by 'the common sense'; the common sense is not a separate sense over and above the several particular senses, but is said to be 'a nature common to diverse organs'.[70] Although what is represented by the common sense is not regarded by Leibniz as 'confused',[71] the palpable fact remains that it is after all *sense*-represented, according to him. The empirical character of his account is obvious enough.

It is time to return to Kant's first space argument. Once its historico-philosophical background has been clear, we have not to wait long to realize wherein lies its final pungency : it lies in its implicit rejection of Leibniz's principle of individuation. To appreciate that the crux of the matter concerns the *principium individuationis,* we need only isolate the *essential point* in the Leibnizian-Wolffian account of the idea of space.

3.5.4 The essential point in the Leibnizian-Wolffian account of the idea of space : it is a relational-cum-reductionist account

Against Newton, or Clarke, Leibniz and his followers maintain that space is nothing independent of the things said to be in it,[72] but a relational system consisting in a certain order, a certain sort of relation, among such things. Accordingly they try to account for the *idea* of space in terms of a representation of a certain sort of *mutual relation* among sensible objects (otherwise called 'phenomena' by Leibniz). How this mutual relation which is represented is to be described,–whether it should be described as the relation of coexistence or of *nebeneinander* or of externality–, is not with them a question of the first importance, though it is of some importance, as we shall see.[73] What is of the first importance to them is just the point that the idea of space derives from the representation of a certain sort of mutual relation among sensible objects themselves. Negatively their contention is that this idea does not derive from the representation of anything independent of the sensible objects, nor again from the representation of even any relation between such objects and something else or parts of something else called space. This is not, however, to deprive us of our right to say that sensible objects occupy, or even are represented as occupying, different parts of space, i.e. different places. The point of the contention is that the so-called places, or parts of space, are not parts of anything ontologically underlying the sensible objects in question, but are rather the positions or situations of the sensible objects themselves in relation to one another,[74] and that accordingly our representation of objects as in different places is not the representation of any relations between the objects and the parts of some ontological absolute called space, but is rather the representation of mutual relations among the objects themselves. This, then, is the *essential point* in the Leibnizian-Wolffian account of the idea of space : that this idea derives from the representation of a certain order, or mutual relations, among sensible objects of a certain sort (say, simultaneously given visible or tangible objects), and that our so-called perception of the different places of objects is ultimately reducible to, or logically dependent upon, the said representation of the mutual relations among sensible objects themselves.

This account makes the idea of space *empirical* in that it essentially refers to the representation of relations among *sensible* objects otherwise called by Leibniz *phenomena.* Now this view is doubtless not vitiated by 'obvious circularity' ; and this question is whether it is vitiated by unobvious circularity.

3.5.5 Towards a deeper study of Kant's first space argument

The Leibnizian-Wolffian view in question can be effectively countered on the score of circularity itself if it can be maintained that the representation of *relations* at all among sensible objects of a certain sort itself *presupposes* the representation of those objects *as in different places.* What we are going to try to show in the next section is that exactly this is the all-important fundamental point on which Kant's first space argument does turn. The words 'outside . . . one another' occurring in its proof (and capitalized by Sidgwick) suggest a somewhat superficial interpretation of it, which we adopted before only in preference to the psychological-temporal interpretation of the argument and which we found really useful in its own way within a certain range. But we can no longer allow those words to distract our attention from the deeper contention implicit in Kant's argument, which is, as we shall work out shortly, that *relations* at all among sensible objects of a certain sort cannot be represented unless those objects are individuated, and they cannot be individuated unless they are already represented *as in different places.* It will be seen that by insisting on the logical priority of the representation of the *different places* of certain sensible objects over that of their relations to one another, Kant in his present argument has launched a subtle attack on the Leibnizian principle of individuation.

3.6 Delving Deeper into Kant's First Space Argument

There are in Kant's work two versions of his space argument under examination, one in the *Inaugural Dissertation* and one in the Transcendental Aesthetic of the *Critique.* Either version is better than the other in this or that respect. What we propose to do now is to construct a third version that shall combine the virtues of the original two and thus place Kant in a clearer light. For our immediate purpose, we shall confine ourselves only to the decisive part of the proof of Kant's argument. Let us compare the following two partial extracts from the two original versions of the proof :

(1) The *Dissertation* version (§15A) : 'I cannot conceive . . . things as outside one another unless I arrange them in different parts of space'.

(2) The Aesthetic version (B 38) : '. . . in order that I may be able to represent them (sc. "certain sensations") as outside and alongside[75] one another, and accordingly as not only different but in different places, . . .'.

Combining the felicities and avoiding the infelicities of these two versions, we get the following third version :

(3) 'I cannot represent certain sensible objects as outside and alongside one another unless I represent them as not only different but as in different places'.

Upon this third version, Kant's proof has indeed a great deal of viability; it has sufficient flexibility to lend itself to being appropriately recast and pitted against whatever form the Leibnizian-Wolffian or kindred account[76] of the idea of space may present itself in. Thus it is possible to add to the words 'as outside and alongside one another' occurring in Kant's proof the words 'or as together involved in any relation or order among themselves' without altering the spirit and mitigating the polemical force of the proof. It is even possible to expunge the words 'as outside and alongside one another' and rewrite the proof as : 'I cannot represent certain sensible objects (e.g. certain visible things) as together involved in any relation or order among themselves[77] unless I represent them as not only different but in different places'. All this will become clear by the end of this section.

Let us begin with our version (3), which is less a reconstruction of Kant's proof than an interweaving of his two original versions. That this third version is more suggestive and as such better than the two original ones has to be shown in the first place. It need hardly be said that in beginning with this third version we are of course obliged to work with Kant's words 'as outside and alongside one another' and the order or relations among sensible objects that they signify, namely, the order or relations of externality and adjacency. Subsequently it will be seen, however, that these words and the specific order or relations they signify are not essential, and that Kant's first space argument in its own right expansively installs itself on a broader spectrum. Now, as for the superiority of the third version over Kant's two original ones, this can be shown on the basis of the following two considerations.

(a) The word 'accordingly' in the phrase 'accordingly as not only different but in different places' occurring in the Aesthetic version of Kant's proof is liable to be misleading : it may cause on the part of some a failure to notice, or even a refusal to admit, that the phrase here introduces a *condition,* and a necessary condition at that. As the combined study of Kant's two original versions of his proof indicates and as will be clearer in what follows, a necessary condition[78] of the representation of a certain sort of relations (order) among sensible objects is, for Kant, the *representation* of these sensible objects *as not only different but in different places.* In other words, the sensible objects cannot be represented as related or ordered in a certain way *unless* they are represented as not only different but as in different places. In this respect the *'unless'*–construction in the *Dissertation* version is better than the *'accordingly'*–construction of the Aesthetic, and so has been preferred by us.

(b) But the *necessary condition* in question has been stated in the *Dissertation* in a less suggestive way than in the Aesthetic. In this respect the Aesthetic gives us an improved version. In this version the phrase introducing the condition is 'as not only different but in different places', whereas in the *Dissertation* it is simply 'in different parts of space' meaning 'in different places'. The Aesthetic version, then, adds 'as different' to 'in different places' ;[79] and the question arises about the significance of this addition. For us the significance of this addition consists in suggesting that the deeper point at issue between Kant and his opponents is, in the case under consideration, connected with the problem of *individuation* of sensible objects. *Pace*' some eminent scholars, we are taking the words 'as different' in the sense of 'as numerically different'.[80] The addition of these words made in the Aesthetic enables us to see what the *Dissertation* keeps concealed, namely, that Kant's central contention in his first space argument comes to this : Since sensible objects cannot be represented as involved in a certain kind of relations or order (say, of mutual externality and adjacency) unless they are individuated, that is, represented *as different* (as numerically different, to be more precise) and since they cannot be individuated, represented as numerically different, unless they are represented *as in different places*, the idea of space is already presupposed in the representation of an order of sensible objects, and so cannot without circularity be derived empirically from such order.

Kant's contention as just now paraphrased is not, to be sure, clear enough. Or rather, it is not precise enough. A more precise restatement of it remains to be attempted.

One is required here to give a little thought to Kant's general position on the problem of individuation. 'Being represented as in different places' is not, for him, a necessary condition for the individuation of items of *every* kind. He insists on this necessary condition for individuation only in the case of (i) *sensible* objects that are (ii) *simultaneously* given. That this is his general position will be substantiated later on, and at present reference is being made to it only to underline the backing that we think it gives to his first space argument before us. In this argument, he is talking of 'sensations' and 'appearances', which shows that he has in view just *sensible* objects. And, moreover, by saying here of 'certain' sensible objects that they are represented 'as outside and alongside one another', he is saying, by implication, though not by explicit statement, that the sensible objects being particularly considered by him are *simultaneously* presented, i.e. that they are coexistent sensibles. To say 'A and B are outside and alongside one another' is indeed to imply 'A and B *zugleich sind'*. The proof of his first space argument, then, hinges on this general point, to be explained and examined in due course, that simultaneously given sensible objects cannot be individuated except by reference to their individuating spatial locations. If it be still objected that Kant does not express himself exactly in this way in his first space argument, it may be replied that it is not then clear how otherwise his phraseology itself in this argument can be convincingly explained. Why does he hold in this argument that sensible objects that are represented as outside and alongside one another are required to be not only different but as in different places ? The question is really about the justification to be offered for his employment of so complex a phrase as 'not only different but in different places'. The answer already given before can now be spelled out as follows : With respect to sensible objects given at the same time the representation of any mutual relation (or 'relation to one another', as he says in the introductory paragraph of the metaphysical exposition of the concept of space,[81]) and therefore the representation of such specific mutual relation as that of externality and adjacency presupposes the representation of those sensible objects *as other than one another* (that is, in his words, *'as different'*, which we take to mean *'as numerically different'*), and the representation of simultaneously given sensible objects as other than one another (as numerically different) presupposes the representation of them *as in different places*. In short, sensible objects given at the same time cannot be represented as related to one another at all, and *a fortiori* as outside and alongside one another, unless they are individuated through being represented as in different places. Were the proof of Kant's first space argument stated in this way, it would in principle remain the same argument and yet be less involved and so more precise.

It will have been clear that it does not matter much for Kant whether the space-empiricistic view (if we so call it) that he purports to combat in his first space argument is stated in terms of the representation of an order of mutual *externality* (out- sideness) or an order of *coexistence* among sensible objects. The word 'coexistence' clearly indicates that the sensible objects in question are *simultaneously* given; whereas the word 'outsideness' indicates this only by way of implication. The point that the concerned sensible objects are *simultaneously* given is indeed of some importance;[82] and to express this point the word 'coexistence' is no doubt better suited. Otherwise, however, the word gives no extra advantage ; thus it is not the case that a formulation of the Leibnizian-Wolffian view by use of this word makes it the less vulnerable to the Kantian sort of attack on the ground of circularity. For Kant's is an insidious form of attack, in his present argument, on the Leibnizians, being an attack, as we have been saying, on their principle of individuation. The fundamental point at issue between Kant and the other party is whether sensible objects are individuated necessarily by reference to their qualitative differences or by reference to their spatio-temporal locations. Kant opts for the second alternative and adopts the view that simultaneously given sensible objects are individuated necessarily by reference to their *difference of spatial locations.* Upon this view, an empirical account of the idea of space in terms of the representation of any order or relations at all among simultaneously given sensible objects,–that is, broadly speaking, a reductionist account of this idea on the lines of relational analysis–, has of course to be disallowed on the score of circularity.

The nature of our next task is plain enough ; to consider the arguments that Kant has elsewhere given in repudiation of the Leibnizian principle of individuation, namely, the *principium identitatis indiscernibilium.* His first space argument upon the interpretation it has finally come to receive in the foregoing exposition will become more meaningful if it is shown that his attack on the Leibnizian principle of individuation has a history in the course of which his first space argument itself crystallizes and becomes a factor in the further development of that history from a complex phase of which light radiates, in a demonstrably non-circular manner, to illumine that argument again. Since tracing that history is a matter of more time than we can afford, we may confine ourselves to the major issues involved in so far as they bear on the epistemology of space-representation and go to constitute, on the Kantian side of the controversy, a real source of strength for his first space argument under consideration.

NOTES :

1. D. P. Dryer, *Kant's Solution for Verification in Metaphysics,* 1966, pp. 173-174.
2. Below, 5.3 (penultimate paragraph).
3. Although at A xii Kant suggests that his *Critique* is not meant to be polemical, the fact remains that in this work he has, more than once in matters of detail, offered refutations of others' views; cf. his 'Refutation of Idealism' (B 274ff), 'Refutation of Mendelssohon's proof . . .' (B 413ff). As for his first space argument, the *negative* character of its first and last sentence strongly suggests that it embodies a refutation of some actual view.
4. The word 'deduction' here is to be taken in the wider sense of 'explanation' or 'account'. For an analogous use by Kant, see B 127, where he criticises Locke for having 'deduced them [the pure concepts] . . . from experience' ; 'deduced from' here means 'explained in terms of'.

5. Cf. Paton, *Kant's Metaphysic of Experience,* 1951, I, 110 n. 5.
6. See above, 2.2.
7. Kemp Smith, *Commentary,* 1918, p. 101.
8. *Ibid.*, p. 86 n. 3.
9. § 14, 1; Handyside, *Kant's Inaugural Dissertation and Early Writings on Space,* 1929, pp. 53f.
10. G. Martin, *Kant's Metaphysics & Theory of Science,* 1955, p. 29.
11. § 15, A; Handyside trans., p. 59.
12. Martin, *loc. cit.*
13. Below, 14.1.2.
14. Henry Sidgwick, *Lectures on the Philosophy of Kant and Other Philosophical Lectures & Essays,* Macmillan, London, 1905, p. 39.
15. *Ibidem.*
16. *Critique,* A 23 = B 38.
17. A 709 = B 737.
18. We say 'part of the import' because of the reason stated below in (a)(i) and (a)(ii) of note 20.
19. The attempted derivation of the idea of space from the representation of an order of externality among sensible things is obviously circular (assuming that 'externality' signifies spatial externality), even although this obvious circularity can be avoided by reformulating the account in question by saying that the idea of space derives from the representation of a certain sort of order among sensible things which, once we have already acquired the idea of space, we describe as the order of externality. In 5.1, we shall see, however, by way of replying to R. C. S. Walker, that even such a reformulated account commits an unobvious circularity in the sense that it cannot avoid presupposing the idea of space ultimately.
20. In our reply to Sidgwick we have not disputed his view that the word 'outside' (*ausser*) in Kant's first space argument means spatial externality, i.e. location at a different place. For one thing, Kant often, though not always (as we shall see in 7.2), uses this word or its cognates in the spatial sense. For another thing, Kant's first argument in his *Inaugural Dissertation* (§14, 1) provides by analogy some sort of exegetical support for the spatial interpretation of the word 'outside' in

his first space argument. In that argument on time he exploits the temporal notion conveyed by 'the word *after*' (Handyside trans., p. 54). Sidgwick, then, by emphasizing the spatial notion of the word 'outside' in Kant's first space argument has done nothing purely arbitrary. [And many sympathetic commentators also do interpret that word spatially ; cf. e.g. Paton, *op.cit.*, pp. 110-111 ; J. Kemp, *The Philosophy of Kant*, Oxford University Press, London, 1968, p. 17.]

Nevertheless it may be useful, for prevention of misunderstanding, to note two things here :

(a)(i) As we shall come to see towards the end of this chapter, Kant's first space argument does not essentially depend upon a commentary on the meaning of the word 'outside'. It has indeed a deeper aspect which does not even depend upon the use of the word 'outside' (or 'beside', or the like). When this deeper significance is brought to the fore, it will be clear that the idea of space is presupposed in any attempt to derive it empirically from any sort of order or relations whatever among sensible objects of a certain kind.

(ii) In the light of that deeper significance, it will also be clear that even if the word 'outside' is considered crucial to Kant's first space argument, but interpreted differently so as to signify objective otherness or discriminability rather than spatial externality, the argument still serves to support the conclusion that the idea of space has a special enough status to deserve to be regarded as a priori (see below 5.3, fourth paragraph.)

(b) While discussing Kant's second space argument, we shall have occasion to point out the ambiguity of the word 'outer' (*aüsseren*) in the Kantian usage. We shall see that the word 'outer' in that argument demands to be taken rather in the sense of, say, 'objective' than in the sense of 'spatial' if an essential contention of that argument is not to be missed. The confusion that thus arises as to the exact meaning of 'outer' will of course be discussed. (See below, 7. 2.)

21. L. W. Beck, *Early German Philosophy*, 1969, p. 269.

22. T. D. Weldon, *Introduction to Kant's Critique of Pure Reason*, Clarendon Press, Oxford, 1945, p. 84 n.

23. M. W. Calkins, *The Persistent Problems of Philosophy*, Macmillan, London, 1923, pp. 200, 520; H. Cohen, *Kants Theorie der Erfahrung*, Berlin, p. 95, cited by E. Caird, *The Critical Philosophy of Immanuel Kant*, 1909, Vol. I, p. 266 n.

24. This is the title of an article by K. Groos in the Kant-Studien 5 (1900), pp. 177-81.
25. The point is too familiar to require substantiation; let us only refer to L. W. Beck, *Early German Philosophy,* 1969, p. 467 n.
26. Cf. K. Groos's article referred to in note 24 above.
27. See Caird, *op. cit.*, p. 265.
28. 'But my senses convey to me only the impressions of colour'd points, disposed in a certain manner' Hume, *A Treatise of Human Nature,* ed. Selby–Bigge, Clarendon Press, Oxford, 1967, p.34. '. . . 'tis from the disposition of visible and tangible objects we receive the idea of space, . . .'; (p. 35). A misleading sentence in the *Treatise* is : '. . . the idea of extension is nothing but a copy of these colour'd points, and of the manner of their appearance'; (p. 34). The phrase 'is a copy' is here misleading; it should not be taken literally; it simply means 'is an abstract of'; indeed, how can there be a copy of 'the manner' in which impressions appear ? Hume puts his view more clearly in the case of time; see p. 36 (last para) of his book, and also N. K. Smith, *The Philosophy of David Hume,* Macmillan, London, 1960, chap. xiv. The idea of space is for Hume no more a copy of any impression or impressions than the idea of time.
29. See John Laird, *Hume's Philosophy of Human Nature,* Methuen, London, 1932, p. 70.
30. See, e.g. Laird, *op. cit.*, pp. 70–72.
31. Although the word 'contiguous' does not necessarily have a spatial sense, it seems that, as used by Hume in his account of the idea of space, the word, at least sometimes, bears this sense; cf. the passage alluded to in note 32 below.
32. *Treatise*, p. 236.
33. The view that Kant's present argument is directed against Wolff is also an old one; it was held, e.g. by John Watson, *The Philosophy of Kant Explained,* 1908, pp. 81–83.
34. § 15, D; Handyside trans., p. 62.
35. *Critique*, A 273 = B 329. *I* [talies not in the text].
36. The phrase 'relations of appearances, alongside . . . one another' (in Kemp Smith's trans.) is replaceable by 'relations of outer appearances' and 'abstracted from experience' by 'empirically obtained'.
37. We repeat that by 'Leibnizians' we here primarily mean Wolff. Whether

Kant's present argument is also consciously directed against *Leibniz* (as Caird, *op. cit.*, p. 265, suggests) will be considered later; see 3.5.3 below.

38. § 15, D; Handyside trans., p. 62.

39. Some might object to the word 'presupposed' on the ground that the relevant actual clause of Kant's has for its exact translation, not 'the representation of space must be *presupposed*', but 'the representation of space must already *lie at the basis* of this (*Grunde liegen*)'; cf. Dryer, *op. cit.*, p. 174 n. 4 & also n. 3. But without troubling whether Kamp Smith's rendering here is an unexceptionable *translation,* we may surely accept it at least as a not wrong *paraphrase* of Kant's clause in question; and our purpose is then still served.

40. *Early German Philosophy*, 1969, pp. 266-270.

41. *Ibid.,* p. 267.

42. *Ibid.,* p. 257.

43. *Ibid.,* p. 267.

44. Cf. Kant's *Inaugural Dissertation,* § 15, D.

45. *Ontologia,* Frankfurt, 1730, § 589.

46. Should it be objected that Wolff's definition reduces, on this interpretation, to the tautology that space is the order of simultaneous things in so far as they are simultaneous, it might be replied that its implication is perhaps as follows : space is the order of simultaneous things such that it is not independent of, or anything apart from, the coexisting (simultaneous) things in question.

47. Cf. Leibniz's *New Essays Concerning Human Understanding,* trans., A. G. Langley, Open Court, Chicago and London, 1916, bk ii, ch. 13, sect. 17, p. 153.

48. 'The Controversy between Leibniz and Clarke' ('Mr. Leibniz's third paper', para 4) in *Gottfried Wilhelm Leibniz : Philosophical Papers and Letters,* trans. and ed. L. E. Loemker, Chicago University Press, 1956, vol. I, p. 1108. For Leibniz's full account of the origin of the idea of space, see § 47 of that 'Controversy'.

49. The qualification 'considered as existing together' in the previous sentence is perhaps meant to suggest that the spatial order exists only in dependence upon, not apart from, the coexisting things concerned. As he says in the opening sentence of the paragraph in which the passage quoted occurs : '. . . I hold space to be something merely relative . . .'

50. See note 37 above.

51. It may be noted incidentally that there is a close similarity between Kant's theory that the ideas of space and time are, though original, yet acquired and the Leibnizian principle of virtual (i.e. potential) innateness. But it is doubtful whether this similarity is to be explained in terms of Leibniz's influence on Kant, as it is explained by W. Windelband in his *A History of Philosophy,* trans. J. H. Tufts, Macmillan, New York, 1957, pp. 465f. For the notion of 'original acquisition' might have been suggested to Kant by what 'the teachers of natural right' say; cf. Kant's *On a Discovery,* trans. Allison, 1973, p. 135, [AK. VIII. 221].

52. See above, 3.4.

53. § 14, 5; Handyside trans., p. 57.

54. Cf. our observations in 3.4 (para 8) above.

55. *Critique,* A 275 = B 331.

56. A 273 = B 329.

57. A 275-76 = B 331-32.

58. A 264 = B 320.

59. A 267 = B 323.

60. A 268 = B 324.

61. *Ibidem.*

62. A 276 = B 332.

63. See G. G. Brittan, Jr., *Kant's Theory of Science,* 1978, pp. 87-88.

64. Loemker ed. II, 888-898.

65. On the Aristotelian distinction between the particular senses and the common sense herein made use of by Leibniz, see *Aristotle's de Anima in the Version of William of Moerbeke and the Commentary of St. Thomas Aquinas,* trans. K. Foster and S. Humphries, Yale University Press, New Haven, 1959, pp. 347-356.

66. Loemker ed., I, note 323 (on p. 583).

67. Loemker ed., II, p. 892.

68. *Ibid.,* p. 890.

69. See above, 3.5.1 and note 48.

70. Leibniz 'On the Elements of Natural Science', Loemker, I, p. 442.

71. Leibniz, 'What is Independent of Sense and Matter', Loemker, II, p. 890; see also the piece referred to in note 55 above (Loemker, *loc. cit.*).
72. See Alexandre Koyre', *From the Closed World to the Infinite Universe*, Johns Hopkins, Baltimore, 1968, p. 250.
73. See note 82 below.
74. For the difference, in this respect, between Newton and Leibniz, see A. Koyre', *Newtonian Studies,* University of Chicago Press, 1968, p. 105 (the second quotation, and the second para in the third quotation, from Newton, and note 3 on the same page).
75. The words 'and alongside' (*und neben*) are added by Kant in the second edition.
76. By 'kindred account' we mean any form of relational-cum-reductionist account (of the idea of space).
77. Recall the cautious formulation of the Leibnizian-Wolffian view as given in the last section.
78. The expression 'necessary condition', and *a fortiori* the expression 'presupposition' (used before), are susceptible of different senses; see Brittan, *op. cit.*, pp. 34-37; Arthur Pap, *Elements of Analytic Philosophy,* Macmillan, New York, 1949, pp. 402ff.

    The exact sense in which we are using the former expression here is made clear later on in 4.1.2.3, pp. 151ff.
79. We take Kant's phrase 'as not only different but in different places' to mean 'as different and as in different places', not 'as not different, but as in different places'. The latter construing is unlikely, and yet it seems to be implied by Paton's interpretation of Kant's argument. He says : 'To know things (whether sensa or objects) as outside and beside one another is not merely to know qualitative differences between them : it is to know them as in different places . . . Kant's main argument is that the *particular* spatial and temporal relations in which sensa (and consequently objects) are given cannot be reduced to mere qualitative differences . . .'; Paton, *op. cit.,* p. 111. Surely, Paton does not mean here that to know things as outside and beside one another is to know them as not only qualitatively different, but also as in different places; he rather means that it is to know them not as qualitatively different, but as in different places. Upon this our remarks are as follows :

    (1) The reason why Paton is led to adopt the above interpretation is that he takes 'different' in its first occurrence in Kant's phrase 'as not only different but as in different places' *to refer to qualitative*

differences (see *ibid.,* p. 111 n. 3). But we are going to take the word 'different' in question to refer to *numerical difference;* see the next note below.

(2) In Paton's own exposition the words 'merely' and 'mere' seem only decorative; they might be treated as if they were non-existent.

(3) It is indeed Kant's view that the particular spatial relations cannot be reduced to mere qualitative differences; but Paton does not explain how and where Kant develops this view, and why he needs to appeal to this view in his first space argument. As for ourselves, we shall come to consider this view in the sequel; but we shall come to it from a different route; see below, pp. 190-192.

80. Kemp Smith in his *Commentary,* 1918, p. 99, (though not in his Translation of the *Critique)* translates the word *verschieden* in Kant's phrase *nicht bloss verschieden, sondern als in verschiedenen Orten* as '[qualitatively] different', the square brackets here being used by Kemp Smith himself', and S. Körner in his Pelican on *Kant,* 1960, p. 34, translates it as 'qualitatively different'; but this is definitely misleading. The word in its second occurrence as an adjective of 'Orten' can by no means be translated as 'qualitatively different' (since one part of space *qua* space is for Kant 'completely similar' to another part, see *Critique,* A 264 = B 320), and so it would be strange if the word in its first occurrence almost immediately before its second appearance conveyed a different notion. Nor can it be said that the German word *verschieden* itself suggests qualitative difference; for in that case the expression *numerischen verschiedenheit* (meaning numerical difference) would be un-German; yet Kant sometimes does use it, see *Kritik,* (A 263) = B 319.

81. '. . . We represent to ourselves objects as outside us, and all without exception in space. In space, their shape, magnitude, and *relation to one another* are determined or determinable'. (Emphasis added). A 22 = B37.

82. That the point is of some importance to Kant has already been stated; but what is meant here is that it is of some importance to Leibniz and his followers, because, on their view, the spatial order, unlike the temporal one, manifests itself only among things existing *at the same time.*

Two peculiar difficulties of this view, which are usually overlooked, are these :

(i) In so far as the view associates space with the order of simultaneity (or coexistence) and time with the order of succession only, it comes to imply that simultaneity is not a mode of *time*. We are led to think that it regards succession only as an original mode of time and simultaneity (or coexistence) as simply the negation of succession. The view is rejected by Kant in his *Inaugural Dissertation* in a long footnote (to § 14, 5), from which only two sentences may be quoted : 'What is simultaneous is not made simultaneous simply by not being successive. For when succession is taken away there is removed a certain conjunction of things within the temporal series, but there does not on that account at once arise another real relation, such as is the conjunction of all in the same moment'.

(ii) If simultaneity or coexistence is to be considered, as it has to be, a mode of time, the order of coexistence must of necessity be reckoned *temporal* (cf., for requisite clarification, the entire footnote to § 14, 5 of the *Dissertation*); and this being so, the spatial order *qua* spatial cannot be distinguished from the temporal order as such by being entitled the order of coexistence. The difficulty is so patent that it is hard to imagine that the Leibnizians could be unaware of it. Whether or not they were aware of it, the sole escape-route for them lay through (conscious or unconscious) adoption of the view that the word 'coexistence' when used in the description of the spatial order connotes not merely existence at the same time, but existence side by side (i.e. spatial contiguity) as well.

Presumably for this reason Kant often paraphrases the Leibnizian-Wolffian view of space by avoiding the word 'coexistence' (which happens to be ambiguous between mere simultaneity and side-by-sideness) and using instead the word *neben* (meaning alongside or beside); mark the expression *und neben* that he inserts in the proof of his first space argument in the second edition of the *Kritik* and his expression *neben* in the A 40 = B 56-57 passage of the *Kritik* (already discussed at length before), where he puts the view in question as the view which regards 'space and time as relations of appearances, alongside or in succession to one another *[neben oder nach einander]* . . .

CHAPTER FOUR

KANT'S FIRST SPACE ARGUMENT (Continued)

4.1 Kant's Critique of the Leibnizian Account of Individuation

(A Study of the Background, and, through It, of the Inherent Strength of Kant's First Space Argument)

The need for a study of Kant's critique of the Leibnizian account of individuation in the context of his first space argument has already been explained. As a summary of that explanation are added the words that form the subtitle of this section. Kant's first space argument as it stands is very brief, and so its real strength is not apparent. Its real strength, which is here called its 'inherent strength', has its source in the various arguments by which he has rejected the Leibnizian account of individuation; for, upon the interpretation we have adopted, it essentially depends upon such rejection. In this section very little will be explicitly said about his first space argument itself; and this is because we are here concerned only with unearthing the considerations that we think lie at the back of it.

The Leibnizian account of individuation means Leibniz's principle of individuation along with some of the consequences drawn by him by application of this principle. Kant has criticized this principle in his different writings in a variety of ways. Sometimes he examines and rejects the arguments by which the principle is supported. Sometimes he rather accepts the principle in one of its aspects and applies it against Leibniz himself to arrive at results that contradict the latter's relational account of space. Sometimes, again, he seeks to show how the principle, which is no doubt valid in some applications, is extended by its author[1] to cases where it is not only out of place, but invalid.

4.1.1 The Leibnizian account : an exposition

It will be well to begin with some explanation of Leibniz's principle : that of the identity of indiscernibles. The principle means that indiscernibles, that is, things without any discernible differences, are identical. Leibniz opposes this principle to the Thomistic view that 'there are . . . things different *solo numero*'.[2] According to his principle, then, no two things are just numerically different, which is to say that any two things are *qualitatively* different, i.e. different in respect of their internal determinations.

As it stands, the principle is *ontological.* Leibniz's statement, 'There is no such thing as two individuals indiscernible from each other',[3] is ontological in that it only says what kind of things there are or are not in the Universe. As such, it does not say how *we distinguish* things. An *epistemological* counterpart of this Leibnizian principle is embodied in the Bradleyan dictum 'There is no distinction without difference', which means that we cannot distinguish things except by reference to their qualitative differences.[4] The question is whether Leibniz also allows his principle to bear this epistemological import. The question is important for purposes of this Study. What is of relevance to this Study is not whether all things in the Universe are or are not qualitatively different, but whether it is the case that no two things whatsoever can be distinguished by us except by reference to their qualitative (internal) differences.

The question is difficult to answer. Although the principle of indiscernibles is primarily applicable to the Leibnizian substances (i.e. monads), Leibniz applies it also to things which are not for him substances, but appearances of classes of substances, namely, to 'sensible things'.[5] Thus he says that 'two leaves in a garden or two drops of water perfectly alike are not to be found'.[6] Let us consider the principle of indiscernibles in this latter application and inquire if it is Leibniz's view that sensible things can *never* be distinguished by us except by reference to their qualitative (internal) differences. A careful study shows that he sometimes allows that we do not always discern qualitative differences between things and that such things are distinguished through their spatio-temporal positions. Thus in the *New Essays* (bk ii, ch. 27, sect. 1) he observes : 'Thus although time and place (that is to say, external relation) enable us to distinguish things, which we do not readily distinguish by themselves, the things are none the less distinguishable in themselves'.[7] This might be paraphrased by saying that although, epistemologically speaking, we do not always discern qualitative differences between things and so are led to individuate them by reference to their spatio-temporal positions, yet, from the ontological viewpoint (or, in other words, from the viewpoint of God's discernment), there *are* qualitative differences between the things in question. Hence, it seems that the principle of indiscernibles remains to the end purely ontological and that as such it is out of place in the epistemological discussion of the sort we are concerned with.

But the matter can hardly be so simplified. For in the same paragraph of the *New Essays* Leibniz hastens to make another observation, which raises a complication. He observes that 'it is rather by means of the things that we must distinguish one place or time from another, for in themselves they are perfectly alike'. The complication that arises is this : how to make intelligible to ourselves the Leibnizian contention that sensible things sometimes, being qualitatively indistinguishable for us, are distinguished by reference to their spatio-temporal locations, and that the spatio-temporal locations in their turn, being in themselves indistinguishable, are distinguished by reference to the diversity of the occupying sensible things ? So far as we can see, the only way to make it intelligible is by reference to his theory of perception. He admits 'unconscious [insensible] perceptions', and holds 'that *noticeable perceptions* . . . come by degrees from those which are too small to be noticed'.[8] And in the Introduction to his *New Essays* he explicitly says that it is in virtue of insensible perceptions that individual things 'must always differ more than *numero*'.[9] His view, then, comes to this : when sensible things are not readily distinguishable by themselves and so are apparently distinguished by their spatio-temporal locations, they are really distinguished by their unconsciously or insensibly perceived qualitative differences. In his controversy with Clarke, Leibniz sometimes appeals to a microscope : 'Two drops of water or milk, viewed with a microscope, will appear distinguishable from each other'.[10] This, interpreted in the light of his theory of perception, means that a microscope brings under noticeable perception minute qualitative differences that were only subconsciously or insensibly apprehended with the naked eyes.[11] It now seems that it will not do simply to dismiss Leibniz's principle of the identity of indiscernibles from our consideration on the ground that it is after all an ontological principle without any bearing on our epistemological investigation. Leibniz's epistemology is so linked up with his ontology that his principle of individuation is as much in place in the former as in the latter.

It will be appropriate now to consider how Leibniz deduces his principle of indiscernibles, and how his adoption of this principle influences his epistemology of space-perception.

In more than one work[12] Leibniz says that his principle of indiscernibles follows ultimately from the consideration that in every true proposition the predicate (i.e. the concept of the predicate) is expressly or virtually contained in the subject (i.e. the subject-concept). He says : 'This is what the philosophers call *in-esse* when they say that the predicate *is in* the subject'.[13] Now the concept of the subject must include that of the predicate in such a way that anybody who perfectly understands the concept of the subject will of course also understand what predicates belong to the subject. 'This being premised, we can say that it is the nature of an individual substance or complete being to have a concept so complete that it is sufficient to make us understand and deduce from it all the predicates of the subject to which the concept is attributed'.[14] An individual substance, then, has a complete concept that is sufficient to identify it.[15] If we, with our limited understanding, do not comprehend the complete concept (or 'haecceity') of an individual substance and therefore fail to deduce all the predicates that can truly be affirmed of it, the omniscient God does comprehend such a complete concept and sees in it the basis of all the truly affirmable predicates of it.[16] Since, now, an individual substance has a complete concept such that it is sufficient to identify it, no two substances can have the same complete concept. No two substances, therefore, can be perfectly alike. Different substances having different complete concepts must differ in respect of the qualities (attributes) that go to constitute their distinctive complete concepts. This is the principle of the identity of indiscernibles.

A difficulty arises here. Since according to the principle of indiscernibles two substances or individuals are to be distinguished from each other by comparison of their complete concepts and a complete concept is admittedly of infinite complexity so that an exhaustive analysis of it may surpass *our* capacity, how can we distinguish one substance or individual from another ? Leibniz's reply to this is that a complete analysis of the concepts of two substances is practically unnecessary for purposes of distinguishing them. As Parkinson elucidates this point by means of an example :

> For example, suppose that someone mentions a person whom he calls 'Alexander', and that we think that he is talking about Alexander the Great. To discover that he is in fact talking about (say) the son of Priam, it is only necessary to note that some of the predicates he ascribes to Alexander are predicates of Paris, but not of Alexander the Great, and this can be done without any very lengthy inquiry into what he means by 'Alexander'.[17]

Since an exhaustive treatment of the principle of indiscernibles does not belong to our assignment, we may omit certain points, important as they are, about it, and pass on to note how this principle relates to the topic of space, in which we are interested.

When Leibniz says that there are no two things perfectly alike, his statement considered in relation to sensible objects implies that any two things differ in respect of their internal properties and not merely in respect of their spatio-temporal locations. As he puts it : 'Besides the difference of time and place, there must always be an *internal principle of distinction*'.[18] The question is whether this is a *logical* consequence of the principle of indiscernibles. It will be seen by and by that this is not. After deducing this principle in the manner stated above, Leibniz, by way of a further explanation, says in his paper entitled 'First Truth' that the reason why any two individual things differ more than numerically 'must be sought in some differences within themselves.'[19] He argues that 'there *are no purely extrinsic denominations* which have no basis at all in the denominated thing itself. For the concept of the denominated subject necessarily involves the concept of the predicate. Likewise, whenever the denomination of a thing is changed, some variation has to occur in the thing itself'.[20] It thus seems that the principle of indiscernibles *logically* involves the suggestion that any two things differ in respect of their *internal* determinations. But difficulties arise from Leibniz's own way of working with this principle. He applies the principle to sensible objects which are admittedly perceived to be in space and time, and holds that any two of them differ in their internal properties and not *merely* in their spatio-temporal locations. Evidently he first considers sensible objects in the abstract, i.e. without regard to their places and times, and applies to them the general principle that any two things differ in their internal properties; then he considers the sensible objects in the concrete, i.e. in their places and times, and holds that since they already differ in their internal properties, they do not differ *merely* in their spatio-temporal locations. But the difficulty that arises is that he sometimes allows that things can be perfectly alike, internally quite alike, if considered in the abstract. Thus he allows that there can be perfectly alike triangles, circles, etc. in so far as these are considered in the abstract. 'So geometry is right', he says, 'in studying similar triangles, even though two perfectly similar material triangles are never found'.[21] Likewise he distinguishes between abstract spaces and abstract times, on the one hand, and concrete ones, on the other, and admits that the former are perfectly alike, while denying this of the latter. To quote him : 'The parts of time and place considered in themselves are ideal things, and therefore they resemble one another like two abstract units. But it is not so with two concrete ones, or with two real times, or two spaces filled up, that is, truly actual'.[22] It is, then, clear that, with regard to abstract units which are not truly actual, Leibniz does not hesitate to admit that two such things can be, and are, perfectly alike. Returning to the sensible objects, we find that such objects, if considered apart from their spatio-temporal locations, are also abstract units and not truly actual. If the places filled by sensible objects are considered in themselves apart from such fillings, they are said to become abstract units and to cease to be truly actual; but then the same thing must be said of the sensible objects also if they are considered in themselves apart from their places (no matter how the word 'places' is defined). There is, then, no *logical* reason why sensible objects considered in the abstract cannot be perfectly alike, if their places considered in the abstract can be. Hence, there is no logical reason why sensible objects *in the concrete* must invariably differ *otherwise than merely in their spatio-temporal locations.* The supposition is natural that the reasons for Leibniz's statement,–namely, 'Besides the difference of time and place, there must always be an internal principle of distinction'–, are, if there are any, extralogical.

The supposition is confirmed when Leibniz is found to observe in very clear terms that it is *not absolutely impossible* for sensible objects to be perfectly alike, but that such indiscernibles do not in fact exist. He appeals here to his principle of sufficient reason. He says :

> [1] When I deny that there are two drops of water perfectly alike, or any two other bodies indiscernible from each other, I don't say 'tis absolutely impossible to suppose them but that 'tis a thing contrary to the divine wisdom, and which consequently does not exist.[23]
>
> [2] And 'tis a great objection against indiscernibles that no instance of them is to be found.[24]

Leibniz denies that there really exist, or are to be found, in different places indiscernible things, because such things on his view will not be produced by God. He argues as follows : On the supposition that there are three 'equal and perfectly alike' bodies, it is indifferent which is put in which place; that is, they may be placed in any order whatever and so 'they will never be placed in any order by him who does nothing without wisdom'. 'But then, he being the author of things, no such things will be produced by him at all, and consequently there are no such things in nature'.[25]

It remains to point out how Leibniz's account of individuation influences his epistemology of space-perception. Since, according to him, sensible objects are in principle distinguishable or identifiable by means of their internal qualities, and their places are not distinguishable or identifiable except by reference to them, he is led to award a priority to our idea of sensible objects over our idea of space. The idea of space reduces, on his account, to that of a certain kind of order or mutual relations among sensible objects. He seeks to show 'that in order to have an idea of place, and consequently of space, it is sufficient to consider' among sensible things 'certain relations and the rules of their changes, without needing to fancy any absolute reality out of the things whose situation we consider'.[26] The details of this relational and reductionist analysis of the idea of space may be ignored; for, according to Kant, as will be clear in the sequel, this analysis is mistaken more in principle than in detail.

4.1.2 Kant's criticisms of the Leibnizian account

4.1.2.1 Kant's criticism in the Nova Dilucidatio

To Kant the principle of indiscernibles in its application to sensible objects has always appeared to be a 'spurious law', as he dubs it in so early a work as the *Nova Dilucidatio* (1755).[27] In this work he says that he is 'concerned to refute' it. The first argument he brings against it is this :

> Perfect identity of two things requires identity of all marks or determinations both internal and external. From this complete determination who will except place ? However the internal characteristics of things may agree, if those things are distinguishable in respect of place, they are not identical.[28]

The point of this argument must not be misunderstood. Kant is not suggesting here that the difference of places has to be reckoned as a qualitative difference of sensible objects, if the term 'qualitative difference' is taken to mean what it usually does, namely, difference in respect of internal properties. The import of his argument, as can be confirmed by a careful examination of its context, is that there is no *logical* justification for the Leibnizian contention that perfect agreement in internal characteristics implies identity. So long as the logical possibility remains open that perfect agreement in internal characteristics may go with difference in spatial locations, the former sort of agreement cannot be held to be a sufficient condition for identity. And that the above-mentioned *logical* possibility does remain open is already admitted by Leibniz himself; we have already quoted him saying that the supposition of indiscernible (internally quite alike) things existing in different places is *not absolutely impossible.* His contention is that it is, though logically possible, still not a fact that there are indiscernibles in different places. Now, if this Leibnizian contention be true, then of course Kant's argument would have no more than a logical interest. But is it true that the existence of indiscernibles in different places *is not a fact*? The question is worth pursuing.

Whether or not something is a fact has to be settled ultimately by appealing only to the facts. Leibniz, however, would not allow the matter under consideration to be settled that way. His is a stronger contention than the one to the effect that the existence of indiscernibles in different place *is not a fact;* for him it *cannot be a fact.* This 'cannot' is not of course logical, in the narrower sense of the term 'logical', as is plain from the preceding discussion; it is an *ontological* 'cannot'. Leibniz's appeal here is to the wisdom of God, as was also previously noted. His argument is that there is no sufficient reason why God should have assigned different places to substances[29] that are otherwise perfectly alike. Kant in his criticism of this argument says that it reduces the principle of indiscernibles to a 'spurious law'. He turns the tables on Leibniz by observing that this law is 'refuted' 'by the fitness of divine wisdom' itself.[30] For the things which we consider similar, such as water, gold, etc., 'should agree perfectly as to their homogeneous and internal characteristics' is 'both suitable to their identity of use and function, for the upholding of which they are designed'.[31] He contends further that the assumption of 'some hidden and imperceptible diversity' in things of which the qualitative differences are indiscernible for us amounts to the assumption that 'God has something by which he himself distinguishes the parts of his work';[32] this also for Kant is not in accord with the fitness of divine wisdom.

The last point made by Kant is particularly noteworthy. He is not impressed by the Leibnizian doctrine of hidden and imperceptible diversity. In order to show that Leibniz's principle of indiscernibles is not merely ontological, but has an epistemological import as well, we were led, we may recall, to stress his doctrine of unconscious ('insensible') perception. As was noted, when we apparently do not discern qualitative differences in two things, we really subconsciously perceive such differences, according to Leibniz. On coming to Kant, however, we now see that he lets Leibniz's epistemological doctrine of insensible perception run into the ontological doctrine of sole discernibility by God, and criticizes Leibniz accordingly. It seems, therefore, that Kant so far looks upon the Leibnizian principle of indiscernibles as purely ontological; and this being so, the desirability of our examining this principle at some length in the epistemological context of Kant's space-argument comes again to be doubtful. The reply that may be made here is this; Kant's criticism stated above of the Leibnizian doctrine of hidden diversity involves the suggestion that if we are to individuate things by their qualitative diversity, it is necessary for us to be able to discern such diversity and that where we cannot discern, there the principle of indiscernibles is useless; for there is no question of our waiting on the faith that there is still some diversity hidden from us, though discerned by God. It may be noted that in the *Nova Dilucidatio* section under consideration Kant admits, with an implicit allusion to Leibniz's microscope-experiment, that perfectly alike leaves of one and the same tree are hardly to be found. He says that his only contention is that it is idle to dogmatize that the principle of the identity of indiscernibles must hold in all cases without exception.[33]

Kant's criticism of the principle of indiscernibles in his *Nova Dilucidatio* can be summed up by saying that, in its application to sensible objects having positions in space, it is neither logically nor metaphysically sound.

4.1.2.2 Kant's criticism in the essay of 1768

We now pass on to Kant's famous essay of 1768 entitled 'On the First Ground of the Distinction of Regions in Space', where his criticism of the Leibnizian account of individuation has a very close bearing on the problem of space. There is a noticeable peculiarity in his treatment of the principle of the identity of indiscernibles in this essay : he does not directly attack the principle, nor does he even mention it by name. Although there can be no doubt that the principle does receive here a certain sort of treatment, how the treatment should be described is not easy to decide. Some commentators point out that in this work Kant does not reject the principle, but rather accepts and utilizes it to his own advantage.[34] It will be seen in the end, however, that there is a sense in which he here does reject the principle.

He begins by calling attention to things that are indistinguish-able for us in all respects except in their orientation in space. He particularly considers 'incongruent counterparts', which are pairs of things such that one in each pair is, or may be, perfectly like the other in that pair in all respects except 'that the surface which bounds the one cannot possibly bound the other',[35] e.g. an object and its image in a plane mirror, the left and right hands of the same human body, etc.[36] To such incongruent counterparts he applies, clearly, though not expressly, the principle of the identity of indiscernibles, or rather, its corollary that otherness involves discernibility, and then proceeds on this basis to draw an anti-Leibnizian conclusion or conclusions regarding the nature of space and even the nature of the *idea* of space. We say 'an anti-Leibnizian conclusion or conclusions', because some commentators distinguish different theses in Kant's essay in question : for example, Garnett distinguishes 'four theses'.[37] These four theses all concern, however, the nature of space, and no one of them is about the nature of the idea of space. This is because Garnett is a party to the controversy among commentators on the issue whether Kant's main object in this essay is to establish 'that space is absolute and real' or that the idea of it is a priori (non-empirical) and intuitive (non-conceptual).[38] Garnett has preferred to take the former side of this controversy. We do not want to try to resolve the controversy decisively; but we do not see how it can be wrong to say that Kant's interests here are not merely ontological, but epistemological as well, and that on the epistemological side, although it is doubtful whether he is as yet reflectively making separate uses of the two dichotomies of a priori-empirical and intuitive-conceptual, he is at least contesting the view that the idea of space is empirical. He clearly holds that space is absolute (not relative), and that as such it 'is not an object of an outer sensation, but a fundamental concept which first makes all such sensations possible'.[39] How far 'his Newtonianism' evident here, as Vleeschauwer calls it,[40] is going to be retained in his later teachings is again a problem; but his apriorism regarding the idea of space to which we are here introduced for the first time is a view he 'will adhere to without change for the rest of his life'.[41] The similarity of the view conveyed through his words quoted above with his first space argument in the *Inaugural Dissertation* and the

Critique of Pure Reason may be noted for what it is worth.[42] The quoted words constitute one of the two sentences of Kant's at the end of his 1768 easay that have evoked the mentioned controversy among the commentators as to the chief burden of this essay; but even if those two sentences were non-existent one could not still afford to miss an aspect of the Kantian contention in this essay that has a clear bearing on the nature of the idea of space. It is this aspect, quite ignored by Garnett as it is, which is of chief importance to us; it is connected with Kant's overall assessment in this essay of the Leibnizian principle of individuation. G. Brittan aptly explains it by saying

> that the existence of incongruent counterparts shows that the principle of the identity of indiscernibles cannot be used in a non-circular way to individuate objects and to construct space in terms of them, for the only differences that incongruent counterparts display are *spatial* differences.[43]

The bearing of this on the nature of the *idea* of space is obvious enough : 'It is in this sense', Brittan goes on, 'that space is an *a priori* concept. The individuation of objects depends on their occupying spatial positions; therefore the concept of space cannot be "reduced" to an order of objects'.[44]

Some elucidation of Kant's contention in this essay will now be in order. Only the respects that are relevant to the present Study will be emphasized.

Kant's contention is that there can be such objects as are otherwise 'perfectly equal and similar'[45] and yet not congruent, and that such objects are distinguishable only by reference to space. Since there is a discernible difference between a pair of incongruent counterparts consisting in the fact, though only in the fact, that the surface bounding the one cannot possibly bound the other, – in short, in the fact that they cannot be superimposed –, they are not identical, according to the principle of the identity of indiscernibles itself. Kant concedes that the discernible difference between them is 'an inner difference',[46] and C. D. Broad explains this by saying that it is in fact a difference in respect of their 'intrinsic spatial properties' :[47] the surface of a thing being a boundary to its extension is *intrinsic* to it, and hence, e.g. the two hands of the same body that differ in their surfaces differ in virtue of their intrinsic spatial properties. The question is whether the discernible inner difference between incongruent counterparts is explicable on the lines laid down by the author of the principle of indiscernibles.

The principle of indiscernibles signifies, as we saw, that the reason for the difference between any two individual things 'must be sought in some differences within themselves'. But Kant contends that the 'inner ground' for the discernible difference of a pair incongruent counterparts does not lie *within either* of them. If the grounds for the difference between the two hands in our example are to lie within their inner constitution, these must lie in the *relations* among the parts of the hands considered severally; but 'in this respect', Kant says, 'everything may be completely identical in the two cases'.[48] As he elaborates it :

> The right hand is similar and equal to the left, and if we look at one of them by itself, all the proportions and positions of its parts relatively to one another and at the magnitude of the whole, a complete description of it must also hold for the other in every respect.[49]

[If this example is demurred to, reference may then be made to a hand and its image in a plane mirror.]

There is, then, no way of explaining the discernible inner difference of a pair of incongruent counterparts on the Leibnizian principle, which yet professes to be a principle of inner differences. A further point made by Kant is that the difference cannot be explained at all along the lines of Leibniz's reductionist-cum-relational analysis as such of space. For Kant, if the intrinsic spatial difference between the two hands in question cannot be explained, as just now seen, in terms of the *relations among their parts,* it cannot also be explained in terms of the *relations between this pair of things and some third thing* (on the same level). This is a particularly noteworthy point, because it might be argued that the two hands can always be distinguished in our universe by their differing relations to a third thing, inasmuch as the thumb of one is closer to it than its fingers, while the fingers of the other are closer to it than its thumb. But Kant thinks that the difference between rightness and leftness is such an irreducible one that we can well conceive of a universe containing only a single hand which is nevertheless either right or left.[50] In that conceivable universe, there is no *other* thing besides the single hand to relate to it, and yet it is 'impossible' that the hand should be 'indeterminate' in respect of the characteristic of rightness or leftness;[51] 'it is necessarily either a right or a left . . .'. Remnant here objects to Kant by saying that 'in a universe which contained nothing but a single hand, it would not just be empirically undecidable whether that hand were left or right; it would be strictly indeterminate'.[52] To this a reply has come from a recent expositer of Kant's, C. S. Walker, who points out that

> Kant would say that Remnant had followed Leibniz in failing to see that there is an irreducibly ostensive element in the meanings of 'left' and 'right'. A left-handed and a right-handed glove look different regardless of their relations to other things, and a left-handed and a right-handed universe would look different too.[53]

It is indeed true that the meaning of 'left' and 'right' are at first learnt by reference to one's body; but the peculiarity of left-handedness or right-handedness is, Walker points out, 'immediately obvious without reference to my body or to anything else'.[54]

The intrinsic spatial difference between a pair of incongruent counterpart is, for Kant, explicable only in terms of their differing relations to the 'absolute, primary space'.[55] They differ not other-wise than in their absolute orientation in space.

The ontological conclusion drawn here by Kant is that space is not reducible to the relations of bodies; for bodies stand in relations to one another ultimately in virtue of their relations to (orientation in) space. Their relations to space 'cannot . . . be immediately perceived', he says;[56] and this is intelligible in the light of his remark that 'absolute space is not an object of an outer sensation'; this, by the bye, raises the question whether in his essay under consideration he regards space as an object of *pure intuition*. This question cannot be answered more than conjecturally. But to the question whether he here regards the idea of space as at least *a priori*, his characterization of space as 'primary', which means that it is irreducible, and his observation about it that 'it is a fundamental concept which first makes all such sensations possible', leave us in no doubt whatever that the answer to be given is, 'Yes'.

The epistemological import of Kant's contention in this essay is for us immediately more relevant than his ontological conclusion (or conclusions); and let us see what we have gained in this regard. Leibniz's attempted deduction of the idea of space from the representation of a certain sort of order or relations among sensible objects is based on the view that such objects are necessarily identifiable by means of their internal properties only. Kant's discussion of incongruent counterparts has served to show that this view in its generality is tenable if account is also taken of such internal properties as are essentially dependent on their positions in space. If pairs of incongruent counterparts differ in their internal properties, their only differing internal properties do depend on their positions in space. It is clear that if the principle of the identity of indiscernibles is to be set up as a general principle of individuation of objects and yet the idea of space to be reduced to that of a certain sort of order among objects, then circularity is unavoidable in the end.

It remains to consider the question whether there is a sense in which it can be said that Kant in his 1768 essay has *rejected* the principle of the identity of indiscernibles. In taking up this question we are trying to redeem a promise made earlier. Now, on the basis of our previous exposition of this principle, we can say that the following are the two main claims associated with it by its author :

(1) Any two individual things have some discernible difference between them; and

(2) The discernible difference has its grounds entirely within each of them.

What Kant does in the 1768 essay with the help of his sophisticated example of incongruent counterparts is to accept (1), but to reject (2). It is worthy of note in this connexion that the way he here partly accepts and partly rejects the principle of indiscernibles is not in the least irreconcilable with his total rejection of this principle, in its application to sensible objects, elsewhere, namely, earlier in the *Nova Dilucidatio* and later on in the *Critique*. Elsewhere when he insists that two drops of water, for example, are sometimes quite alike in respect of both quality and quantity, he doubtless denies that there is a discernible difference in the indicated sense between them; nevertheless, even there he could, only if he would, as much emphasize that the two drops of water differed discernibly as he does emphasize in 1768 that incongruent counterparts, despite their being 'perfectly equal and similar', differ discernibly. For the two drops of water did differ discernibly in the same way that a pair of incongruent counterparts do, namely, in their orientation in space. Two drops may be mutually as alike as a drop and its image in a plane mirror, and yet the former are between themselves as different discernibly as the latter pair of things which are evidently incongruent counterparts. As for the main ground relied on by Kant elsewhere in his rejection of the principle of indiscernibles, namely, that things that are otherwise perfectly alike are distinguishable ultimately (irreducibly) by their locations in space, this also has its parallel in the 1768 essay.

4.1.2.3 Kant's criticism in the Critique

It is time to turn to the *Critique* to see how Kant here deals with the principle of the identity of indiscernibles. A difficulty here is that his criticism of this principle comes at a much later section than the Transcendental Aesthetic, where he is within his rights to presuppose his doctrine already established in the Aesthetic that space and time are formal a priori subjective conditions of sensible intuition. The reason why this makes a difficulty is that the present discussion is being conducted only in the interests of his first space argument which occurs at the beginning of the Aesthetic, where his transcendental-idealist doctrine of space and time cannot already be presupposed. We are therefore required to explore the possibility of so reconstructing his arguments against the Leibnizian principle as to make them free of their dependence, when such dependence is found, upon the transcendental-idealist doctrine of space and time. That this can be done is suggested by the fact that his opposition to the Leibnizian principle of indiscernibles long antedates, as we have seen, his formulation of the transcendental-idealist doctrine of space and time.

In the *Critique* Kant argues in the first place that the representation of internal difference of quality and quantity (that is, broadly speaking, of qualitative difference) is not a necessary condition for the individuation – or, as he puts it, for the representation of numerical difference – of sensible objects, since the representation as in different places is, in the case of such objects, a sufficient condition of individuation. This argument is nothing new, nor is it of much importance, apparently,[57] for our purposes; what we rather need is an argument to the effect that the representation as *in different places* is a *necessary condition* for the individuation of sensible objects given at the same time, – a necessary condition in the *austere sense*, however, that is, in a sense not derived from the transcendental-idealist doctrine that space is a formal a priori subjective condition of sensible intuition.

The following passage is one among many where Kant urges only that the representation *as in different places* is a *sufficient condition* for the individuation of sensible objects given at the same time :

> . . . even if there is no difference whatever as regards the concepts, difference of spatial position at one and the same time is still an adequate ground for the *numerical difference* of the objects, that is, of the objects of the senses. Thus in the case of two drops of water we can abstract from all difference (of quality and quantity), and the mere fact that they have been intuited simultaneously in different spatial positions is sufficient justification for holding them to be numerically different.[58]

Obviously, the argument stated in this passage does not already presuppose the doctrine that space is a formal a priori subjective condition of certain sensible intuition. It is not much different in spirit from the sort of criticism that appeared in the *Nova Dilucidatio*. There are no doubt lines in the *Critique* that may suggest that Kant sometimes supports this argument by appealing to his special doctrine of space already established in the Aesthetic; e.g. '. . . plurality and numerical difference are already given by space itself, *the condition of outer appearances*'.[59] [Italies not in the text.] But, for one thing, the italicised portion can be given an austere interpretation, and need not be given a transcendental-idealist interpretation;[60] and for another thing, the lines just quoted may at any rate be ignored in the present discussion, and the essentially neutral longer passage cited above will suffice.

Let us pass on to investigate whether the *Critique* offers any considerations purporting to show that the representation as in different places is a *necessary condition* in the austere sense, and not merely a sufficient condition, for the individuation of simultaneously given sensible objects.

The passages that we are about to quote and study may not immediately present before us in any clear form the sort of considerations we are looking for. But if, bearing in mind that they appear in an expressly anti-Leibnizian context, we analyse them properly, the looked-for considerations will, it is hoped, ultimately crystallize. Kant writes :

> [1] Whether things are identical or different, in agreement or in opposition, etc., cannot be established at once from the concepts themselves by mere comparison . . .[61]
> [2] Leibniz . . . compared the objects of the senses with each other merely in regard to understanding, taking them as objects in general. *First*, he compared them in so far as they are to be judged by understanding to be identical or different. And since he had before them only their concepts and not their position in intuition (wherein alone the objects can be given), and left entirely out of account the transcendental place of these concepts (whether the object is to be reckoned among appearances or things in themselves), it inevitably followed that he should extend his principle of the identity of indiscernibles, which is valid only of concepts of things in general, to cover also the objects of the senses . . .[62]
>
> [3] Leibniz *intellectualised* appearances . . .[63]
>
> [4] The principle of the identity of indiscernibles is really based on the presupposition, that if a certain distinction is not found in the concept of a thing in general, it is also not to be found in the things themselves, and consequently that all things which are not distinguishable from one another in their concepts (in quality or quantity) are completely identical (*numero cadem*).[64]

> [5] . . . the above so-called law [i.e. the principle of the identity of indiscernibles] is no law of nature. It is only an analytic rule for the comparison of things through mere concepts.[65]

These passages can be best studied in the light of our previous exposition of the principle of the identity of indiscernibles. Let us recall the way that Leibniz has deduced this principle and made use of it. We have seen that Leibniz has deduced this principle from the view that every individual substance has a complete concept which is sufficient to identify it and that this view in turn is deduced from the view that in every true proposition the concept of the predicate is already contained in that of the subject. It follows that different substances have different complete concepts and so different qualities connoted by these different concepts. Hence Leibniz is led to hold that the numerical difference of two substances is determinable only through comparison of their concepts or qualities. And he holds this, as also has already been observed, not only with respect to metaphysical substances (monads), which are in Kant's words 'intelligibilia, i.e. objects of the pure understanding',[66] but also with respect to phenomenal objects, which are in Kant's words 'objects of the senses'.[67] It is also worth noting that as regards qualitative difference, in the narrower sense of the term 'qualitative', between two things of any kind, it is Leibniz's professed view that this can be represented only by an act of comparison; thus he says that 'quality presents something to the mind which can be known in a thing separately and can then be applied to the comparison of two things . . .'.[68] One can now appreciate the force of Kant's criticism. He contends that the principle of the identity of indiscernibles is valid only of objects of the pure understanding and that it is a mistake to extend it uncritically to the objects of the senses. With respect to the objects of the pure understanding, the question does not arise how they are *given,* since they are on the level of conception, and not on that of intuition. We have only their concepts at our disposal; and so we can distinguish, or individuate, them by a mere comparison of their concepts, or the qualities signified by their concepts. About them it is indeed true that the representation of qualitative difference is a necessary condition for the representation of numerical difference. But the case is different with the objects of the senses. They cannot be treated in a purely intellectualist fashion as mere things in general. With respect to them, 'we are not concerned to compare concepts', Kant says.[69] For purposes of their individuation, we cannot begin by comparing their concepts or qualities : they have to be given, and given separately. It is necessary that they be given (intuited) separately before they allow of being compared with respect to their qualities. Their separateness of presentment in intuition is both a *sufficient* and a *necessary* condition of their individuation : 'a sufficient condition', because if they are intuited separately, their numerical difference is *ipso facto* established; and a 'necessary condition', because unless they are intuited separately, they, as objects of the senses, are not given at all to be in any way considered.

Kant's argument here turns upon the making of a fundamental distinction between the objects of the senses and those of the pure understanding, that is, between intuition and conception.[70] Herein lies the crux of the matter; for Leibniz does not recognize any such distinction. He holds the doctrine that there is ultimately no difference in kind, but at most one in degree, between conception and intuition, thought and sense. Sensation, for him as for Wolff, is nothing but a confused and obscure conception. This doctrine has been trenchantly criticized by Kant in the Transcendental Aesthetic as well as in the *Inaugural_Dissertation* as being not only false, but responsible for 'a completely wrong direction' given 'to all investigations into the nature and origin of our knowledge'.[71] His criticism of this doctrine occurs no doubt in a transcendental-idealist context ; it is nevertheless at bottom theory-neutral. Let us consider only the following sentence taken from the *Dissertation* : 'Moral concepts, for instance, though of this confused character, are known not by experience but by the pure intellect itself.'[72] He explains this in the *Critique* by saying that the concept of 'right', for example, is indeed very obscure and yet not empirical, but intellectual.[73] Anyone not committed to any special theory of space and time can easily appreciate, in the light of this example given by Kant, that an obscure conception and a sensation are not the same. Once therefore we dismiss the prejudice that conception and intuition, thought and sense, are non-different, we can easily acknowledge, with Kant, the right of the objects of the senses to be treated in a fundamentally different manner from the objects of the pure understanding. We can also make sense of Kant's view that not all distinction is conceptual and qualitative.[74] There is, for him, as has been noted, a pre-logical mode of intuitional distinction,[75] so to say, whereby objects of the senses are individuated : it is their separateness of presentment in intuition.

It remains to introduce the crucial point – a point which we fear will raise difficulties–that separateness of presentment in intuition involves a reference to (or better, a representation of) space and time. The point is crucial because it shows that since, as we have seen, separateness of presentment necessarily and sufficiently serves to individuate sensible objects, it is *the representation of space and time* that holds the real key to the individuation of such objects. The main difficulty here is that Kant, in the post-'Aesthetic' section of the *Critique* under consideration, explains the point just now introduced not quite in a theory-neutral manner. He says :

> A location *b* can contain a thing which is completely similar and equal to another in a location *a*, just as easily as if the things were inwardly ever so different. Difference of locations, without any further conditions, makes the plurality and distinction of objects, as appearances, not only possible but also necessary. Consequently, the above so-called law [i.e. the principle of the identity of indiscernibles] is no law of nature.[76]

Kant is here saying that objects in so far as they appear to the senses (that is, are intuited) are distinguished in sense sufficiently and necessarily by their difference of spatio-temporal locations. But why is their intuitional difference necessarily due to their difference of locations ? A clear answer is provided in a later remark : 'these locations are conditions of . . . intuition . . . ; they do not, however, belong to the concept but entirely to sensibility'.[77] Here, obviously, his special doctrine of space, namely, that space is a formal a priori subjective condition of sensible intuition, is already presupposed. It is presupposed, not indeed through the words 'locations are conditions of intuition', for these could be given an austere interpretation, but through the words which refer to their (locations') ultimate connexion with *sensibility*, and so to the view that space is a form of sensibility. The difficulty we are here confronted with has to be resolved.

A simple way to resolve the difficulty is to maintain that it is possible to argue, and that it is imaginable that Kant also might have argued if only he was required to do so in an austere context, that the separateness of presentment in intuition *develops of its own accord* into the representation of a difference of locations in space and time. One such argument has actually been worked out by Johnson, who in the end observes that the view taken by him

> is so far equivalent to Kant's in that I regard space and time as the conditions of the otherness of sense-experiences upon which the possibility of cognising *determinate* spatial and temporal relations depends, and that this characteristic of space and time is what constitutes Sense-Experience into a manifold, i.e. a plurality of experiences, which we can proceed to count as many only because of their separate presentment.[78]

But one may not be satisfied with Johnson's procedure, since one may think that he has expressed himself more in an assertoric than in an explanatory fashion. What we propose to do next is therefore to attempt a different sort of reconstruction of Kant's argument for the view that the representation as in different places is a necessary condition for the individuation of simultaneously given sensible objects. The reconstructed argument will be based partly on the considerations presented in the post-'Aesthetic' section of the *Critique* under examination and partly on some external considerations.

That argument, to put it bluntly, is that the representation as in different places is, in the case of simultaneously given sensible objects, a necessary condition of individuation in the sense that it is the *only* sufficient condition of that. Kantian scholars are aware that Kant sometimes recognises a sense of 'necessary condition' such that, as Brittan puts it, 'a necessary condition is a sufficient condition, "necessary" in the sense that it is the *only* sufficient condition'.[79] Kant's procedure in such cases is briefly described by Brittan in these words : 'More generally, Kant sometimes begins with a pair of alternatives delimited by the law of excluded middle, and then tries to show that only one of the alternatives accounts for the knowledge we do in fact have'.[80] To come to the point now : As regards the individuation of things, only two views were current at the time of Kant : one was the ancient view with which he was ever impressed, namely, that the principle of individuation is bound up with space and time; and the other was the view endorsed by Leibniz, namely, the principle of indiscernibles. These two views have always provided Kant with the only pair of alternatives to be considered. It is to be expected therefore that if Kant thinks he is able to show that the representation of qualitative differences is neither a sufficient nor a necessary condition, whereas the representation as in different places is a sufficient condition, of the individuation of simultaneously given sensible objects, he should feel authorized to conclude (for lack of a third alternative) that the representation as in different places is the *only* sufficient, and in this sense a necessary, condition of individuation of the sort of objects in question. Our task is to try to ascertain whether Kant has actually been able to show this, and whether he has been able to show this without invoking his special doctrine of space and time.

Now, one of the passages quoted earlier[81] has already shown us that for Kant the representation as in different places is a sufficient condition and that the representation of qualitative differences is not a necessary condition for the individuation of simultaneously given sensible objects. It remains to inquire whether, for him, the representation of qualitative differences, even though it is not a necessary condition, may not yet be regarded as a sufficient condition for the individuation of such sensible objects. We are here required to do two things : (i) to try to be sure of Kant's actual view, and (ii) to state his reasons for this view in as austere a manner as possible.

(i) Kant's view : Let us quote once again, for convenience of comparison, two of his statements and examine them closely :

> . . . the above so-called law [i.e. the principle of the identity of indiscernibles] is no law of nature. It is only an analytic rule for the comparison of things through mere concepts.
>
> [A 272 = B 328.]

> Whether things are identical or different . . . cannot be established at once from the concepts themselves by mere comparison. . . [A 262 = B 318.]

The first sentence in the first passage implies that the principle of indiscernibles has no bearing upon *the objects of the senses.* The second sentence in this passage implies that the principle has bearing 'only' upon objects represented through 'mere' concepts (which Kant sometimes calls 'intelligibilia').[82] In the second passage the important word is 'things', which without doubt comprehends within its reference *the objects of the senses.* And the words 'the concepts themselves' in this passage stand not merely for the concepts themselves, but for *the qualities or attributes signified by the concepts, and these qualities or attributes alone.*[83] So the second passage comes to mean, among other things, that the numerical identity or difference of the objects of the senses cannot be established by reference to their qualities (i.e. qualitative identity or differences) *alone.* It is clear that, with regard to sensible objects, Kant does not accept the view that qualitative difference is a *sufficient condition* for numerical difference. [Previously we have seen that, with regard to the same kind of objects, he does not also accept the view that qualitative difference is a *necessary condition* for numerical difference. We thus see that the representation of qualitative difference is for him neither a necessary nor a sufficient condition for the individuation of sensible objects.] And this is confirmed by the above-quoted first passage.

(ii) The reasons for Kant's view that the representation of qualitative difference is not a sufficient condition for the individuation of sensible objects : It is tempting to argue that, since it is true that if sensible objects are represented as qualitatively different, they are also represented as numerically different, the representation of qualitative difference is a sufficient condition for their individuation. But the conclusion does not follow, and, moreover, will soon be seen to be based upon an uncritical presupposition. If the representation of qualitative difference is rightly to be regarded as a *sufficient condition* for the individuation of sensible objects, it must be possible to hold that such representation, *without any further conditions,*[84] serves to individuate the sensible objects. The question is whether it can be held.

The Kantian answer is, No. Something else does and must go with the very representation of the qualitative difference of the sensible objects; it is their separateness of presentment in intuition, as has already been noted before. When we are just concerned with logically comparing mere concepts, or objects represented through mere concepts, the concepts themselves suffice to reveal their internal determinations, i.e. the qualities (or attributes) signified by them.[85] With regard to the objects of the senses, however, their separate presentment in intuition is a necessary presupposition of the very possibility of the representation of their qualitative difference.[86] So if in the case of sensible objects the requirement of the representation of qualitative difference is to be satisfied, it can be satisfied in such a way as to preclude the conclusion that it is a *sufficient condition* for their individuation. The view that it is a sufficient condition for their individuation either overlooks the presence of the necessary additional factor called their separateness of presentment or altogether abstracts from this factor; in either case it surreptitiously treats the objects *of the senses* as objects *in general*. An abstract rule, which is derived from a mere comparison of concepts, to the effect that items differ numerically if and only if they differ qualitatively[87] is quite unexceptionable in the field of concepts; and the supposition that the rule must also apply to the objects of the senses is based on a surreptitious *intellectualization* of them. But such intellectualisation is uncritical.[88] Since, then, the view that the representation of qualitative difference is a sufficient condition for the individuation of sensible objects is thus ultimately based upon an uncritical presupposition, it is for Kant a view 'which the critical reason cannot recognise'.[89] So he cannot accept this view. He sets it aside, and in this sense rejects it.[90]

Conclusion : It is just now seen that, and why, Kant rejects the view that the representation of qualitative difference is a sufficient condition for the individuation of sensible objects. As to the other view that the representation as in different places is a sufficient condition for the individuation of sensible objects, there is nothing in it to offend the critical reason, and so Kant can accept it, and we have previously seen that, and how, he accepts it. So the conclusion on his part is that the representation of qualitative difference *is not*, whereas the representation as in different places, is, *a sufficient condition* for the individuation of sensible objects. In the absence of a third alternative, the further conclusion follows that the representation as in different places is the *only* sufficient condition, and in this sense *a necessary condition,* of the individuation of simultaneously given sensible objects.

4.1.2.3.1 Some difficulties considered

An objection that might be made to the above reconstructed argument is that it is at the mercy of some overlooked alternative. This objection cannot be regarded as good until a third alternative neglected by Kant is produced. We for ourselves are not aware of any eligible third alternative here.

No doubt Russell in his *Human Knowledge : Its Scope and Limits* has mentioned under the heading 'The Principle of Individuation' *three views.*[91] The first view is the Leibnizian principle of the identity of indiscernibles; the second is the Thomistic view endorsed by Kant, and the third is, in Russell's own words, that 'numerical diversity is ultimate and indefinables'.[92] But this third view is not a third alternative in the required sense; it does not give us a third alternative principle of individuation, does not put up, that is to say, a third candidate for the status of either a necessary or a sufficient condition for the individuation of objects, whether of objects in general or of objects of the senses. So Kant's omission to consider a third alternative still remains a challenge to others to produce it.

A difficulty arises, however, from Russell's discussion of the principle of individuation in his book under reference, and it may incidentally be considered here. He maintains that the second view, which one may call the Thomistic-Kantian view, 'may be ignored',[93] because, as he says, it 'is reducible to either the first or the third according to the way in which it is interpreted.'[94] It is, he argues, reducible to the third view – namely, that numerical diversity is ultimate and indefinable – if one takes, e.g. the absolute view of space (and time), because on the absolute view 'two different points are exactly alike in all their qualities, and their diversity must be that bare numerical diversity contemplated in the third' view.[95] This is no doubt a serious contention; and we may put it a little otherwise to make its seriousness evident. Let it be asked : If things are distinguishable by their places, how are the places in turn distinguishable ? Here arises this difficulty : On the absolute view, two places, which may be equal in size, are quite alike qualitatively, and so are not distinguishable qualitatively, nor are they distinguishable by reference to their places, since, being places, they have no places. So they are distinguishable by reference to themselves, which is as good as saying that their numerical diversity is ultimate and indefinable. Now, Kant does admit that 'one part of space, although completely similar and equal to another part, is still . . . a different part';[96] but he finds in it rather a confirmation of his view that 'plurality and numerical difference are already given us by space itself',[97] that is, of his view that the ultimate ground of differentiation of items (things and places) is non-qualitative and spatial.[98] One may say that Kant here virtually admits that so far as the numerical diversity of places is concerned it is ultimate and indefinable; but it will be unfair to stop short and say nothing further. For Kant, the numerical diversity of places is ultimate and indefinable only in the sense that is *not conceptually explicable*; and this fact is for him immensely significant : it suggests the view that places are distinguished by sense through pure intuition.[99] The view that space and places are pure intuitions will be explained and discussed later on.[100] Here we may only observe, in fine, that Russell's contention, namely, that the second view is reducible to the third, is wrong in so far as it insinuates that the second view is unimportant, and that, for a student of Kant, the second view is (i) reducible to the third view only if the latter is taken to mean that numerical diversity is, ultimately, not conceptually explicable, and (ii) is thus a pointer to the view that numerical diversity is, ultimately, based upon pure sensible spatial (or spatio-temporal) intuition.

It remains to consider Russell's other contention that the second view (the Thomistic-Kantian one) is, from another angle, reducible ultimately to the first (i.e. the Leibnizian one). The view that 'if A and B differ in spatio-temporal position, then A and B are two' is shown to be reducible to the Leibnizian one by arguing that A and B are nothing but bundles of qualities, where the term 'qualities' is used in the wider enough sense to include spatio- temporal positions too.[101] Upon this interpretation of 'qualities', A and B that differ in spatio-temporal position differ in their qualities. But this interpretation of the term 'qualities' is less an interpretation of its usage than a plea for its misuse; and thus a reduction of the Thomistic-Kantian view to that of Leibniz, resting as it does upon a misuse of the term 'qualities', may be brushed aside as being in the end a terminological trifle. We shall have occasion to develop and justify this criticism in a subsequent context.[102]

Meanwhile, for the sake of maintaining clarity of line a summing up of the discussion made in the last and the present chapter will be useful.

4.2 A Summary of Chapters 3 and 4

In his first space argument Kant contends that the idea of space is already presupposed in our representation of sensible objects as outside and beside one another, and therefore cannot be derived empirically from such outer relations. This contention appears to Sidgwick as trivial. But Sidgwick fails to appreciate that Kant's argument serves to expose the obvious circularity in the Wolffian sort of analysis of the idea of space. Wolff attempted an empirical deduction of the idea of space by arguing that the idea derives from our representation of a certain order of mutual *externality* among simultaneously presented sensible objects. The circularity of such a deduction is obvious, and is exposed in Kant's first space argument without any mention of Wolff, though. Wolff's view is no doubt capable of a more guarded formulation; but such formulation leads to Leibniz's reductionist-cum-relational analysis of the idea of space, which analysis, despite Leibniz's higher-level pan-innatism, is definitely empiricistic in effect. According to it, the idea of space reduces to that of a certain order or relation of coexistence (in the sense of simultaneous existence) among sensible objects.

This account of the idea of space is not obviously circular. This is not to say, however, that it is obviously not circular. In theory it avoids circularity only by basing itself upon an untenable principle of individuation; it is not too difficult a task for Kant to set aside that principle, and show that Leibniz's reductionist account of the idea of space does after all suffer from circularity. Kant's first space argument, *upon a closer examination*, shows itself as involving a subtle attack on the Leibnizian principle of individuation, namely, that of the identity of indiscernibles. On Kant's view, the principle of indiscernibles is indisputable only in its application to intelligibilia (objects of mere conception), but turns out to be a spurious law of nature when its application is uncritically extended to the objects of the senses. Kant's main contention in his first space argument is that the idea of space is not without circularity reducible to or deducible from the representation of a certain sort of order or mutual relations among sensible objects, since these objects cannot be individuated except by reference to their individuating spatial locations.

NOTES :

1. It is customary to regard Leibniz as the 'author' of the principle of indiscernibles, although the principle 'is an extension of Scotism'; see Loemker, *Gottfried Wilhelm Leibniz : Philosophical Papers and Letters,* 1956, vol. II, p. 1208 n. 426.
2. 'The Controversy between Leibniz and Clarke, 1715-16' (Leibniz's fifth paper; para 26) in Loemker, II, 1140.
3. 'The Controversy' (Leibniz's fourth letter' ; para 4) in Loemker, II, 1117.
4. As W. E. Johnson (*Logic, Part I,* Dover Publications, N. Y., 1964, p. 194 n. 1) says : 'If the Leibnizian and the Bradleyan principles can be in any way distinguished, it is that the former is ontological and the latter epistemological'.
5. See, e.g. 'The Controversy' (Leibniz's fifth paper ; para 23) in Loemker, II, 1139.
6. *Ibidem.*
7. R. Latta, *Leibniz : The Monadology and Other Philosophical Writings,* Clarendon Press, Oxford, 1898, p. 377 No. 96.
8. Latta's translation, p. 377.
9. *Ibidem.*
10. 'The Controversy between Leibniz and Clarke' (Leibniz's fourth letter ; para 4) in Loemker, II, 1117.
11. It may be noted that what is insensibly apprehended is for Leibniz apprehended, although we are not aware of this fact. In other words, an unconscious perception for Leibniz '*is* a state of consciousness, but is unconscious in the sense that we are not aware of it'; B. Russell, *A Critical Exposition of the Philosophy of Leibniz,* London, 1949, p. 156.

12. Namely, in his papers (i) 'First Truths' (Loemker, I, 411ff.), (ii) 'Discourse on Metaphysics' (Loemker, I, 465ff.), (iii) 'Correspondence with Arnauld' (Loemker, I, 508ff.).
13. 'Discourse on Metaphysics', sect. 8 (Loemker, I, 471).
14. Loemker, I, 472.
15. This means that there is a complete concept of an individual by means of which it is sufficiently identifiable. The complete concept of an individual reflects its 'haecceity'; cf. *ibidem.*
16. *Ibidem.*
17. G. H. R. Parkinson, *Logic and Reality in Leibniz's Metaphysics,* Clarendon Press, Oxford, 1965, pp. 128-129.
18. *New Essays,* bk ii, ch. 27, sect. 1 (Latta, p. 377 no. 96).
19. 'First Truths', Loemker, I, 413.
20. *Ibid.,* pp. 413-414.
21. *Ibid.,* p. 413.
22. 'The Controversy between Leibniz and Clarke' (Leibniz's fifth paper; para 27) in Loemker, II, 1140.
23. 'The Controversy' (Leibniz's fifth paper; para 25) in Loemker, II, 1140.
24. Loemker, II, 1139.
25. 'The Controversy' (Leibniz's fourth letter; para 3) in Loemker, II, 1117.
26. 'The Controversy' (Leibniz's fifth paper; para 47) in Loemker, II, 1146.
27. In F. E. England, *Kant's Conception of God : A Critical Exposition of Its Metaphysical Development Together with a Translation of the Nova Dilucidatio,* George Allen & Unwin, London, 1929, Appendix, p. 244. [All references in what follows to the *Nova Dilucidatio* are to 'Proposition XI' therein.]
28. *Ibid.*, p. 243.
29. I.e. to sensible 'things' or 'bodies' which Leibniz sometimes 'prefers' to call 'corporal substances' (see 'Conversation of Philare'te and Ariste', in Loemker, II, 1015).
30. *Nova Dilucidatio,* England trans., p. 244.
31. *Ibidem.*
32. *Ibidem.*
33. *Ibidem.*
34. See, e.g. Garnett, *The Kantian Philosophy of Space*, 1939, p. 114 (last para) and p. 115 (lines 4-7).

35. Kant, 'On the First Ground of the Distinction of Regions in Space', trans. Handyside in *Kant's Inaugural Dissertation and Early Writings on Space,* 1929, p. 27.
36. *Ibid.*, pp. 26-27.
37. Garnett, *op. cit.* p. 112. These four theses are : '(1) there is necessary or absolute space; (2) it is real or actual; (3) it is independent of the existence of matter; and (4) it is the first ground of the possibility of the compositeness of matter.'
38. Vaihinger and Kemp Smith are on the former side of the Controversy, while Riehl and Kuno Fischer are on the latter side, see Garnett, *op. cit.*, pp. 117f.
39. Handyside trans., p. 28.
40. Herman–J. de Vleeschauwer, *The Development of Kantian Thought–The History of a Doctrine,* trans. A. R. C. Duncan, Thomas Nelson and Sons Ltd., Edinburgh, 1962, p. 48.
41. L. W. Beck, *Early German Philosophy,* 1969, p. 450.
42. It is this similarity in view of which it was observed in the last chapter (see above, p. 108) : '. . . his [Kant's] attack on the Leibnizian principle of individuation has a history in the course of which his first space argument itself crystallizes. . .'.
43. Brittan, *Kant's Theory of Science,* 1978, p. 88.
44. *Ibidem.*
45. Handyside trans., p. 26.
46. *Ibid.,* p. 27. Cf. also Kant's Prolegomena, § 13, Beck trans., 1976, p. 33, 1127-28.
47. C. D. Broad, *Kant : An Introduction,* ed. C. Lewy, Cambridge, 1979, p. 38.
48. Handyside trans., p. 27.
49. *Ibid.*, p. 26.
50. As Kant puts it (see Handyside trans., pp. 27-28) : 'Nevertheless if we conceive the first created thing to be a human hand, it is necessarily either a right or a left, and to produce the one a different act of the creating cause is required from that whereby its counterpart can come into being'.
51. *Ibid.*, p. 28.
52. P. Remnant, 'Incongruent Counterparts and Absolute Space', *Mind* N. S. 72 (1963), p. 399; also cited by R.C.S. Walker, *Kant,* 1978, p. 47.

53. Walker, *Kant,* p. 47.
54. *Ibidem.*
55. Handyside trans., p. 28.
56. *Ibidem.*
57. 'Apparently', because later on we shall see that this really is of considerable importance.
58. *Critique,* A 263-264 = B 319-320.
59. A 264 = B 320.
60. The expression 'condition of outer appearances' may be taken just in the sense of 'form of outer appearance', and then a distinction may be made 'between "form of appearance" and "form of sensibility", the latter alone implying the subjectivity of space and time'; Paton, *Kant's Metaphysic of Experience,* 1951, I, 103. An analogous problem is considered below on pp. 220-221.
61. A 262 = B 318.
62. A 271-272 = B 327-328.
63. A 271 = B 327.
64. A 281 = B 337.
65. A 272 = B 328.
66. A 264 = B 320.
67. A 272 = B 328 : 'the objects of the senses (*mundus phaenomenon*)'.
68. Leibniz, 'On Analysis Situs', Loemker, I, 392.
69. *Critique,* A 263 = B 319.
70. This distinction is epistemological (or, as Kant says, 'transcendental' ; see *Critique,* A 44 = B 61-62). It is not 'logical' as Leibniz and Wolff suppose (*ibid*), nor is it, despite Kant's talk of 'objects' here, ontological (cf. *Critique,* B 311). Cf. also Graham Bird, *Kant's Theory of Knowledge,* Routledge & Kegan Paul, London, 1962, pp. 19, 53.

    What is essential to Kant's present criticism of Leibniz is the recognition of a fundamental distinction between sense and understanding, sensible intuition and conception, sensation and conception, and not any concern with the question whether there *are* objects of the pure understanding (i.e. of mere conception).
71. *Critique,* A 44 = B 61.
72. §7, Handyside trans. p. 48.
73. A 43-44 = B 61.

74. Consider the following taken from Kant's criticism of Leibniz in his *Fortschritte der Metaphysik seit Leibniz und Wolff* (as translated by Latta, *op. cit.,* p. 169 n. 3) :

'Leibniz could not admit that we could still distinguish them [i.e. internally quite alike sensible things] through their places in space . . . Leibniz could not admit this, for he recognizes no other distinction among things than that which is made through notions [*Begriffe*], and refuses to allow any way of representation specifically distinct from this, such as intuition . . .'

If we translate *Begriffe* in the last sentence by 'concepts', we come to see that, for Kant, not all distinction is conceptual (or, for that matter, qualitative).

It may be noted incidentally that Kant admits three kinds of distinction : 'logical' 'physical', and 'pure intuitional'. The first two kinds of distinction are explained in his 'The Mistaken Subtility of the Four Syllogistic Figures', sec. vi, trans. by T. K. Abbott in *Kant's Introduction to Logic and His Essay on the Mistaken Subtility of the Four Figures,* Vision Press, London, 1963, pp. 93f. The third kind of distinction is connected with his theory that space and time are conditions of otherness of sensible objects.

75. Cf. Kant's statement at A 270 = B 326 of the *Critique* : 'The conditions of sensible intuition . . . carry with them their own differences'. This, taken in the minimum of meaning (i.e. in a strictly austere sense), implies that he recognizes a non-conceptual mode of sensible distinction in intuition.

76. A 272 = B 328.

77. A 282 = B 338.

78. *Logic, Part I,* 1964, p. 24. Cf. Sections 2, 3, and 4 in full of the chapter from which the passage is quoted.

79. Brittan, *op. cit.,* p. 34.

80. *Ibidem.*

81. P. 143.

82. Kant's reference to such objects is transcendental, not ontological (cf. note 70 above), and is polemically significant in the context of his criticism of Leibniz.

83. This is how indeed Kant sometimes uses the word 'concepts' in the Amphiboly – section under consideration. Thus his expression, e.g. 'things which are not distinguishable from one another in their

concepts (in quality or quantity) are . . .', at A 281 = B 337, shows that he is using the word 'concepts' in the sense of 'qualitative and quantitative determinations (signified by concepts)'. Using the word 'quality' in the comprehensive sense of 'attribute', we may say, therefore, that Kant is here using the word 'concepts' in the sense of 'qualities or attributes (signified by concepts)'.

84. The expression 'without any further conditions' (*ohne weitere Bedingungen*) is borrowed from A 272 = B 328 of the *Critique,* where, as the context shows, Kant is concerned with maintaining that something is a sufficient (as well as a necessary) condition of something else. The expression embodies (as we take it) his recognition of the demand that if 'a' is to be sufficient for 'x', then no other factor or condition shall strictly be necessary for 'x'. On the legitimacy of this demand, cf. C. D. Broad, *Scientific Thought,* London, 1952, p. 500.

85. Cf. Kant's observation at A 279 = B 335 : 'If we reflect in a merely logical fashion, we are only comparing our concepts with each other in the understanding, to find whether both have the same content . . .'.

86. Kant's statement, e.g. at A 279 = B 335, namely, 'we must either abstract from any and every object (as in logic), or, if we admit an object, must think it under the conditions of sensible intuition', *if taken in its context and in the minimum of meaning* (i.e. in an austere sense, with which alone we are at present concerned), can be paraphrased and expanded as 'we must either abstract from any and every object (as in logic), or, if we are concerned with the objects of the senses, must note their separateness of presentment in sensible intuition prior to the consideration whether they have, or have not, the same qualitative content'.

87. This rule is derived from a comparison of concepts in this way : If one concept fully agrees with another in respect of its internal content, i.e. in respect of the qualities signified by it, then these are one and the same concept; and if one concept does not agree with another in that qualitative way, then these are two different concepts.

88. This is uncritical even in the austere sense, inasmuch as it is based upon the ignoring of the fundamental distinction between sense and conception, a distinction which one not already committed, or without even having to be committed, to Kant's transcendental idealism can be expected to endorse, as we have seen.

89. A 270 = B 326.

90. It will be argued by some that the view under reference *cannot be*

rejected, because, being based upon an uncritical presupposition, it can be neither accepted nor rejected. Even if the presupposition be false, the view cannot still be rejected, though again it cannot be accepted.

We cannot discuss this argument lest we should be carried far afield. But we may point out that Kant is at any rate entitled to express his non-acceptance of that view by saying 'It is not that the representation of qualitative differences is a sufficient condition for the individuation of sensible objects'. The most that can be said is that the expression of his non-acceptance by rather saying 'The representation of qualitative differences is not a sufficient condition for the individuation of sensible objects' is misleading, since it is not then clear whether the negation here is intended to be external or internal.

Of course, to make the above remarks and yet not to introduce certain consequential changes into what we have said before and after is equally misleading. But I think there is another aspect of Kant's criticism which is worth emphasizing. A reason has been already stated for rejecting (not merely for not accepting, but for rejecting) the view that the representation of qualitative differences, *without any further conditions,* serves to individuate the objects of the senses; and that reason is not too weak, surely. It is after all reasonable to admit on more or less neutral grounds the distinction between sensible intuition and mere conception and to maintain that the objects of the senses, as such objects, cannot be represented as qualitatively different unless they are *also* separately presented in intuition. This being so, it is not unreasonable to reject the view just mentioned. And if it is not unreasonable to reject this view, it is not unreasonable to reject the view that the representation of qualitative differences is a *sufficient condition* for the individuation of sensible objects.

91. Bertrand Russell, *Human Knowledge,* etc., Simon and Schuster, New York, 1948, 6th paperback printing, p. 292.
92. *Ibidem.*
93. *Ibid.*, p. 293.
94. *Ibid.*, p. 292.
95. *Ibidem.*
96. *Critique*, A 264 = B 320.
97. *Ibidem.*
98. Cf. the sentence in the *Critique* immediating succeeding the one

referred to in Note 96 above and *also* the whole passage at A 263-64 = B 319-20.

99. Cf. Kant's analogous treatment of the difference between incongruent counterparts (that 'cannot be made intelligible by any concept, but only by . . . relation . . . to intuition') in the *Prolegomena*, § 13 (second para), Beck trans., pp. 33-34.

100. In 5.2.2 and Chapter 9.

101. Russell, *op. cit.*, pp. 292-293. Cf. A. Pap, *Elements of Analytic Philosophy*, 1949, p. 73, 11.25-26. On Leibniz's view about spatial positions, Broad's remarks are illuminating : '. . . ultimately Leibniz must hold what Johnson would call a form of the adjectival qualitative theory. The real basis of the phenomenon of spatial position must be certain pure qualities in the substances which we perceive as bodies'. See C. D. Broad, *Leibniz : An Introduction*, ed. C. Lewy, Cambridge University Press, 1979, p. 61.

102. See 5.2.3.

CHAPTER FIVE

KANT'S FIRST SPACE ARGUMENT (Continued)

In this chapter Kant's first space argument is examined in some further detail. A recent criticism of this argument is considered first.

5.1 An Examination of Walker's Criticism of Kant's First Space Argument

Walker criticizes Kant's argument in question (along with his first argument on time) as follows :

> He [Kant] starts by claiming that it would be impossible to acquire any notion of space by abstraction from experience, because if we are to represent objects as spatially located 'the representation of space must already be presupposed' (A 23/B 38); and similarly with time (A 30/B 46). This is hardly convincing. Obviously we cannot think of objects as spatio-temporally located without having the ideas of space and time; but we may still have acquired these ideas by observing objects which now, after having performed the abstraction, we can think of as located spatio-temporally. In just the same way one cannot think of an object as red without having the idea of redness; but redness is Kant's paradigm of an empirical concept, acquired by abstraction from the observation of things which once we have the concept we can describe as instances of redness. So the argument fails even to show that space and time are a priori in the genetic sense.[1]

Walker's criticism has to be restated, since, as it stands, it is an *ignoratio elenchi.* Kant's first space argument is, as we have amply seen, mainly concerned with rejecting a reductionist-cum-relational account of the idea of space. If this is remembered, it may be easier to discern what exactly Kant says in this argument. Walker fails to notice that Kant does not say, much less argue, in his first space argument, that the representation of space must already be presupposed in the representation of objects as spatially *located.* What the second sentence of Kant's argument, which is depended upon by Walker, actually comes to is this : the representation of space must already be presupposed in the representation of eertain sensible objects as outside us and as themselves outside and beside one another in so far as such representation involves that of the sensible objects as not only different, but in different places. Kant's contention here is, in other words, that the representation of space must already be presupposed in the representation of the outer or spatial relations of sensible objects through the representation of the objects concerned as in different places. Walker's criticism, then, involves a confusion between 'that *through* which the representation of space must be presupposed' and 'that *in* which the representation of space must be presupposed' according to Kant's first space argument.[2]

Walker, then, is required, for the sake of strict accuracy, to restate his criticism by recognizing that Kant's main contention in the present argument is not that the idea of space must be presupposed in the representation of objects as spatially located, but rather that this idea[3] is presupposed in the representation of certain relations of sensible objects, namely, their outer or spatial relations.[4] Walker, however, might now take the radical empiricistic view that spatial or outer relations are themselves objects of empirical perception (or, as he says, 'observation'), and say that the idea of space derives empirically from the perception of spatial relations in the same way that the idea of redness derives empirically from the perception of red items.[5] A precise statement of such a criticism of Kant might take the following form :

The idea of space is no less empirical than that of redness. Exception is not usually taken to the view that the idea of redness derives empirically from the perceptions of red items, even although in this account the word 'red' is already used in the phrase 'perceptions of red items'. The reason is that the word 'red' in 'perceptions of red items' is used only to mention or mean what occurs[6] non-linguistically in our experiences. Similarly, no exception need be taken to the statement that the idea of space is empirically obtained from the outer or spatial relations of outside, beside, etc. For such words as 'outside', 'beside', or even 'outer or spatial relations' just as truly as the words like 'red', 'green', etc. mean (stand for) something that occurs non-linguistically in objects of perception.[7]

In reply to the above objection it may be said that the supposed analogy between the idea of space and the idea of redness breaks down at a crucial place. To be able to see this it is necessary to distinguish between the two senses in which the idea of space (or, to use Kant's expression, 'the representation of space') is presupposed in our perceptions of outer or spatial relations[8] : the trivial sense in which the representation of space *qua* the concept of spatiality[9] is presupposed in our perceptions of certain relations as outer or spatial relations[10] (that is, in our description of them as outer or spatial relations, or more determinately, as the spatial relations of outside, beside, etc.), and the non-trivial sense in which the representation of space *qua* the intuition of space (or more specifically, the intuition of places) is presupposed in our perceptions of outer or spatial relations prior to our determination of them as such relations. The intuition of space is presupposed in our perceptions of outer or spatial relations in this way : the perception of an outer relation between sensible objects presupposes[11] the representation of these objects as numerically *different,* and the representation of these objects as numerically different presupposes the intuition of them *in different places,* which implies that the places in which they are intuited are also intuited along with them. That this is so, and that this is Kant's actual view, should be clear from the discussions in Chapters 3 and 4 except for the point that the different places in which the sensible objects have to be intuited are themselves intuited. This point, that places are objects of *intuition,* is not stressed by Kant in his first space argument, but nevertheless needs to be taken into account for reasons to become clear soon. Deferring discussion of this point as well as a detailed examination of the other points to avoid digression, it is necessary to return to the supposed analogy between the idea of space and the idea of redness. The analogy holds only between what has been called the trivial sense in which the *concept* of space (i.e. spatiality) is presupposed in our perceptions of certain relations as spatial relations and the corresponding sense in which the *concept* of redness is presupposed in our perceptions of certain items as red items. But the analogy breaks down with respect to what has been called the non-trivial sense in which the *intuition* of space is presupposed in our perceptions of spatial relations. For it cannot analogously be said that the *intuition* of red is presupposed in the perceptions of red items. And this cannot be said because the perceptions of red items from which admittedly the idea of redness derives being themselves intuitions of red, it would then amount to saying that the intuition of red is presupposed in the intuitions of red. Against the objection under consideration, then, one may in fine say this : The idea of redness is without doubt empirical in that it derives empirically from perceptions of a certain kind which we, on the reflective level once we have already acquired the concept of redness, describe as 'perceptions of red items'. As to the idea of space, however, one cannot similarly say that it derives empirically from our perceptions of relations of a certain kind which we, on the reflective level once we have already acquired the concept of spatiality, describe as 'perceptions of spatial relations', because the very perceptions of relations of the sort in question would not be possible at all on the pre-reflective level without our having *intuitions of places,* and so, as Kant says, without already presupposing the representation of space.[12]

It is time to turn to a detailed examination of Kant's argument. It remains to see in particular what can be said for and what against it in the light of some contemporary philosophical discussions on spatial relations and positions.

5.2. A Detailed Examination of Kant's Contention that the Representation of Outer Relations of Sensible Objects13 Presupposes14 That of the Sensible Objects as Not Only Different, but in Different Places

For the purpose of a critical examination, Kant's contention can be logically analysed into the following two parts :

(1) The representation of outer relations of sensible objects presupposes that of the outer objects as *different,* and (2) the representation of the outer objects as different presupposes[15] their representation as *in different places.* (That 'their representation as in

different places' here strictly means 'the intuition of them in different places' is a point of further detail, which also has to be discussed.)

These two parts are but the logical moments of one psychological process, and are here distinguished because a complex or involved argument cannot be examined all at once. We begin with an examination of the first part.

5.2.1 Outer relations and numerical difference

There can be no doubt that the representation (or, if one prefers, the apprehension) of a relation presupposes that of the things or terms related. One may doubtless distinguish between a *relating relation* and *a relation per se,* and say that a *relation per se* has no connexion with the terms;[16] but then one should note further that the so-called relation *per se* has only to be 'considered as a term'.[17] A relation *per se* (i.e. a relation *in* itself) is only considered in the abstract, while a relating relation (i.e. a relation actually relating) is apprehended in the concrete. Our present concern is with the perceived outer relations; and since these are apprehended in the concrete situation of outer experience, these are of course relating relations, i.e. relations actually relating the outer objects. Outer relations, that is to say, are apprehended as relations relating the outer objects. Now to proceed further, the apprehension of outer relations presupposes that of the concerned outer objects as *different.* (Difference here means numerical, not qualitative, difference,[18] or, to adopt Johnson's phrase, 'existential otherness'). If outer relations cannot be apprehended *per se,* but only with respect to outer objects, the outer objects involved in the apprehension of the outer relations must be given to our awareness, explicit or implicit, as numerically *different,* or existentially other than, one another.[19] In examination, or rather vindication, of this contention, the following considerations may be brought forward :

If outer objects are not apprehended as *different,* it will follow, to use an early argument of Russell's, that we apprehend outer relations with respect to numerically one and the same object, i.e. that we apprehend one and the same object as outside itself, beside itself, to the right or left of itself; – which is absurd.[20] It might be objected that these outer relations are often actually apprehended even within one and the same object. Thus, when we perceive a single piece of paper as an object consisting of two parts, a right-hand and a left-hand part, the two parts are apprehended within one and the same object, and yet one part appears as outside or beside another even within this one object. Any such objection, however, would be trite and irrelevant. The single piece of paper seen as one and the same object is not apprehended as outside or beside itself; only its parts appear as outside or beside one another; but then the two parts are apprehended as *numerically different.* It is no doubt true that the two parts are apprehended as being within one and the same object, but what is worth notice is that the outer relation of outside or beside that is apprehended is apprehended not with respect to this one and the same object, but as between its two different parts only. The two parts within one and the same object imply a diversity in a unity, where diversity refers to the parts and unity to the object as a whole; but though these diverse parts, as parts of one object, imply in a sense the unity of the object, the relation holding between the parts does not imply this unity but only the diversity of the parts. We shall only meddle matters by arguing that since the parts belong to the one object, the relation between them also belongs to it. 'A belongs to B' may mean : 'A is in B', or 'A is of B', or 'A is both in and of B'. The parts are both in and of the one object; but the relation between the parts is only *in* the one object, but not of it.[21.]

Other difficulties similar to the one mooted above can be anticipated and easily disposed of, and we may thus be persuaded, as was Russell at least in the autumn of 1911,[22] of 'the maxim that every spatial relation implies diversity of its terms, i.e. that nothing is to the right of itself, or above itself, and so on'.[23] Russell, however, it is necessary to note, was not consciously deciding in favour of Kant, and his chief concern was simply to support the conclusion that there must be particulars as well as universals : '. . . given two white patches, one of which is to the right of the other, it will follow that there is not a single thing, whiteness, which is to the right of itself, but that there are two different things, instances of whiteness, of which one is to the right of the other'.[24] But whatever his purposes, he regarded it as 'the self-evident fact',[25] elsewhere referred to by him as 'synthetic a priori general truth',[26] 'that certain spatial relations imply diversity of their terms'.

This, it hardly needs stating, well corroborates Kant's view that the apprehension of outer relations presupposes that of the outer objects as *different.*

Any objection designed to question the propriety of our reference to Russell on the ground that his problem was very different from Kant's would be otiose, because on the main point that spatial relations can be apprehended only between numerically different objects there is clear harmony between Russell as quoted and Kant. It should not be presumed Russell's maxim that spatial relations imply diversity or numerical difference of their terms was only ontological without the epistemological significance that the *apprehension* of spatial relations implies the *apprehension* of different objects as terms. For the spatial relations spoken of by him were, in spite of his concern with the ontological problem of the relations of universals and particulars, 'perceived spatial relations' or 'spatial relations of objects of perception', i.e. spatial relations as *apprehended.* The only relevant difference here is that whereas his emphasis was on the *perceived* (as he said that the perceived spatial relations involved the numerical difference of the objects), our emphasis is on the *perceiving* (as we say that the apprehending of the spatial relation involves the apprehending of the numerical difference of the objects). But this difference in emphasis does not indicate any opposition, but only difference of purposes at hand.

5.2.2 On the nature of the representation of places

What falls to be considered next is the second part of Kant's contention that the apprehension of the outer objects as *different* involved in the apprehension of their relations presupposes their apprehension as *in different places.* The contention has been explained in detail in Chapter 4; and nothing need be added to that explanation. It only remains to consider here the question whether absolute places or positions are perceived or not.[27] In the article of Russell's used above in favour of the first part of Kant's contention Russell argues that if absolute space is admitted, one can of course say that it is the difference of places that accounts for the numerical difference of objects; but unfortunately 'perceived space is certainly not absolute, i.e. absolute positions are not among objects of perception'.[28] In the *Critique* Kant, however, holds that space and even places are objects of *intuition*.[29] They are not among objects of perception like chairs and tables; nevertheless they are for him directly apprehended by the mind in virtue of its own principle of intuition. This is a view at which Kant has arrived after a long struggle. In his famous essay of 1768 he comes to adopt for the first time the Newtonian view that space is absolute by way of arguing, against Leibniz, that outer objects cannot be individuated except by reference to their orientation in absolute space; but in this work he is yet to achieve clarity regarding the nature of our *mode of apprehension* of space. He observes that 'absolute space is not an object of an outer sensation, but a fundamental concept which first makes all such sensations possible' and that there are 'difficulties surrounding this concept, if we attempt to comprehend its reality – a reality which is sufficiently intuitable to inner sense – through ideas of reason'.[30] These remarks are, as L. W. Beck aptly says, 'very obscure, but very important'.[31] These are very important, as showing that Kant is struggling towards the view that space is apprehended by a priori intuition. In his later writings, the *Dissertation* (1770) and the *Critique*, Kant adheres to the view that space is absolute[32] and as such is not an object of outer sensation and is nevertheless intuitable to some sense, but he corrects the previous view that it is intuited by inner sense, and comes to maintain that it is intuited a priori by outer sense.[33] This view that space is an object of pure intuition is duly supported by him by some specific arguments, which cannot be discussed at present. But it may be pointed out here that the view represents a natural culmination of his previous reflections. Since, as is suggested by his essay of 1768, outer objects cannot be individuated except ultimately by reference to their location in different places,[34] it is clear that the individuating places are themselves *somehow* immediately apprehended, and since, as is also hardly to be disputed, absolute places are not objects of sensation, it is clear, moreover, that places, in so far as these are immediately apprehended, are so apprehended independently of sensation.[35] And this points to the view that places are apprehended by pure intuition.

This pure intuition theory is something which the majority of thinkers, however, are not prepared to accept. They seek to 'define' places or locations by means of relations among physical objects. Reference may be made to Russell's perspective theory. This theory will be examined later on.[36] Here, however, it is necessary to remark that the question whether the perception of objects originally carries the immediate consciousness of their places should not be confused with the question whether such immediate consciousness of their places or locations is the dependable basis for the determination of their exact or right places or locations. Reference may also be made to A. S. Eddington's words : 'Location is not something supernaturally revealed to the mind; it is a kind of conventional summary of those properties or relations of objects which condition certain visual or tactual sensations'.[37] According to Eddington, our awareness of location is not a direct intuition, but an inference from observations of the relations of objects. He says that our view of the direct experience of locations is a superstition that has come down to us from ape-like ancestors. Now, here also the remark to be made is that the question whether we are immediately aware of location in space should not be confused with the question whether this awareness is the dependable basis for the determination of *right* location. Seeing that our immediate awareness of locations is often deceptive, scientists have bothered about the precise method of determining right locations; this method happens to be different from the ordinary or obvious method of immediate awareness, and so it is concluded that we have no immediate awareness of locations. But the conclusion is not warranted. If immediate intuition of the relations of objects can be admitted, why not also immediate intuition of their locations ? Indeed we immediately experience not only the spatial relations of objects[38] but also their positions or locations in space; and however unprecise such expressions as 'locations', 'positions' or 'places' may be, places must have to be regarded as ostensibly definable, and so as objects of intuition, at some stage or other if an infinite regress of the bad sort is to be avoided.[39] Consequently any attempts at explaining places as inferences or as logical constructions or as entirely definable by means of the mutual relations of objects are bound to be unsuccessful. Our immediate intuitions of locations require to be supplemented by other methods for the determination of right locations; but that is a different matter. Immediate intuitions of locations or places cannot indeed be regarded as empirical perceptions for certain reasons; but then the legitimate hypothesis is that they are pure intuitions. To decry such pure intuitions as mystical intuitions or as supernatural revelations will be only to betray a refusal to understand.

5.2.3 Some difficulties (as posed by Russell's later views about spatial relations and positions) answered

It is necessary to turn now to consider the difficulties that emerge from Russell's disavowal[40] of the view that has been utilized above in favour of the first part of Kant's contention. In stating Russell's revised view, certain things have to be mentioned which are not related to the present inquiry, but it is hoped that the relevant point will not fail to be noticed. He now holds

> . . . that spatial and temporal relations, such as *to-the-left-of* or *before*, should not imply diversity. This causes difficulties . . . I think they can be overcome, but only by admitting as empirical and doubtful certain propositions which have seemed certain such as 'if A is to the left of B, A and B are not identical, . . .'.[41]

His innovation upon the previous view is 'that qualities suffice, without our having to suppose that they have instances. Incidentally, we have reduced to the empirical level certain properties of spatio-temporal relations which threatened to be synthetic *a priori* general truths'.[42] Thus, as against his previous view according to which every spatial relation implies diversity of its terms so that redness, for instance, cannot be outside itself, to the right of itself, etc., his present view holds

> . . . that redness can have to itself one or more of those spatial relations which, according to common sense, no 'thing' can have to itself. Redness may be to the right of redness, or above redness, in the immediate visual field; redness may be in America and in Europe, in physical space.[43]

Formulated with reference to the problem of universal *vs.* particulars – although this problem is not of immediate relevance to the present study –, the contrast between the two views is this : for the earlier view, redness cannot be in two places at once, all that occupy different places being instances of redness; but, for the later view, redness can be in two places at once. That is to say, whereas for the old view, there are particulars as well as universals, the new view admits only universals, and not particulars as well. When we perceive two exactly similar red patches, can we be sure, Russell now asks, that we are not perceiving *numerically one and the same* red patch in different places ? He admits that his present view cannot be better proved than his previous one, but argues that it is a clear gain in *logical parsimony*[44] if we can maintain that we perceive, and that there is, one and the same (i.e. not merely qualitatively, but also numerically, identical) redness in different places.

The view just mentioned is relevant to this Study to the extent that it disputes (i.e. renders 'doubtful') the foregoing account of spatial relations. One may no doubt say that there is no reason to be worried about this new Russellian view because even if, as it holds, we apprehend outer relations with respect to numerically one and the same object in different places, we have still, during apprehensions of outer relations, the idea of space presupposed under the awareness of different places. But the difficulty is that Russell has in the actual working out of his view given a disappointing account of *places.* He reduces a 'thing' as commonly conceived to a *complex or bundle of qualities,* where the term 'quality' is used broadly enough to include spatial (and temporal) relations and positions (and dates). Obviously, different *places* have under Russell lost their special status. Whereas we tend to regard a 'thing' as having qualities and not as defined by them, but by *spatio-temporal position* as if the latter were not itself a thing or quality, but what was occupied by it, Russell, on the other hand, suggests that there are only qualities, or rather, complexes of qualities among which spatial (and temporal) positions (and dates) also are to be reckoned. He says :

> places in the momentary visual field . . . are absolute, and are defined by relation to the centre of the field of vision. They may be defined by the two relations right-and-left, up-and-down; these relations, at any rate, suffice for topological purposes.[45]

These relations defining *places* are also called 'differing qualities' by Russell : '. . . there are in the visual field a number of differing qualities of up-and-downness and a mumber of differing qualities of right-and-leftness. Any one of the former we will denote by "Q" and any one of the latter by "Ꝗ".[46] The place-defining qualities have again been otherwise called 'angular co-ordinates' : '. . . let the angular coordinates of the one patch in visual space be Q, Ꝗ, and those of the other Ꝗ', Q' . . . . The angular coordinates of an object in the visual field may be regarded as qualities'.[47] According to Russell, a 'place' as defined by qualilties Ꝗ is, by a 'harmless avoidance of circumlocution', itself to be considered a 'quality'. The implication of this view of different places as *qualitative differences* seems disastrous for Kant's argument. In Russell's analysis our awareness of redness (e.g.) as *in different places* is not strictly the awareness of red-quality *in* non-qualitative spaces (i.e. places), but the awareness of red-quality *compresent* or *overlapping with*[48] space-qualities; – in other words, far from being the awareness of red-quality *in* places that are not themselves qualities, but are presupposed by them, it is the awareness of red-quality overlapping with space-qualities as if both the red-quality and the space-qualities had the same status in experience. That a real difficulty has arisen can be appreciated through the following consideration. Some may hastily argue that, since in his revised view Russell has admitted, contrary to his earlier contention, that absolute places or positions are perceived, Kant's doctrine is rather likely to be supported. But nothing can be farther from truth. There is a marked discrepancy of views between Kant and Russell concerning the very implication of admitting absolute space. According to Russell, for absolute places or positions to be objects of perception means that in the apprehension of (e.g.) redness in two places, this place and that place should respectively be constituents of two different complexes, one complex consisting of a red patch and this place, and another complex consisting of a red patch and that place, that is to say, this place should be one quality overlapping with the red-quality in one complex and that place should be another quality overlapping with the red-quality in another complex. All this suggests that, for Russell, in the theory of absolute position, different places (i.e. differences of places) should be reckoned among qualitative differences.

According to Kant, however, belief in absolute positions does not involve the consequence of space being regarded as a quality; on the contrary, it involves the opposite consequence of abandoning the view of space as a quality.[49] Indeed what is of vital importance to Kant is this latter view that particular places are not mere qualitative differences; and consequently what contradicts this view would constitute a formidable difficulty for him. That is why, Russell's new view that places are qualities, or constituents of complexes of qualities, becomes a great difficulty for Kant's argument. If different places signify mere qualitative differences overlapping or compresent with other qualities like redness etc., then the apprehension of the outer relation, say, to-the-right-of, between redness and redness (e.g. in 'redness is to the right of redness') may involve the apprehension of the redness in different places[50] in the sense that the apprehension of the redness should be compresent with that of the space-qualities,[51] and yet Kant's ultimate contention will not stand. For even though in this way it can be maintained that the apprehension of the said outer relation presupposes the idea of space under the awareness of different places or different space-qualities, nevertheless if it be asked how the different space-qualities themselves are apprehended, there shall be no escape from answering with a good grace that their apprehension is only *empirically* intelligible : the space-quality (=, say, 'this place') and the red-quality being constituents of the same complex or bundle of qualities, the space-quality cannot be assigned a *unique* status in experience. And in this way Kant's elaborate argumentation will meet with an eventual defeat : the idea of space will remain far from having been shown to be *a priori.* It may be objected that the foregoing difficulty can at any rate be ignored, because the problem in Kant's first space argument is not whether the apprehension of *different places* is empirical or non-empirical, but whether the apprehension of outer relations in any way presupposes the idea of space. But such an objection will only betray laziness and escapism, and cannot be entertained in a *detailed examination* of Kant's argument, and, moreover, it should be noted that the difficulty is considered only in passing on to the examination of Russell's revised thesis that we can apprehend outer relations with respect to numerically one and the same object.

The mentioned difficulty makes it necessary that an attempt should be made to show that different places cannot really be reduced to mere qualitative differences. Since Russell shows *places* to be qualities by arguing that the former are definable by means of certain spatial relations, which again are but 'differing qualities', it is obvious that he has as the first step reduced the spatial relations to qualitative differences. It is remarkable that Paton in his interpretation of Kant's first space argument itself has taken this argument to mean primarily that spatial relations cannot be reduced to mere qualitative differences. But it is regrettable, as we had also occasion to note previously,[52] that Paton has not rendered quite clear the chief points, namely, the why and how, of Kant's argument. First, he has not made clear why Kant should at all argue against the reduction of spatial relations to 'mere qualitative differences'; it is not enough for purposes of clarification that Kant has argued thus. Secondly, he has not explained why for Kant spatial relations 'cannot be reduced to mere qualitative differences'. Paton, then, although he says that there is in Kant an argument against the reduction of spatial relations to qualitative differences, does not enable us to use it in need. What, now, is to be said against Russell, that is, against his description of spatial relations, which are said to define places, as differing qualities and of places also as qualities ? The first remark to be made is that in calling the said relations qualities, he has given us nothing that can be truly called a *reason* or an *argument.*[53] It is true that he thinks the description of the said relations as qualities enables him ultimately to construct a theory that has many attractive advantages, but this hardly makes acceptable that description, which demands an antecedent independent justification especially because he himself has elsewhere emphasized the distinction between relations and qualities.[54] Now, as regards the resulting view that *places* are qualities, it will suffice to quote the following criticism urged by Arthur Pap :

> [Russell extends] the usage of the word 'quality' to spatial positions and dates; and surely such extended usage of the word can hardly be distinguished from a misuse of the same. For, the word 'quality', and its synonym 'property', are normally used in such a way that it is logically possible for a quality to have several instances, although it may in fact have only one

> instance. But surely the same place cannot be in two places at once, nor can the same temporal instant be supposed to occur twice – unless temporal instants be confused with kinds of events. 'Having polar coordinates (x, y) with respect to the sun' is, indeed, a predicate, and with a pardonable stretch of the ordinary meaning of 'quality' it may be said to designate a spatial quality. But then we cannot *identify* the place of the planet described by means of such a predicate with the spatial quality. Different places may stand in the same spatial relations just as different persons may stand in the same kinship relations. If 'point 0' were synonymous with 'the ordered triplet of coordinates (x_1 y_1 z_1)', it would be nonsense to speak of the coordinates *of* the point, for thus one would speak of the coordinates of a set of coordinates.[55]

The view that *places* are qualities having been shown to be unsatisfactory, the denial of the special status enjoyed by spatial positions, instead of being prized, should be regarded as perfunctory.

It remains to examine Russell's main thesis that a spatial relation can be apprehended with respect to numerically one and the same object; because it is not possible to rest satisfied with the bare remark that in the apprehension of outer relations the idea of space is presupposed under the awareness of different places; for how can we be aware at all of *different places* except as the places or positions of *different* terms of outer relations ? Of course, the purpose of defending the Kantian argument under review will be achieved only by reference to the awareness of *different places* in the context of the awareness of outer relations; but, lest some should protest that the awareness of *different places* does not come pure and simple, it is no otiose addition to maintain that we have this awareness as presupposed in the awareness of *different* terms between which we apprehend outer relations; and, since the terms can often be qualitatively alike, how can we apprehend *different* terms if not as *numerically different ?* Russell argues that when, on apprehending two patches of a given shade of colour, say, redness, we declare that redness is to the right of redness, redness as such is not twofold :

> If we see simultaneously two patches of a given shade of colour, we shall say : 'this and that are precisely similar in colour'. We shall have no doubt that one of them is *this* and the other *that;* nothing will persuade us that the two are one. This, however, is a puzzle that is easily resolved. What we see is not merely a patch of colour, but a patch in a given visual direction. If 'this' means 'a patch in such a direction' and 'that' means 'a patch in such another direction', these complexes are different, and there is no reason to infer that the bare colour is twofold.[56]

This argument that the bare colour is not twofold is meant to suggest that the colour, though it appears in different places, is numerically one and the same. Obviously the argument is based on a confusion between the instances and the common nature. Perhaps this criticism would be repudiated by Russell as being quite irrelevant on the ground that according to him 'qualities suffice without our having to suppose that they have instances'. But this view that qualities suffice owes whatever plausibility it has to the supposed reduction of a 'thing' as commonly understood to a complex of qualities, where the term 'quality' is stretched enough to include spatial and temporal relations and positions, and the untenability of the view that spatial positions or places are qualities has already been shown. (The view that a thing is a complex of qualities is objectionable, because whereas a thing cannot be in two places at once, qualities being of the nature of universals[57] can, and Russell has sought to obviate this objection by making the place a quality and including this quality in the complex to which the thing is reduced; consequently the rejection of the view that places are qualities involves the rejection of the view that a thing is a complex of qualities, and, for that matter, of the view that qualities suffice, without our having to suppose that they have instances.) The aforementioned criticism, therefore, cannot be brushed aside as irrelevant. Indeed, the colour that Russell considers to be not twofold can only be colour in the sense of colouredness, which signifies the conceived one common nature of the two perceived colours in the visual field. As Joseph, by way of criticizing Russell, puts it :

> . . . in regard both to relations and attributes . . . we are very

> apt to confuse the instances and the common nature. And we often denote them by the same name; 'colour' means particular colours when I speak of the colours in last night's sunset'; it also means colouredness; every distance is a particular distance, but their common nature is called distance also. We do not make this confusion in regard to substances ; men and horses are instances of their kinds; and individual men or horses are so much more obviously different from one another than individual likenesses or distances or ultramarines that we cannot overlook in them the distinction between the manifold individuals and the one common nature. But perhaps this distinction is more readily seen in substances because individual substances are something more than instances of their kind. The true instances of human nature are the human natures of individual men; but the human nature of Caesar is *what* Caesar is; and sensible individual substances at any rate we do not seem to discriminate altogether by *what* they are.[58]

Against Russell's view that we apprehend the outer relation of (e.g.) to-the-right-of with respect to one and the same redness, what may be said now in close connexion with the main problem before us is as follows. When we apprehend redness to the right of redness, we evidently apprehend two terms as terms of this 'relating' relation, and admittedly we apprehend these in different places. Awareness of *different* (i.e. separate) terms in *different* (i.e. separate) places is the necessary presupposition of the awareness of any outer relation whatever. In this sense *the idea of space* is *presupposed* in the apprehension of outer relations. Perhaps Russell might admit all this and yet stick to his position. He might admit that in order to apprehend redness to the right of redness it is necessary to apprehend two terms, and yet maintain in the end that the two terms are not really two items (entities). He might argue : 'Difference is first perceived when we perceive the relation. Later on this difference may be denied and numerical identity established'. We incline to think nevertheless that Russell, in speaking, in the way that he does, of numerically one and the same redness with respect to which we apprehend the outer relation of to-the-right-of, has only *intellectualized* what are in fact *sensible* data,[59] and that this intellectualization creeps quite unawares into his so-called 'empirical generalizations' concerning spatio-temporal relations. We may accordingly conclude that his claim to 'have reduced to the empirical level certain properties of spatio-temporal relations which threatened to be synthetic *a priori* general truths' has not been substantiated.

5.3 Concluding Remarks on Kant's First Space Argument

The preceding study of Kant's first space argument has shown that many of the objections urged against it are based upon superficial interpretations. The interpretation that we have ultimately come to adopt has been explained and defended in detail. Kant's argument upon that interpretation does, as indeed any philosophical argument must, raise difficulties; and we have sought to state them as clearly as possible. Attempts to overcome them have also been made, and we believe such attempts have not been perfunctory. So the argument has surely considerable strength.

The question now is whether we should accept it. Here we feel called upon to make the following observations.

The argument has shown that the idea of space does not derive from (or, in other words, is not reducible to) the representation of the relations of a certain sort of sensible objects. But this does not justify the strong conclusion that this idea is not empirical. The only legitimate conclusion that can be drawn is that this idea is not empirical in the way that the relational-cum-reductionist analysis of it suggests that it is. As to the strong conclusion, we cannot accept it until we are persuaded that the other available major empiricistic accounts of the idea of space are all of them vitiated by circularity by already presupposing this idea in the attempted empirical deductions of it. The task of examining such other accounts we reserve for the final chapter.

Kant's present argument has, however, another aspect which is worth emphasizing. The argument raises a problem of considerable philosophical importance, namely, that of individuation of sensible objects in experience. If we accept Kant's view that such individuation presupposes ultimately the representation of space (and time), we have to say that this representation, as a presuppositional factor in our experience of distinguishable sensible objects, enjoys a unique status such that the recognition of it as 'a priori' cannot be unjustified. Kant's statement in his first space argument that the representation of space is presupposed in the representation of sensible objects as outside us and as outside and beside one another has, as will be clear upon a deeper reflection, the implication that without the representation of space the very possibility of objective sensible experience is unintelligible. For objective sensible experience is the experience of sensible objects that can be discriminated from ourselves and from one another; and the deeper point of Kant's argument is that such discrimination involves the individuation of the sensible objects (i.e. the representation of them as numerically different), and that such individuation (i.e. representation of them as numerically *different*) is not possible without ultimately representing them as *in different places* and therefore without presupposing the idea of space.

The thesis of Kant's first space argument – 'Space is not an empirical concept which has been derived from outer experience'–is sometimes interpreted (e.g. by D. P. Dryer)[60] as suggesting that the idea of space is unlike an empirical concept such as, for example, that of redness. This suggestion is subsidiary, but has some importance. The force of this suggestion can be best appreciated in the light of the foregoing discussion. Avoiding niceties, we may in this connexion make the following remarks. An empirical concept is formed, directly or indirectly, through comparison of a number of sensible items presented in experience, reflection upon what they have in common, and abstraction from their differing features.[61] This procedure presupposes that the sensible items in question, which are considered together for comparison etc., are represented in experience as numerically other than one another. Now the main contention of Kant's present argument is, as we have amply seen, that sensible items of the sort in question cannot be represented as other than one another without being represented as *in different places*, and therefore without already presupposing the idea of space. Clearly, the idea of space being thus presupposed in the procedure of empirical concept-formation cannot itself be of the same kind as an empirical concept.

For further considerations for the view that the idea of space is not empirical, we have to turn to Kant's second space argument, which we begin to study in the next chapter.

NOTES :

1. R. C. S. Walker, *Kant,* 1978, p. 29.
2. It may be asked, 'If the representation of space is not also presupposed *in* the representation of different *places,* how can the former representation be presupposed in that of outer relations even *through* the representation of different places (or, *through* the representation of objects as in different places) ?' In reply it may be conceded that it is indeed Kant's view that the representation of space is presupposed *in* the representation of *places*; but it must be pointed out that this is true only in a particular sense, although a fundamental sense, and that in this sense the view is simply *assumed* by Kant in his first space argument, reserving its legitimation for his third space argument. In explanation of the qualification 'in a particular sense', the following observation may be made. The word 'space', in the usage followed by (but not confined to) Kant, is ambiguous between 'space (i.e. the one whole space)' and 'a space or spaces (i.e. a part, or parts, of space, which is, or are, commonly called a place, or places)' ; cf. Leclere's article 'The Meaning of "Space" in Kant' in L. W. Beck, ed., *Proceedings of the Third International Kant Congress,* D. Reidel, 1972, pp. 393-400. This being so, the idea (representation) of space, in the second sense of 'space', is only another name for the representation of places, so that it is already shown that the idea of space, in this sense, is presupposed in the representation of outer relations if it is shown (as it is shown in the first space argument) that this representation of outer relations presupposes that of the related objects as in different *places.* But it does not follow that the idea of space, in the first sense of 'space', is presupposed in the representation of outer relations if it is only shown that this representation presupposes that of the related objects as in different *places*; something more needs to be shown, indeed namely, *that the representation of different places presupposes in its turn the idea of the one whole space.* This further point is not established in Kant's first space argument; it is established in his third space argument, which is yet to be considered. Since, however, 'space' for Kant primarily means the one whole space, we have to say that, in his first space argument under consideration, he, in so far as he argues that the idea of space is presupposed in the representation of outer

relations through the representation of the related objects as in different places, simply *assumes* a connexion between the idea of space (i.e. the idea of the one whole space) and the representation of places, and that the legitimation of this assumption is deferred till his third space argument.

Walker, then, fails to distinguish between what Kant actually seeks to establish in the first space argument and what he just *assumes.* As such his criticism serves to obfuscate Kant's main contention in the present argument.

3. Or more accurately, the idea of places.
4. We are here ignoring the point that, according to the logic of Kant's first space argument (as expounded before), the idea of space is presupposed in the representation of any *mutual relations* whatever among sensible objects presented together.
5. This emendation will preserve the spirit of Walker's criticism, surely, and at the same time make it directly relevant to Kant's first space argument.
6. This word ('occurs') is borrowed from Russell, cf. note 7 just below.
7. See B. Russell, *An Inquiry into Meaning and Truth,* Penguin Books, Harmondsworth, 1965, p. 325 : 'It seems that there is no escape from admitting relations as parts of the non-linguistic constitution of the world; . . . Such words as "before" and "above", just as truly as proper names, "mean" something which occurs in objects of perception'.
8. For Kant also, spatial (and temporal) relations are objects of perception in the sense of intuition, (the difference being that they are for him objects of pure intuition; cf. Paton, *Kant's Metaphysic of Experience,* 1951, I, 105, last para).

To obviate misunderstanding it is perhaps necessary to point out here that the view that spatial relations are *intuited* is not incompatible with the view that the representation of spatial relations among sensible objects presupposes (necessarily involves) the representation of the sensible objects concerned as not only different but in different places. The latter view need not be taken to suggest that the representation of spatial relations is a complicated intellectual exercise. For consistently with the latter view it can be said that the representation of a spatial relation between sensible objects is a comprehensive *intuition* analysable into the intuition of the spatial relation, that of the concerned sensible objects, and that of their places. (This will be clear by and by.) The latter view in question is no doubt required to say that the intuition of the spatial relation would not be possible without the intuition of the concerned sensible objects and that the intuition of the concerned sensible objects (in the plural) would not be possible without intuiting them in different places. But the allocation of priorities here is not to be understood in a temporal sense; it is to be understood, on the level of this explanatory account, in what it is customary to call a logical sense.

9. Whether Kant can admit the *concept* of spatiality will be discussed in connexion with his third space argument. It is a satisfaction to see that Walker also has argued the point that Kant can; see Walker, *op. cit.*, pp. 42-43.

10. Such perceptions, which are more than mere intuitions, may be called *determinate* perceptions.

11. On the word 'presupposes' in this clause and in the next, see notes 14 and 15.

12. We may point out once more that if we take the word 'space' as referring to spaces, i.e. places (cf. note 2 above), the intuitions of places themselves constitute the representation of space. If, however, the word 'space' is taken in what is for Kant the more fundamental sense of the one whole space, then, to anticipate the results of his third space argument, the intuitions of places *presuppose* the representation of space; and the point to be emphasized here is that the representation of space (in this sense), which is presupposed in the intuitions of places is for Kant *not a concept,* but a singular representation, i.e. an *intuition.*

13. We use the expression 'sensible objects' in lieu of Kant's 'sensations' *(Empfindungen)*; cf. 3.2, pp. 74-76.

14. We use the word 'presupposes', though Kant's own expression is 'mithin' meaning 'accordingly', because the latter expression is liable to be misleading; see above, p. 103.

    We use 'presupposes' as short for 'has for its necessary condition'.

15. In this part of Kant's contention, 'presupposes' is short for 'has for its *only* sufficient condition'. Of course, 'the *only* sufficient condition' is also 'a necessary condition' for Kant; see Chapter 4, p. 151.

    About this second part of Kant's contention, it may be pointed out that Sidgwick's objection on the score of triviality should no longer bother us, because Kant's view here is not that the objects in question would not count as *outer* unless they were represented as occupying different places, but rather that they cannot be individuated (represented as numerically different) unless they are represented as in different places. We have previously noted (see above, p. 105) that the objects in question are sensible objects, and that, since we are considering them as involved in such outer relations as outside and beside one another, they are coexistent (i.e. simultaneously given) sensibles; and we have seen that with respect to simultaneously given sensible objects as such it is Kant's view that they cannot be individuated unless they are represented as in different places.

16. For an explanation of the distinction between a relating relation and a relation *per se,* see B. Russell, *The Principles of Mathematics,* George Allen & Unwin, London, 1956. sect. 54, p. 49.
17. Russell, *The Principles of Mathematics,* p. 50.
18. See above, p. 104 and note 80 to Chapter 3.
19. It may be asked : Are not one-term relations possible ? Our reply is that, first, one-term relations are difficult to conceive, and, secondly, if they are possible, they are to be distinguished from the relations like the outer relations under consideration. See also Russell, *The Principles of Mathematics,* chap. iv., sect. 53.
20. Cf. Arthur Pap, *Elements of Analytic Philosophy,* 1949, p. 73.
21. Compare : 'When the shect of paper is perceived as consisting of two halves, . . . these two halves are combined into a complex whole by means of a spatial relation which holds directly between the two halves . . .' Bertrand Russell, *Logic and Knowledge, Essays 1901–1950,* ed. R. C. Marsh, George Allen & Unwin, 1956, p. 115.
22. The view we are referring to, though it was adopted by Russell in 'On the Relations of Universals and Particulars' read as the Presidential Address to the Aristotelian Society (of London) in the autumn of 1911, is subsequently abandoned by him. We shall come to examine his later view in due course.
23. *Ibid.*, p. 115.
24. *Ibid.*, pp. 115-116.
25. *Ibid.*, p. 124.
26. The passage in which the phrase occurs is quoted below.
27. I.e., intuited or not.
28. *Logic and Knowledge,* ed. Marsh, p. 116.
29. See *Critique*, B 136a : 'Space and time, and all their parts, are *intuitions,*

. . .'. By 'their parts' Kant here means places and times. Some Kantian scholars, however, think that although Kant regards space as an object of intuition, he does not, at least in the Transcendental Aesthetic, regard the parts of space also as objects of intuition. This view will be examined and rejected in connexion with his third space argument.

30. Handyside trans., 1929, pp. 28-29.

31. *Early German Philosophy*, 1969, p. 450.

32. But he differs from Newton in not being able to accept in the end the latter's additional views that space is objective and ontologically primitive (irreducible). Kant's theory in these later writings, as compared with that of Newton, is that space is absolute, epistemologically primitive and ultimately subjective. See L. W. Beck, *Early German Philosophy*, 1969, p. 450.

    Even Russell, in a different work (*The Principles of Mathematics*, 1956, p. 446), admits, on the authority of Vaihinger, that 'Kant, in the *Critique*, appears to have advocated the theory of absolute position'.

33. This view that space is an object of sense (i.e. sensible intuition), but not of sensation, obviously, casts doubt upon many more or less commonly accepted equations such as 'datum of sense = empirical datum', 'sense = sense-organ', 'sense-intuition = sensation', 'sensible intuition = empirical intuition', etc.

34. See above, pp. 135-6, 140.

35. On the point that the place of an object is immediately apprehended and yet not apprehended through sense-affection, cf. *Reflexionen Kants zur Kritischen Philosophie* (ed. Erdmann, 1884), Bd. II, No. 403.

36. See 14.1.3

37. A. S. Eddington, *The Nature of the Physical World*, Cambridge University Press, 1944, p. 18.

38. Cf. note 7 above.

39. Compare A. Pap (*Elements of Analytic Philosophy*, 1949, pp. 72-73) : 'To be sure, the role of unprecise denotation is minimized with the help of coordinate systems. Instead of *pointing to a spatial position* we can describe it in terms of three numbers coordinated with the distances from three intersecting perpendicular axes. But if the position of the intersection (the so-called "origin" of the coordinate system) were determined in the same manner, the origin of a larger coordinate

system would have to be determined *by pointing*, otherwise *an infinite regress* would ensue . . .' [A] pure coordinate language in which no *indicator* terms, like "here" . . . etc. occur would, therefore, seem to be an impossible ideal'. [Emphasis added by us.]

40. 'I no longer think that there are any spatial or temporal relations which always and necessarily imply diversity'.—Note added by Russell in 1955 at the end of the article 'On the Relations of Universals and Particulars', which we have many times referred to.

41. Russell, *An Inquiry into Meaning and Truth,* 1965, p. 92.

42. *Ibid.*, p. 98.

43. *Ibid.*, pp. 94-95.

44. Cf. note added by Russell in 1955 to his article 'On the Relations of Universals and Particulars' already referred to; (Marsh's ed., p. 124.)

45. *An Inquiry into Meaning and Truth*, 1965, p. 325.

46. *Ibid.*, p. 319.

47. *Ibid.*, p. 93.

48. Russell intends a distinction between 'overlapping' and 'compresence' by preferring the former in connexion with space and the latter in connexion with time : 'We now require a relation of "overlapping", which plays a part in the construction of perceptual space analogous to that played by compresence in private time'. (*Ibid.*, p. 319) Nevertheless we are not wrong in saying 'compresent or overlapping with space-qualities' because Russell remarks : 'The relation of compresence, which exists between percepts, may be supposed to exist also between any two physical events which overlap in space-time. A "point" in space-time may be defined as a group of events having the following two properties : (1) any two of the group are compresent, (2) nothing outside the group is compresent with every member of it'. (*Ibid.*, p. 321).

49. This should be clear from his discussion of incongruent counterparts in the essay of 1768. As T. D. Weldon (in his *Introduction to Kant's Critique of Pure Reason,* 1945, pp. 64-5) puts it : '. . . if we are to draw any distinction at all between them [i.e. incongruent counterparts], we are bound to take for granted the existence of an absolute space in which both exist. To do this, however, involves giving up the notion of space as a predicate or quality of things, for it would appear that things must be regarded as presupposing space and not vice versa'.

50. Because the object (here redness), if the outer relation is to be apprehended with respect to it, must have to appear in different places.
51. 'Places' being for Russell qualities, different places are called different *space-qualities.*
52. See note 79 to Chapter 3.
53. It is this lack of a clear-cut argument that shall explain our abstention from a detailed criticism of Russell.
54. Cf. his *The Problems of Philosophy,* Oxford University Press, London, 1968, chap. 9., p. 54.
55. *Elements of Analytic Philosophy,* 1949, pp. 73-74.
56. *An Inquiry into Meaning and Truth,* 1965, p. 104.
57. That qualities are universal is a widely accepted view among western philosophers (though many Indian philosophers regard the qualities of what we ordinarily call particular things as particular and not universal).

    For some discussion, we may here refer to G. E. Moore, 'Are the Characteristics of Particular Things Universal or Particular ?' (a symposium article reprinted from the *Proceedings of the Aristotelian Society,* Supp. vol. 3, 1923) in his *Philosophical Papers,* George Allen & Unwin, London, 1959, pp. 17-31.
58. H. W. B. Joseph, *An Introduction to Logic,* Clarendon Press, Oxford, p. 28.
59. What we called in the last paragraph a confusion between the instances and the common nature is a consequence of this intellectualization.
60. See above, 3.1., p. 72.
61. See above, p. 10 and note 23 to Chapter 1.

CHAPTER SIX

KANT'S SECOND SPACE ARGUMENT

6.1 Statement of the Argument and Some Preliminary Observations

Kant states his second space argument in the Metaphysical Exposition as follows :

> Der Raum ist eine nothwendige Vorstellung a priori, die allen äusseren Anschauungen zum Grunde liegt. Man kann sich niemals eine Vorstellung davon machen, dass kein Raum sei, ob man sich gleich ganz wohl denken kann, dass keine Gegenstände darin angetroffen werden. Er wird also als die Bedingung der Möglichkeit der Erscheinungen, und nicht als eine von ihnen abhängende Bestimmung angesehen, und ist eine Vorstellung a priori, die nothwendiger Weise äusseren Erscheinungen zum Grunde liegt. [Kritik, B 38-39.]

In Kemp Smith's translation, this is rendered as follows :

> Space is a necessary a priori representation, which underlies all outer intuitions. We can never represent to ourselves the absence of space, though we can quite well think it as empty of objects. It must therefore be regarded as the condition of the possibility of appearances, and not as a determination dependent upon them. It is an *a priori* representation, which necessarily underlies outer appearances. [*Critique*, A 24 = B 38-39.]

The burden of the present argument is the *necessity* of the representation of space. What is particularly problematic is not whether, if the representation of space is necessary[1] and recognized to be such,[2] it is appropriate to characterize it as 'a priori' in the austere sense of this expression,[3] but whether this representation is necessary at all.

As to the necessity of the representation of space, considerations bearing upon it lie implicit in the second sentence of this argument. The pre-eminent importance of this sentence justifies Kemp Smith's calling it 'the *nervus probandi* of the argument'.[4] A systematic and comprehensive study of the argument is therefore possible mainly by way of a detailed analysis of this sentence.

Before entering upon the proposed analysis of that crucial sentence, however, it is necessary to safeguard ourselves against an error that is not infrequently made as regards the exact import of this argument. The error in question consists in reading into the conclusion of this argument the transcendental-idealist significance of the apriority of space and then complaining that the conclusion does not follow from its premise or premises. It is surely an error, because in the Metaphysical Exposition Kant is concerned with the apriority, *only in the austere sense,* of the representation of space. In recent times, the error is made by Strawson[5] (even although he has been otherwise helpful to us in many ways in this Study). A sophisticated version of this error, however, is presented by J. T. Baker. He maintains that no adequate appraisal of Kant's second space argument is possible without relating it to 'an important historical tradition which may be said to have started with More'.[6] And he comes to commit the error mentioned above (along with some other errors) in his effort to set forth the peculiarity of Kant's argument as compared with a similar argument of More's. Let us see how exactly the error arises in Baker's exposition, how it may also arise otherwise, and how it can be avoided.

6.2 Henry More and Kant : A Comparison (A Corrective to Some Misapprehensions on the Import of Kant's Argument in Question)

As has been pointed out by Baker, although there is no definite evidence to show that Kant was acquainted with More's work, the probability that he was is high and is 'increased by the fact that More published a fairly complete Latin edition of his works for Continental perusal'.[7] The relevant portion from More's argument quoted by Baker in both its English and its Latin versions is here cited in its English version only :

> Hy (obares). But it (space) is so imaginary that it cannot possibly be dis-imagined by human understanding. Which methink should be no small earnest that there is more than an imaginary being there.
>
> Bath (ynous). For this [space] will be necessarily, though all matter were annihilated out of the world. Nay, indeed this is antecedent to all matter nor anything else can be conceived to be but in this. In this are all things necessarily apprehended to live and move and have their being.[8]

Now, clearly, all of More's statements about (1) the impossibility of dis imagining space, (2) the possibility of thinking of the annihilation of all matter from space, (3) the antecedence (i.e. the status-as-condition) of space in relation to all matter, and (4) the conceptual dependence of all things (in the ordinary sense of 'things') on space have their parallels in Kant's second space argument. Kant also says (1) that we can never represent the absence of space, (2) that space is thinkable as empty of objects, (3) that space must be regarded as the condition of the possibility of appearences, and (4) that the representation of space necessarily underlies outer appearences. These parallelisms make the supposition natural (whether or not justified) that Kant is influenced by More.

Nevertheless the question how the arguments of the two philosophers differ is more important. It will be appropriate to begin by examining Baker's suggestion. He says that the arguments of the two philosophers 'differ in assigning differing subjects to the predicate "necessary". "Necessity" for More is metaphysical, for Kant logical'.[9] That is to say, space as the bearer of the predicate 'necessary' is for More a 'metaphysical entity' and for Kant a 'logical entity'.[10] The point is explained by Baker thus : space for More 'necessarily exists as the metaphysical framework of the external world', whereas for Kant 'space necessarily exists as the logical framework of our knowledge of the external world'.[11] We have to try to see what further light can be obtained on the difference here suggested.

Analysing the context of More's argument, Baker points out that it is directed against the Cartesian identification of space (or extension) with matter.[12] The thought-experiment on which More's argument is based is designed to show that the relation between space and matter is completely asymmetrical[13] : for example, we cannot dis-imagine space, although we can conceive all matter annihilated. Such asymmetry makes their identity out of the question. More's rejection of their identification is bound up with his assertion of the metaphysical priority of space. He adopts the view that space is real (when he says that 'there is more than an imaginary being there'), that space is real independently of matter (when he says, 'For this will be necessarily, though all matter were annihilated'), that space is not only real independently of matter, but an antecedent condition, that is, a presuppositional framework for the existence of all matter (when he says : 'this is antecedent to all matter nor anything else can be conceived to be but in this'). He is thus led by the thought-experiment undertaken by him to draw a metaphysical conclusion about the nature of space. What is particularly noteworthy is that it is only from the conceptual priority of space over all matter and the conceptual dependence of all matter upon space that More concludes to the metaphysical priority of space and the metaphysical dependence of all matter upon space. Obviously, the conclusion is a *non sequitur.* Baker rightly points out that the more result of a thought-experiment, namely, that space cannot be dis-imagined by us, does not justify the conclusion that space is an ontological reality capable of subsisting on its own. He comes to maintain – and in this suggestion comes to read too much into Kant's argument under consideration, as we shall see – that this *non sequitur* of More's is of a kind that Kant seeks to avoid in his second space argument : 'The *non-sequitur* of the Cambridge Platonist was precisely the type of metaphysical presumption that Kant wished to end by the force of his *Critique*'.[14] Baker hastens to add : 'But in the argument he may have borrowed [from More] we have . . . a recurrence of the fallacy when the argument was rewritten'.[15] This amounts to saying that Kant in his logical reconstruction of More's metaphysical argument has avoided More's *'non sequitur'* only on the basis of another of his own. Kant, in Baker's estimate, has done no more than transmute More's metaphysical concept of space into a logical or epistemological one.[16] The thought-experiment about space justifies, for Kant (as Baker understands him), not any conclusion about what space is independently of our knowledge situation, but only a conclusion about the logical status of space in relation to our knowledge. As Baker puts it :

> The argument of the Transcendental Aesthetic reaches no positive metaphysical conclusion but is content to show the logical meaning of space for knowledge. That of which we are aware is *in* space categorically, not physically. The necessity of Kantian space is the necessity that accompanies the positive arrangement of noetic material. Necessity for More reaches beyond this conclusion by its necessary ignorance of Kantian logic and psychology.[17]

The passage just now quoted from Baker makes only difficulties, however. Although we have been taking his expression 'logical' in the wider sense of 'epistemological', his other expressions 'positive arrangement of noetic material' and 'is *in* space categorically' create confusions. They particularly lay his crucial phrases such as 'the logical meaning of space for knowledge', 'Kantian logic', and, in a different paragraph quoted earlier, 'logical framework', open to suspicion. The suspicion is that the word 'logic' is used in its narrow Kantian sense, and that accordingly the adjective 'logical' is used not merely in the negative sense of 'non-metaphysical', nor again merely in the ordinary positive sense of 'epistemological', but in the specific Kantian sense of 'intellectual', or rather, 'intellectual-cum-formal'. The suspicion is confirmed as we find Baker saying that space for Kant is 'a category',[18] 'a part of the intellect',[19] 'is in logical relation . . . to understanding',[20] and so on. It is not, therefore, more surprising that Baker should complain of 'the recurrence of the fallacy' of *'non sequitur'* in Kant's second space argument. For no one will deny that the argument is quite unable to bear the weight of the suggestion that space is a category of the understanding, or that it is a logical, in the sense of a categorical, framework necessary for the knowledge of external objects.

There remains something to be said on behalf of Baker, however. That space for Kant is *not* a 'category' of the understanding is so well known that it is hard to assume ignorance of it on the part of Baker.

It is probable that Baker has picked up the expression 'understanding' from More's passage and chosen to use it throughout his article in the same neutral sense of 'cognitive subject', and that as regards the word 'category' in the Kantian context, he has used it in just the general sense of 'form', and as regards the word 'logical', his use of it is approximately in the wider sense of 'epistemological', a sense that writers on Kant sometimes prefer to express by using the word 'transcendental'. In that case, one may no doubt accuse Baker of having made use of systematically misleading expressions, but one cannot, on that account, brush aside his suggestion from further examination.

Baker's suggestion, put in a less misleading terminology, is that the necessity that Kant ascribes to space (i.e. to the representation of space) in the second space argument is its epistemic or transcendental necessity exhibited by it as a *formal* prior condition of the possibility of outer appearances (where the word 'appearances' is not indicative of an old-fashioned metaphysical context, but simply means 'sensible objects'). In other words, Kant in this argument is moving from the necessity of the representation of space to the apriority of space in the transcendental-idealist-cum-formalist sense of being prior in us to the appearance of noetic material as external objects, that is, prior in us as a form with which noetic material has of necessity to be invested, so to say, in order to appear as outer objects.

Whether such interpretation can legitimately be put on Kant's second space argument will be considered soon (this being indeed our chief concern in this entire discussion); here only a few words are needed to show that some such interpretation is really at work in Baker's mind. Supposing that his favourite term 'logical' means approximately the same as 'epistemological', his statement that Kant, unlike More, looks upon space as a 'logical entity' boils down to the statement that Kant finds for the necessity and priority of space in relation to objects an exclusively epistemological relevance. This is to say that whereas for More space has a 'meaning' (status) not only in the context of knowledge, but also beyond it, its sole meaning for Kant lies in the context of knowledge. The Kantian argument, let us recall Baker's words, 'is content to show the logical meaning of space for knowledge'. And it is with a view to showing the 'meaning of space for knowledge' that Kant in his present argument has sought, according to Baker, to 'attach' space to the mind; for if space is attached to the cognitive subject, it is not free to have a status beyond the limits of knowledge. The view that Kant has sought to do this in his present argument is rested by Baker on Kant's statement that we can quite well think space as empty of objects. As Baker says : 'In the effort to attach space as necessary not only to all objects before the mind but to the mind itself we are informed of the psychological ability to conceive empty space'.[21] Baker is thus once again in a position to complain that the Kantian conclusion is a *non sequitur* (i.e. 'that the argument overreaches itself and proves too much'[22]) : the assertion as to our psychological ability to conceive empty space is simply based upon an 'introspective report',[23] and this report, though it may exhibit the 'unique peculiarity of Kant's own intellect',[24] hardly justifies the conclusion that space necessarily attaches to the mind.

A further criticism urged by Baker is that Kant's assertion as to our ability to conceive empty space simply assumes 'that space is attached or "adheres" to the mind',[25] or else it 'is hard to understand what meaning this could have for Kant',[26] and 'that such an assumption reduces the entire second argument to a *petitio principii*'.[27]

The last criticism, however, is hardly consistent with the immediately preceding one. A slight examination reveals in it the following steps :

First : It is just an 'assumption'[28] on the part of Kant that we can conceive space as empty.

Second : This assumption is not intelligible ('is hard to understand') except on the further 'assumption'[29] that space necessarily adheres to the cognitive subject. [That is, space as necessarily adhering to the subject can conceivably be empty of objects.]

Third : This further assumption – that space necessarily adheres to the cognitive subject – happens to be Kant's intended conclusion in his present argument [in so far as the apriority in the logical sense (i.e. transcendental-idealist sense) of space consists in 'the logical relation of space to understanding'[30] (i.e. in the formal adhesion of space to the cognitive subject)].

Fourth : So Kant's argument involves a *petitio principii.*

It requires little reflection to see that the first step in the above criticism contradicts Baker's preceding criticism on the ground of a *non sequitur.* In the preceding criticism he has said that Kant's assertion as to the psychological ability to conceive empty space rests upon an introspective report; but how can that which is alleged to be an 'introspective report' on the part of Kant be called again a mere 'assumption' on his part ? It may be contended that what is apparently an introspective report on Kant's part is really not such, but an assumption pure and simple. Even then, however, the two criticisms are not consistent with each other, for the simple reason that if the conclusion of an argument is a *non sequitur,* it, or its equivalent, cannot be also presupposed by a premise of that argument.

In view of the greater weight attached by Baker to the preceding criticism on the score of a *non sequitur,* he should have rested content with it, and withheld his criticism on the score of a *petitio principii.*

As for his criticism on the score of a *nón sequitur,* it is valid only if the interpretation that Kant's second space argument is intended to conclude to the necessary adhesion of space to the mind is itself justified. But we do not think that it is justified. As the interpretation is not confined to Baker, but is adopted by many a commentator, we cannot dismiss it off-hand without some discussion.

The interpretation amounts to saying that Kant, in moving from necessity to apriority in his second space argument, uses the term 'a priori' in its full Critical significance that covers not only its austere sense (in which the representation called a priori is simply independent of experience), but also its transcendental-idealist sense (in which what is thus represented is as a form prior in us to experience). The fatal defect of this interpretation is that it ignores totally Kant's distinction between his 'expositions of the concept of space' and his 'conclusions' from those expositions.[31] Anyway, we are required to investigate what considerations might be adduced in support of this interpretation.

(i) In a passage (A 20 = B 34) preceding the second space argument Kant observes that 'form must lie ready for the sensations *a priori* in the mind, and so must allow of being considered apart from all sensation'.

This observation, which was discussed in certain respects in Chapter 2, is here quoted again because of the noticeable similarity between its second part and one of Kant's statements in the second space argument, namely, that we can quite well think space as empty of objects. It is noteworthy that in the quoted observation the fact, if it is a fact, that space (or time) *allows of being considered apart from all sensation* is connected with three things at once, namely, apriority, formality, and subjectivity. This, it may be said, does something to confirm the interpretation of Kant's second space argument that is under examination.

Against this, we may point out, however, that in the introductory section of the Aesthetic from which the quoted observation is taken Kant is concerned more with proclaiming what he has to establish than with actually establishing it.[32] His observation in question has not the status of an argument, surely. It only serves to put us, by way of anticipation, in early possession of the main theme of the Aesthetic. The apriority (in the austere sense), formality, and subjectivity of space and time, which are to be established step by step in the course of the Aesthetic, are all of them just announced here in advance. The second space argument, however, occurs as a step in the sequence of arguments developed in the Aesthetic, and since this is to be reckoned among the beginning steps only, it would be overhasty to try to extract from its conclusion as much as is adumbrated in the first part of the quoted observation.

(ii) Again in favour of the transcendental-idealist interpretation of the import of Kant's second space argument, attention might be called to a statement occurring in the argument itself, namely, this : 'It [space] must therefore be regarded as the condition of the possibility of appearances . . .'. The phrase 'condition of the possibility of appearances' is, as is well known, often used by Kant interchangeably with 'form of appearance', and the latter phrase in its application to space means, as Kant has explained later, 'the subjective condition of sensibility, under which alone outer intuition is possible for us.'[33] It might be argued, therefore, that the formality and subjectivity of space are also intended by Kant besides its apriority in the austere sense in the conclusion of his second space argument through the use of the phrase 'condition of the possibility of appearances'.

Against this, we may say that even if Kant is taken as maintaining in his second space argument that space is an a priori form of appearance, he need not be taken as expressing here the view that space is a subjective form of sensibility; and it may be noted that it is through this latter view alone that Kant's transcendental idealism-cum-formalism regarding space finds its definite expression. 'Form of appearance' has to be distinguished from 'form of sensibility'. Paton, in his effort to 'make Kant's exposition a little tidier than it actually is',[34] distinguishes these phrases by saying : 'There is a clear distinction between "form of appearance" and "form of sensibility", the latter alone implying the subjectivity of space and time'.[35] As regards Kant's second space argument, Paton's view is that the argument is intended to conclude not only that the representation of space is a priori in the austere sense, but also that space is a form or condition of appearances in the neutral sense that objects of experience have of necessity to be presented in space.[36] This is the most that one can say legitimately about the import of Kant's second space argument.

The upshot of the discussion is that the transcendental-idealist view to the effect that space is a subjective form of sensibility must not be projected into the conclusion of Kant's second space argument and that therefore the conclusion cannot be criticized on the score of a *non sequitur* in the way done by Baker.

Baker is doubtless right in saying that Kant's argument unlike that of More does not draw a metaphysical conclusion, Kant's argument is indeed out and out epistemological. And since this is so, we suggest that it should be judged mainly in terms of the success or failure of its claim to have established the apriority, in the austere sense, of the representation of space. Baker contends, however, that Kant's argument fails even to establish the apriority in the austere sense of the representation of space.[37] Whether this contention is sound remains to be seen. For this purpose a thorough examination and analysis of the Kantian argument will be required.

6.3 'Kant's Proof' in This Argument

As has already been pointed out, 'the *nervus probandi*' of Kant's second space argument is stated in its second sentence. It enshrines the considerations relevant to the supposed *necessity* of the representation of space, such necessity being crucial to the issue whether this representation is a priori or not. Following Kemp Smith, we may, in the present discussion, refer to this sentence as 'Kant's Proof'.[38] ['Kant's Proof' serves to abbreviate 'the sentence giving expression to the fact through which Kant proves his thesis'. Some prefer to call it 'Kant's premise'.]

Kant's proof contains two parts : (1) 'We can never represent to ourselves the absence of space', and (2) 'we can quite well think it [space] as empty of objects'. The question is whether the two parts must be considered together or can be treated in separation. Without denying that either of them cannot by itself contribute what both of them can, we take the view that each has an independent claim to our concentrated attention. It is not that Kant's proof is without bearing on the *necessity* of the representation of space unless it is taken as a whole. It will be seen that its first part in itself has a sufficient bearing thereupon to point to the *apriority*, in the austere sense, of the representation of space. This is to say that the first part does not require the support of the second to play its role adequately; and this implies that the second part can justify its position in Kant's proof only by having some independent relevance to the *necessity* of the representation of space. All this will be clear in the sequel.

The advantage of considering separately the two parts of Kant's proof is obvious. There are critics who reject Kant's second space argument simply by rejecting the second part of his proof.[39] They do not see that even if this part of the proof fails, Kant's argument may still stand in virtue of the first part of the proof. There is no justification indeed for rejecting Kant's argument before clearly showing that both the parts of the proof are untenable.

It becomes our task now to analyse and examine each part of the proof as thoroughly as a detailed Kant-exegesis requires.

NOTES :

1. A representation (idea) is for Kant necessary mainly in the sense that it yields an 'objective ground of the possibility of experience'; cf. 1.3, p.11; also below, pp. 304ff. [This point, in the case of the representation of space, will be progressively clear in the next Chapter.]
2. Necessity can be, as it is for Kant, a *criterion* of apriority only if it is recognised, i.e. represented. [Kant explains this point, in the case of a proposition, by saying : '. . . if . . . a proposition which in being thought is thought as *necessary,* it is an *a priori* judgment'; *Critique,* B 3, The expression 'thought as necessary' is noteworthy.]
3. For an explanation of this sense of 'a priori' see above, pp. 13-14.
4. See his *Commentary,* 1918, p. 104.
5. See his *The Bounds of Sense,* 1966, p. 89.
6. J. T. Baker, 'Henry More and Kant : A Note to the Second Argument on Space in the Transcendental Aesthetic', *Philosophical Review* 46 (1937), p. 303.
7. Ibid., p. 299 n. 3.
8. Cited by Baker from More, 'Divine Dialogues', 2nd ed., 54-55; see Baker, *op. cit.,* pp. 299-300.
9. *Ibid.,* p. 306.
10. Cf. *Ibidem.*
11. *Ibid.,* p. 304.
12. *Ibid.,* p. 298.
13. *Ibid.,* p. 304.
14. *Ibidem.*
15. *Ibidem.*
16. *Ibid.,* p. 306.
17. *Ibid.,* p. 303.
18. *Ibid.,* pp. 306, 305.
19. *Ibid.,* p. 302.
20. *Ibidem.*
21. *Ibid.,* p. 301.
22. *Ibidem.*
23. *Ibidem.*

24. *Ibidem.*
25. *Ibid.*, p. 301.
26. *Ibid.*, p. 302.
27. *Ibidem.*
28. Mark the word 'assumption' in Baker's phrase 'the assumption of the possibility of "empty" conceptual space', *ibid.*, p. 302.
29. *Ibid.*, p. 301, last para, second sentence.
30. *Ibid.*, p. 302.
31. Cf. above, pp. 3, 14.
32. Cf. Paton, *Kant's Metaphysic of Experience*, 1951, Vol. I, pp. 93-94 and note 1 to p. 94.
33. *Critique*, A 26 = B 42.
34. Paton, *op. cit.*, p. 101.
35. *Ibid.*, p. 103.
36. Cf. *Ibid.*, p. 114.
37. See below, pp. 300-302.
38. Kemp Smith, *Commentary*, p. 105.
39. See, e.g. Prichard, *Kant's Theory of Knowledge*, 1909, pp. 42-43.

CHAPTER SEVEN

KANT'S SECOND SPACE ARGUMENT (Continued)

7.1 The Import of the First part of 'Kant's Proof' in the Second Space Argument (The Relative or Conditional Necessity of the Representation of Space)

The first part of Kant's proof in question, – 'We can never represent to ourselves the absence of space' –, is, as it stands, extremely misleading. It has led some commentators to suppose that Kant is denying here that the non-existence of space can be conceived at all.[1] A consequence of this supposition is the view that the proof is intended to show the absolute or unconditional necessity of space.[2] Needless to say, the proof upon this view is vulnerable to severe attacks.[3]

But the supposition, and the view to which it leads, are wrong. That the supposition is wrong can be shown by reference to Kant's explicit pronouncements elsewhere. Thus, besides his hypothetical clause at B 461 of *Critique*, 'if . . . space in general . . . be set aside', we have his categorical statement about space in the *Nachträge* : 'We can prove that its non-existence is not *self-contradictory*'.[4] At A 619 = B 647 of the *Critique* he observes that it is only by 'transcendental subreption' that 'space . . . is taken as something absolutely necessary, existing in its own right, and as an object given *a priori* in itself'.

So the view that space is absolutely or unconditionally necessary in the sense that its non-existence is inconceivable is not Kant's.[5] The view can be ascribed to, say, Henry More.[6]

The necessity with which Kant is concerned in the first part of his proof is not the necessity of the existence of space as such, but that of the representation of space for experience of a certain sort. In the conclusion of his argument under examination Kant says, with regard to the representation of space, that it 'necessarily underlies outer appearances'. The representation of space can indeed underlie outer *appearances* only in so far as it underlies the *experience* of outer appearances, that is, outer *experience* in general. Kant's point is, as will progressively be clear, that the representation of space is a priori as necessarily underlying, in the sense of yielding a necessary condition of the possibility of, outer experience.[7] The first part of his proof in this argument is, we maintain, elliptical and can be expanded in some such way as 'We can never represent to ourselves the absence of space from outer appearances' and may then be paraphrased as 'we can never represent to ourselves the possibility of non-spatial outer experience'. Whether the proof as so construed is trivial will be examined in the next section. Before that what is needed is to provide some textual support for the two points that the necessity that Kant seeks to establish in the first part of his proof in question is the relative or conditional necessity of the representation of space for outer appearances, and that, in this context, the proof has an epistemic slant so as to permit the translation of his talk of 'outer appearances' into talk of 'outer experience'.

On the first point, one may profitably consult the first part of Kant's proof in the corresponding argument for time. It is : 'We cannot, in respect of appearances in general, remove time itself.'[8] What is noteworthy is that instead of saying simply 'We cannot remove time itself' Kant adds the qualification 'in respect of appearances in general'. This makes it clear that he intends to bring out not the absolute or unconditional necessity of time, but its relative necessity in respect of appearances in general (i.e. both inner and outer appearances). An analogous interpretation of the first part of his proof in the second space argument is, then, not only possible, but in strict accord with his real intention. One has to recognize therefore an ellipsis in this part of the proof; and it has already been indicated how the omitted portion is to be supplied.

On the second point, attention may be called to certain relevant words in Kant's third space argument in the *first edition* of the *Critique*, which may be regarded as a follow-up of his second space argument under consideration. There he relates his doctrine of the '*a priori* necessity of space' to the refutation of the view that 'this representation of space [is] a concept acquired *a posteriori*, and derived from outer experience in general'.[9] Here the expressions 'representation of space' and 'outer experience' have to be noticed; and it is important to notice them not only for the purpose in view, but also for other reasons. We have to guard once more against the transcendental-idealist interpretation of Kant's doctrine of the *a priori* necessity of space as expounded in his Metaphysical Exposition of the Concept of Space. By 'a priori necessity of space', Kant really means, in the context of this Exposition, the a priori necessity of the *representation* of space, where 'representation of space' signifies not that space itself is a representation, but that it is an object of representation. The opening sentence of his second space argument, 'Space is a necessary *a priori* representation . . .', may suggest that space itself is a representation, – a suggestion which, though quite in keeping with his ultimate transcendental idealism regarding space, is altogether out of keeping with the spirit of his Metaphysical Exposition. In this Exposition he is not concerned with showing that space is a priori in the sense of being, as he elsewhere puts it, itself 'nothing but a representation',[10] but that it is a priori in the merely austere sense that the representation *of* it is not 'derived from outer experience in general'.[11] Similarly when Kant concludes in the second space argument, 'It must therefore be regarded as the condition of the possibility of appearances', his words 'It' (i.e. 'space') and 'appearances' may again encourage the transcendental-idealist interpretation that *space* is a condition of the possibility of (that is, a subjective formal determinant of) outer *appearances.* But what he can properly be taken to mean here is just that the *representation of space* is necessary for *the representation of (outer) appearances* (i.e. for outer *experience* in general); for so much is sufficient for his intended austere conclusion here that the representation is not 'derived from outer experience'. Under the circumstances, the first part of his proof under examination, as expanded before to 'We can never represent to ourselves the absence of space from outer appearances', is best construed as 'We can never represent to ourselves the absence of the representation of space from outer experience' and can be briefly paraphrased as 'We can never represent the possibility of non-spatial outer experience'. In examining this proof in what follows, we need not always quote it as so paraphrased; it will be enough to recognize the exegetical soundness of the paraphrase when it is adopted.

7.2 Is the First Part of 'Kant's Proof' as Explicated by Us Really Tautological ?

The first part of Kant's proof under examination in the form in which he himself has stated it is not tautological; but if, in the light of the foregoing considerations, we expand it as 'We can never represent the absence of space from outer appearances', or explicate it as 'We cannot represent the possibility of non-spatial outer experience', it appears to be tautological.[12] This, however, is no reason why our expansion or explication of it should be considered wrong. For, in the first place, the expansion or explication is so far from being arbitrary that it has already been found that it is clearly required by the text, and, in the second place, an appearance of tautology after all attaches originally to some of Kant's own sentences in the second space argument, namely, to the opening sentence and the conclusion, since, surely, it is apparently tautologous to say that the representation of space necessarily underlies 'outer intuitions' or 'outer appearances'. Let us then squarely face the question whether the first part of Kant's proof as expanded or explicated above is really tautological.

The question has to do primarily with the meaning of 'outer'. Kant not infrequently takes 'outer' to mean *spatial.*[13] In one place in the *Critique* he comes very near to providing a definition of 'empirically external objects' by saying that they are 'things which are to be found in space'.[14] From this angle indeed we have, in the case before us, the tautology that we cannot represent the absence of space from things to be found in space, or, that we cannot represent the possibility of non-spatial spatial experience.[15]

The difficulty arises, then, not mainly because of the employment of the word 'outer' but because of the supposition, very natural and not at all ill-founded, that Kant usually prefers the definition of 'outer' as 'spatial'. There are, however, some who define 'outer' not as 'spatial', but as 'objective as distinguished from the subjective.'[16] There is evidence to show that even Kant also *sometimes* tends to take 'outer' in the sense of *objective, i.e. of objects which are other than states of consciousness.* Such evidence will be cited before long, and the question of Kant's consistency or inconsistency with respect to the use of the expression 'outer' will be considered too. Meanwhile some preliminary remarks by way of clarifying one or two points will be in order.

We may first note Kant's use, in the second part of his proof in the present argument, of the word 'objects' (*Gegenstände*). The word is used there in lieu of his favourite term 'outer appearances', and there can be no doubt that it is used in a fairly strong sense : when it is said that we can think space as 'empty of objects', the objects referred to are obviously not *any* items of experience, but such as have positions in space. Objects in this sense are commonly identifiable sensible particulars which are other than states of consciousness. In this connexion the expression 'outer intuitions' in the opening sentence of his present argument is noteworthy. It indicates that the objects he has in mind are, as objects of *intuition,*[17] and hence as distinguished from mere sensa, commonly identifiable particulars. Consider what he says at B 44 of the *Critique* : '. . . the sensations . . ., since they are mere sensations and not intuitions, do not of themselves yield knowledge of any object'.[18] Sensations, he goes on to say, 'may, indeed, be different for different men' (B 45). The implication is that objects as intuitions (that is, as represented by intuitions)[19] are items in a commonly sharable experience, which we may briefly call 'objective experience';[20] and Kant suggests that particular items cannot attain to this status of objectivity without having positions in space.[21] To return to the point at issue : the appearance of tautology in the explicated first part of Kant's proof in his present argument can be avoided by paraphrasing it further as : 'We can never represent the possibility of non-spatial objective experience'. Kant could indeed avoid needless complications by avoiding the word 'outer' in the present argument and using instead some such other word as 'objective'. The point needs to be amplified a little further.

As has been pointed out by Strawson, there is an intimate connexion between what may be called Kant's 'spatiality thesis' and his 'objectivity thesis'.[22] The objectivity thesis is 'that experience must include awareness of objects which are distinguishable from experience of them in the sense that judgements about these objects are judgements about what is the case irrespective of the actual occurrence of particular subjective experiences of them'.[23] The spatiality thesis is 'that the objects referred to [in the objectivity thesis] are essentially spatial'.[24] The objectivity thesis is argued for in the Transcendental Analytic; and, in the Metaphysical Exposition of the Concept of Space, it is just taken for granted, and is altogether devoid of the Copernican or typically Critical implication. Now, the true import of the first part of Kant's proof in the second space argument is that objects, in the sense defined in the objectivity thesis, are necessarily spatial, that is, that objective experience must be spatial. This statement has, for Kant at least, the status of a synthetic a priori one. This is not to suggest, however, that in the Metaphysical Exposition Kant has anything to do with the problem of the synthetic a priori; we simply emphasize that the statement in question is not in any sense tautological.

It remains to give some exegetical support to the suggestion that the word 'outer' in Kant's present argument be construed as 'objective'. Let us reflect on the following sentence in the *Inaugural Dissertation* : 'Of these concepts, the one [i.e. space] properly concerns the intuition of an object, the other [i.e. time] a *state*, namely, that of representation.'[25] The relevant point to be noticed is once again Kant's use of the word 'object'. An *object* is distinguished from a *state* of consciousness. Obviously, by 'an object' Kant means here a sensible objective particular, which is other than a state of consciousness. Let us now compare the statement of the *Dissertation* that space properly concerns the intuition of an *object,* which is other than a state of consciousness, with his more familiar statement in the *Critique* as well as elsewhere that space properly concerns *outer* intuition. It becomes clear that by 'outer intuition' Kant, at least sometimes, means the same as 'intuition of an object which is other than a state of consciousness', or what is more to the point, that by 'outer' Kant, at least sometimes, means *objective, i.e. of an object which is other than a state of consciousness.* This serves to support our suggestion that the word 'outer' in Kant's second space agrument might, in conformity to his occasional practice, be eliminated in favour of some such other word as 'objective'.

The difficulty raised by the observation that by 'outer' Kant, at least sometimes, means *objective* concerns the qualification 'at least sometimes'. We are led to suspect that there is some confusion on the part of Kant as regards the exact meaning of 'outer'. On the one hand, he sometimes virtually defines 'outer' in terms of space,[26] and seems to make use of this sort of definition in his implicit criticism of other philosophers, e.g. in his implicit criticism, in the first space argument, of Wolff's empirical deduction of the idea of space;[27] on the other hand, he sometimes badly needs, and perhaps assumes the possibility of, a definition of 'outer' in different terms, namely, in terms that do not already contain a reference to space : this is so in his second space argument, and in his important doctrine that space is a form of outer intuition.[28] We think, however, that the definition of 'outer' as 'objective', instead of as 'spatial', not only is sometimes needed and even assumed by Kant, but *would have sufficed for all his purposes.* His first space argument has already been found to have a deeper aspect that does not depend at all on the view that 'outside' means *spatial* externality, that deeper aspect being rather connected with the problem of individuation of objects,[29] and when in the *Critique* he later on says that 'empirically external objects' are to be entitled 'things which are to be found in space', this statement might not have had the status of a *definition* of 'external' or 'outer' (in its empirical employment[30]) as 'spatial'; for in that passage (A 373) he is *primarily* concerned with distinguishing 'empirically external' things from 'those which may be said to be external in the transcendental sense', and for this purpose his characterization of the former as 'things which are to be found in space' is still amply justified even if the concept of empirically external things and that of things to be found in space be considered no more than reciprocal concepts, that is, concepts having the same sphere (extension).[31] It will soon be seen that even if 'outer' is not defined as 'spatial', it is still possible for Kant to maintain that whatever is outer (that is, empirically outer) is *necessarily* spatial. [And, needless to add, it is possible to use 'outer' and 'spatial' in the empirical context interchangeably, as he often does, and as we, following him, have sometimes done.[32]] Let us try to make this clear.

'Outer' is regularly contrasted by Kant with 'inner'. So far 'outer' means non-inner, i.e. objective as distinguished from subjective.[33] The 'outer-inner' contrast in this sense is to be distinguished from the 'outer-inner' contrast in a different sense, where, – e.g. when a spatial object is said to have an inner side as well as an outer –, 'inner' does not mean the same as 'subjective' and, for that matter, 'outer' has not the same meaning as 'objective as distinguished from subjective'. It is the outer-inner contrast in the former sense, and not in the latter sense, that is under consideration in the present discussion and is relevant to Kant's term 'outer' in the second space argument. Now 'outer', in contrast with 'inner' in the sense of the subjective, might well be *defined* as 'objective'.[34] Were Kant to adopt and adhere to this definition, he would not be debarred then from maintaining what he wanted to maintain, namely, that the outer[35] is *necessarily* spatial. On the definition of 'outer' as 'objective', the proposition that *the outer is objective* is no doubt analytic, but the proposition that *the outer is spatial* is not. The latter proposition would nevertheless remain, on independent grounds, necessary a priori, according to Kant. And it is the apriority, and this alone, of this proposition that should suffice on his view to render intelligible the fact that the term 'spatial' is *necessarily* applicable to anything[36] to which the term 'outer' is applicable. The point needs a little clarification. Let us attend to the following words of Kant's : 'A predicate which is ascribed to a subject by means of an *a priori* proposition is thereby asserted as belonging *necessarily* to it (inseparable from the concept of it)'.[37] It is noteworthy that, instead of saying 'an analytic proposition', Kant says here 'an *a priori* proposition'. It is for him the mark of an a priori proposition *qua* a priori, no matter whether it is analytic or synthetic, that its predicate concept is *inseparable* from its subject concept. If the proposition is analytic, this inseparability is due to the fact that the predicate concept is contained (in the sense of being intensionally involved) in the subject concept, and if the proposition is synthetic, it is due to some other reason.[38] Coming now to the proposition that *the outer is spatial,* or rather, that *the outer is necessarily spatial,* this is for Kant *an a priori* proposition, and it is the apriority alone of this proposition that should on his view be a sufficient reason why the term 'outer' cannot be applied to anything[39] to which the term 'spatial' cannot be applied. This being so, the necessary substitutability of 'spatial' for 'outer' need not be construed as the synonymy of these terms or as implying the analyticity of the proposition that the outer is necessarily spatial.[40]

It is a welcome result for Kant that the proposition that the outer is necessarily spatial is on his view, when properly analysed (or reconstructed), *non-analytic,* though a priori. Indeed when he concludes in the second space argument that space 'is an *a priori* representation, which necessarily underlies outer appearances', he, in thus asserting a necessary connexion between the representation of space and outer experience, does not intend to assert a merely analytic connexion. Although, as has been admitted before, in the Metaphysical Exposition of the Concept of Space, Kant is not concerned with the issue of the synthetic a priori, the conclusion he draws in the second space argument belonging to this Exposition is rendered altogether trivial if the necessary connexion he there asserts between outer experience and the representation of space is not, at least in intention, a non-analytic (synthetic) a priori connexion.

To sum up : We admit that 'outer' is not a well-defined term in Kant and that his different uses of it are not always consistent. There are reasons to believe, however, that Kant could consistently adhere to the meaning of 'outer' as objective on all occasions without detriment to any of his theses. The first part of his proof in the second space argument may well be paraphrased finally as 'We can never represent to ourselves the possibility of non-spatial objective experience, And this is not tautological.

7.3 Whether Non-spatial Objective Experience Is Conceivable Or Not (Kant and Strawson : A Comparison)

We have just now seen that the first part of Kant's proof in question reduces, on careful scrutiny, to the contention that the possibility of non-spatial objective experience cannot be represented by us. This all-important contention shows him to be, if, we may borrow L. W. Beck's words, 'one of the most contemporary of the great philosophers of the past'.[41] It is well known that Strawson also in the second chapter of his *Individuals* tries to establish the thesis that the possibility of objective experience cannot be conceived, by us at least, except on analogy with space. Although in this book he is not specifically concerned with a defence of Kant and makes only an incidental reference to the first part of Kant's proof in the second space argument, there can be little doubt that Strawson's is essentially a Kantian theme. Even in his brief reference to Kant, he has not failed to remark that the problem he has taken up is 'in form and partly in content . . . Kantian'.[42] One expositor of Kant, namely, Walker, however, thinks otherwise; his view will be discussed later on.

Strawson considers the model of a No-Space world, namely, a purely auditory universe, in which the sole experience is that of a sequence of sounds.[43] This shows that we can conceive the possibility of some kind of non-spatial experience; but this does not disprove Kant's contention, which is (as has been found) rather that we cannot conceive the possibility of any kind of non-spatial *objective* experience. A purely auditory universe merely presents an auditory chaos in which, as such, there is no room for the distinction of the objective from the subjective, of the non-inner from the merely inner. In short, it is as such not a world of objective particulars. However, the conditions of knowledge of objective particulars can be fulfilled for a purely auditory experience by introducing into this world a non-temporal dimension analogous to the spatial dimension of our familiar world. This non-temporal dimension is necessary 'for, so to speak, the housing' of reidentifiable objective particulars, necessary 'for objects which are not themselves intrinsically spatial, such as sounds, as well as for objects that are'.[44] To this end, Strawson introduces into the auditory universe what he calls 'the master-sound'.[45] The master-sound is the auditory device for reidentifying sound-particulars, and consequently for making the purely auditory experience into an objective experience. It is the necessary non-temporal dimension which is analogous to our familiar spatial dimension. If this auditory analogue to our spatial dimension is unlike the latter in certain respects, this only shows that the features which are common to both are the only features which are absolutely necessary for the possibility of any objective experience conceivable by us.

It thus appears that we cannot represent (i.e. make intelligible) to ourselves the possibility of objective experience without the help of the idea of space. The difficulty, however, is that Strawson's view has been subjected to a searching criticism by Bennett, among others, and, further, that there is one interpretation of Kant's second space argument on which Strawson's view, if it is true, is of no use for it. So an examination of Strawson's view both in itself and in relation to Kant's argument will be in order.

Bennett objects 'that Strawson's theory is analytic if it is true at all'.[46] By 'Strawson's theory' he means the view that what is outer must be spatial. It must be quickly pointed out that Bennett does not mean to regard Strawson's view as analytic in the straight- forward definitional sense, that is, 'by including "spatial" in the definition of "outer", his definition of 'outer' being 'objective', 'of something other than oneself'.[47] It is for him analytic in a different sense. He distinguishes between two kinds of analytic truths : obviously (i.e. trivially or elementarily or definitionally) analytic and unobviously analytic.[48] He regards Strawson's view as unobviously analytic.[49] But his notion of unobvious analyticity is not quite clear. He seems to mean by it derivability by steps from a number of other truths which are in themselves elementarily or obviously analytic.[50] This being so, Strawson's view can be shown to be unobviously analytic if it can be completely demonstrated by being deduced from a number of elementarily or obviously analytic truths. But Bennett comes near confessing that this can hardly be done. For he contends that Strawson's view 'cannot be proved conclusively', inasmuch as in holding such a view 'one is inevitably at the mercy of the overlooked possibility'.[51] This amounts to the confession that a complete demonstration through analytic deduction of the Strawsonian view is not feasible.

Does then Bennett rest the alleged unobvious analyticity of the view in question on some other consideration ? But that too is not at all clear.[52]

Let us therefore attach greater importance to Bennett's other contention that Strawson's theory is of a kind that is not conclusively provable. He argues that it is a theory of a kind where one cannot be sure that one has exhausted all possibilities : 'In such a case, one is inevitably at the mercy of the overlooked possibility . . .'. The objection, again, is too brief to be fully clear. Perhaps he means this : in order to be sure that what is outer (i.e. objective) must be spatial, we have to explore all possible no-space worlds, because some of these may not require any such devices as the master-sound which resemble our familiar spatial dimension. To this the following reply may be made :

> But Strawson introduces this Master Sound, this auditory device, not because of the nature of the particular no-space world he is investigating, but because he is looking for the possibility of objective particulars. So it seems we will meet precisely the same difficulty and have to offer similar devices as solutions, no matter what type of no-space world we invent. Certainly it seems that Strawson has hit upon the most profitable universe to use as an example.[53]

There is, however, still another objection raised by Bennett. He says :

> I do not see how one could reconstruct Strawson's argument about the concept of spatiality so as to turn it into a treatment of an intuited particular called 'Space'. Apart from his desire for a synthetic theory, therefore, Kant has a further reason for denying that the Aesthetic is a Strawson-type exercise in conceptual analysis.[54]

What Bennett means comes to this : The auditory world, in so far as it is *objective*, is no doubt *spatial* in some sense (even 'in a fairly strong sense')[55], but it is certainly not a part of our familiar physical space, but is at best like it (analogous to it) 'in certain formal respects';[56] and this shows that Kant's theory that space is an intuited particular is in jeopardy. There is for Kant only one Space which is an intuited particular, and the so-called diverse spaces we can think of are spatial not by formally resembling the one Space, but by being parts of it. This theory, Bennett contends, cannot be reconciled with Strawson's theory that objectivity requires spatiality. This objection is surely a formidable one. It will be considered in its proper place, namely, in connexion with Kant's third space argument, and it will be seen that it is difficult to accept Kant's view that all conceivable spaces are but parts of one and same intuited space, and that yet his pure intuition theory is after all maintainable.[57]

At present we are concerned with Kant's second space argument, and it is the relevance of Strawson's view to this argument that deserves consideration. It has already been said that there is one interpretation of this argument which makes the Strawsonian view, if it is true, quite useless for it. That interpretation is due to Garnett. Before we turn to it, an examination of Walker's view of Strawson's relation to Kant remains in arrear.

7.4 The Issue of 'Experience without Space' Considered Further (An Examination of Walker's Comparison of the Kantian View with that of Strawson)

Walker maintains that on the question whether 'experience without space' is possible the Kantian position is that it is possible, and that in this Kant may not be wrong,[58] although 'that he is wrong is argued by Strawson, among others'.[59] Clearly, if Walker is right, then we have been wrong in the foregoing exposition in more than one way. Let us disentangle the different points involved in Walker's view and examine briefly each in turn.

(a) Walker says about Kant :

> He considers it a possibility that there might be beings whose experience was neither spatially nor temporally ordered. We impose the forms of space and time upon our intuition, and that is why they are a priori for us, but beings of another kind might impose alternative forms instead.[60]

Walker is referring here to a passage in that part of the Aesthetic where Kant has drawn 'Conclusions' from his Metaphysical and Transcendental Expositions of the Concept of Space. Kant there (A 27 = B 43) says that 'we cannot judge in regard to the intuitions of other thinking beings, whether they are bound by the same conditions as those which limit our intuition and which for us are universally valid'. Clearly, Kant's talk here of other thinking beings than human is metaphorical; what he is really doing is to recognize, in a metaphorical way, the logical possibility of a non-spatial form of experience. But the important question is whether he regards this form of experience, or rather, the non-spatial form of *objective*61 experience, as in any way intelligible to us. Kant puts his view more clearly in a later passage in the *Critique* :

> Other forms of intuition than space and time . . . even if they should be possible, we cannot render in any way conceivable and comprehensible to ourselves; and even assuming that we could do so, they still would not belong to experience—the only kind of knowledge in which objects are given to us.[62]

Kant is saying that we cannot make intelligible to ourselves the idea of a non-spatial 'form' of intuition, far less the idea of a non-spatial sort of objective experience. Walker in taking Kant 'to allow the possibility of forms of intuition different from our own' fails to note that although Kant allows this possibility in some sense, there is yet a more important (typically Kantian) sense in which he emphatically disallows this possibility. In other words, Walker has ignored the all-important Kantian distinction between 'logical' and 'real' possibility.[63] [This distinction may be utilized here, with a little adaptation, however.[64]] For Kant, logical possibility consists in the mere absence of contradiction, and real possibility consists (if, indeed, we may put it thus) in constructibility, that is, roughly speaking, in capability of exhibition in intuition and imagination.[65] Now when he allows the possibility of a non-spatial non-temporal form of objective experience, he allows only its logical possibility, but not its real possibility. He allows its logical possibility in the sense that the idea of it does not involve a contradiction, and he disallows its real possibility in the sense that we cannot render 'conceivable and comprehensible to ourselves' (that is, imaginatively construct) a scheme of any such experience. [The view will be examined before long.]

(b) We may now consider Walker's view of Strawson's relation to Kant, namely, that Strawson is concerned with showing Kant to be 'wrong'.

Walker is undoubtedly right in taking Strawson to hold that space, or a close analogue of space, is necessary for the possibility of experience in the sense of objective experience, that is, that non-spatial[66] objective experience is not possible. Now since Walker thinks that Kant does allow the possibility of such an experience, he concludes that Kant for Strawson is wrong. Walker's error here has already been pointed out : he fails to see that Kant allows only the logical, but not the real, possibility of such an experience. As for Strawson, it is not known how he would appraise the Kantian distinction between these two sorts of possibility. But on the issue of experience without space he is expressly in substantial agreement with Kant in both the *Individuals* and *The Bounds of Sense.* The question he asks in the former work, 'Could there be a scheme, providing for a system of objective particulars, which was wholly non-spatial ?'[67] is not merely the question whether the scheme of a non-spatial objective experience is possible in the sense that the idea of it is free from logical contradiction. He observes : 'When I say, "Could there exist such a scheme ?" I mean "Can we make intelligible to ourselves the idea of such a scheme ?" '[68] The question even so clarified may not be clear enough just as the comparable Kantian notion of real possibility may not be sufficiently clear. But this much is clear that Strawson's is not a mere formal *logical* inquiry. When he says in the other work, 'There are limits to what we can conceive of, or make intelligible to ourselves, as a possible general structure of experience',[69] he does not mean that the determining of such limits is a formal logical undertaking. He calls it a 'philosophical undertaking' and remarks : 'No philosopher has made a more strenuous attempt on it than Kant'.[70]

In fine, it may be said that Strawson, in spite of his many important departures from Kant, does not at all argue to prove him 'wrong', as Walker imagines, on the issue of experience without space, but rather does something that serves to remove the 'element of unexplicitness'[71] in the development of Kant's view that non-spatial objective experience is not possible in the sense of being representable to ourselves or capable of being made intelligible to ourselves.

(c) What falls to be examined next is Walker's criticism of Strawson's view in question; for, on our interpretation, any such criticism must apply to Kant's view as well.

The criticism is that non-spatial experience of objects is possible, because all that is required for the application of the concept of an object is that our experience must be ordered, but it need not be spatially ordered. His words may be quoted for the convenience of subsequent examination :

> If we are to find it useful to apply the concept of an objective particular which is reidentifiable over time, we need to have a certain sort of regularity in our experience allowing for a pattern of more or less gradual change . . . For beings like ourselves the sorts of regularity the spatial dimensions allow, and which lead us to think of objects as existing elsewhere when we are not perceiving them, are particularly easy and natural; alternative regularities are the more difficult to see as regularities of the relevant kind the more dissimilar they are to these spatial ones. For percipients radically different from ourselves quite other dimensional orderings, and hence other sorts of regularity, might be far more natural than space, and might make the hypothesis of unperceived particulars useful for them in circumstances remote from those in which we employ it.[72]

If this criticism is intended to establish only that the idea of a scheme of non-spatial objective experience involves no logical contradiction, then, for reasons stated before, we need have no concern with it. It can have interest for us only if it allows of being construed as offering an affirmative answer to the question asked by Strawson, but answered by him in the negative, namely, 'Can we make intelligible to ourselves the idea of such a scheme ?' But then there is nothing in Walker's criticism to show that an affirmative answer to this question is justified. He has argued that *percipients radically different from ourselves* can presumably make intelligible *to themselves* the idea of a scheme of non-spatial objective experience. But this is hardly relevant as a criticism of Strawson, and, on our interpretation, of Kant. Neither Strawson nor Kant denies, or is even concerned with denying, that beings of another kind can make intelligible to themselves the idea of such a scheme of experience. The only thing they are concerned with denying, and do deny, is that *we* can make intelligible to ourselves the idea of such a scheme. Strawson has clearly said that he is not concerned with devising 'wildly speculative answers' to questions 'about hypothetical beings at all', and that his only object, in seeking to explore the No-Space world, is to try to ascertain 'the extent to which, and the ways in which, *we* might find it possible to reinterpret, within a part of our experience, some of the most general conceptual elements in our handling of experience as a whole.'[73] As regards Kant, he too lets us see that it is none of his business to speculate about hypothetical 'thinking beings'; for he clearly says that 'we cannot judge' about their conditions.[74] And when he hypothetically considers,[75] though not as fully as Strawson, a scheme of non-spatial objective experience, his object also is to emphasize what *we*[76] can or cannot make intelligible to ourselves.[77] Returning to Walker, then, it may be said that he has failed to separate the two questions : (1) 'Can *we* make intelligible *to ourselves* the idea of a scheme of non-spatial objective experience ?' and (2) 'Can *beings of another kind* make intelligible *to themselves* the idea of such a scheme ?'

It has sometimes been contended (e.g. by Don Locke) that it is rather Strawson, and in a similar way Kant, who have failed to separate those two questions.[78] This contention may be put in the form of the following objection without altering its spirit, and then a reply to it may be attempted.

OBJECTION : If we are to determine whether the idea of space is one of the necessary conditions that make objective experience possible, we cannot rest content with the first of the two questions formulated above. Even if it is true that *we* cannot make intelligible *to ourselves* the idea of a scheme of non-spatial objective experience, it does not follow that the idea of space is *necessary*, and so *a priori* in the austere sense of this term. For the question 'Can *we* make intelligible *to ourselves* the idea of a scheme of non-spatial objective experience ?' is really a question of the form whether or not it is, *in fact*, possible for *us* to interpret what we perceive in a certain way; and

> whether or not it is, in fact, possible for us to interpret what we perceive in a certain way . . . may. . . depend on what knowledge and concepts we possess already, for it may be possible for *us*, drawing on the conceptual scheme we have developed for application to what we now perceive, to interpret

> some new and unusual perceptual world, e.g. Strawson's auditory universe, in terms of a non-solipsistic conceptual scheme, when a being with no previously acquired concepts and knowledge would be extremely unlikely to do so.[79]

REPLY : The objector thinks that in order to establish the conclusion that the idea of space is *necessary* (and so *a priori* in the austere sense), so strong a premise is required as that we not only cannot make intelligible to ourselves, but can conceive that beings of another kind too cannot make intelligible *to themselves*, the idea of a scheme of non-spatial objective experience. On his view, the mere statement that we cannot make intelligible to ourselves the idea of such a scheme is not strong enough for that conclusion, since it fails to rise above the sphere of factuality or contingency, being restricted to reporting what is not in fact possible for us, particularly, to do. His use of the clause, 'whether or not it is, in fact, possible for us to interpret . . .'. which is evidently crucial in the statement of his case, is noteworthy. It suggests a special category of possibility or impossibility, namely, factual possibility or impossibility, and the question is what this can mean.

One may here consider, for example, a well-attested scientific statement, such as that sound does not move faster than light. One may say that it is in fact impossible that sound moves faster than light.[80] The point of regarding this as factually impossible, instead of simply as false, may be to stress the scientific law-character of the original statement. In this sense factual impossibility is like what Karl Popper calls 'musical impossibility' : 'It is like the impossibility of a four-beat rhythm in a classical minuet, or the impossibility of ending it on a diminished seventh or some other dissonance'.[81] In other words, the point of regarding the negation of the well-attested scientific statement as factually impossible is virtually to stress that the statement, as expressing a natural law, *'expresses a structural property of our world;* a property which prevents the occurrence of certain logically possible singular events, or states of affairs of a certain kind . . .'.[82] But although we may agree that it is factually impossible, in the explained sense, for sound to move faster than light, the state of affairs in question is nevertheless possible not merely logically, but really or transcendentally[83] in the

Kantian sense, – in the sense that we can quite well comprehend it, that is, represent it to ourselves.[84] In contemporary terminology, we can intelligibly construct a model of a world in which sound moves faster than light.

The notion of factual impossibility being thus delimited, little doubt remains regarding the status of the statement underestimated by the objector, namely, that we cannot make intelligible to ourselves the idea of a scheme of non-spatial objective experience. Manifestly, it is a pointer to a kind of impossibility that is stronger than mere factual impossibility. It goes to show more than that it is just an empirical law that objective experience is spatial. Were this such, we could indeed do what the statement in question denies that we can : construct an intelligible model of a non-spatial objective world (scheme) of experience.

The objector's main contention, however, seems to be that the statement in question, which might well be called the Kantian-Strawsonian statement, is as much about *us* (human beings) as it is about the relation between the idea of space and objective experience, and that, *qua* a statement about *us,* it is surely factual, expressing, as it does, a quasi-psychological brute fact about our imaginative capacity and conceptual ability : indeed, what we can or cannot make intelligible to ourselves is a matter of our *de facto* power of imagination and comprehension.

Against this contention, the following two points may well be made :

(i) It is not strictly accurate to say that the Kantian-Straw-sonian statement in question is as much about *us* as it is about the relation of the idea of space and objective experience, if 'as much' is to mean *in the same sense.* For the statement 'we cannot make intelligible to ourselves the idea of a scheme of non-spatial objective experience' is, in virtue of its context, to be construed as 'we cannot make intelligible to ourselves the denial of the relation that obtains between the idea of space and objective experience', and, in the latter, the locution 'we cannot make intelligible to ourselves the denial of' is rather a term of epistemic appraisal than a term for what such appraisal is *about.* The latter statement, which is the more explicit equivalent of the Kantian-Strawsonian statement under consideration, is an appraisal-statement *about* the relation between the idea of space and objective experience, *with the comment* that we cannot make intelligible to ourselves the denial of it (i.e. of that relation), and *with the inplication* that it, the relation, is necessary, Clearly, the statement is not *in the same sense* (that is, on the same level of reckoning) about *us* as it is about the relation between the idea of space and objective experience. To suppose that it is about *us,* seeing that the words 'we' and 'ourselves' occur in it, is to ignore the fact that the appraisal-locution 'we cannot make intelligible to ourselves the denial of', of which those words are constituents, does not occur there primarily and materially (just as the expressions 'objective experience' and 'space' do), but is rather a philosopher's general formal tag used in statements designed to show the necessity of whatever it is that may be concerned.

[It has to be admitted, however, that there is a line of interpretation of particularly the Kantian statement 'We can never represent to ourselves the absence of space . . .' upon which the word 'we' in it is as much integral to its matter (content, or primary intention) as the word 'space'.[85] Needless to add, such an interpretation reads the transcendental-*idealist* suggestion into Kant's statement in view, and has the effect of foisting on him the error of begging the issue.]

(ii) At a secondary level of thinking, of course, the Kantian-Strawsonian statement under consideration deserves to be regarded as being about *us*; the question is whether, from this point of view, it is appropriate to classify it as *factual.* If the label 'factual' is to mean the same as 'contingent or empirical', it can be properly attached, according to our standard, only to a statement that admits of being intelligibly denied. Incidentally, it may be pointed out that our objector has not rejected the standard itself, though in his converse use of it he has rather overcharged it by demanding that a strictly non-factual statement shall be one that does not admit of being intelligibly denied by *any* person, human or other. He here assumes that we, human beings, can intelligibly discourse about what beings other than human can or cannot make intelligible to themselves. The is an assumption which Kant and

Strawson reject, and it will soon be seen that the basis of this rejection is not factual (i.e. empirical), but transcendental (in that broad, nowadays familiar, sense of this expression in which it, by itself, does not involve a commitment to transcendental idealism[86]).

The moot-question before us is whether we can make intelligible to ourselves the *denial* of the Kantian-Strawsonian statement regarded as a statement about *us* : whether, that is, we can intelligibly to ourselves deny that we cannot make intelligible to ourselves the idea of a scheme of non-spatial objective experience. Now, it must be conceded that there is no *logical contradiction* in the supposition that our conceptual ability might have been otherwise; e.g. in the supposition that if we were beings of another kind than we are, then we (i.e. the hypothetical other beings) could make intelligible to ourselves (i.e. to themselves) the idea of non-spatial objective experience. But, free from contradiction as this supposition is, it is yet *devoid of any intelligible content for us* : in entertaining this supposition we are only thinking emptily.

It is worth emphasizing here that, in inquiries into the foundations of our (human) knowledge, operation with the criterion of intelligibility or unintelligibility of states of affairs is our unavoidable *pis aller*, and that our pronouncements on intelligibility or its lack are within proper bounds only when couched in terms of reference *to ourselves*. The question may be raised whether even the formal-logical criterion of consistency or inconsistency itself is not reducible to that of intelligibility or unintelligibility. The tangle of issues that this question is sure to produce can be avoided, however, by making a concession to each side : by recognizing that, besides a purely logical variety of unintelligibility ('logical impossibility' or 'inconsistency'), there is an unintelligibility of another sort stronger yet than mere 'factual impossibility', namely, the one that Kant qualifies as 'real' or 'transcendental' (the latter expression bearing again a broad sense, which is compatible with Strawson's quasi-Kantianism). We are forced to say, therefore, that the Kantian-Strawsonian statement under consideration regarded as being about *us* is not factual in the sense of being intelligibly deniable by us, but transcendental.

As regards the idea of space, – to conclude our reply to the objection under reference –, the view that it is necessary for objective experience (and so a priori in the austere sense) is only strengthened by having been temporarily shaken. The view has, admittedly, not the force of a formal logical principle; it is never- theless stronger than an empirical law. In a sense (the transcendental sense) one can say that, of necessity, the idea of space is necessary for objective experience.

7.5 Complications Arising from Garnett's Interpretation of Kant's Second Space Argument

We understand that the Strawsonian view that outer (i.e. objective) experience must be of a spatial[87] world corroborates the Kantian view that the possibility of such an experience without the representation of space cannot be represented by us. But difficulties arise again owing to Garnett's interpretation of Kant's second space argument. Garnett maintains that Kant's argument in question, when closely examined, shows itself to be 'a direct defense of the necessary Euclidean nature of space in pure geometry, in applied Newtonian science, and in the empirical intuitions of daily life . . .'.[88] By saying that we cannot represent the absence of space, Kant means, according to Garnett, that we cannot represent the absence of the necessarily three-dimensional Euclidean space. If so, the Kantian argument makes a stronger claim than the Strawsonian view, since the latter only claims, as Bennett puts it, 'that outer experience must be of a spatial world . . . though there is no privileged number of dimensions, nor a privilege for Euclid's or any other geometry'.[89] The question now is whether Garnett's interpretation of Kant's argument is correct.

7.5.1 An examination of Garnett's interpretation

Garnett maintains that Kant's second space argument is concerned with a threefold necessity : 'the necessary character of space, its necessary relation to the knowing subject and its necessary relation to outer intuitions'.[90] In so far as the argument has to do with the necessary character of space, it has to be analysed properly before one can see that it means that space 'necessarily has the nature that it has, whatever that nature may be (i.e. it is homaloidal)' and that 'it must be so represented'.[91] More specifically, it means, according to him, that space 'is necessarily three-dimensional, continuous, uniform, etc. – in a word, Euclidean – and must be so represented'.[92] Garnett is well aware that such an interpretation 'is apt to be too hastily dismissed' (as it is done by Vaihinger) on the ground that the doctrine of necessity of space with the above implications has properly no place in Kant's 'metaphysical exposition' and finds expression only in the 'transcendental exposition'.[93] But he argues that the two expositions differ at most in 'procedure and type of argument', and not in being concerned with 'two different kinds of space as objects of investigation'. That is to say, the term 'space' has for Kant a definite and specific connotation that cannot be supposed to vary from one exposition to another, because in both the expositions the same kind of space is in question; and this being so, Kant's view in the second space argument that we cannot think away space surely points to 'a constraint to represent space as it is, not merely as without any specific connotation'.[94] As Garnett puts it : 'It is not that some connotatively indeterminate space cannot be thought away, but space with its connotatively necessary, and its denotatively singular, nature cannot be thought of as absent'.[95] Kant's statement that we cannot represent space as absent signifies, according to Garnett, not merely that space has a necessary relation to the representing subject, but also that 'space is and must be represented as it is, and not otherwise'.[96] The *Nicht-anders-denken-könnens* of space in this way connects with its *Nicht-Hinweg-Denkbarkeit.*

Garnett's interpretation certainly reads more into Kant's second space argument than it actually expresses. The context of this argument demands, as was previously seen,[97] that we should understand his statement 'We can never represent to ourselves the absence of space' in the sense that we can never represent the absence of space from outer intuitions (appearances). And this expresses only the *relative necessity* of space. The argument contains nothing to show that it gives expression to what Garnett calls the *absolute necessity* of space in the sense that space must be represented not otherwise than as it is, specifically as Euclidean.[98] The question is, why should Garnett read so much into Kant's present argument ? One reason given by him is, as just noted, that space which Kant says cannot be thought away is not 'connotatively indeterminate', is not 'without any specific connotation', with the suggestion that within this specific connotation is to be included the character of being Euclidean. It is fairly clear that Garnett is here under the influence of the view that the representation of space is for Kant 'temporally prior to experience', which means, in Kemp Smith's words, that the idea of space is 'innate in conscious form'.[99] On this view indeed the idea of space is already there in the mind in its full-fledged form, that is, as connotatively determinate. At one point of his discussion of Kant's second space argument Garnett observes that if this argument is 'stripped of the theory of the apprehension of space temporally prior to sense experience', the only conclusion it then yields is 'that space is empirical and necessary'[100] – a conclusion different from that which Kant has actually drawn. This observation shows that Garnett has in fact brought the theory of the psychological-temporal priority of the representation of space to bear upon Kant's second space argument. Since it is of the essence of this theory that the representation of space lies in us 'in its entirety' and not as 'a mere potential disposition', it is only too natural that Garnett should read into Kant's second space argument the suggestion that the representation of space 'which the mind must carry out' is a representation that is in it in its entirety, i.e. as *fully determinate*. But the theory of the psychological-temporal priority of the representation of space has already been rejected in the second chapter. We have seen that the idea of space is for Kant not temporally prior to sense-experience; and here it will suffice to observe, in Paton's words, that the priority of space and time 'does not mean that our ideas of space and time are necessarily explicit. They may be "obscure" *(dunkel)*, that is, not immediately present to consciousness'.[101]

To the question why Garnett should choose to read so much into Kant's second space argument, still another shred of reply is provided by the following statement of his : 'Considered alone, the theory of the necessary nature of space leaves every feature of space unspecified. Neither a non-empirical, nor an intuitive, nor an (sic.) Euclidean, nature is implied in the argument'.[102] The import of this statement is that if 'the theory of the necessary nature of space' in the sense that space is and must be represented *as it is* (as Euclidean, to be specific) is to be excluded from Kant's second space argument, then the theory of its 'non-empirical nature' also should be excluded ; for the non-empirical nature also is *not implied* there. But what are we to make of the statement that the non-empirical nature of space (which is short for 'the non-empirical nature of the representation of space') is not implied in Kant's second space argument ? Obviously, it cannot be taken to mean that Kant himself has not intended the non-empirical nature of space in the argument; for his intended conclusion is clearly that 'Space is a necessary *a priori* representation'. Perhaps the statement means that the non-empirical nature of space is not warranted by Kant's second space argument alone : we have already referred to Garnett's observation that Kant's second argument *alone* yields just the conclusion 'that space is empirical and necessary'. Garnett writes :

> Abandoning the first argument, the necessary, empirical nature of space would result [from Kant's second space argument].[103] If there are necessary elements which are discoverable in experience and if space is one of these, then space would be empirical and necessary. The necessary nature of space would be discoverable immediately as experienced.[104]

Here the following comments may be made :

(a) If Kant's sccond space argument does not warrant the conclusion that space has 'a non-empirical nature' in the sense, as defined by Garnett, that the apprehension of it is temporally prior to sense-experience, it does not matter at all. Kant does not intend, and so has not tried, to establish that conclusion. The non-empirical nature, or apriority, with which Kant is actually concerned in his conclusion is to be understood in logical, and not in temporal-psychological, terms.

(b) Garnett in saying that Kant's second argument considered alone yields the conclusion that 'space is empirical and necessary' is taking the word 'experience' (or 'empirical') in a wider sense than is appropriate in the present context. Garnett himself admits this : 'Space would be yielded in experience *(widely construed)*, and yet it would be impossible to think of space as absent'.[105] That in the wider sense of 'experience' space is involved in experience is not denied by Kant, and that is why he insists in more than one place on the need for a transcendental isolation of space from experience or empirical knowledge or empirical intuition (widely construed) by an elimination of the merely empirical.[106] Indeed, if space is discovered in objective experience, it is not just as the objects are. Space is not so much discoverable *in* experience as it (i.e. the representation of it) is *at the basis of* experience.[107] The relative necessity of space, which is explicitly asserted in Kant's second argument, definitely shows that space has a *unique status* in experience.

(c) In addition to saying that space is discoverable in experience, Garnett has said that 'the necessary nature of space' is 'discoverable immediately in experience'. But is 'necessary nature' ever immediately experienced ? One may seek to *explain* necessity in terms of experience and its laws, but it is useless to try to *discover it immediately* as being there. [It may be argued, again, that the necessity of apprehension consists in the *apprehension* of necessity; to which our reply is that if 'experience' be here substituted for 'apprehension', the sense of 'experience' is then overstretched even beyond what has been called above the wider sense of 'experience'. One may extend the sense of 'experience' in this way, if one pleases; only then one cannot operate with the distinction between empirical and non-empirical representation.]

In the light of the above examination of Garnett's interpretation we can see that its bases are unsound. So we are forced to reject it. Reverting to Strawson's defence of the view that outer (in the sense of objective) experience is essentially spatial, we may reassure ourselves that this defence does serve to provide a genuine corroboration of the view expressed in the first part of Kant's proof in the second space argument. We may now take leave of this part of Kant's proof and turn to the second. If some further words are still needed, after the discussion that has been made, to overcome any lingering doubt whether the first part of Kant's proof by itself *without the cooperation of the second part* is sufficient to support the conclusion that the idea of space is a priori in the austere sense, these will be added in a general discussion to be made in the final section of the next chapter.

NOTES :

1. G. S. Fullerton, The Doctrine of Space and Time', *Philosophical Review* 10 (1901), § 1 ('The Kantian Doctrine of Space'), p. 118, Cf. also H. Sidgwick, *Lectures* on *the Philosophy of Kant,* 1905, p. 42.
2. This means that space exists necessarily in its own right. For a different account, see below, 7.5.1.
3. See Fullerton, *op. cit.,* pp. 118-119.
4. *Nachträge zu Kants Kritik* (ed. B. Erdmann, 1881) XVII, cited and translated by D.P. Dryer, *Kant's Solution for Verification in Metaphysics,* 1966, p. 175 n. 3. It may be noted that some (e.g. Fullerton, *op. cit.,* p. 119) do regard the representation of the non-existence of space as 'self-contradictory'.
5. See also John Watson, *The Philosophy of Kant Explained,* 1908, p. 84.
6. See 6.2 (above), and also A. Koyre', *From the Closed World to the Infinite Universe,* 1968, pp. 148, 150-151.
7. Herein lies the link between Kant's second space argument and his first space argument which concludes : '. . . outer experience is . . . possible at all only through that representation [i.e. the representation of space]', A 23 = B 38.
8. A 31 = B 46.
9. A 24.
10. A 385; cf. also A 374.
11. Cf. A 24, A 23.
12. We are using the word 'tautological' here not in the strict Kantian sense, but in the ordinary sense as given in *The Concise Oxford Dictionary,* Oxford University Press, Calcutta, 1977, p. 1185. In the latter sense, tautology consists in 'Saying . . . the same thing twice over in *different* words . . .', [italics used by us]. In this sense, the first part of Kant's proof as explicated by us appears to be tautological in so far as it seems that the word 'outer' means the same as 'spatial'.

    In the Kantian sense, however, a tautological proposition is an *explicitly* analytic (or identical) proposition such as *Man is man* (Kant's example). In his *Logic* (Compiled by Jäsche), § 37 (trans. Hartman and Schwarz, 1974, p. 118), Kant distinguishes between explicitly analytic (or identical) and *implicitly* analytic (or identical) propositions, and regards the former alone as 'tautological'.

    So a statement that can justly be called 'tautological' in the ordinary sense may not be so called in the Kantian sense. In the latter sense it has rather to be called an implicitly identical or analytic statement.

The problem before us is whether the first part of Kant's proof as explicated by us really is tautological in the ordinary sense, i.e. an implicitly identical statement in the technical Kantian sense.

13. Cf. below, seventh paragraph of this section.
14. A 373. (The passage concerned is commented on below.)
15. The word 'tautology' is used in this sentence in accordance with the Kantian sense, following Paton, who says : '. . . since "outer" means "spatial", it [i.e. the Kantian statement under consideration] looks like the tautologous statement that there can be no spatial experience apart from space'. – *Kant's Metaphysic of Experience,* 1951, vol. I, p. 146.
16. Cf., e.g. Jonathan Bennett, *Kant's Analytic,* Cambridge University Press, 1966, pp. xi, 42.
17. It is fairly clear that Kant's word 'intuition' here is used in what we have previously called the wider sense of 'empirical intuition' as distinguished from the narrower sense of it. For the distinction between these two senses, see above, note 62 to Chap. 2, p. 70.
18. For some discussion of the sense in which intuition for Kant yields *knowledge* of an object, see Manley Thompson, 'Singular terms and Intuitions in Kant's Epistemology', *Review of Metaphysics* 26 (1972), pp. 314-43.
19. On the ambiguity of the word 'intuition', cf. 1.4.
20. Kant's term for 'objective experience' is simply 'experience'. At 110 of the *Critique* he says that 'experience' stands for 'one and the same general experience'. The phrase translated by Kemp Smith as 'one and the same general experience' is translated by Paton (*Kant's Metaphysic of Experience,* 1951, I, 452) as 'one and the same universal experience'. Paton takes the phrase as signifying a commonly sharable human experience; cf. *ibidem.*
21. The role of what Graham Bird (in his *Kant's Theory of Knowledge,* 1962, p. 133) calls 'the generalising function of concepts' in objective experience is ignored in the Aesthetic. What Kant here does is to emphasize the role that intuition in space (and time) has in such experience. As to sensations, these, considered in themselves, are for Kant subjective; but, surely, he does not mean that they are not available for objective knowledge. They are, in his view (cf. his *Critique*

of Judgement, Introduction VII, trans. J. C. Meredith, Clarendon Press, Oxford, 1980, p. 29), *capable of becoming elements of objective knowledge,* and are in this respect to be distinguished from pleasure and displeasure which are subjective 'representations' incapable of becoming such elements. But sensations come to be elements in objective knowledge in so far as they are viewed as revealing qualities of objects *having positions in space and time;* cf. Paton, *Kant's Metaphysic of Experience,* vol. II, pp. 135 (first para, 11. 9-11), 137 n.4. In this sense, clearly, intuition in space (and time), as distinguished from 'mere' sensation, plays, according to Kant, an objectivating role in knowledge.

22. Strawson, *The Bounds of Sense,* 1966, p. 24.
23. *Ibidem.*
24. *Ibidem.*
25. § 15, *Corollary;* Handyside trans., 1929, p. 64.
26. *Critique,* A 373; but see below.
27. See above, p. 79.
28. H. W. Cassirer (in his *Kant's First Critique,* George Allen & Unwin, London, 1978, p. 30) observes : 'Kant says of space [at A 34 = B 50] that it is the form of outer intuition. But this tells us precisely nothing, . . .'. Cassirer says further (see *ibidem)* that 'it is impossible to attach much importance' to Kant's statement in question. This criticism is based on the supposition that Kant here means by 'outer' the same as 'spatial'. But we contend that this is an over-simplification.
29. See note 20 (a)(i) and (ii) to Chap. 3., and pp. 100, 106-107 above.
30. That is, in its application to objects of possible experience, as distinguished from its transcendent (or, as Kant says, transcendental) application to things in themselves. (It need hardly be stated that 'empirical' in 'empirical employment' is opposed not to 'a priori', but to 'transcendent'.)
31. On 'reciprocal concepts', see Kant's *Logic,* § 12 (Hartman and Schwarz trans., p. 104).
32. E.g. in Chap. 5.
33. Surely, by 'inner' (in its empirical employment) Kant does not *mean* the same as 'temporal'; he rather means *in us, i.e. in the mind.* Cf. his observation : 'Inner sense, by means of which the mind intuits itself or its inner state . . .'; *Critique,* A 22 = B 37.

34. The wish to reserve the meaning of 'outer' as *objective* for its transcendental application to things in themselves fails to do justice to the fact that Kant not seldom uses even the word 'objective' empirically (i.e. non-transcendentally). At A 28 = B 44 he says that space, although 'subjective', 'could be entitled [at once] objective [and] *a priori'* : here 'objective' stands for empirically objective (i.e. non-transcendentally, or non-transcendently objective).
35. In the empirical sense.
36. In the empirical sense.
37. Quoted and translated (from Kant's *Uber eine Entdeckung)* by Dryer, *op. cit.,* p. 100 n.l. In H. E. Allison's translation (1973) of Kant's work in question, see p. 141; [AK. VIII, 228-229]. Cf. also the last three lines of the first para on p. 141 of Allison's translation.
38. Cf. L. W. Beck, *Studies in the Philosophy of Kant,* Bobbs-Merrill, Indianapolis, 1965, pp. 99ff. ('Remarks on the Distinction between Analytic and Synthetic').
39. In the empirical sphere. [In this discussion we are concerned with the empirical employment of 'outer'.]
40. Although, in the Kantian context, 'necessary' must not be equated with 'analytic', the equation is sometimes made, however, by critics, (as has been shown, in a different connexion, by Beck, *op. cit.,* pp. 100-101).
41. L. W. Beck, ed. *Kant's Theory of Knowledge,* D. Reidel, Dordrecht-Holland, 1974, Preface, p. vii.
42. Strawson, *Individuals,* Methuen, London, a University Paperback, reprinted 1969, p. 62.
43. For Strawson's arguments for the view that a purely auditory world is a No-Space world, see *ibid.,* pp. 64ff. The view is based mainly on the consideration that sounds 'have no intrinsic spatial characteristics'; *ibid.,* p. 65.

    For an examination of alternatives to Strawson's view in question, see R.M.P. Malpas, 'The Location of Sound', in R. J. Butler, ed., *Analytical Philosophy, Second Series,* Basil Blackwell, Oxford, 1965, pp. 131-144.
44. Strawson, *Individuals,* p. 74.
45. *Ibid.,* p. 76.
46. Bennett, *Kant's Analytic,* pp. 41-42.
47. *Ibid.,* p. 42, also p. xi.

48. Cf. *ibid.,* pp. 7-8, and also Strawson, 'Bennett on Kant's Analytic', *Philosophical Review* 77 (1968), p. 333.
49. Bennett, *op. cit.,* p. xi.
50. Cf. *ibid.,* p. 8., 11.11-14.
51. *Ibid.,* p. 43.
52. Cf. Strawson's article in *Philosophical Review* 77 (1968), pp. 334f.
53. Don Locke, 'Strawson's Auditory Universe', *Philosophical Review* 70 (1961), p. 519. Don Locke in his turn, however, has raised some objections against Strawson. One such objection (repeated by him elsewhere) is considered below.
54. Bennett, *op. cit.,* p. 62.
55. *Ibid.,* p. 41.
56. *Ibid.,* p. 63., cf. the whole para referred to here.
57. See below, p. 366.
58. Walker, *Kant,* 1978, p. 30 : 'It is not so clear that Kant is wrong . . .'.
59. *Ibidem.*
60. *Ibidem.*
61. We add here 'objective' in the light of our previous exposition of the Kantian view.
62. A 230 = B 283.
63. B xxvi note, A 596 = B 624 note. The 'real possibility' is also called by Kant 'transcendental possibility'; see A 244 = B 302, A 610 = B 638.
64. An adaptation or adjustment is called for, because the notion of real possibility is for Kant strictly relevant to *objects* or *things* (A 219-220 = B 267), whereas what is required here is to apply this notion to *forms of intuition* or to *experience.* The following observations may be of use :

    (1) While speaking of objects as really possible, Kant indeed speaks of them as objects of possible experience. So the real possibility of objects suggests a corresponding possibility of experience. Cf. A 219 (end), and also Paton, *Kant's Metaphysic of Experience,* vol. II, p. 354, third para.

    [In relevant cases, Kant himself wants his talk of 'objects' to be construed as his talk of the 'experience' in which objects are known; cf. his observation at B xvii : '. . . the objects, or what is the same thing, . . . the *experience* in which alone, as given objects, they can be known, . . .' (the emphasis added by Kant himself).]

(2) In actual practice, Kant does not keep the application of the notion of real possibility confined to objects. Thus in B xxvi n. he extends its application to a *concept,* equating the real possibility of a concept with its 'objective validity' (which is sometimes also called 'objective reality', and, in the case of an a priori concept, also again 'transcendental truth'; A 221-222). Accordingly, an inquiry into the objective reality (or validity) of suggested alternative forms of intuition or kinds of experience may, without committing an outrage upon the Kantian usage, be as well called an inquiry into their real possibility. Talk of real possibility in such cases is, admittedly, not exact; it is not, however, unnatural, and it need not indicate or cause confusion.

65. Cf. L. W. Beck, 'Lovejoy as a Critic of Kant', *Journal of the History of Ideas* 33 (1972), pp. 481 (last para), 482.

66. One may or may not qualify 'non-spatial' here as 'neither spatial nor quasi-spatial', since what is quasi-spatial is in some important respects *spatial.*

67. *Individuals,* p. 62.

68. *Ibid.* p. 60.

69. *The Bounds of Sense,* p. 15.

70. *Ibidem.*

71. *Ibid.,* p. 51.

72. Walker, *op. cit.,* pp. 33-34.

73. *Individuals,* p. 63. The emphasis on the word 'we' is laid by Strawson himself.

74. A 27 = B 43.

75. At A 230 = B 283.

76. Strawson has sometimes expressed doubts whether the personal pronoun 'we' as used by Kant in the *Critique* refers to human beings or to supersensible timeless beings; see *The Bounds of Sense,* pp. 247f. For critical comments on this, see H. E. Matthews, 'Strawson on Transcendental Idealism' in R.C.S. Walker, ed., *Kant on Pure Reason,* Oxford University Press, 1982, pp. 145f.

It may be noted further that when, with regard to hypothetically considered alternative forms of intuition or kinds of experience, Kant says that we cannot make them intelligible to ourselves, it is fairly clear that he is speaking from *the human standpoint* (the same standpoint from which Strawson is speaking on p. 63 of his *Individuals).* Kant's statement at A 27 = B 43 to the effect that 'we cannot judge in regard to the intuitions of other thinking beings' is made expressly 'from the human standpoint'; see A 26 = B 42.

77. If, incidentally, it be asked, 'How can one *consider* (i.e. conceive) a scheme which for one is unintelligible (i.e. inconceivable) ?', the answer may be given by calling attention to the ambiguity of 'inconceivable' as has been pointed out by Karl Popper on p. 429 of his *The Logic of Scientific Discovery,* Hutchinson of London, 8th impression, Oct. 1975.

78. Cf. Don Locke's article, 'Strawson's Auditory Universe', *Philosophical Review* 70 (1961), and also his *Perception and our Knowledge of the External World,* George Allen & Unwin, London, 1967, p. 224.

79. Don Locke, *Perception,* etc., p. 223.

80. Cf. Hughes and Cresswell, *An Introduction to Modal Logic,* Methuen, London,, 1972, p. 23.

81. Popper, *op. cit.,* p. 430.

82. *Ibid.,* p. 432.

83. It need hardly be stated that the word 'transcendentally', here does not mean 'transcendently' i.e. that the use of the word 'transcendental' here is different from its use as embodied in, e.g. the phrase 'transcendental employment'.

    [Logical possibility, for Kant, is strictly the possibility of *propositions or concepts,* whereas transcendental possibility is the possibility *de re.* This is a restriction which we have already begged permission not to abide by. In the present case, we have applied the notion of logical possibility to a state of affairs and this may not be objected to, since this need not cause confusion.]

84. Or, in still other words, can 'exhibit' it in imagination.

85. On this interpretation, the statement implies that space 'must be grounded in our subjective organisation' (See Kemp Smith, *Commentary,* 1918, p. 103) or that space is necessarily connected with the intuiting subject (see Garnett, *The Kantian Philosophy of Space,* 1939, p. 181).

86. On the question whether Kant's *transcendental idealism* is to be set aside in favour of, say, Strawson's quasi-Kantianism, we are not required in this work to express any opinion. [Matthew's article referred

to in note 76 shows that *transcendental idealism* can be defended as against Strawson's attack.]

87. Or, 'quasi-spatial'; cf. *The Bounds of Sense,* p. 29. But see note 66 above.
88. Garnett, *op. cit.,* p. 178.
89. Bennett, *op. cit.,* p. 41.
90. Garnett, *op. cit.,* p. 176.
91. *Ibid.,* p. 177.
92. *Ibidem.*
93. *Ibidem.*
94. *Ibidem.*
95. *Ibid.,* p. 178.
96. *Ibid.,* p. 177.
97. In 7.1.
98. Garnett, *op. cit.,* p. 177.
99. Kemp Smith, *Commentary,* 1918, p. 93.
100. Garnett, *op. cit.,* p. 181.
101. Paton, *Kant's Metaphysic of Experience,* 1951, vol. I, p. 110 n. 4.
102 Garnett, *op. cit.,* p. 178.
103. *Ibid.,* p. 179.
104. *Ibid.,* p. 181.
105. *Ibid.,* p. 179. [Emphasis ours.]
106. *Critique,* A 2, B 2, B 5-6, A 20-22 = B 35-36.
107. Cf. Paton, *Kant's Metaphysic of Experience,* vol. I, p. 152 (fifth para).

CHAPTER EIGHT

KANT'S SECOND SPACE ARGUMENT (Continued)

As we come to consider the second part of Kant's proof (that is, premise[1]) in the second space argument, we find that it has been so frequently and sanguinely criticized that the impression is left that there is no doubt whatever about its precise significance. An attempt is made in this chapter to provide both a corrective to this impression and a critical commentary on this part of Kant's proof. At first certain difficulties associated with this part of the proof are set forth, and then a way out of them is suggested. Before leaving this chapter, a final estimate of Kant's second space argument as a whole is offered.

8.1 Doubts about the Exact Import of the Second Part of 'Kant's Proof' (The problem of its Bearing on the Supposed Necessity of the Idea of Space)

The second part of Kant's proof under review is : 'we can quite well think it [space] as empty of objects'. The question of the truth of this statement is secondary to that of its meaning or significance. First of all we have to consider how it bears, if it bears at all, on the stated necessity of the representation (idea) of space. Necessity consists in the exclusion of a possibility : thus, for example, the first part of Kant's proof in the present argument has shown, in the light of what turned out to be its adequate and consistent interpretation, the necessity of the idea of space by excluding the possibility of representation of the absence of space from objects, that is, the possibility of non-spatial objective experience. What possibility, now, is excluded by the second part of his proof? It says just what we *can* do, not what we cannot; in other words, it rather asserts than excludes a possibility. So its bearing, if any, on the *necessity* of the idea of space is not clear.

Under the circumstances, we have to go outside Kant's second space argument and try to find out if some external help can be got.

The following passage taken from one of his Introductory sections in the *Critique,* where in the course of a general discussion devoted to the criteria of apriority he specifically considers *inter alia* the necessity-cum-apriority of the idea of space, may here be relevantly considered for what it is worth :

> Such a *priori* origin is manifest in certain concepts, no less than in judgements. If we remove from our empirical concept of a body, one by one, every feature in it which is [merely] empirical, the colour, the hardness or softness, the weight, even the impenetrability, there still remains the space which the body (now entirely vanished)[2] occupied, and this cannot be removed. Again, if we remove from our empirical concept of any object, corporeal or incorporeal, all properties which experience has taught us, we yet cannot take away that property through which the object is thought as substance or as inhering in a substance (although this concept of substance is more determinate than that of an object in general). Owing, therefore, to the necessity with which this concept of substance forces itself upon us, we have no option save to admit that it has its seat in our faculty of *a priori* knowledge. [B 5-6].

The last sentence of this passage is not without relevance to the 'concept' (idea) of space. For the context of the passage clearly allows one to read 'the concept of space or of substance' for 'this concept of substance' in the last sentence.

The passage ostensibly holds a key to the second part of Kant's proof in the second space argument, inasmuch as his statement in the passage to the effect that space remains over even if the object occupying it is ideally removed is strikingly similar to his statement in the latter that we can quite well think space as empty of objects (or more literally, we can quite well think 'that there are no objects in it'). In the former the asserted fact that 'there still remains the space which the body (now entirely vanished) occupied' is explicitly interpreted by Kant in terms of a 'cannot' (that is, an impossibility), as is clear from his additional clause 'and this cannot be removed'. It is in this asserted impossibility of removing space by removing its occupants that he sees the 'necessity' (and therewith the apriority) of the idea of space. Analogously, it is permissible, it seems, to maintain that his statement in the second space argument that we can quite well think space as empty of objects is, in intention, equivalent to, or convertible into, a 'cannot'-statement such as that space *cannot* be thought away by thinking away the objects from it. The absent bearing of the statement at issue on the asserted necessity of the idea of space is now apparently in its place.

But if the rationále for the second part of Kant's proof under examination is to be drawn from the quoted passage, which may henceforth be referred to as 'the B 5-6 passage', we have only disappointing results to come by in the final analysis. The reasoning employed in that passage is unpersuasive and has not the least tendency to show that the idea of space is *necessary.* In that passage, he starts by distinguishing several factors that are represented, namely, (1) 'the colour', (2) 'the hardness or softness', (3) 'the weight', (4) 'the impenetrability', and (5) 'the space', and then he argues that 'if we remove, one by one' all the factors except the last, the last factor 'still remains'. This tautological statement altogether fails to establish that the representation of the last factor as contradistinguished from that of the others is *necessary.* No doubt, if all the factors except the last are removed, the last still remains; but then likewise if the first factor is removed, the second (as well as the rest) remains, and yet it cannot be maintained that the representation of the second factor unlike that of the first is necessary or even a whit less contingent. It has to be seen what there is to say in reply to this objection.

The most likely reply from the Kantian side is that the last factor (namely, 'space') is, strictly speaking, not just one among the many enumerated factors, but has an outstanding peculiarity that gives it rather an underlying than a collateral status. Thus although it is true that if the first factor is removed, the second, for example, remains, the second is nevertheless like the first in respect of the liability to removal : it also *can* be removed; that is to say, if it remains over, it simply *is not* removed, but not such as to warrant our saying of it, 'And this cannot be removed';–whereas if 'the space' that was occupied by the ultimately vanished object remains, it does not simply happen to be not removed; it, as Kant says, 'cannot be removed'.

This reply is of dubious value, however. For it seems that Knat's clause about space, 'and this cannot be removed', is pressed to yield far beyond its proper capacity. This clause, as it occurs in the B 5-6 passage, is essentially context-bound, and it is possible to be misled by it in momentary forgetfulness of its context. The context is that if the given colour, hardness, etc., in short, the object, be removed, the space that was occupied by the object remains; and to say in this context, 'And this cannot be removed', is, *in default of any further observations,* only to say with an emphasis that the space does remain. 'This cannot be removed' may mean either that this cannot be removed *by removing the other factors,* or, that this cannot be removed *by any means* : in the former case, the 'cannot' is qualified or conditional, while in the latter, it is unqualified or unconditional. Now the context of the passage permits only the first interpretation; for nothing like an argument or an explanation is given here to support the second interpretation. Since Kant's clause under scrutiny, considered in itself without regard to its context, is amenable to the second interpretation, it is eminently possible to slide into this interpretation from the contextually legitimate first in the haste to conclude that the idea of space is necessary; and it very much seems to be the case that Kant has taken here this overhasty step.

There are also other difficulties to be pointed out. The necessity of the idea of space that comes to be suggested by the above-mentioned second interpretation of Kant's clause about space that 'this cannot be removed' may be called 'unconditional necessity'. We have just now seen that the actual contents of the B 5-6 passage are too meagre to warrant the ascription of such necessity to the idea of space. By analogy there is little (and, on an internal view, there is nothing) in the *second part of Kant's proof in the second space argument* to warrant the same ascription to the same. It remains to see what harm ensues from neglect of this fact.

It will be pertinent to recall here some of Kant's own observations noted in the last chapter. We have noted that he has unequivocally observed elsewhere that space *simpliciter* can very well be thought to be absent (i.e. ideally removed) without contradiction, and that a kind of 'transcendental subreption' is responsible for the view that space is unconditionally necessary in itself.[3] These pronouncements on his part were allowed to influence largely our interpretation of the *first part* of Kant's proof in the present argument : thus we were forced to treat it as elliptical (supplying the omitted words according to the dictates of the available evidence) lest we should read into it the suggestion of the contraband unconditional necessity of the idea of space. On coming now to the *second part* of this proof, we find ourselves equally obliged, or even more, to exercise caution. It is tempting to interpret this part of the proof on analogy with the above-noted *second interpretation* of Kant's crucial clause about the irremovability of space in the B 5-6 passage, and thereby to confer credibility on unconditional necessitarianism regarding the idea of space. But this interpretation will be untenable for two reasons : first, this is on reflection as unwarranted as the second interpretation of Kant's crucial clause in the B 5-6 passage really is; and second, this is contradicted by Kant's explicit pronouncements elsewhere, as recalled above, against the unconditional necessitarianism regarding the idea of space.

Attention has to be called now to a chaos, which in the meantime has arisen. If the just-discredited interpretation of the second part of Kant's proof under examination is, from one perspective, un-Kantian, it is, from another perspective, very nearly Kantian, since it is analogically suggested by what we have lately had grounds to believe to be *Kant's own* implicit, though ill-advised, interpretation (the already noted second interpretation) of the crucial clause in the B 5-6 passage. We cannot avoid confessing, therefore, that a muddle has at length occurred owing to Kant himself. It would not do, however, to stress this confession overmuch ; the fact remains that Kant's overall attitude to the doctrine of the unconditional necessity of the idea of space is one of emphatic rejection and sedulous avoidance, despite his occasional aberration as in his B 5-6 passage.

If it be asked whether there is anything that can extenuate Kant's aberration in the B 5-6 passage, the fair reply is that there is. Only then we have to rely on a new analogy.

In the corresponding argument (second argument) on time in the *Critique* Kant writes : 'Appearances may, one and all, vanish; but time (as the universal condition of their possibility) cannot itself be removed'.[4] If the bracketed phrase is ignored, this argument is clearly one in type with that about space contained in the B 5-6 passage considered above. Without the qualification or condition inserted within the brackets, the argument appears to convey the unconditional necessity of the idea of time : such indeed is the inherent suggestive force of the residual clause 'time cannot itself be removed' that it is apt to make that interpretation look very natural. The bracketed qualification serves to show that the necessity of the idea of time implied by the asserted irremovability of time is conditional, not unconditional, Now, in so far as it is fair to assume that Kant considers the case of space to be similar to that of time (except, of course, in respects that, we all know, have been clearly pointed out by him[5]), we may say, on the analogy of his argument on time under reference, that the second part of his proof in the second space argument, for all the inadequacy of its actual contents and the incidental vagueness of its implications, is intended indeed to convey the *conditional necessity* of the idea of space. The B 5-6 passage no doubt presents an obstacle to this view; but why should it be supposed that the analogy provided by it outweighs the analogy derived from the argument on time ? In the light of this new analogy, it is allowable, if not *de rigueur*, to attempt the following emendation-cum-paraphrase of the second part of his proof in the second space argument :

'Outer appearances may, one and all, vanish; but space (as the condition of their possibility) cannot itself be removed.'

It is hoped that this paraphrase, which is by no means arbitrary, will serve to compensate for Kant's aberration (or, virtual aberration) in the B 5-6 passage from his professed commitment only to *conditional* necessitarianism regarding the idea of space.

It would be well if the discussion could stop here. But an incidental problem arises, namely, whether the above paraphrase of the second part of Kant's proof in the second space argument makes satisfactory sense. It is not hard to see that there is here a mixing up of two modes of talk. These may be distinguished as follows. To say that space, as the condition of the possibility of outer appearances, cannot be removed is to say that it cannot be removed if outer appearances (objects) are to be represented, and this is not to say that it cannot be removed even if such objects are themselves removed (even if outer appearances all vanish). Talk of the ideal irremovability of space as the condition of the possibility of outer appearances is talk of the necessity of the representation of space relatively to the situation where outer appearances are represented, whereas talk of the ideal irremovability of space despite the ideal removal of outer appearances is talk of the necessity of the representation of space in and for itself. In the former case, the conditional necessity of the idea (representation) of space is implied; and in the latter case, what is implied is the unconditional necessity of that idea. The paraphrase under consideration allows these two implications to run into each other by a subtle amalgamation of these two modes of talk. It is for that reason open to suspicion.

A more explicit form of the mixing up of those modes of talk can be found in the following passage from the *Prolegomena* :

> . . . if we remove from the empirical intuitions of bodies and their alterations (motion) everything empirical, that is, belonging to sensation, space and time still remain, which are therefore pure intuitions that lie *a priori* at the basis of the empirical. Hence they can never be omitted; . . .[6]

In this passage Kant is saying that space remains over even if objects (bodies) are removed; and he concludes that space 'can never be omitted', which looks like the ascription of an unconditional or absolute necessity to the representation of space. But his other words (which also are part of his conclusion), namely, 'lie *a priori* at the basis of the empirical', supposing that 'a priori' here is not to be taken in the objectionable psychological-temporal sense, suggest that the necessity to be ascribed is not unconditional, but conditional. [This unintelligible position begins no doubt to be less unintelligible as the passage is continued; but since that continuation is in the direction of his formalistic idealism, we cannot in the present connexion profit by following it through.]

8.2 On the Idea of Empty Space, and on the Strength of the Second part of 'Kant's Proof' under Examination

We have seen that Kant's statement, in the second part of his proof in the second space argument, that we can quite well think of empty space, does not by itself throw any light on the necessity of the idea of space. A key of a kind to this statement is provided by the B 5-6 passage in the *Critique*, but what we come to find upon turning that key is far from satisfactory. For the statement then comes to convey the unconditional necessity of the idea of space, which cannot be reconciled with his professed allegiance only to conditional necessitarianism regarding that idea. The detection of this inconsistency is indeed the worst factor in the sum of unwelcome results of the investigation made in the last section. The point of the inquiry now is whether those difficulties may not be avoided and a more or less satisfying net result achieved by following a different technique, namely, a change of perspective or of the mode of analysis. This is not to suggest that Kant's statement under consideration in the second space argument needs to be altogether de-linked in thought from its counterpart in the B 5-6 passage. There is in any case a connexion between the two; but the difficulties have arisen because in neither the one nor the other is there any clear indication to show that the idea of empty space, the idea that space remains over even if its filled contents vanish, is rather conditionally necessary for the possibility of experience of objects than unconditionally necessary in and for itself. Surely we are badly in need of such an indication. So long as the idea of empty space is interpreted as 'the idea of space in and for itself', one cannot avoid reading into it the suggestion of unconditional necessitarianism and therewith the difficulties met with in the last section. The task ahead of us is therefore to try to see, from a different perspective, whether the idea of empty space has not for Kant a *rationále* such as can bring into relief its conditional necessity, that is, its status as a presuppositional factor in objective experience.[7] If this project of our task fails to look promising, this only shows that the task is difficult; and it is our hope that the requisite clarity will emerge when the task nears its completion. We propose to start, however, not by a direct plunge into the projected task, but, with a view to a gradual advance, from a familiar point, namely, consideration of the question whether empty space is really thinkable. This question has an independent topical interest, too.

In the history of philosophy the idea as well as the existence of empty space has been a topic of great controversy. Descartes who identifies extension with body denies both the existence and the conceivability of empty space. He argues that from our ordinary talk of empty space it must not be assumed that empty space or vacuum 'in the philosophical sense of the term, that is, a space in which there is no substance'[8] is really thinkable. Ordinarily we use the term to denote, not a place where there is nothing, but 'only a place in which there is none of those things we presume ought to be there'.[9] Thus when we speak of an empty pitcher, we simply mean a pitcher empty of water, though it is full of air; when we say of a fish-pond that there is nothing in it, we simply mean that it is empty of fish, though it is full of water ; and so on.[10] The question is whether empty space in the philosophical sense defined above is thinkable, and here Descartes's answer is in the negative. An idea of absolutely empty space is for him self-contradictory. He says :

> . . . it is not more contradictory to conceive a mountain without a valley than such a cavity without the extension it contains, or this extension apart from an extended substance, for, . . . of nothing there can be no extension.[11]

Descartes argues that if there were an absolutely empty space between two bodies, they must touch each other, and that

> it is manifestly contradictory for two bodies to be apart, in other words, that there should be a distance between them, and this distance yet be nothing; for all distance is a mode of extension and cannot exist without an extended substance.[12]

Descartes's argument against the conceivability of empty space comes to this : space with nothing in it is a mere extension apart from an extended thing, but there can be no extension of nothing. In other words, the idea of an extension that is an extension of nothing is self-contradictory.

Not much reflection is needed to see the logical error involved in this argument. The error has been clearly exposed by Clarke. His criticism is stated by Alexandre Koyre' as follows : '. . . according to Clarke, the Cartesians . . . are making a logical error in identifying the *vacuum* with *nihil* : space void of matter is undoubtedly space in which there is nothing, but this does not make it itself nothing . . .'.[13] In the same spirit, Voltaire protests : '. . . it is not true that the *Void* is nothing; it is the *locus* of bodies, it is space . . .'.[14]

The Leibniz-Clarke controversy on empty space may here be ignored,[15] because the discussion brings in a reference to God.

A natural objection to the view that we can think of empty space is that we cannot form an image of it. This sort of criticism acquires a great deal of philosophical respectability from the image theory of thinking developed by Hume. Those, however, who admit the conceivability of empty space are unperturbed by such a criticism. Voltaire, for example, retorts : 'I cannot form an image of myself as a thinking being either, and this does not preclude me from being convinced that I think'.[16]

Let us avoid further historical details and turn to Kant next.

The standard objection to Kant's statement under examination –'we can quite well think it [space] as empty of objects' –has been clearly stated by Prichard, who says that the statement is 'simply false', no matter whether 'think' means *believe* or *make a mental picture of.*[17] But this objection is a clear example of an *ignoratio elenchi* ; for by 'think' Kant means neither of the two things supposed by Prichard. Kant has explicitly argued in the Transcendental Analytic that the existence of an empty space cannot be proved. He maintains that an absolutely empty space can neither be 'perceived' by itself nor be 'inferred' from anything in experience. Nor is it legitimate on his view 'to postulate it in order to explain any difference'.[18] All this shows that Kant neither *believes* in an absolutely empty space nor allows for the possibility of a memory-image of it. And the drift of his discussion in the Analytic passage is incompatible with any suggestion that he may admit the psychological possibility of otherwise forming *a mental picture* of an empty space. His clear contention is that no sort of support of an empty space can 'be derived from experience'.[19]

Nevertheless Kant's statement under examination stands in need of interpretation. In this connexion, the following passages quoted from the Transcendental Analytic may profitably be consulted. After studying these passages, we shall be able to return to Kant's second space argument with a new insight.

> [1] . . . what corresponds in empirical intuition to sensation is reality (*realitas phaenomenon*); what corresponds to its absence is negation = 0. Every sensation, however, is capable of diminution, so that it can decrease and gradually vanish. Between reality in the [field of] appearance and negation there is therefore a continuity of many possible intermediate sensations, the difference between any two of which is always smaller than the given sensation and zero or complete negation.[20]

> [2] . . . from empirical consciousness to pure consciousness a graduated transition is possible, the real in the former completely vanishing and a merely formal *a priori* consciousness of the manifold in space and time remaining.[21]

The import of these passages is clear : A sensation (i.e. sensum)[22] that fills a place and a time being represented as having a degree, it follows from the concept of degree that many intermediate sensations are possible between the given sensation and its complete negation. The complete negation of the sensation is thus thinkable. What is true of the sensation in question is true of any other sensation. So the complete negation of sensation as such is thinkable. This thought involves for Kant the idea of empty space and empty time.[23] The reason is this : the degree of a sensation is a quantity peculiar to itself; the more or less of a sensation is not the more or less of the filled space; for a smaller degree of a sensation can fill as much space as the greater degree does.[24] Since the quantity of a sensation is independent of the quantity of space, the complete negation of sensation through gradual diminution of its quantity does not entail the negation of the space (and the time) originally filled by it. Hence the idea of the complete negation of sensation gives rise to the idea of empty space. Kant asserts that empty space is 'pure' space *qua* object of 'pure consciousness'.[25]

Paton has emphasized another aspect of the Kantian doctrine in question. Although this presupposes Kant's theory of categories and of synthesis, it is worth a little reflection, because it makes clear Kant's view as to the role of the idea of empty space and time in the cognition of determinate objects. Paton writes :

> Reality (when schematised) is the given quality which fills time (and space), while negation is the empty time (and space) which is filled. For a determined object we require the combination of the two. I think Kant holds that the object both fills and does not fill time (and space), so far as its qualities have a degree and have not a greater degree; so that there are different degrees in which we combine reality and negation . . . in order to have a determinate object under the category of limitation.[26]

This perhaps needs some explanation. Although in the context under consideration Kant speaks of the category of *reality*, this category, according to Paton, would here 'be better called the category of *limitation*, that is, of *reality* combined with negation.[27] The infinite judgement of the form 'S is non-P' with which Kant connects the category of limitation has for its import that in a judgment we both affirm and deny, and in so doing delimit or determine reality. A determinate object therefore must 'somehow be characterised by a combination of being and not-being'.[28] Now being in space and time lies ultimately in sensation (or the sensum)[29] and its correlate non-being consists in empty space and time.[30] The combination of being with non-being required for a determinate object is accordingly rendered possible, on Kant's view, through the synthesis of sensation with pure (i.e. empty) time and space. The implication of this view is clearly stated by Paton in the words : 'Kant seems to infer from this that when we know an object, time and space are neither completely filled nor completely empty, so that an object must always exhibit in itself a determinate combination of being and non-being'.[31]

It must be added that the foregoing considerations do not yield any empirical 'proof of an empty space or an empty time'. As Kant says :

> If all reality in perception has a degree, between which and negation there exists an infinite gradation of ever smaller degrees, and if every sense must likewise possess some

> particular degree of receptivity of sensations, no perception, and consequently no experience is possible that could prove, either immediately or mediately (no matter how far-ranging the reasoning may be), a complete absence of all reality in [the field of] appearance.[32]

For Kant, then, a complete absence of sensation, and for that matter, an absolutely empty space is thinkable, although this thought is neither a perception nor any empirical image nor otherwise grounded upon empirical evidence. While admitting the thinkability of empty space, he nevertheless holds that it is not necessary to assume its *existence* 'to explain any difference'.[33]

All the same we have to face the question : What is the status of the statement that every sensation has a degree that is capable of gradual diminution ? The importance of the question lies in the fact that the idea of empty space connects with the idea of the complete negation of sensation and that the latter idea in turn connects with our reflection on the truth that every sensation has a degree that could be less and less till it vanished. The question regarding the status of this truth is whether this truth is merely contingent and empirical. The point of still lingering concern is that if it be merely a contingent truth, it fails to be a strong enough base for the idea of empty space to justify an appeal to this idea, if such an appeal be made (as it is made in Kant's second space argument), in proof of the *apriority* of the idea of space.

Now as to Kant's official answer to the question, it is that the truth under consideration is synthetic a priori. For him, the truth is in a special sense to be called an 'anticipation of perception' : 'in a special sense' because it is particularly remarkable that something is knowable a priori about what is precisely the a posteriori element in knowledge, namely, sensation.[34] Now, the difficulty that we have to overcome is that the truth in question rather looks like an empirical generalization. As Bennett puts it :

> This, however, merely says that our sensation *are* like that : it states an empirical fact, and has no place in Kant's apparatus of a priori principles. He provides no arguments for the

> impossibility of a world in which nothing is ever dim or in-between, in which there is only one level of pain, say, and only three degrees of saturation for each colour.[35]

Bennett, however, is not unaware of the kind of reply that is likely to be made on behalf of Kant; for he concedes : 'Perhaps Kant would reply that even in such a world there would be "a continuity of many *possible* intermediate sensations" : such intermediate sensations need not actually occur but they must always be possible'.[36] But still he contends : 'This would make Kant's talk about "forestalling experience" look rather feeble'.[37] To this we may reply that Kant in 'Anticipations of Perception' is not concerned at all with the *extent* to which experience can be forestalled;[38] he is just concerned with the general point that every sensation has a degree and is in principle capable of diminution, and with the implications of the general point. And for our present purpose approval of the award of a non-empirical status to this general point is enough.

Before returning to Kant's second space argument, it remains to emphasize that although in 'Anticipations' he is speaking of sensation, his primary concern is not to examine the nature of sensation as such, but to establish a necessary feature of every *object* of experience.[39] He says : 'In all appearances sensation, and the *real* which corresponds to it in the object (*realitas phaenomenon*), has . . . a degree'.[40] By 'the *real* which corresponds to it in the object' he means the sensed *quality* of the object.[41] His view, as Paton puts it, is 'that when we are aware of anything in space and time, it must have a quality distinct from being spatial and temporal'.[42] This quality, be it colour, or sound, or smell, or whatever, is of course represented a posteriori.[43] There may be disagreement as to the exact nature of the quality, and this is allowed by Kant by calling it 'empirical quality'.[44] But, he says, we can know a priori that the quality, whatever it be, must have a degree.[45] The following comment made by Paton may serve to mitigate further any persisting doubt on this point.

> I find it hard to think my belief in degrees of sensible qualities due merely to generalisation from experience. No doubt I could not have such a belief apart from experience; but just as

> I know, when I see a line, that a shorter line is possible, so I seem to know, when I see [e.g.] a shade of colour, that a paler shade is possible, and that the paler shade could fill the same area and last for the same time. And it seems as reasonable to say that there is an infinity of possible paler shades between any given shade and zero, as it is to say that there is an infinity of possible shorter lines between any given line and zero. We may well hesitate nowadays to assert that we know anything *a priori,* but is there any ground for saying that one of these statements is known *a priori* and the other not ? And can we really maintain that either of these statements rests on precisely the same basis as the statement that forget-me-nots are blue ?[46]

To return to Kant's second space argument : he there says that we can quite well think space as empty of objects, but does not explain his statement. A good explanation is now obtained from his 'Anticipations of Perception'. Any determinate object in space and time must have a quality or qualities distinct from being spatial and temporal, and this quality, or each of these qualities,[47] must have a degree, which in principle allows of gradual diminution till complete vanishing. We can thus think that an object in space could gradually vanish in respect of its sensed qualities without affecting the extent of space filled by it, that is, by its sensed quality or qualities. Moreover, to recall Paton's words, 'the object both fills and does not fill time (and space), so far as its qualities have a degree and have not a greater degree'. This shows that the idea of non-filled space underlies the idea of a determinate object.

The strength of the second part of Kant's assertion in the second space argument under examination lies in the fact, as Lotze suggests,[48] that in order to account for the thinkability of empty space it is not necessary to accept the atomistic or mechanical theory of matter, since empty space is thinkable even according to the dynamical theory of continuously filled space. It must not be supposed, however, that the *Critique* in any part is concerned with offering a defence of the dynamical theory. It is not the job of 'pure philosophy' to do so.[49] For Kant's treatment of this theory, one is required to consult indeed the Second Division of his *Metaphysical Foundations of Natural Science.*[50]

To bring the discussion of this section under some sort of perspective now : We have seen that Kant's statement that space can be thought of as empty of objects is intelligible and defensible. But we may ask, after all that has been said, whether it is right to *conclude* that the idea of empty space is a priori. To an empiricist this idea is either non-existent[51] or at most existent as a complex idea which is free from contradiction. If now we find that there are reasons to believe that this idea is not merely self-consistent, but stronger than that, we may conclude that this idea, being not amenable to the empiricistic analysis, is a priori. At this point we have to inquire whether the discussion of this section goes to show that the idea of empty space is *necessary* in any way : either unconditionally or conditionally. If an affirmative answer is available, it will be clear that the idea of empty space is stronger than a merely self-consistent idea such as the idea of, say, a two-side figure[52] (the latter sort of idea being not *necessary* either unconditionally in itself or conditionally in relation to the possibility, or intelligibility, of objective experience), with the implication that the idea of empty space is a priori. (As for the question whether the discussion of the present section at length enables us to avoid what at the beginning of this section we called the unwelcome results of the last section, we shall consider this too.)

Let us, then, ask, to begin with, whether the idea of empty space is unconditionally necessary. We have seen that the conceivable complete negation, through gradual vanishing, of sensed qualities that fill space does not by itself amount to the negation of space; but from this it does not follow that space itself cannot possibly be negated otherwise. Thus the unconditional necessity of the idea of empty space is not established. This is not, however, any serious matter, because, as we have seen, Kant, when reflective, is not at all interested in this sort of necessity.

The more important question is whether the exposition in this section goes to show in a way the *conditional* necessity of the idea of empty space. On account of the difference in the mode of analysis between the last section and the present, a significant difference in results emerges, to which attention may be called. In the last section we were concerned with the alleged necessity of the idea of space in the light of Kant's contention in the relevant B 5-6 passage of the *Critique* that space remains over if objects occupying it are ideally removed, and we could not make intelligible to ourselves the suggestion that the idea of space as empty of objects might be regarded as conditionally necessary in some sense. There was a sufficient reason for this : the sort of analysis that was there made led us to consider only one possibility and ignore another. We considered one possibility in this way : since the idea of empty space is the idea of space with no objects represented as being in it, this idea cannot be a necessary condition of the possibility (i.e. intelligibility) of the representation of objects; that is to say, since the contemplated situation is *ex hypothesi* one in which no objects are represented, the question how the representation of objects is intelligible in the situation does not arise. We did not then consider another possibility, namely, this : even while we are actually representing objects and so considering filled space (i.e. space filled by the qualities of the represented objects), the idea of empty space serves, as an independent necessary background, to make intelligible the representation of determinate objects or the representation of the filled space (space filled by the qualities of the represented objects). In the present section we have, following Kant, analysed the idea of empty space in such a way that serves to show that this idea is a presuppositional factor in terms of which objective experience as necessarily involving the representation of space-filling qualities of objects is properly intelligible. If, as has been implied before, we are under the necessity of thinking that objects in respect of their sensed qualities cannot fill space except in degrees that are, at least in principle, capable of gradual diminution to complete negation = 0, then, to quote Lotze's defence of Kant's second space argument under examination, 'it is certain that we cannot imagine objects in space without conceiving its empty extension as a background . . . ; although no remembered image of a perception of it is possible . . .'.[53] May it not be said, in fine, then, that the idea of empty (that is, pure) space is a necessary condition[54] of the possibility, in the sense of intelligibility, of objective experience ?

8.3 Concluding Remarks on Kant's Second Space Argument

The tendency of the foregoing examination of Kant's second space argument has been to show that his intended conclusion to the apriority, in the austere sense, of the idea of space is warranted by the considerations implicit in his proof. Objections to the effect that the conclusion is a *non sequitur* are often due to misunderstanding about the word 'a priori' in this argument. If the transcendental-idealist construction is put upon this word, then of course the conclusion is a *non sequitur*; but we have frequently argued before that this construction is out of the question. Another piece of misunderstanding derives, we have seen, from the psychological-temporal interpretation of the same word 'a priori', on which too the conclusion of the argument is a *non sequitur*; and we have amply seen that this interpretation is mistaken. Let us now examine briefly some criticisms of Kant's argument under consideration.

With reference to Kant's statement in this argument that the representation of space necessarily 'underlies all outer intuitions', Baker observes : 'The only conclusion safely reached is the psychological "simultaneity" of space-perceptions with perceptions of objects',[55] and

> Psychological necessity of this kind has no relevant connection to that which is prior to experience, for this part of his proof is given over to a demonstration of what is *in* experience taken perceptually.[56]

This criticism obviously rests on the supposition that 'a priori' means for Kant temporal priority to experience; and this supposition is wrong.

At times no doubt Baker seems to stay away from the psychological-temporal interpretation of 'apriority' and to take it in the austere sense of *independence* of experience; but then he criticizes the Kantian argument in a similar vein :

> The *non sequitur* of the argument is glaring; for, if the necessity of space perceptually and conceptually considered is from the 'adhesion' of space to our perceptual and conceptual objects, how is it possible to advance the conclusion that space is independent of appearances ?[57]

The interpretation underlying this criticism perhaps calls for a little explanation. Kant's statement, 'We can never represent to ourselves the absence of space', is taken by Baker 'to include both percepts and concepts',[58] that is, to assert the necessity of the representation of space for both the perception and the conception (in the loose sense of imagination) of objects; and his criticism of Kant amounts to this : the necessity of space for our percepts and concepts (in the loose sense of images) is scarcely logical and signifies no more than the involvement of the representation of space *in* our perceptions and conceptions (imaginations) of objects, and this being so, the conclusion that the representation of space is independent of experience is unjustified. This criticism, free from misunderstanding about the word 'a priori' as it may be, suffers yet from misunderstanding about the associated Kantian notion of necessity. For the 'cannot' in Kant's statement, although it is not a logical 'cannot', is not for that reason a merely psychological or empirical one. We have already tried to show in the last chapter that the true import of the Kantian statement in question is that although the idea of a scheme of non-spatial experience of objects does not involve a logical contradiction, it is still incapable of being rendered intelligible to ourselves. This view cannot be effectively criticized on the score that it involves a psychological or quasi-psychological appeal to our intuitive or conceptual abilities, because when the problem is that of determining the epistemic status of a certain sort of representation, an appeal to our representational abilities in the sense of what we can or cannot represent is inevitable,[59] and it is a mere terminological issue whether we should describe such an appeal as psychological or quasi-psychological or epistemic. The view in question can only be effectively countered by producing a model of a non-spatial system of objective experience with the claim that it is quite intelligible to us. But that has not been done by Baker. Were Kant's statement merely factual, its negation could at least be made intelligible to ourselves through construction of an appropriate model. Against Baker, then, we must say that Kant has not argued from the fact of the involvement of the representation of space *in* our objective experience to the conclusion that this representation is independent of experience; he has rather argued from the 'real' impossibility of non-spatial objective experience to the conclusion that the representation of space is a presuppositional or 'underlying' factor of objective experience :[60] the 'independence' of space signifies just this status of it as a presuppositional factor.

As Kemp Smith' *Commentary* still remains influential for indeed many good reasons, a word or two in explanation of our disagreement with him on the appraisal of Kant's second space argument will be in order. What, in the context of this argument, we have called the relative or conditional necessity of the representation of space for objective experience is called by him its 'objective necessity';[61] and he contends that Kant's argument really is not, though it may appear to be, one from objective necessity to apriority, since then the argument would be untenable.[62] This contention is quite unexpected of him, because on the interpretation that he has himself preferred to put on this argument, the argument is *for him* still untenable. Anyway, we should like to consider one of the reasons why he thinks the Kantian argument, regarded as being one that moves from *objective* necessity to apriority, is untenable. The point is clearly stated by him in the case of Kant's second argument on time and is intended to be applicable *mutatis mutandis* to the latter's second argument on space. He writes :

> It is indeed possible that Kant himself regarded this objective necessity of time as contributing to the proof of its apriority. But no such argument can be accepted. Time may be necessary to appearances, *once appearances are granted.* This does not, however, prove that it must therefore precede them *a priori.*[63]

We may only substitute 'space' for 'time' to achieve what we want. Now this criticism is doubtless unanswerable on the temporal interpretation of apriority; for there is of course no transition from *the necessity for appearances* to the *temporal priority to those appearances.* But since the temporal interpretation of apriority is wrong, the criticism is beside the point. We think nevertheless that, even if apriority is understood in the non-temporal sense of independence of experience, Kemp Smith's criticism implicitly raises a question that needs to be considered.

That question is : What is the connexion between objective necessity and apriority ? Unless the connexion is clear, Kant's transition from the contention that space is necessary for appearances to the conclusion that it is a priori – that is, his transition fro the contention that the representation of space is necessary for the experience of objects to the conclusion that this representation is a priori (independent of experience) –remains unexplained.

The following argument presented by H. E. Allison may relevantly be considered here (by way of a preliminary).

> The connection between being a condition of experience and being a priori is analytic for Kant, as being such a condition is precisely what is meant by saying that a 'concept', e.g., space or time, is a priori. While propositions are said to be a priori in so far as they are necessarily true, concepts or representations have this status in so far as they provide necessary conditions, and that which they necessarily condition is human experience. But if something is a condition of experience, it is absurd to claim that it is derived from experience. For to claim that it is so derived would be to suppose that it is possible to have experience before and apart from one of its conditions, and this is obviously contradictory. Thus, in so far as a representation is shown to be a condition of experience, it is *eo ipso* shown not to have its origin in experience,. . .[64]

Allison's exposition, however, invites difficulties. First, there are concepts claiming to be a priori (e.g. the concept of a spirit) which do not yield, according to Kant, a condition of the possibility of experience.[65] (Whether their *elements* are related to such a condition[66] is another question.) So being a condition of experience is not what is meant by Kant's saying that a concept is a priori. By saying that a concept is a priori he *means* simply that it is independent of (or, not derived from) experience.[67] Secondly, sensation is reckoned by him (Kant) as a 'representation'[68] and as being among the 'conditions of experience',[69] and yet is not regarded by him as an a priori representation.[70] So Paton writes : '. . . we can no more have experience without sensation than we can have experience without space and time. What is the special necessity which belongs to space and time, and not to sensation ?[71]

We think that the difficulties can be avoided by expressing Kant's view thus : If a concept or representation yields a necessary condition of experience[72] in the sense of a condition of the objectivity thereof, it is an a priori concept or representation. (The converse may not be true.) He says : 'Concepts[73] which yield the objective ground of the possibility of experience are for this very reason necessary'.[74] [To this we may add : 'And if they are thus recognized as necessary, they are a priori'.] Now to be an objective ground of the possibility of experience is to be a condition of the possibility of experience of *objects* in the strict sense. Kant says : 'Everything, every representation even, in so far as we are conscious of it, may be entitled object'.[75] But he quickly points out that this is not an object in the strict sense.[76] A representation, which is an object of consciousness, really is a state in the mind. An object in the strict sense must be distinguished from a mental state in this or that subject, and must be common to all.[77] There is a link between objectivity and intersubjectivity (or universality).[78] To come now to sensation, it is, on Kant's view, a condition of experience only as yielding the indeterminate matter for it, but not as having any part to play in conditioning the objectivity thereof. Sensa yielded in sensation are, in the ultimate analysis, only changes in the subject,[79] and they do not feature out in objective experience except in so far as they are viewed as presenting the reals in space and time. The representations of space and time and the categorical concepts are *objective conditions* of experience[80] in a way in which sensation is not. Herein lies the special necessity of the former that gives them a dignity not belonging to the latter. As for the representation of space, its role in objective experience has been highlighted in our foregoing exposition. Its necessity for experience, which Kemp Smith calls its 'objective necessity', being such, we can well understand why Kant regards it as a priori, that is, as 'independent of experience and even of all impressions of the senses'.[81]

Of the two parts of Kant's view in the Metaphysical Exposition of the Concept of Space, namely, that the representation of space is a priori in the austere sense, and that it is non-discursive or intuitive, the first part has kept us engaged so far. With our turn to his third space argument (in the second edition of the *Critique*) in the next chapter, the second part of his view will begin to be the chief point of concern.

NOTES :

1. See above, p. 222.
2. For Kant, although a body is not a mere bundle of sense qualities, there can be no body without sense qualities.
3. See above, p. 226.
4. B 46.
5. In the Transcendental Aesthetic *passim.*
6. *Prolegomena to Any Future Metaphysics,* § 10, the Carus translation revised with an introduction by L. W. Beck, Bobbs–Merrill, 1976, p. 31.
7. The notions of necessary condition and presupposition are not distinguished in this argument.
8. Rene' Descartes, 'The Principles of Philosophy', pt. II, § xvi, in *A Discourse on Method, etc.,* trans. John Veitch, 'Everyman's Library, No. 570,' London, 1949, p. 207.
9. *Ibid.,* pt. II, § xvii, (p. 207).
10. *Ibidem.*
11. *Ibid.,* pt. II, § xviii, (p. 208).
12. *Ibidem.*
13. A. Koyre', *Newtonian Studies,* Chicago, 1968, p. 165.
14. Cited by Koyre', *op. cit.,* p. 168.
15. For a brief report of this controversy, see Koyre', *op. cit.,* pp. 166-167.
16. Cited by Koyre', *op. cit.,* p. 168.
17. Prichard, *Kant's Theory of Knowledge,* 1909, pp. 42-43.
18. *Critique,* A 172 = B 214.
19. *Ibidem.*
20. A 168 = B 209-210.
21. B 208.
22. 'Sensation' here means not sensing, but the sensum; see Paton, *Kant's Metaphysic of Experience,* Vol. II, pp. 137f.
23. Paton, *op. cit.,* p. 140 and n. 1.
24. Cf. *Critique,* A 143 = B 182-3, B 216; see also Paton, *op. cit.,* p. 140 and n. 6.
25. S. Alexander (*Space, Time, and Deity,* vol. I., Humanities Press, New

York, 1950, p. 39. n. 1) admits that 'pure Space' is conceivable by some kind of apprehension'.

26. Paton, *op. cit.,* pp. 148-149.
27. *Ibid.,* p. 48, and see *Critique,* B 111.
28. Paton, *op. cit.,* p. 49.
29. For explanation, see *Critique,* A 373-374.
30. Paton, *op. cit.,* p. 49.
31. *Ibid.,* p. 50. n. 1.
32. *Critique,* A 172 = B 214.
33. Cf. Paton, *op. cit.,* pp. 154f.
34. *Critique,* B 208-9.
35. J. Bennett, *Kant's Analytic,* 1966, p. 172; cf. also Walker, *Kant,* 1978, p. 95.
36. Bennett, *loc. cit.*
37. *Ibidem.*
38. Cf. Paton, *op. cit.,* p. 146.
39. Cf. *ibid.,* pp. 135, 120.
40. *Critique,* A 166.
41. *Critique,* A 176 = B 218, and Paton, *op. cit.,* pp. 135 n. 3, 137f.

    Here a question arises : How can sense qualities, which are for Kant subjective, be yet qualities in objects ? For a discussion of the nature of Kant's commitment to the subjectivity thesis as to sense qualities, see Ingrid Stadler, 'Perception and Perfection in Kant's Aesthetics', in R.P. Wolff, ed., *Kant,* 1968, pp. 339-383. Ernst Cassirer's comments on the 'subjectivity of the sensuous qualities' (in his *Substance and Function* and *Einstein's Theory of Relativity,* trans. W. C. Swabey and M. C. Swabey, Dover edition, 1953, pp. 274f.) seem to have a Kantian flavour and may well be consulted.
42. Paton, *op. cit.,* p. 140.
43. Cf. A 175 = B 217, A 714-15 = B 742-43.
44. A 175 = B 217.
45. A 176 = B 218.
46. Paton, *op. cit.,* p. 145.
47. But cf. *ibid.,* p. 144 n. 2.
48. Hermann Lotze, *Metaphysics,* English trans. edited by Bernard Bosanquet, Oxford, 1884, bk. II, chap. 1, pp. 179-180.

49. Cf. Paton, *op. cit.,* p. 155.
50. For a critical study of Kant's treatment of the theory in question, see G. G. Brittan, Jr., *Kant's Theory of Science,* 1978, pp. 149ff.
51. Hume, for example, denies that we have, or can have, the idea of empty space. As he says : '. . . we can form no idea of a vacuum, or space, where there is nothing visible or tangible'. See his *A Treatise of Human Nature,* ed. L. A. Selby-Bigge, Oxford, 1967, bk. I, pt. ii, sect. v, p. 53. For an examination of Hume's view, see C. D. Broad, 'Hume's Doctrine of Space', *Proceedings of the British Academy 47* (1961), pp. 171ff.
52. *Critique,* A 220-221 = B 268.
53. Lotze, *op. cit.,* p. 180.
54. See note 7 to this Chapter.
55. J. T. Baker, 'Henry More and Kant' : A Note to the Second Argument on Space in the Transcendental Aesthetic', *The Philosophical Review* 46 (1937), p. 302.
56. *Ibid.,* p. 301.
57. *Ibid.,* p. 302.
58. *Ibidem.*
59. Cf. above, p. 256.
60. We may observe once more that no distinction between a necessary condition and a presupposition is made in Kant's present argument. The important point is that the represen- tation of space is for Kant a constitutive necessary condition of objective experience, both a determining condition of and an objective ingredient in it.
61. Kemp Smith, *Commentary,* 1918, p. 104.
62. *Ibid.,* p. 124 (third para, first sentence).
63. *Ibid.,* p. 124 (first para).
64. H. E. Allison, *The Kant-Eberhard Controversy,* 1973, p. 79.
65. Cf. *Critique,* A 96. Allison, however, might argue here in the way that Paton does in note 3 to p. 197 of his *Kant's Metaphysic of Experience,* vol. I., ix § 5. But even Paton's note referred to here raises questions that cannot be settled without making some distinctions.
66. Cf. *Critique,* A 96.
67. See A 86-87, where Kant says of 'pure *a priori* concepts' that they are 'independent of experience, . . . in a position to show a certificate of

birth quite other than that of descent from experiences'. Cf. again B 166-167, where Kant says of a priori concepts that experience does not make them possible, that they are 'independent of experience', that 'the ascription to them of an empirical origin would be a sort of *generatio aequivoca'*.

68. A 320 = B 376.
69. B 266.
70. Cf. A 42 = B 60, A 167 = B 209.
71. *Kant's Metaphysic of Experience,* vol. I, p. 153.
72. I.e. experience in general; cf. Kant's phrase 'conditions of experience in general' at B 271.
73. The word 'concepts' here covers the representations of space and time as well as the categories; cf. A 92-93 = B 124-125.
74. A 94 = B 126.
75. B 234f.
76. Cf. B 235.
77. Cf. B 142 (end), and also B 44-45.
78. Cf. *Prolegomena,* §§ 18-19.
79. *Critique,* B 45.
80. The phrase 'objective conditions of experience' is Kant's own; see B 271.
81. This phrase as giving the meaning of 'a priori' occurs at B 2.

CHAPTER NINE

KANT'S THIRD SPACE ARGUMENT

9.1 Statement of the Argument and Preliminary Observations

Kant's third space argument (in the second edition[1]) runs :

> Der Raum ist kein discursiver oder, wie man sagt, allgemeiner Begriff von Verhältnissen der Dinge überhaupt, sondern eine reine Anschauung. Denn erstlich kann man sich nur einen einigen Raum vorstellen, und wenn man von vielen Räumen redet, so versteht man darunter nur Theile eines und desselben alleinigen Raumes. Diese Theile können auch nicht vor dem einigen allbefassenden Raume gleichsam als dessen Bestandtheile (daraus seine Zusammenseezung möglich sei), vorhergehen, sondern nur *in ihm* gedacht werden. Er ist wesentlich einig, das Mannigfaltige in ihm, mithin auch der allgemeine Begriff von Räumen überhaupt, beruht lediglich auf Einschränkungen. Hieraus folgt, dass in Ansehung seiner eine Anschauung a priori (die nicht empirisch ist), allen Begriffen von demselben zum Grunde liegt. [*Kritik,* B 39.]

This, in Kemp Smith's translation, is rendered as follows :

Space is not a discursive or, as we say, general concept of relations of things in general, but a pure intuition. For, in the first place, we can represent to ourselves only one space; and if we speak of diverse spaces, we mean thereby only parts of one and the same unique space. Secondly, these parts cannot precede the one all-embracing space, as being, as it were, constituents out of which it can be composed; on the contrary, they can be thought only as *in* it. Space is essentially one; the manifold in it, and therefore the general concept of spaces, depends solely on [the introduction of] limitations. Hence it

> follows that an *a priori,* and not an empirical, intuition underlies all concepts of space. [*Critique*, (A 24-25 = B 39)]

The thesis of this argument, as stated in its first sentence, may be restated[2] more precisely by saying that the original representation (idea) of space is not a discursive,[3] or general, concept,[4] but a pure intuition.[5] Two comments will be in order here. First, it is better to say, as Kant himself often does, that *the representation (idea) of space* is an intuition than that *space* is an intuition. For intuition as a mode of representation is to be distinguished from the object of such representation (i.e. intuitum).[6] Space is an intuition only in the sense of an intuitum, that is, secondarily in the sense that the idea of it is an[7] intuition. Secondly, by saying that space (i.e. the idea of space) 'is not . . . a general concept', Kant does not deny that we have a 'general concept of spaces' : he clearly admits such a general concept in the fourth sentence of this argument. What he really means is, as will be clear by and by, that the general concept of spaces is ultimately derivative upon the intuition of space, so that the *original (ursprüngliche)* idea of space is not a general concept, but an intuition.[8] (This interpretation is disputed by Garnett, whose view will of course be examined later on.)

9.2 Analysis of This Argument

The first part of Kant's present argument cites the *oneness* of space as a ground for the thesis. The second part can be taken either as a further clarification of that ground[9] or as also containing an independent ground for the thesis. Some (e.g. Vaihinger and Kemp Smith) take the second part in the latter way, and their exposition will be considered later.[10] At first it will be well to consider the argument as a whole.

It has to be ascertained why Kant insists that space 'is essentially one'. It is very often held that Kant insists on this point with a view to making use of what may be called the uniqueness criterion of intuitivity.[11] Unlike a general concept, which applies, or is applicable, to any of an indefinite number of individuals through certain common features or marks, an intuition is a mode of awareness that relates immediately to a single individual.[12] That is why, it is held, Kant insists on the essential oneness or uniqueness of space as a ground for the intuitivity of the idea of it. We, however, think, mainly on the basis of Kant's corresponding argument in the *Inaugural Dissertation,*[13] that in the present argument Kant is primarily making use of the singularity criterion of intuitivity,[14] where singularity is to be understood more in contrast with generality than with plurality. This is of course ultimately a matter of emphasis; nevertheless it is an emphasis required for a correct appreciation of the perspective of Kant's argument in question.

Kant himself says towards the end of the present argument that space is essentially one in the sense that the different particular spaces, and therewith the general concept of spaces, arise through limitation of the one space.[15] This means that the different particular spaces are not strictly independent factors,[16] but can only be represented as limited portions, or secondary parts,[17] of the one whole space. And this means that the representations of the particular spaces are not prior to, but rather presuppose, the representation of the one whole space. As to the general concept of spaces, it is, as Kant leaves this to be understood by us, derived from the representations of the particular spaces, which are its instances;[18] and since, as is said above, the representations of the particular spaces presuppose the representation of the one space, the general concept of spaces too ultimately presupposes that representation.[19] As the representation of the whole space in this way 'underlies' the very possibility of the general concept of spaces, the whole space is not itself represented discursively through the general concept of spaces, but is rather represented non-discursively (i.e. immediately) as singular.[20] As an immediate singular representation,[21] the representation of it is intuitive.

Using modern terminology, it may be said that in this argument Kant is maintaining that space is not an extensional whole (that is, a class)[22] but an individual, and that the original representation of it is in the nature of an immediate representation of an individual. This seems to be the dominant significance of the argument. Some explanation of this is obviously called for; and for this purpose it will be well to put the argument into its historico-philosophical perspective.

9.2.1 The historico-philosophical perspective of the argument

The main perspective is provided by para 47 of Leibniz's fifth paper in the Controversy between Leibniz and Clarke.[23] There he gives a particular account of the idea of space. He first explains how we arrive at the idea of 'the same place' and hence the idea of different places.[24] Thereafter he observes that *space* is the sum-total of *places* : '. . . that which comprehends all those places is called *space*'; '. . . *space* is that which results from places taken together'.[25] This means that we reach the idea of space by some sort of mental addition of places to one another. This view may be paraphrased in modern terminology as follows : the idea of space is logically dependent upon that of places, i.e. particular spaces, being the idea of an extensional whole, or class, of spaces arrived at on the basis of the general concept of spaces (much as the idea of the extensional whole, or class, of men is arrived at on the basis of the general concept of men, i.e. manness.)

Clearly, this sort of view adopted by Leibniz can be rejected if the following points are made :

(a) Space is not an extensional whole, or class, of spaces such that the particular spaces are members contained under it. It is rather a non-extensional, individual, whole such that the particular spaces are parts contained in it.

(b) The particular spaces are not prior to space. That is, the representations of the particular spaces rather presuppose the representation of the one whole space.

(c) The general concept of spaces too is not prior to the idea of the whole space.

It takes but a moment's reflection to see that all these three points are made in Kant's third space argument :

(i) The second sentence of the argument says that the diverse spaces are 'parts' of the one space. The end of the third sentence says that the spaces are represented as being '*in* it' (i.e. *in* the one whole space).

(ii) The third sentence asserts the priority of the whole space over the particular spaces. The fourth sentence says that spaces arise through limitation of the one whole space. This implies that the representations of the particular, or limited, spaces presuppose the representation of the one unlimited space.

(iii) The fourth sentence says also that the general concept of spaces presupposes the representation of the one space.[26]

According to Kant, then, the original representation of space is that of the whole space.[27] This representation is an intuition, because it is an immediate representation of an individual. And it is an immediate representation of an individual, because, for one thing, the representation of the whole space is not that of a class, but of an individual, and, for another thing, the representation in question is not discursively reached through the general concept of spaces. All this will be clear in the sequel.

An additional point made by Kant is that the representation of the whole space, which is an intuition, is an *a priori* intuition. Its apriority connects presumably with its being the *underlying*, or presuppositional, factor in the representations of spaces, that is, of places.

Against Kant's argument under consideration, a serious objection has been urged by Prichard. This objection deserves to be examined first and in some detail.

9.3 Examination of Prichard's Objection that the Whole Space is Not an Object of Intuition and that the Idea of It is Reached Rather Conceptually

Prichard develops his objection in the following way.

The test of perception (i.e. intuition)[28] for Kant is that it relates to an individual, which 'is unique' in the sense that 'there is only one of it',[29] whereas conception,[30] being the awareness of a universal, relates to 'a plurality of instances'.[31] Since 'space, in the sense of the one all-embracing space, i.e. the totality of individual spaces'[32] is one, it must be, according to Kant, something perceived and not conceived. But really 'we do not perceive space as a whole'.[33] Individual spaces are no doubt perceived, and

> it is reflection on the general nature of space, the apprehension of which is involved in our apprehension of individual spaces

> or rather of bodies in space, which gives rise to the apprehension of the totality of spaces, the apprehension being ar act, not of perception, but of thought or conception.[34]

> We should, then,

> distinguish (a) individual spaces, which we perceive; (b) the nature of space in general, of which we become aware by reflecting upon the character of perceived individual spaces, and which we conceive; (c) the totality of individual spaces, the thought of which we reach by considering the nature of space in general.[35]

These distinctions are quite general, and apply to all characteristics of objects.

> Thus, with respect to colour it is possible to distinguish (a) individual colours which we perceive; (b) colouredness in general, which we conceive by reflecting on the common character exhibited by individual colours and which involves various kinds or species of colouredness; (c) the totality of individual colours, the thought of which is reached by considering the nature of colouredness in general.[36]

Thus the distinction between universal and individual, and therefore also that between conception and perception, can be drawn 'with respect to any characteristic of objects', no less with respect to colour than with respect to space.[37] A possible objection is that space is essentially one, whereas colours are many. But the essential unity of space only means that all individual bodies in space are spatially related to one another. Correspondingly in the case of colour also, we find that 'all individual coloured objects are related by way of colour, e.g. as brighter and duller'.[38]

To Prichard's objection stated above the following reply may be made from the point of view of Kant.

The parallel drawn between individual colours and individual spaces is wrong. The perceived individual colours are strictly independent factors, which the individual spaces are not. The perception of an individual colour does not presuppose the awareness of the totality of colours, but the 'perception' (i.e. intuition) of an individual space presupposes the awareness of the one whole space. This statement needs a defence, so far as its latter part is concerned. In respect of the former part, it requires no defence so long as we are concerned with Prichard, even though here too it is possible to raise certain complications (e.g. from the point of view of Bradley's dialectic of relation and quality).

The defence of the statement in its latter part may be attempted as follows : Kant's view need not be interpreted as meaning that the awareness of the whole space is the psychological prius of the apprehensions of individual spaces. He says that the multiplicity in space depends solely upon limitations. This statement at the first glance suggests that we are, to begin with, aware of space as an all-pervasive spread and then come to think of the individual spaces as what are carved out of it. But this suggestion is liable to be misleading.[39] What Kant really means is that we intuit the individual spaces as the limited parts of a single whole wherein they necessarily fall. It might be objected that although we *know* the individual spaces *as* limited, we do not *intuit* them as such. The reply to this is that our admitted knowledge of the individual spaces as limited has an intuitive foundation : the limited character of the spaces is not imposed on them by our thinking, but is rather discovered in them. Now to intuit them thus, that is, as limited, is not possible except on the basis of some awareness of an unlimited single whole. This awareness of the unlimited single whole being presupposed in the apprehensions of the limited spaces is as much immediate[40] as are the latter, and is for that reason to be regarded as equally intuitive.[41] As Paton puts it : 'The intuition of spaces as necessarily limited presupposes a pure intuition of one all-embracing space'.[42]

It may be argued that if an awareness of the whole space is logically presupposed[43] in our intuitions of the individual spaces, we should rather put the matter by saying that the whole space is 'conceptually apprehended only as the presupposition of our limited intuitions'.[44]

In replying to this objection, it should first be pointed out that it is not strictly the whole space but an awareness of the whole space that is the logical presupposition of our limited intuitions, i.e. intuitions of limited spaces; and the awareness of the whole space is the logical presupposition of the limited intuitions in the sense explained below. The explanation of this sense may be prefaced by drawing the distinction between our awareness of the whole space and our knowledge that this awareness is presupposed in our limited intuitions. Now Kant's actual position is that our awareness of the whole space is immediate and intuitive, although our knowledge that this awareness is presupposed in our limited intuitions is discursive or based on reflective analysis. When it is said that the awareness of the whole space is the logical prius of our intuitions of limited spaces, what is meant is that the awareness of the whole space is really involved in the intuitions of the limited spaces, although we may not be explicitly aware of this fact. (To cast doubt on this statement is to embrace the wrong assumption that every consciousness is *explicitly* self-conscious.)[45] Now what logical, or reflective, analysis does, is to enable us to be aware of the fact that the awareness of the whole space is really involved in the intuitions of limited spaces. Here the awareness that comes from reflection is without question discursive, but this awareness is not the awareness of the whole space, but an awareness of the second order, being some kind of philosophical knowledge (or, reflective theory, so to say,) about the nature of our awareness of the whole space.[46]

The crux of Prichard's contention is that the whole space 'is not object of perception'; this is his particular reason for a summary dismissal of Kant's argument in the end.[47] But there is no use denying that the whole space is 'perceived' if individual spaces are admitted to be perceived. It is essential to Prichard's objection that individual spaces are 'perceived'. He refers to them as 'individual spaces, which we perceive', and proceeds to develop his objection on this basis; but that these spaces are perceived he is unable to state without qualification. He has stated it thus : 'We perceive individual spaces, or rather, individual bodies occupying individual spaces'.[48] What this qualification is meant to signify is not quite clear. Perhaps Prichard means that individual spaces are perceived along with the individual bodies occupying them. Here again his emphasis may not be on individual *bodies*; for although individual colours are not bodies, he might as well say that in (e.g.) visual perception individual spaces are perceived along with the individual colours occupying (i.e. filling) them. It is Prichard's explicit contention that we perceive individual spaces as we perceive individual colours. (We may recall here his parallel expressions 'individual spaces, which we perceive' and 'individual colours which we perceive'.) Now, that an individual colour or colours are perceived is a view that finds an easy acceptance; for, setting aside Kant's definition of 'objects of perception', we ordinarily mean thereby 'objects (or items) so occupying (or filling) space in relation to the percipient that the latter has sensuous consciousness of them'.[49] But if one were to work with this notion of 'objects of perception', one would have simply to deny that individual spaces were perceived at all. For these spaces, unlike individual colours, could be neither supposed to occupy (or fill) space[50] nor be supposed to be sensuously apprehended[51] in the sense of being apprehended through some sense-organ.[52]

In the circumstances, one might seek to retain the view that individual spaces are perceived by depriving the above definition of 'objects of perception' of its clarity and imparting to it a certain vagueness somewhat as follows : 'objects which are so existent in relation to the percipient that he actually beholds them'. Both the terms 'existent' and 'actually behold' in this definition are vague, and yet it is not difficult to show that such a definition has actually been used by many philosophers. Thus Taylor, who regards individual spaces as 'perceptual'[53] or 'presentation-spaces',[54] has clearly proceeded upon some such definition as this; indeed, the very term 'actually behold' is borrowed from him.[55] And that such a requirement as the above for an object being considered an intuitum, or an object of perception, is implicitly laid down by Prichard also is suggested by a footnote in his book. There he admits that 'our distinct apprehension of an individual space is always bound up with an indistinct apprehension of the spaces immediately surrounding', but points out that 'our indistinct apprehension cannot be supposed to be of the whole of surrounding space'.[56] Here his reason for the admission that an individual space is intuited together with the denial that the whole space is intuited seems to be that, unlike the whole space, an individual space is so existent in relation to the percipient that he actually beholds it. But, now, this notion of an object of perception is, as already pointed out, quite vague; and it has been noticed that if its vagueness were removed, then, although an individual colour could be said to be 'perceived', an individual space could not be so said. Prichard speaks of individual spaces as 'perceived', but exactly how they are perceived needs an elucidation, which he has not provided.

Prichard has, however, suggested, as already noted, that individual spaces are perceived along with their occupants. But this suggestion can be made workable only through the following interpretation of it. We intuit neither an individual colour itself nor an individual space by itself. What we intuit can be rather described as, say, 'some coloured patch here'. 'This colour' and 'this space' (or 'here') are subsequent distinctions drawn on the basis of the concrete presentation. They are not, however, *made* by the distinction, but are only reflectively cognized as what were already there. We can say, although to say this is to make a reflective judgment, that the awareness of this colour and that of this space are originally both of them intuitive, one of them involving the other. This being so, an individual colour and the individual space occupied (filled) by it are not such that we are psychologically aware of them as presented distinctly from each other. If we regard both of them as objects of perception (i.e. intuition), it is because our reflection shows that the representations of both of them were originally immediate (i.e. conceptually unmediated). In other words, the statement that they are objects of perception is only a reflective judgement about the nature of our original representation of them, and not a report descriptive or indicative of the actual manner of their being presented or given to our consciousness.

Now to come to the point : if an individual space can be said to be perceived on the ground that the awareness of it is immediately involved in the admittedly intuitive awareness of, e.g. an individual colour, it has to be maintained that being immediately involved in some acknowledged perception or intuition is sufficient to entitle any awareness to be regarded as perceptual or intuitive. But then the awareness of the one whole space is no less intuitive than that of an individual space. For the awareness of the one whole space also is immediately involved in acknowledged intuitions, namely, in what Prichard acknowledges to be the intuitions of individual spaces. Our knowledge of the limited character of individual spaces must have, as has already been pointed out, an intuitive foundation, and, therefore, it can be said – although this saying is a reflective judgement – that we intuit individual spaces as limited; and such intuitions of limited spaces presuppose an immediate awareness of the unlimited whole space. We say 'immediate awareness of the unlimited whole space' because this awareness is not conceptually mediated, that is, not mediated by the general concept of spaces, as is clarified below.

Prichard has said that the apprehension of the totality of spaces (i.e. of the one whole space) is an act of conception, and not of perception, inasmuch as it is reached by considering the nature of space in general, of which in turn we become aware by reflection on the character of the perceived individual spaces. This view is untenable. It is true that the awareness of the totality of (e.g.) colours is reached by considering the nature of colouredness in general,[57] i.e. through the general concept of colouredness. The totality of colours is represented through conception of the general nature of colouredness. To be more precise, the idea of the totality of colours is obtained by coupling with the general concept of colour (or colouredness) the concept of totality or all. Now it is permissible to say this because the general concept of colour (or colouredness) is not itself derived by presupposing the awareness of the totality of colours : it is derived ultimately from perceptions of individual colours, and these perceptions in their turn do not presuppose the awareness of the totality of colours. The case of space, however, is rather different. Prichard's statement that the awareness of the totality of spaces is reached conceptually by considering the nature of space in general can be paraphrased by saying that the awareness of the one whole space is reached through the general concept of spatiality[58] (coupled, of course, with the general concept of wholeness or totality, although Prichard has failed to point this out). This view is surely untenable (as involving circularity), because the general concept of spatiality presupposes the awareness of the one whole space. Kant has explicitly argued that the many spaces, and *'therefore the general concept of spaces'*, depend solely on the limitation of the one whole space. This means, as has been pointed out before,[59] that the general concept of spaces (or spatiality) is derived from our intuitions of individual spaces, and that since such intuitions, as limited intuitions, presuppose the representation of the one unlimited space, the general concept of spatiality also presupposes the latter representation. The latter representation is thus conceptually unmediated. So Kant says : '... an *a priori* ... intuition [of the one whole space] underlies all concepts of space'. [What has prevented Prichard from accepting this argument is his attribution to Kant of the obviously untenable view that a perceptual awareness of the one unlimited space is temporally and psychologically prior to the intuitions of spaces.[60] Kant's actual view is, to repeat, that the intuition of the one unlimited space is logically presupposed in the intuitions of limited spaces and so in the formation of the general concept of spaces, whether or not we are explicitly aware of this fact.]

Summarizing : Our awareness of the one whole space must somehow be an intuition; for it cannot be reached through *conception* of the nature of space in general. The intuition of the one whole space is the ultimate presupposition of even the general concept of spatiality.

9.4 The General Concept of Spaces

It has been pointed out that, according to Kant' 'the general concept of spaces', by which he has been taken to mean the concept of spatiality, presupposes the pure intuition of the one whole space. The problem is whether it is fair to suppose Kant to have admitted a general concept of spatiality at all. The problem arises on account of Garnett's denial that Kant has anywhere admitted a general concept of spatiality. The reply that has already been made to Prichard by saying that the general concept of spatiality itself presupposes for Kant the idea of the one space is not, however, in the least affected by the problem in question; for, unlike Garnett, Prichard has not complained of the impropriety of supposing that Kant admits a general concept of spatiality.

Although Kant says that space is not a general concept, but a pure intuition, he does not deny that there is a general concept of spatiality, but only maintains the primacy of the intuition of space over this general concept. This seems to be a quite natural interpretation of his argument in question; and the interpretation has been accepted by a great many eminent scholars.[61] The significance of the relevant Kantian statement that the manifold spaces, and therefore the general concept of spaces, rest solely on the limitation of the one space could not be better brought out than in the following words of Paton's :

> His [Kant's] argument seems to be (1) that one common mark of the many different spaces is that they are necessarily limited; and (2) that consequently our concept of spatiality is derived from our immediate intuition of spaces as necessarily limited. The intuition of spaces as necessarily limited presupposes a pure intuition of one all-embracing space. Hence our concept of spatiality presupposes a pure intuition of one all-embracing space.[62]

Garnett, however, contends that Paton's interpretation, 'interesting' as it is, is not germane to Kant's argument. Garnett's arguments against what he calls Paton's 'unhappy distinction between space and spatiality'[63] call for an examination.

9.4.1 Comments on Garnett's criticism of Paton

Garnett argues that Kant could not be taken to mean 'that space is both a conception (*Begriff*) and an intuition (*Anschauung*)' in view of the latter's explicit utterance at A 320 = B 377 of the *Critique* 'that knowledge is either an intuition or a conception (*intuitus vel conceptus*)'.[64] This objection is due to a misunderstanding. Paton does not mean that space for Kant 'is both a conception and an intuition'. What he means is simply that we have for Kant primarily an intuition of space (i.e. the one whole space), also intuitions of spaces (i.e. individual spaces), and secondarily a general concept of spaces. Kant himself clearly mentions three things in his third space argument : 'space' (or 'the one all-embracing space'), 'the manifold in it' (or 'diverse spaces', i.e. individual spaces), and 'the general concept of spaces'. What Paton has done is to substitute the expression 'our concept of spatiality' for the Kantian expression 'the general concept of spaces'. The general concept of spatiality, or of spaces, is derived from the intuitions of individual spaces and has for its instances such spaces. Individual spaces are primarily represented by intuition, and not by the general concept of spaces of which they are the instances; for this general concept is itself derivative upon the intuitions of the individual spaces. Thus, in the light of Paton's interpretation, the following are the implications of Kant's argument in question :

(1) Space is not a concept. That is, the one whole space is not indirectly represented through the general concept of spaces.

(2) Space is an intuition. That is, the one whole space is represented by intuition. (Were it not intuited, the individual spaces *qua* limited could not be intuited.)

(3) Spaces are both intuitions and concepts. That is, the individual spaces are primarily apprehended by intuition, and are secondarily instances of the general concept of spaces, which is derived from the intuitions of them.

To credit Kant, then, with the admission of the general concept of spatiality or of spaces is not to make him surrender his view that the one space is an intuition.

Garnett has argued further that 'Kant nowhere denied that we have a conception of spatiality, but he also nowhere affirmed it, because he did not mention spatiality at all.'[65] It is indeed true that Kant has nowhere mentioned 'the concept of spatiality'. But Paton is very well aware of this. What Garnett has overlooked is that Paton has elsewhere given a reason for Kant's not using that expression and for his own substitution of 'the concept of spatiality' for Kant's 'the concept of spaces in general' :

> . . . Kant habitually uses concrete rather than abstract words for the purpose of indicating particular concepts. Thus he speaks, not of the concept of spatiality (as I have done for the sake of clearness), but of the concept of 'spaces in general'. Similarly he speaks of the concept of 'body' or the concept of 'the body'.[66]

A really serious argument offered by Garnett is this :

Particular spaces *qua* particulars, far from revealing any such

> notions as spatiality or limitedness, indicate a tampering by the mind with the given space, and tell us nothing about the latter . . . . Far from indicating that there is a general conception of spatiality, the limited nature of spaces shows that they are not features of space at all, for their limitedness contradicts its limitlessness.[67]

Garnett is here saying that for Kant particular, or individual, spaces are not intuited, but are rather read by the mind into the given space and so are indicative of 'a tampering by the mind with the given space'. The implication of this contention is clear enough. Upon Paton's interpretation the general concept of spatiality is derived from the intuitions of individual spaces; and so this interpretation assumes that for Kant the individual spaces are intuited. Garnett is maintaining that this assumption is false, and that, therefore, Paton's distinction between space and spatiality is at bottom un-Kantian.

This contention that individual spaces are for Kant not intuited is of great consequence, and calls for a detailed examination. The examination is attempted in a separate section to which it is entitled.

9.5 Are the Parts of Space Intuited ?

Garnett in maintaining that Kant in his third space argument does not regard the parts of space (that is, particular spaces) as objects of *intuition* calls attention to Kant's statement that the parts of space are merely 'thought of as in it' (i.e. in space) [*in ihm gedacht*].[68] He interprets Kant's view about the parts of space in the third space argument as follows :

> As in the corresponding view in the *Dissertation,* the parts are not given features of the intuition : only the whole is given. Thinking of spaces as in space is the process of delimitation by the mind of the wider given whole of space. The conception of the parts and the general conception of all parts refer to nothing in the intuition. 'This' space and 'that' space are merely space. There is nothing in space corresponding to the 'thisness' which our minds read into it. The conception of 'thisness in

> general' lacks *a fortiori* all reference to space. When by a process of delimitation the mind thinks of parts of space as in space, what really lies back of each such conceived part is the one space.[69]

This interpretation by Garnett of Kant's view in question does not, however, square with Kant's own interpretation of the view; for Kant has clearly said : 'Space and time, and all their parts, are *intuitions,* and are, therefore, with the manifold which they contain, singular representations (*vide* the Transcendental Aesthetic)'.[70]

Against Garnett, the following points may be made :

(a) In the phrase 'thought of as in it' (*in ihm gedacht*), Kant's emphasis is not on 'thought', but on 'in it' (as anybody can verify by reference to B 39 = A 25). The word 'thought' can even be replaced by 'represented' ; for Kant means just that spaces can be represented as *in* it (space). He thinks that this serves to bring out the essential unity of space and the priority of the representation of space to that of spaces.

Kant denies the priority of the representation of spaces to that of space. In denying this, he does not mean to assert, however, as Garnett thinks he does, the temporal priority of the representation of space to that of spaces; nor is he obliged to assert that. There are four possibilities in this regard.

(1) The representation of spaces is temporally prior to that of space;

(2) The representation of spaces is logically prior to that of space;

(3) The representation of space is temporally prior to that of spaces;

(4) The representation of space is logically prior to that of spaces.

Kant denies (1) and (2), but is not necessarily led by this to assert (3). Garnett, however, attributes (3) to Kant. For reasons stated in Chapter 2, we think that Kant's position is better expressed by (4).

If Garnett is wrong in holding that for Kant the intuition of the whole space is temporally prior to the representations of spaces, his contention that the latter representations are subsequent conceptual distinctions (or rather, tamperings with the given space) cannot be right.

(b) Garnett says that '"this" space and "that" space are merely space.' He means here that they are not qualitatively different, and as such are not really different.[71] When we think of these spaces, which really are not different from each other, 'what really lies back of each such conceived part is the one space'.

This argument overlooks the distinction between qualitative and numerical difference, and as a result attributes to Kant a patent falsehood. It is false that when we think of this space and that space, we have in either case only the one whole space in mind. In a passage to be quoted shortly, Kant shows himself anxious to avoid this falsehood, and says that this space and that space are different numerically, even although they are qualitatively similar. What is more important, he even regards them as given in intuition itself in their numerical distinction (i.e. otherness). This no doubt raises the question whether any distinction is possible on the level of *intuition.* But the question is based on the assumption that all distinction is due to conception and is qualitative; and this assumption is wrong according to Kant, who, in the passage to be quoted, criticizes Leibniz for failing to admit that sensibility has its own mode of distinction.[72] On Garnett's interpretation, one has to attribute to Kant what Kant himself regards as the error of Leibniz. Kant says in his *Fortschritte* :

> Leibniz could not admit that we could still distinguish them [A and B which, in respect of all their internal characteristics of quality and quantity, are entirely alike] through their places in space (just as it is possible to perceive quite similar and equal spaces outside of one another without being able to say that they are one and the same space, for otherwise we could put the whole of infinite space into a cubic inch and less). Leibniz could not admit this, for he recognizes no other distinction among things than that which in made through notions [*Begriffe*], and refuses to allow any way of representation distinct from this, such as intuition [*Anschauung*], and more especially intuition a priori.[73]

The points to be noticed in the above extract are the following:

(1) Kant says here that we 'perceive' (intuit) spaces. (It is not that we can only conceive them.)

(2) The spaces are quite similar and may be equal, and yet are different (other than one other) intuitively.[74]

(3) Kant here specially points out the absurdity of supposing that spaces (this space and that space) are 'one and the same space'.[75]

These three points very strongly tell against Garnett's interpretation.

(c) Garnett does not content himself with saying that for Kant the parts of space are not intuited, but conceived. He adds that they for Kant 'indicate a tampering by the mind with the given space'. One may want to know how Garnett arrives at this interpretation. The explanation follows :

Space for Kant, as Garnett maintains against Paton, is not really 'made up' of parts.[76] The so-called parts of space are not its real parts, but parts only 'in a figurative sense'.[77] They are not originally involved in the intuition of space, but are subsequently read into it by the mind. Clarke explicitly says that they are the results of *imagination,* and exactly the same view, Garnett opines, is expressed by Kant in different language by saying that they are the results of *thought*[78] (cf. 'in ihm gedacht').

On Garnett's interpretation, then, the parts of space are not intuited, but only imagined.

But the question arises : What is the role of imagination here ? Imagination for Kant is capable of two roles : the role of intuition and that of synthesis. In the first role, it 'belongs to *sensibility*', and in the second, it 'is an expression of spontaneity'.[79] Now in representing the particular spaces, does imagination play the intuiting role or the synthesizing role ? The latter cannot be the case. For synthesis is out of the question where there is no presented multiplicity, and in the case before us, there is, on Garnett's hypothesis, no presented multiplicity at all. Nor would it do for Garnett to say that the particular spaces are, so to speak, *analysed* out of the prior-given intuition of the one space, since analysis, for Kant, presupposes synthesis,[80] which in the present case is out of the question, as just noted. To be clear : Upon Garnett's interpretation, what is originally given is space without spaces, i.e. space without multiplicity; this being so, there are no items to be synthesized into a whole, and accordingly there is no whole, in the strict sense of this term, to be analysed. Ultimately, then, we come to see that Garnett has no alternative but to hold that imagination in representing the particular spaces plays an intuiting role.[81] This is to say that the particular spaces are for Kant intuited.

It might be said that Garnett's main point is rather that 'this' space and 'that' space 'refer to nothing in the intuition', that is, that they are merely imagined in the sense that corresponding to them no objects are really given in intuition.

But this reply would be futile. For the point made in it is equally applicable to the one space. On Garnett's interpretation, what is originally given in intuition is the one space, and not the spaces in it. But space without spaces in it is also space without any sensible objects in it. It is, in short, mere space, which Kant sometimes calls 'pure space' (*der reine Raum*).[82] Now it is noteworthy that 'pure space' and 'pure time' in this sense are, according to Kant, *not* really intuited at all.[83] He holds that corresponding to these expressions no objects (*keine Gegenstände*) are given in intuition. He even holds that considered as intuitions they are 'nothing', *ens imaginarium*.[84] They are 'something, as forms of intuition', but not as 'objects which are intuited'.[85] To Garnett's point, then, that spaces for Kant 'refer to nothing in the intuition', the rejoinder is that the one pure space also for Kant refers to *nothing* in intuition. From this point of view indeed the one space and the spaces in it are in the same boat.

It is not that the Kantian passage just referred to has altogether escaped Garnett's notice. He does indeed consider it, but in a different chapter specially devoted to showing how Kant again and again contradicts himself by holding different views of the nature of space. He maintains that the view expressed by Kant in the passage in question is a new development which is irreconcilable with the position of the Aesthetic (as also with a different position elsewhere in the Analytic). The newly developed view of this passage, he says, involves 'the abandonment of the contention that it [space] is *given* at all',[86] and indeed 'marks the collapse of the theory of a pure intuition contemplated by the mind either prior to, during, or after, experience . . .'.[87] In this passage Kant, as Garnett understands him, holds that space is a *mere* form of empirical intuition, and not a pure intuition at all, 'not directly given at all';[88] 'not given at all' in the sense that it is not given either apart from objects or along with them or still otherwise.

In reply to Garnett it may be said that although in the passage under consideration (B 347 = A 290) Kant says that space *apart from objects* is nothing intuited or given, he does not say, as anybody can verify, that space is 'not given at all', that space even along with objects is not given. The difficulty experienced by Garnett in connexion with this passage is entirely due to his wrong interpretation of Kant's view in the Aesthetic. He interprets Kant's view in the Aesthetic as being that space is a pure intuition in the sense that it is given temporally prior to empirical intuitions. For him, then, there is only one way in which space can be given as a pure intuition, namely, by being given temporally prior to objects (i.e. empirical intuitions). But that space can be given in this way (as without, or temporally prior, to objects) is what Kant denies in the passage under consideration. So Garnett naturally concludes that in this passage Kant denies that space is given at all. For us, however, Garnett's difficulty does not arise, as we are not wedded, like him, to the theory of temporal priority of pure intuition.

(d) To round out the discussion : We have found nothing in the evidence adduced by Garnett to convince ourselves that the parts of space, for Kant's third space argument, are not the original features of the intuition of space. He has not been able to cite any explicit statement from Kant to the effect that, unlike space, spaces are not intuitions. On the contrary, we have cited at the outset[89] an explicit statement from Kant to the effect that, like space, spaces too are intuitions. It remains to show that the representations of spaces quite satisfy the Kantian criteria of intuitivity.

In the first place, such representation are of particulars (individuals).[90] It is indeed true that the parts of space differ from the one space in that unlike the latter, which is (allegedly)[91] a unique particular, the former are particulars having similars. But this difference does not prevent them from being, *primarily,* objects of intuition. It does not matter if they can also (i.e. secondarily) be instances of a general concept. In the second place, the representations of spaces (parts of space) are immediate. The immediacy of an intuitive representation of a particular consists in the fact that this representation does not depend upon that of any features which the particular in question has, or may have, in common with other particulars.[92] Since nobody maintains that, prior to the representations of spaces, we have a general concept of spaces (encapsulating their common features), the immediacy of their representations is not in doubt. It is indeed true that Leibniz has attempted an *intellectualist*-cum-reductionist account of our idea of *places* in terms of our representation of a certain sort of order among sensibles; this makes the representation of spaces dependent on *discursus;* but the defect of this Leibnizian account has already been exposed in connexion with our discussion of Kant's first space argument.

In the next chapter objections of a different sort to Kant's third space argument are considered.

NOTES :

1. Cf. above, 1.6, p. 26. The reason for not including the last sentence of this argument in the present account has also been stated there.
2. For textual support of this restatement, cf. the last sentence of Kant's fourth space argument in the second edition, B 40.
3. A 'discursive' representation is, according to Kant, a representation of reflection; see his *Logic,* § 1, Hartman and Schwarz trans., p. 96. It may incidentally be pointed out that, for Euler, the idea of space is due neither to reflection nor to sensation, and that such is also Kant's view. For an exposition of Euler's view and a comparison of Kant's view with that, see C.B. Garnett Jr., *The Kantian Philosophy of Space,* 1939, pp. 121ff.
4. A general concept is a *repraesentatio per notas communes;* see Kant's *Logic,* § 1, trans., p. 96.
5. Some have objected to the translation of Kant's term 'Anschauung' as 'intuition' : thus T. D. Weldon prefers the translation of it as 'perception' (see T. Penelhum and MacIntosh, eds., *The First Critique,* 1969, pp. 35f.); some, again, prefer to translate it as 'visualization' (see Hans Reichenbach, *The Philosophy of Space and Time,* trans. M. Reichenbach and J. Freund, the translation being partly checked by H. Reichenbach himself; Dover, New York, 1957, p. 83 n.2). But 'all

attempts to dispense with the translation of *Anschauung* as "intuition" are bound to fail'. –See J. Hintikka, 'On Kant's Notion of Intuition (Anschauung)', in Penelhum and MacIntosh, eds., *op. cit.,* p. 40. On Kant's interest in the term 'intuition', see also Hans-Georg Juchem, 'On the Development of the Term "Intuition" in the Pre-Critical Writings of Kant', in L.W. Beck, ed., *Proceedings of the Third International Kant Congress,* D. Reidel, 1972, pp. 687-690.

6. See above, 1.4, p. 15.
7. The word 'an' in this clause might be omitted.
8. Cf. *Critique,* B 40. For further evidence, see Vaihinger, *Kommentar zu Kants Kritik der reinen Vernunft,* Bd. II, 1892, p. 233.
9. Cf. Paton, *Kant's Metaphysic of Experience,* 1951, vol. I, p. 115 n.5.
10. In 11.1.1.
11. H. A. Prichard takes this criterion to mean that intuition is a representation of which the object 'is unique' in the sense that 'there is only one of it', and he holds that Kant has adopted this criterion; see below, 9.3. A similar view is taken by Walker at least in so far as he criticizes Kant by saying that 'Kant is confusing particularity with uniqueness'; see his *Kant,* 1978, p. 44.
12. *Critique,* A 320 = B 377.
13. § 15, B; Handyside trans., 1929, p. 59.
14. We say 'primarily', because, as will be clear by and by, Kant is also implicitly making use of the immediacy criterion.
15. Moltke S. Gram (*Kant, Ontology, and the A Priori,* Evanston, 1968, p. 30) says : 'Space is limited by one of its parts only in that the part is included by a larger whole'. He points out that this sense of limitation is to be distinguished from that in which a concept is limited by another. A concept limits another 'only by restricting the class of objects which falls under it'; *ibidem.*
16. Cf. Nathan Rotenstreich, *Experience and Its Systematization : Studies in Kant,* Nijhoff, The Hague, 1965, p. 88.
17. Felix Grayeff, *Kant's Theoretical Philosophy,* trans. D. Walford, 1970, p. 42.

    That the limited portions of space are secondary to space is made clear by Justus Hartnack by arguing as follows : 'You can make a table by joining together table legs and a table top, but you cannot construct space by piling different portions of space on top of each other or setting them alongside of each other. This is a priori impossible, because the conditions for setting them "on top of one another" or laying them "beside each other" already presuppose space; the concepts "on top of" and "beside" are themselves spatial concepts'. See Hartnack, *Kant's Theory of Knowledge,* trans. M. H. Hartshorne, Macmillan, London, 1968, pp. 19-20.

18. Cf. Paton, *op. cit.,* p. 116.
19. Cf. *ibidem.*
20. 'Singular' here means something non-general, i.e. an individual.
21. For Kant, intuition is an immediate singular representation; for discussion see above, 1.4, pp. 15-22.
22. For the notion of an extensional whole, or class 'considered in extension', see Johnson, *Logic, Part II,* Dover, New York, 1964, pp. 166-167. He says : '. . . the items in an extensional whole are prior in thought, which appears to be the product of a constructive process'; *ibidem.*
23. Edward Caird (*The Critical Philosophy of Immanuel Kant,* 1909, I, 267f.) and J. Watson (*The Philosophy of Kant Explained,* 1908, p. 85) hold that Kant's present argument is directed against Leibniz. They emphasize different aspects of the argument from what we are about to emphasize.
24. For his explanation of the adoption of this procedure, cf. his own observations towards the end of para 47 of his paper referred to.
25. Trans. by Loemker in *Gottfried Wilhelm Leibniz : Philosophical Papers and Letters,* 1956, vol. II, p. 1146.
26. The fourth sentence should be read together with the fifth. The 'general concept of spaces' spoken of in the former is called in the latter 'concepts of space'; and Kant holds that the intuition of the whole space *underlies* the concepts of space, where 'underlies' means 'is presupposed by'. 'It is difficult to see why "concepts" is used in the plural [in the fifth sentence] – perhaps because space has many common marks'. See Paton, *op. cit.,* p. 116 n.5.
27. Cf. Kant's parallel statement about time at A 32 = B 48 (i.e. in his fifth argument on time, second sentence).
28. Prichard follows Meiklejohn's translation of the *Critique,* in which Kant's term 'Anschauung' is rendered by 'perception' (and the term 'Begriff' by 'conception').

29. Prichard, *Kant's Theory of Knowledge,* 1909, p. 45.
30. On this term, cf. note 28 above.
31. Prichard, *loc. cit.*
32. *Ibidem.*
33. *Ibid.,* p. 46.
34. *Ibidem.*
35. *Ibidem.*
36. *Ibid.,* pp. 46-47.
37. *Ibid.,* pp. 45, 46. [Kant, however, does not regard space as a 'characteristic' of objects.]
38. *Ibid.,* p. 47.
39. Prichard is, in fact, misled by this suggestion as is evident from his observation : 'But he [Kant] reaches his conclusion by supposing that we first perceive empty space and then become aware of its parts by dividing it'. See *ibid.,* p. 45.
40. 'Immediate' here means *not conceptually mediated.* It will be clear towards the end of this section that the representation of the whole space is *not mediated* by the general concept of spatiality. For a general discussion of the question, 'What does the *immediacy* of an intuition mean for Kant ?', see above, pp. 19ff. As for Prichard, he has neglected Kant's immediacy criterion of intuition – perhaps because Kant's use of this criterion in the present argument is not explicit.
41. As already indicated in the last note, this point will be clear towards the end of this section.
42. Paton, *op. cit.,* p. 116.
43. We are using the expression 'logically presupposed' mainly with a view to avoiding the suggestion of psychological-temporal priority. Cf. *ibid.,* p. 116 n.1.
44. These words are taken from Kemp Smith, *Commentary,* 1918, p. 94.
45. That Kant does not maintain that every consciousness is *explicitly* self-conscious is suggested by his remark at B 132 that '"I think"... [is] a representation which must be capable of accompanying all other representations, . . .'. It is noteworthy that he says, 'must be capable of accompanying', not 'must accompany'.
46. For Kant, the representation of space is an a priori intuition, but the

reflective knowledge that this representation is such as 'transcendental knowledge'; cf. A 56 = B 80-81. He does not, however, discuss the nature of such reflective knowledge.

47. Thus he concludes : 'In any case, space as a whole is not object of perception, which it must be if Kant is to show that space, as being one, is perceived; . . .'. Prichard, *op. cit.,* p. 47.

48. *Ibid.,* p. 46.

49. 'Sensuous consciousness' here means consciousness dependent on sensation.

50. Spaces are no doubt *in* space in the sense of being parts of the one whole space, but they do not occupy space in the sense of having locations in different places.

51. Space, and even spaces, are not sensuously (or rather, sensually) apprehended, (even although they are, for Kant, sensibly, or rather, sensitively, apprehended). [Kant, it may be noted incidentally, 'uses three different . . . forms, *sensualis, sensibilis,* and *sensitivus; . . .* While sensual refers to sensation and sensitive refers to the forms of sense (space and time), sensible appears to be employed by Kant in a more general manner as covering both'. See J. Handyside, *Kant's Inaugural Dissertation,* etc., 1929, p. 43 n. 2. As for the term 'sensuous', which we use here synonymously with 'sensual', it is not the case, however, that it is invariably so used in the Kantian literature; thus see, e.g. Gregor's translation of Kant's *Anthropology,* The Hague, 1974, p. 21.]

52. Cf. *Inaugural Dissertation,* § 15, A (last sentence); also S. Alexander, *Space, Time, and Deity,* vol. I., pp. 152-153 : '. . . Spaces and Times are not objects of perception as trees or houses are. We have no sense for Space or Time, nor even in the proper meaning of sensation, for movement; they are apprehended *through* the objects of perception, the things which fill spaces and times, but not *by* sense'.

53. A. E. Taylor, *Elements of Metaphysics,* U. P. 25, Methuen, London, 1961, pp. 243f.

54. *Ibid.,* p. 246.

55. *Ibid.,* p. 243.

56. Prichard, *op. cit.* p. 46 n.1.

57. What 'colouredness in general' consists in it is indeed very difficult to state clearly. See in this connexion the discussion of the views of

Sigwart, Johnson, and Kemp Smith by B. Blanshard in his *The Nature of Thought,* George Allen & Unwin, London, 1955, vol. I., pp. 594ff; cf. also G. E. Moore, *Some Main Problems of Philosophy,* London, 1965, pp. 315-16. On behalf of Prichard and others who speak of colouredness in general, however, it may be observed : '. . .very often we have no way of saying what is common to the things to which the same word applies except by using the word itself'– See A. J. Ayer, *The Problem of Knowledge,* Penguin, 1977, pp. 10-11.

58. Kant's expression 'the general concept of spaces' is perhaps better than the expression 'the concept of spatiality' (taken from Paton), since 'being spatial' is ambiguous between 'being a space' and 'having location in space'.

59. In 9.2.

60. Cf. his observation quoted in note 39 above.

61. See, e.g. Paton, *op. cit.,* pp. 116, 112; D.P. Dryer, *Kant's Solution for Verification in Metaphysics,* 1966, pp. 176f; Strawson, *The Bounds of Sense,* 1966, p. 64; Bennett, *Kant's Analytic,* 1966, p. 62.

62. Paton, *op. cit.,* p. 116.

63. Garnett, *op. cit.,* p. 189.

64. Garnett's translation; *ibid.,* p. 188.

65. *Ibidem.*

66. Paton, *op. cit.,* p. 193. Cf. also his notes 3 and 4 to p. 193.

67. Garnett, *op. cit.,* pp. 188-189.

68. *Ibid.,* p. 186.

69. *Ibid.,* pp. 186-187.

70. *Critique,* B 136a. Emphasis added by Kant himself.

71. As he puts it in a different chapter : '. . . "space" is not qualitatively less than "this space" . . . The only way that "this space" differs from "that" is that "this" is here, and "that" there. That this space is here, means, however, no more than that this space is space. "Here" and "there" are not qualities of space; they are space itself . . . ; "this space" and "that" . . . have exactly the same amount of the character of space'. Garnett, *op. cit.,* p. 126.

72. Cf. also above, p. 148, and notes 74 and 75 to Chap. 4.

73. *Welches sind die wirklichen Fortschritte, die die Metaphysik seit Leibnizens und Wolffs Zeiten in Deutschland gemacht hat?* [Rosenkranz, I, 516; Hartenstein, III, 441.] Cited and translated by Latta in his *Leibniz : The Menadology and Other Philosophical Writings,* 1898, p. 169 n. 3.

74. Cf. *Critique,* A 282 = B 338 : '. . . they do not . . . belong to the concept . . .'.

75. Cf. also *ibid.,* A 264 = B 320 : '. . . one part of space, although completely similar and equal to another part, is still outside the other, and for this very reason is a *different* part, which when added to it constitutes a *greater* space'. [Emphasis ours.]

76. Garnett is here referring to Paton's article in '*Mind*', vol. XLVII. No. 186, p. 234'; see Garnett, *op. cit.,* p. 151.

77. *Ibidem.*

78. *Ibidem.*

79. *Critique,* B 151. On imagination spoken of as 'belonging to *sensibility* (the power of intuitive ideas)', see also Kant's *Anthropology,* bk i, pt. i, § 15, Gregor trans., 1974, p. 32.

80. B 130. [We are entitled to refer to this passage, since we are here concerned only with determining what Kant *means.*]

81. On such intuiting role of imagination, cf. Kant's *Anthropology,* § 28, Gregor trans., p. 44.

    [We are far from thinking, however, that this aspect of the Kantian doctrine of imagination is devoid of difficulties.]

82. *Critique,* A 291 = B 347.

83. See *ibidem.*

84. A 292 = B 348.

85. A 291 = B 347.

86. Garnett, *op. cit.,* p. 218.

87. *Ibid.,* p. 219.

88. *Ibidem.*

89. Above, p. 335.

90. Spaces (the parts of space) are for Kant particulars or individuals for this main reason (as stated by A. H. Smith, *Kantian Studies,* Clarendon Press, Oxford, 1947, p. 10) : 'Space and time are individual wholes of which *all the parts are individualized,* and it is in virtue of this nature of space and time that everything which has genuine location in one or the other is . . . individual . . .'. [Emphasis ours.]

91. We say 'allegedly' because it has not yet been discussed whether it is true that we can represent to ourselves *only one* space (i.e. 'complete space'). The point is discussed in the next chapter.

92. See above, pp. 19-21.

CHAPTER TEN

KANT'S THIRD SPACE ARGUMENT (Continued)

One of Kant's crucial statement in his third space argument, namely, that 'We can represent to ourselves only one space' (that is, only one complete space, to use this expression of Bennett's),[1] has not been examined so far. The problems raised by this statement for Kant's argument in question are considered in this chapter.

10.1 On the Unity of Space

10.1.1 Arguments for plurality of spaces

Bradley, Taylor, Blanshard, Stout, Quinton, and others have denied the essential unity of space.[2] In denying this, not all of them have explicitly argued against Kant's third space argument in question; only some (e.g. Stout and Quinton) have done so. All these philosophers follow the same principle, however, in their arguments for the plurality of spaces. That general principle is this : To say that there is one space or spatial system means that all things in space are spatially related to one another. Accordingly it can be shown that there are, or may be, independent spatial systems if it is shown that there are, or may be, things of a class such that all of them are spatially related to one another, and none of them are spatially related to any of the things that belong to a different class by being all spatially related in their turn to one another. In these circumstances, things of the first class belong to a space that is spatially unconnected witht the space to which things of the second class belong. These two spaces, being spatially unconnected, are not parts of one and the same whole space.

10.1.1.1 Private spaces

In advocating the plurality of (independent) spaces, attention is usually called either to the spaces of sensation or to those of imagination (including dream) or to both, and it is argued that these spaces exist without spatial relation to the common space occupied by the publicly observable physical objects of our waking lives. Quinton gives Russell the credit for familiarizing us with the spaces of sensation.[3] Clear arguments for the admission of 'private spaces' of sense-data and images are also adduced in Moore's *Some Main Problems of Philosophy.*[4]

Kant has sometimes been criticized for ignoring the spaces of sensation. Thus Moritz Schlick says about Kant :

> He invariably speaks, as did Descartes be/fore him, of extension, of Space, and omits any investigation as to whether it may not be necessary to distinguish several space-concepts; first, between the physical and the psychological, and under the latter, between visual-space, tactual-space, etc.[5]

In this connexion, at least one of the arguments offered by Schlick for the plurality of spaces is worth quoting :

> Pain has its own space just as visual sensations have theirs and as do sensations of touch. The fact that several sensations of pain can occur *simultaneously* is sufficient to require us to speak of a 'pain-space'. Every arrangement of simultaneous items is a side-by-side (as opposed to a sequence) and it is customary to call such facts 'spatial'. It is experience which first brings about the coördination of the several spaces of visual and tactual sensations, feelings of pain, etc.[6]

To come now to what are called the spaces of imagination and dream. I dream of objects and events that are spatially related to one another, but stand in no spatial connexion with any of the objects and events of the physical world of our waking lives. In waking life, too, imagination gives us spatial objects which are so far from standing in a spatial arrangement with the objects of the common world that they do not always show a spatial inter- relation even among themselves. The objects of waking imaginations and of dreams are usually called 'unreal', but it is contended that their experienced existence cannot be got rid of by the use of any mere label.[7] As Bradley puts it : 'Their extension and their materiality is, in short, a palpable fact, . . .'.[8]

10.1.1.2 Quinton's two-space myth

Quinton has constructed a two-space myth, which is both interesting in itself and apparently quite damaging to the Kantian doctrine of the unity of space. The myth is this :[9] A person, on falling asleep at night, dreams that he wakes up at the start of a day in a new world, which proceeds coherently according to the known physical laws. Then he falls asleep at night in the new world to wake back in the old world, where he resumes his normal duties. At night again he falls asleep in this world and dreams that he is back to the second world, where he meets the same persons and places as he did on the previous occasion. And the state of affairs described is repeated. The result is that the person's dreams form a coherent history similar to that of his normal waking life. Ordinarily our dreams are set aside as being incoherent and private. But Quinton adds the two characters of coherence and publicity to the person's dream-world by means of details and qualifications that may be omitted here. Now in these conceivable circumstances, it is reasonable to say, Quinton argues, that the person in question alternately occupies two coherent and *public* worlds, or spaces, which are spatially unconnected with each other.

10.1.2 An appraisal of the arguments in question

It remains to see whether the above considerations really lead to a rejection of Kant's third space argument.

10.1.2.1 Comments on the argument from private spaces

The doctrine of the private spaces of sensation in its famous Russellian formulation tends to work against Kant's third space argument in two ways. In the first place, it denies the essential unity of space, and in the second place, it maintains that the public physical space of waking life is a *logical construction,* which implies that it is not 'a pure intuition'. It is this double implication of the doctrine that makes it a genuine source of difficulty for the Kantian view. For it would not do to say that the private spaces of sensation are irrelevant to Kant's argument,[10] and that the common physical space with which alone he is concerned is after all essentially one. Even if the unity of the common physical space be maintained, of what avail should this unity be so long as the possibility remains that this space is a logical construction out of the private spaces of sensation, of which the existence is clearly admitted by calling them 'irrelevant' ?

Russell's doctrine that the physical space is a logical construction will be examined in the final chapter.[11] It will then be plain that its apparent success depends upon the use of circular reasoning, which implies that the whole doctrine should be revised. What needs special mention in the present context is that the very knowledge of a *unitary* objective space is a necessary condition for the admission of any private space or spaces, whether of sensation or of imagination. This necessity can be shown in the following way.

If indeed there are private spaces, then, in the first place, I cannot speak of the private spaces experienced by others, except on the testimony of the others. But then the others must be 'identifiable, and therefore spatially locatable'.[12] And the space in which they – their bodies – are to be located cannot be any of the private spaces experienced by them, but must be a common objective space in which both they and I are. Thus the knowledge of a common objective space is a necessary presupposition of my admission of the private spaces of others. In the second place, I cannot also speak of the 'private space of my own' except by implicitly claiming to know of others' experiences, and therefore without already placing both myself and others in a common objective space.

Of course, if private spaces are admitted, Kant's view that we can represent to ourselves only one space cannot be accepted. For the private spaces cannot be called 'parts' of one and the same space. Nevertheless, the view that the common objective space –that is, the public physical space of waking life – is a logical construction out of private spaces is undermined, and this is a clear gain on the Kantian side. Moreover, the common objective space, the representation of which is presupposed in the admission of private spaces, still remains *unique*. It cannot be regarded, or at least properly regarded, as an instance, with the other spaces as its coinstances, of a general concept of spaces. For there cannot be a general concept of spaces unless we can entertain the possibility of there being many spaces; and this possibility cannot be entertained at all except by presupposing the representation of a *single* objective space where the very experients of *other* spaces exist, as we have seen. It follows that our primary (or, to use the Kantian expression, 'original') representation of space is that of a single objective space, and that this representation, being presupposed in the possibility of representing other spaces and therefore in the possibility of having a general concept of spaces, must be itself non-conceptual. In short, the original representation of space is non-conceptual.

10.1.2.2 Comments on Quinton's myth

To come now to Quinton's myth. Quinton in his cleverly constructed story maintains that the dream-space described by him is in its own way a *public* physical space, which is spatially unconnected with the public physical space ordinarily so called. This claim of the dream-space to be regarded as public has been supported by Bennett :

> In so far as no one else in this world has them, the dreams are admittedly private, but they contain their own public; and to divest the 'dream'-public of epistemological authority because it is only a dream-public is to beg the question. The 'dream'-public might even dismiss my reports of this world as mere dream-fiction; but they would be as wrong to do this as you would be to say that yours is the only real world I have been in. Alternatively, we can suppose that many people in this world share my 'dreams', so that one public confirms the reality of both worlds.[13]

The question is whether Quinton's story is really plausible. The story says that an identical person lives in two worlds discontinuously. It is supposed here that similarity of memory claims is a sufficient condition of personal identity. But this supposition may lead to an incoherence. Bernard Williams says,

> that identity is a one-one relation,[14] and that no principle can be a criterion of identity for things of type T if it relies only

> on what is logically a one-many or many-many relation between things of type T. What is wrong with the supposed criterion of identity for persons which relies only on memory claims is just that' . . . being disposed to make sincere memory claims which exactly fit the life of . . .' is not a one-one, but a many-one, relation, and hence cannot possibly be adequate in logic to constitute a criterion of identity.[15]

Suppose a person A to undergo a radical transformation of character and to make sincere memory claims that exactly fit the life of B. It is equally conceivable that at the same time another person C undergoes a similar change and makes similar memory claims exactly fitting the life of B. If now similarity of memory claims be a sufficient condition of personal identity, it has to be said that A = B and C = B, even although A ≠ C. This absurdity can be avoided, Williams claims, by rejecting the similarity criterion of identity and insisting that spatio-temporal continuity [relative to a previously identifiable frame] is necessary for personal identity.[16]

Swinburne, however, is right in maintaining that in most of our 'ordinary' judgements of identity we do not bother about the logical possibility of reduplication.[17] Accordingly, it is understandable that many will admit that in Quinton's story it is numerically *the same person* that successively inhabits the two worlds described there. Still there are other difficulties.

The two worlds in Quinton's story are *ex hypothesi* immediately successive in one and the same time. It may be noted that Quinton frankly confesses that he cannot conceive more than one time, that is, temporally unrelated times.[18] Now, the temporal successivity of the two worlds in his story urgently calls for an explanation. Succession or alteration presupposes something permanent.[19] Unless there be something continuous or enduring, there can conceivably be no succession, and hence no time.[20] What can this enduring element, this permanent, be in Quinton's story ? He has so constructed his story as to try to leave nothing actually continuous between the two worlds – not even the experient's body.

The man in the story reportedly transfers himself from the one world to the other not by spatial movement or local motion, but by falling asleep. Swinburne says that in principle the man might as well transfer himself to the second world in a flash simply by, say, reciting the opening words of the Koran, and return to the old world, again in a flash, simply by reciting the closing words : this is also a method of transfer otherwise than by making spatial movements.[21] We are here led to ask questions about the location at which, say, the opening words of the Koran are recited and the transfer from the one world to the other is effected. Is it common to both worlds or not ? If it is, the two worlds are after all in the same space; for spaces are the same if there is a common location between them. If it is not common, then the succession that is involved is hardly intelligible. Replacement of one public space by another is hardly intelligible except as replacement at a common location.[22]

Of the two spatial systems described by Quinton, both are alleged to be *public* in the sense that the criterion of publicity consisting in such coherence as makes identification and reidentification of objects possible is satisfied by both. The question is whether it is intelligible that the only link between the two spatial worlds for the man in Quinton's story is constituted by his stream of consciousness. The incisive comment on this point made by K. Ward can only be regarded as justified :

> . . . there cannot be a purely private succession from one public space to a different one; two public spaces must be located in one public space, if there is to be a temporal succession of apprehension between them.
>
> The illusion is managed by treating each experienced (public) space as a (private) experience in a stream of consciousness; so we slip from saying, 'I experience x', to saying, 'x is an experience of mine'. Once this verbal ambiguity has been exploited, the description proceeds quite smoothly. We are led to say that we can have successive (private) experiences of two (public) worlds, and thus the only link between these worlds is my non-spatial experience; and thus

> the worlds themselves are neither co-existent in space nor really continuous in time.[23] But the move should . . . be resisted, for two successively apprehended objective spaces cannot be linked only by a subjective continuity of . . . the form of (my) psychic space.[24]

The so-called different spaces (spatial systems) spoken of by Quinton are of the same kind. The question is whether there is a conceivable way of individuating them. 'Such individuation cannot be spatial, for one kind of space cannot limit a space of a different kind, and individuation within one kind of space is itself spatial',[25] that is, demands recognition of the sameness of space. Nor can the individuation be temporal, since two spaces of the same kind cannot be conceived to be successive in time unless there be a common enduring element, and if there be such an element, the space must be continuous.[26] Nor again can it be said that there is here some inconceivable principle of individuation; for if the difference between them cannot be conceived, they cannot be conceived as different.[27]

Two spaces (spatial systems) of the same kind are no doubt conceivable when, for example, they are the *private* spaces of two persons, since these can be distinguished by reference to their experients. But then, as has been pointed out before, the experients themselves have to be identified and located in one common objective space.[28]

The above consideration lead us to think that Quinton's story is not one on which one can base a serious objection to Kant's third space argument.

10.1.2.3 Space and the different systems of geometry

The present section is perhaps also the proper place for a word on the view, which has not been mentioned so far, that the rise of different systems of geometry demonstrates that there is not one space, but that there are different kinds of space. This view is misleading. Different systems of geometry describe different kinds of space only in the sense of describing different sets of relation in conformity with their respective axioms and theorems, but not in the sense of demonstrating the existence of different spatial systems such that actual objects and events do some of them belong to one system, others to another system, and so on. Spherical geometry describes a curved space only in the sense of describing relations on the surface of a sphere, whereas a different system of geometry describes elliptic space by way of only describing relations on the surface of an ellipsoid, and so on. Thus different systems of geometry speak of different kinds of space, and these different kinds of space only mean the different sets of relation deducible from the axioms and theorems of those different geometrical systems. But that there is actually one space only comprehending all physical objects and events is a view which is not in the least endangered by the descriptions of different sets of relation in the alternative systems of geometry. 'When', as Dryer puts it, 'people speak of modern physics using now one system of geometry and now another, they do not mean that physics is not ascertaining relations among things all of which occupy one space'.[29]

10.2 Bennett's Criticism of Kant's Third Space Argument Considered

Referring to different spaces such as the space of our world and 'the space of a Strawsonian auditory world', Bennett maintains that the Kantian account 'of the logic of "space"'[30] is unsatis- factory. He takes Kant to mean that 'x is spatial' or 'x is a space' must be defined as 'x is a part of Space', where 'Space' is a proper name, which denotes an individual.[31] He then criticizes this account by pointing out that the space of a Strawsonian auditory world is *a space*, even although it cannot be said to be *a part of Space* (i.e. a part of our familiar whole space). The former is a space in the only sense that it is analogous to our familiar space in certain formal respects. So he maintains that 'x is a space' or 'x is spatial' is not to be defined in the Kantian way as 'x is a part of Space', but rather as 'x is *like* Space in certain formal respects'.[32]

We do not think, however, that this is a fair criticism of Kant. The space with which Kant is primarily concerned in his third space argument is termed by Bennett 'Space'.[33] But this space is, as Strawson rightly points out, the space of our familiar physical world.[34] The term

'Space' (with a capital 'S') is, then, to be appropriated to the space of our familiar physical world. Now in our world we distinguish within Space different regions which we call spaces. Each of these spaces is *a space,* and is of course *a part of* Space. As to the space of a Strawsonian auditory world, it is strictly to be called, not *a space,* but rather a Space, since it claims to be not subordinate to, but rather coordinate with, our paradigmatic Space. So if it is not a part of Space (if, that is to say, a Space is not a part of Space), Kant's view that a space is a part of Space is not in the least affected.

Our conception of the space of a Strawsonian auditory world (one might call it $Space_2$ to distinguish it from the space of our familiar physical world, which, then, might be called $Space_1$) no doubt shows that Kant is wrong in claiming that 'we can represent to ourselves only one space' (i.e. only one Space). Kant's major contention, however, is that our original representation of space (i.e. of $Space_1$) is intuitive; and we see that Bennett does not want to dispute this contention. He observes : 'Kant says that the intuition of Space is prior to or more basic than any spatial concepts . . . . We could grant this without granting that "x is spatial" must mean that x is *a part of* Space, for it could mean that 'x is *like* Space in certain formal respects'.[35] But if Bennett grants Kant's main point that we have 'intuition of Space' (i.e. of $Space_1$), it does not matter much whether or not Kant's account of the logic of 'space' is satisfactory.

At this point we may make a digression to redeem a promise made in connexion with Kant's second space argument.[36] We refer to Bennett's appraisal of the relation between Strawson and Kant. With respect to Strawson's theory that a world of objective experience must be spatial, Bennett contends that 'spatial' here means, not '*a part of* Space', but '*like* Space in certain formal respects', and that, therefore, Strawson's is an exercise in conceptual analysis which cannot be reconciled with the Kantian doctrine that we can intuit only one complete Space in which all conceivable spaces must fall as its *parts.* Here our observation is that even if Spaces are conceivable that are not parts of our paradigmatic Space (i.e. of $Space_1$), this, as Bennett himself is prepared to grant, does not falsify Kant's main doctrine that our original representation of the one common objective space of our physical world – of our paradigmatic Space, that is to say – is intuitive.

In what follows, we shall mean by 'space' and 'spaces' the one objective space of our waking life and its parts respectively, as we did in the previous chapters.

10.3 Singular Concept and the Idea of Space

The problem to be considered now is whether granting the unity of space, the idea of space may not yet be regarded as a concept. It may not be a general concept, but may it not be a singular concept ?

Bennett distinguishes three kinds of concept : (i) concepts having many instances (e.g. 'the concept of an ink-well'), (ii) concepts which could have many instances (e.g. 'the concept of a natural satellite of the earth'), and (iii) concepts which cannot have more than one instance (e.g. 'the concept of being the sole ruler of the universe').[37] Concepts of the last sort are sometimes called 'singular concepts' :[38] these are concepts with 'singularity built in'.[39] The existence of such concepts seems to cast doubt on the assumption that the idea of a single object must be an intuition rather than a concept.

Dryer argues that although Kant usually ignores singular concepts, such concepts do not lack that which, according to Kant, distinguishes a concept from an intuition.[40] Thus the concept of *the* tallest building in New York is a singular concept. Now the actual observation of the tallest building in New York is certainly quite different from having a mere thought of that building. When I entertain the concept of the tallest building in New York, 'I represent it to myself as in New York, as a building and in terms of height'.[41] Being in New York, being a building, etc. are the respects in which the tallest building in New York resembles other objects. A singular concept is thus like other concepts in so far as it represents an object indirectly by means of respects in which it resembles other objects; whereas intuition is the direct or immediate representation of a single object. Dryer alludes to this passage in Kant : 'An intuition refers to an object directly and is single. A concept refers to an object indirectly, by means of some respect which may be common to several things'.[42]

Dryer's answer to the difficulty under consideration may not, however, be acceptable to some, who may argue as follows :

Dryer has sought to show that Kant's distinction between intuition and concept is not affected by the existence of singular concepts by pointing out that a singular concept is analysable into a number of general concepts. But a singular concept, analysable as it is into certain general concepts, is nevertheless unlike a general concept, and like an intuition, in that it is not the representation of any of an indefinite number of objects, but the representation of a definite single object. There may otherwise be some distinction between a singular concept and an intuition, and some similarity between a singular and a general concept. But that is quite irrelevant so long as we are considering only the assumption that the representation of a single object[43] must be an intuition.

In answering this objection, it may be admitted, to begin with, that from the *mere* singleness of the represented object one cannot rightly conclude to the intuitivity of the representation. The possibility remains open that the representation is a singular concept of the sort mentioned above. A singular concept of this sort is formed, however, from general concepts. The question is how a concept that is formed from certain general concepts can overcome the generality inherent in each of its constituents and thus become singular. Perhaps it will have to be replied that a certain mode of combination of general concepts comes to acquire a 'singular use' by some sort of convention. A reply along this line is suggested by some remarks of Kant's in his *Logic*.[44] This problem, intrinsically important as it is, may, however, be set aside for the sake of avoiding delay in coming to consider whether the idea of space may not correctly be regarded as a singular concept of the sort in question. It is noteworthy that Kant in the *Inaugural Dissertation* sometimes calls the idea of space 'a singular concept'[45] and sometimes again 'a singular intuition'.[46] This shows that he has no objection to regarding the idea of space as a singular concept, provided it is recognized that it is a concept directly formed from an intuition instead of being indirectly formed from some general concepts. One may here lay down a principle in Dryer's words as follows :

> If a singular concept is not derived from intuition of what is thought by it, it is formed from general concepts.[47]

Thus the concept of the only whooping crane (Dryer's example) is a singular concept formed from general concepts, e.g. by coupling with the general concept of the whooping crane the concept of there being no more than one.[48] As regards the singular concept of the one whole space, however, it cannot be said that it is reached by taking the general concept of spaces and coupling with it the general concept of a whole. For, as has been remarked more than onec before,[49] the general concept of spaces already presupposes the idea of the whole space. [It is, indeed, natural to suppose that the concept of the whole space is obtained by successively apprehending the particular spaces so as to reach the general concept of spaces and then, in the light of the general concept of a whole, arriving at the thought of the whole space. But the peculiarity here, as already noted, is that the very apprehensions of particular spaces, and so the general concept of spaces, presuppose the idea of the whole space.] Now, since, as just seen, it cannot be said that the singular concept of space is formed from general concepts, it has to be said, according to the principle laid down above, that the concept is derived from intuition of the whole space. The idea of the whole space, then, is originally an intuition and only secondarily a singular concept.

It remains to consider certain other aspects of Kant's third space argument, to which we turn in the next chapter.

NOTES :

1. J. Bennett, *Kant's Analytic,* 1966, p. 64.
2. F. H. Bradley, *Appearance and Reality,* London, 1969, pp. 253ff; A. E. Taylor, *Elements of Metaphysics,* 1961, pp. 256-259; B. Blanshard, *The Nature of Thought,* 1955, I, pp. 637-638; G.F. Stout, 'Is the Knowledge of Space *A Priori ?' Proceedings of the Aristotelian Society* 3 (1895), pp. 132-33; A. Quinton, 'Spaces and Times', *Philosophy* 37 (1962), pp. 130-147.
3. Quinton, *op. cit.,* p. 133.
4. G. E. Moore, *Some Main Problems of Philosophy,* London, 1965, chap. ii, esp. p. 42.

5. M. Schlick, 'On the Relation between Psychological and Physical Concepts', in H. Feigl and W. Sellars, eds., *Readings in Philosophical Analysis,* Appleton-Century-Crofts, New York, 1949, p. 394.
6. *Ibid.*, p. 395.
7. Taylor, *op. cit.,* p. 258.
8. Bradley, *op. cit.,* p. 253.
9. See Quinton, *op. cit.,* pp. 141ff.
10. Strawson says that Kant would regard the objection on the ground of private spaces 'as irrelevant'; see *The Bounds of Sense,* 1966, p. 63.
11. In 14.1.3.
12. K. Ward, 'The Unity of Space and Time', *Philosophy* 42 (1967). p. 72.
13. Bennett, *op. cit.,* p. 65.
14. For Williams's observations on the objection that identity is not a *relation* at all, see B. Williams, *Problems of the Self : Philosophical Papers. 1956-1972.* Cambridge University Press, 1976, p. 21.
15. *Ibidem.*
16. *Ibid.,* pp. 4-11, 19.
17. Richard Swinburne, *Space and Time,* Macmillan, London, 1968, pp. 40-43.
18. Quinton, *op. cit.,* p. 147.
19. Cf. *Critique,* A 183 = B 226.
20. Kant says : 'Without the permanent there is no . . . time-relation'. See *Ibidem.*
21. Swinburne, *op. cit.,* p. 46.
22. Cf. Ward, *op. cit.,* pp. 70-71.
23. I.e. in objective time. Although Quinton says that he cannot conceive more than one time, he virtually debars himself from explaining succession *in one time* by denying the continuity in space. This subtle criticism made by Ward in the clause in question is reminiscent of Alexlander's view that the times themselves belong to the one time by their belonging to the one space. See Alexander, *Space, Time, and Deity,* vol. II (reissued 1966), p. 235.
24. Ward, *op. cit.,* p. 73.
25. *Ibid,* p. 72.
26. *Ibidem.*
27. *Ibidem.*

28. *Ibidem.*
29. D. P. Dryer, *Kant's Solution for Verification in Metaphysics,* 1966, p. 165.
30. Bennett, *op. cit.,* p. 63.
31. *Ibidem.*
32. *Ibidem.*
33. *Ibidem.*
34. Strawson, *op. cit.,* 1966, p. 63.
35. Bennett, *loc. cit.*
36. See above, p. 243.
37. Bennett, *loc. cit.*
38. Dryer, *op. cit.,* p. 65.
39. Bennett, *loc. cit.*
40. Dryer, *loc. cit.*
41. *Ibid.,* p. 66.
42. Dryer's translation, *ibid.,* p. 64 n. l. *Critique,* B 377.
43. The expression 'a single object' in the Kantian usage is ambiguous between 'an individual' and 'only one object'. In the present context it is being taken in the latter sense.
44. Kant's *Logic,* § 1, Note 2; Hartman and Schwarz trans., p.96, and cf. M. Thompson, 'Singular Terms and Intuitions in Kant's Epistemology', *Review of Metaphysics* 26 (1972), esp. p. 331.
45. *Inaugural Dissertation,* § 12; Handyside trans., p. 51.
46. § 15, *Corollary;* Handyside trans., p. 64.
47. Dryer, *op. cit.,* p. 233.
48. *Ibidem.*
49. See above, pp. 316, 327-329, 330-332.

CHAPTER ELEVEN

KANT'S THIRD SPACE ARGUMENT (Continued)

11.1 A Supposed Further Aspect of the Argument

In the present argument Kant has said that the parts of space do not precede the one whole space as if they were constituents out of which it could be composed, but can be thought only as *in* it, as arising through limitation of it. Some commentators[1] find in this statement what might be called an additional argument for intuitivity, namely, one from the nature of the whole-part relation : space is an intuition in so far as, unlike a concept, the whole space is prior to its parts. This is called an additional argument, because it presents the priority of the whole space in a special light. In the foregoing exposition also the priority of the whole space was emphasized, but it was done in order to make clear the individuality of the whole space and the immediacy (non-mediacy) of the idea of it. We have seen that the whole space is not a mere class of spaces the idea of which is mediately reached through the general concept of spatiality, because the idea of the whole space is already presupposed in the representations of particular spaces, and therefore also in the general concept of spatiality, which is derived from the latter representations. The additional argument to be considered now presents, however, a somewhat different perspective in emphasizing the priority of the whole space to its parts. This will be clear by and by.

The point of the argument is set forth by Kemp Smith as follows :

> The parts of space cannot precede the one all-comprehensive space. They can be thought only in and through it. They arise through limitation of it. Now the parts (i.e. the attributes) which compose a concept precede it in thought. Through combination of them the concept is formed. Space cannot, therefore, be a concept. Consequently it must, as the only

> remaining alternative, be an intuition. Only in an intuition does the whole precede the parts. In a concept the parts always precede the whole.[2]

This additional argument, as we have called it, rests on a particular view of the contrast between intuition and concept that Kant has not clearly stated in his third space argument. The following reasons, however, mediate in favour of the supposition that it is implicit in the third space argument :

(i) Kant's proof in the third space argument is presented in two parts. The second part can no doubt be taken as a further expansion of the first, and indeed it has been so taken in the foregoing exposition; nevertheless, it may be that it is not a mere expansion of the first part, since its parallel in the case of time has been developed by Kant himself into a separate argument, and that argument (namely, the fifth one on time in the first edition of the *Critique*)[3] suggests a distinction between intuition and concept on the ground that in a concept 'the partial representations come first' (that is, the partial representations precede the whole representation), while in an intuition the parts presuppose the whole.

(ii) The following passage in the Transcendental Dialectic is also noteworthy :

> Space should properly be called not *compositum* but *totum,* since its parts are possible only in the whole, not the whole through the parts. It might, indeed, be called *compositum ideale,* but not *reale.* This, however, is a mere subtlety.[4]

This passage explicitly says that in the case of space the whole is prior to the parts, not the parts to the whole. The whole that is prior to the parts is, strictly speaking, a *totum,* and not a *compositum;* and this suggests that a *compositum* is a whole to which its parts are prior. Now in the second part of his third space argument Kant says that the parts of space are not *constituents* out of which the whole space is *composed,* which means that the whole space is not a *compositum.* This, in the light of the Dialectic passage, means that the whole space is not a whole to which its parts are prior, but one which is prior to its parts. Moreover, if in the third space argument Kant insists that space is not a compositum, it is because he wishes to distinguish it from a concept. And this shows by implication that he thinks a concept is a compositum, i.e. a whole composed out of its constituents, and so one to which its parts are prior. Thus emerges one of Kant's distinctions between intuition and concept, namely, that in the former case the whole is prior to its parts, whereas in the latter the parts are prior to the whole.

These considerations tend to suggest that the additional argument under examination is implicit in Kant's third space argument.

It is nevertheless doubtful whether Kant is steadfast to this argument. Thus in the second edition of the *Critique*,5 he withdraws, from his fifth argument on time relied on above, the clause 'in their case [i.e. in the case of concepts] the partial representations come first', and puts in its place some other clause. It may be that he has come to see on reflection that it is not true of every concept that the parts are prior to the whole. An Idea of reason is regarded by him as a 'concept',[6] and about such an archetypal Idea he says in his *Logic* that it cannot be 'obtained by *composition*; for the whole is here prior to the part'.[7]

The additional argument in question may, therefore, be set aside. The second part of the proof in Kant's third space argument does not on that account lose in importance. It is important in the way already indicated in Chapter 9.

It need hardly be added that, in setting aside the additional argument in question, we do not deny that the whole space is prior to the parts, and not the other way round, and that the idea of it is primarily intuitive (non-conceptual). We may here refer back to what has been said in the first paragraph of the present section. Nor do we deny that on any view that maintains that the whole space cannot be known except through the synthesis of its various parts, the knowledge of the whole space would in a sense be conceptual. In this case, the parts would be prior to the whole space, and this priority of the parts of space would prevent the knowledge of the whole space from being intuitive. This view, unlike the additional argument in question, does not appeal to the doctrine of the 'partial representations' of a concept, according to which parts are prior to the whole in the case of a concept. It is rather based on the doctrine of the necessity of 'part to part synthesis' for our knowledge of the whole. Obviously, such a view as this has an independent claim to consideration.

It may be pointed out that Kant has appealed to the doctrine of part to part synthesis in his Analytic, and held that the knowledge of the whole space demands a successive process of synthesis of part to part. This view apparently comes into conflict with his view in the Aesthetic, which we have endorsed so far, namely, that the representation of the whole space is presupposed in the representations of its parts and is primarily intuitive. This apparent contradiction comes in for discussion in the next section.

11.2 Kant's Aesthetic vs. Analytic

It has been maintained by many critics that Kant's third space argument in the Aesthetic is contradicted by his later observations in the Analytic.[8] The Analytic presents a theory of synthesis, according to which no whole can be determinately known without a successive synthesis of the representations of its parts. While discussing the 'Axioms of Intuition', Kant says, 'I entitle a magnitude extensive when the representation of the parts makes possible, and therefore necessarily precedes, the representation of the whole',[9] ascribes such extensive magnitude *inter alia* to space, and argues that 'the representations of a determinate space or time are generated . . . through combination of the homogeneous manifold and consciousness of a synthetic unity'.[10] The 'synthetic unity' here referred to is the product of a synthetic act, i.e. of a successive process of part to part synthesis. By 'a determinate space' he here means the determinate space occupied by an object. Obviously, Kant does not here speak of the one whole space, i.e. the unlimited whole space; he only speaks here of a limited whole space.[11] A limited whole space is determinately known by being constructed or generated through successive synthesis of part to part. The one unlimited whole space, however, cannot be actually determined or generated by the successive synthesis of part to part, inasmuch as the synthesis here cannot in the nature of the case be completed. But the principle of determinate knowledge is here the same. That is, the one whole space could be determinately known only by virtue of a successive process of synthesis. This looks like a reversal of the teaching of the Aesthetic, according to which the representation of the whole space is prior to the representations of its parts.

T. D. Weldon seeks to resolve the contradiction by saying :

> Space (and also time) regarded as objects of thought are . . . *tota synthetica,* a whole of parts. This is not really inconsistent with the teaching of the *Aesthetic,* which maintains that as objects of sense they are *tota analytica* or wholes which are antecedent to their parts. It is meaningless to ask what they are really in themselves, for in themselves they are nothing.[12]

One can hardly be satisfied with Weldon's reply to the charge of contradiction against Kant. That Kant treats space as a *totum analyticum* in the Aesthetic and as a *totum syntheticum* in the Analytic is precisely the reason why the charge of contradiction has actually been brought by, e.g. Kemp Smith[13] against Kant. Weldon has only reinforced the charge by his attempted reply.

How, then, to reconcile the view of the Analytic with that of the Aesthetic ? The reconcilation will be found by considering that the doctrine of part to part synthesis maintained in the Analytic does not entail the rejection of the view of the Aesthetic that the idea of the one whole space is presupposed in the intuitions of particular spaces. According to Kant's third space argument, the whole space is prior to its parts in the sense that the idea of the whole space is presupposed in the intuitions of particular spaces. As so presupposed, the idea of the whole space is as much immediate[14] as are the intuitions of particular spaces. The intuitions of particular spaces are in their turn presupposed in the successive process of synthesis that supervenes through the act of thought (or imagination). For the synthesis in question is synthesis of the intuitions of particular spaces. Such, then, is the situation : the idea of the whole space is presupposed in the intuitions of the particular spaces, which, again, are presupposed in the successive process of synthesis that imagination starts. It is plain that the idea of the whole space is not generated through, but is rather presupposed in, the successive process of part-to-part synthesis which is oriented towards a *determinate* knowledge of the whole space. As Caird puts it :

> Determination of space and time and of individual objects in space and time can take place only in a successive process of synthesis . . . . At the same time, in this successive process we always presuppose the totality of determination of the object in itself, as the goal towards which in our synthetic process of thought we are tending. While, therefore, the progressive determination of the object appears on the one hand as a synthesis, proceeding *a parte ad totum,* which is never completed : on the other hand, it is equally true that the idea of the whole, as that in, and in reference to, which the part is determined, is implied in the process from the first, and gives to it its interest and direction : and in this point of view knowledge may be said to proceed *a toto ad partes.* The idea of the whole, however, we do not *determine*; in Kantian language, we can never make it an object of knowledge. But the thought of it is the presupposition in all our efforts in determining such objects . . . . It is this idea of a presupposed totality, within which our experience grows, which appears in the *Aesthetic* as the representation of space and time as 'infinte given wholes' by limitation of which particular places and times (and objects as occupying these places and times) are determined.[15]

We might, then, distinguish between the primary or original nature of the idea of the whole space that we possess and the nature of the determinate knowledge of the whole space that we aim at. As the presupposition of the limited intuitions of particular spaces, the idea of the whole space is primarily or originally[16] *intuitive* (i.e. non-discursive) : it is as much immediate as are the intuitions of particular spaces, and is unmediated by, being presupposed in, the synthetic activity of thought, as has been noted above. The *determinate knowledge* of the whole space, however, if we could reach it, would be *discursive,* because the synthetic activity of thought is necessarily involved in the process that tends towards it.

It will perhaps be unfair to stop here without referring at all to Garnett, who has made an elaborate discussion to show that Kant's third space argument is threatened by his theory of synthesis.[17] He first points out and then rejects one possible way of coordinating Kant's views in the *Critique* as a whole. That possible way of coordination is to maintain, as Garnett puts it by saying, 'that in the order of our apprehension the parts of space are given first in the synthesis, whereas upon the completion of the unity of space the whole is found to determine the parts'.[18] This amounts to saying that Kant's third space argument 'would hold for space after it is generated', while his theory of synthesis does 'refer to its nature as we construct it'.[19] But Garnett hastens to reject the suggestion on the ground (already noticed) that the synthesis of parts cannot, in the case of the one whole space, be completed. He argues that since the synthesis of parts cannot here reach the whole, it cannot be said that the whole space would upon completion of the synthesis be found to determine its parts logically or objectively.[20] In the same vein, he observes :

> The contention that the parts are limitations of the whole cannot be established if the synthesis does not reach the whole. The only assurance that the parts of space are not constituent parts[21] must lie in the fact that they are so *given,* and for this to be the case the whole must be given, out of which they may be carved.[22]

Thus, in so far as the process of synthesis cannot in the present case be completed, the possibility remains that the parts of space are the constituent parts (rather than its limitations), and this possibility jeopardizes the intuitiveness of the whole.

In replying to Garnett, it is unnecessary to comment on the possible way of coordinating Kant's views that he rejects, and it will be sufficient to question his statement that unless the synthesis of parts reaches the (one) whole space, we cannot know whether those parts arise by limitation of the whole or not. Since the synthesis cannot be completed, we cannot, he argues, reach the whole so as to determine by examination whether its parts are carved out of it, that is, obtained by limitation of it. But here he assumes that the synthesis begins merely with the parts of space as if nothing more were involved.[23] If this assumption is correct, the idea of the whole space is entirely lacking at the beginning, and cannot arise until and unless the synthesis reaches the whole. But, as has been noted, the idea of the whole space is presupposed in the intuitions of the particular spaces, and so is already there from the first as the guiding principle, so to say, behind the synthesis of parts (that is, synthesis of the intuitions of the parts). Since, then, we do not lack the idea of the whole space, we need not await the completion of the synthesis (which cannot be completed) for that idea to occur. We not merely are already in possession of that idea, but also know its relation to the intuitions of particular spaces : we know that the idea of the whole space is presupposed in the intuitions of the particular spaces. This knowledge enables us to say that the idea of the whole space is intuitive. Garnett's trouble seems to arise from his thinking in terms of a physical analogy. Unless the whole space is actually exhibited before us either through presentation or through construction, we cannot know that its parts are carved out of it; that is, both the whole and its parts must be actually before us in order to enable us to see that the parts arise through limitation of the whole. But this way of looking at Kant may well be given up. For when he says in the third space argument that 'the manifold in space depends solely on limitations', he means that the parts of space *depend on* (i.e. presuppose) the whole space, or, in other words, that the representations of the parts of space presuppose the representation of the whole, and this can be further paraphrased by saying that the idea of the whole space is presupposed in the intuitions of the particular spaces. This idea of the whole space is, as seen before, also implied in the successive process of synthesis which seeks to reach the whole (with a view to a determinate knowledge of it). Thus the intuitiveness of the whole (that is, of the idea of the whole space) is not in jeopardy.[24]

11.3 Concluding Remarks on Kant's Third Space Argument

The different aspects of Kant's third space argument have been examined. Kant's view that we can represent to ourselves only one space cannot be accepted if this is taken to mean that we cannot *conceive* more than one spatial system. It must be admitted nevertheless that the one physical space of our waking life is the paradigmatic space by reference to which, or on the analogy of which, different spaces are conceivable, and that the original representation of this one space is non-conceptual.

One thing to which attention was not called before may well be noted here. In so far as we, in waking life, think of imaginary objects, and are aware of them as imaginary, an additional space called an imaginary space is not needed to house them over and above the common objective space with which we are all acquainted. It would not do indeed to say simply that as imaginary they are nowhere; for they are after all represented as occupying space in our imaginative consciousness, and this state of affairs calls for an explanation. The explanation that A. H. Smith has given seems to be reasonable. He says :

> Two cases should be distinguished. In the one I may imagine an object or objects substituted for those which are actually present, e.g. a pen which is better than that which I now use. Evidently in this case the space in which the imaginary object is placed is the real space of actual objects. In the second case I imagine, let us say, the landscape of *The Faerie Queene.* Here it seems that either I imagine myself looking at a scene or living in a world substituted for that which I know to be real – and if so, this case is not substantially different from the other; or else I imagine this new world as indeterminately located somewhere in the old. The latter is possible, because although I imagine the landscape as located in real space, I know that it is imaginary, not real, and therefore I relate it only imperfectly or indeterminately in my imagination to the form of space as a whole and to its actual occupants. All this is indeed a corollary to Kant's views regarding the connexion of the forms

> of space and time with our consciousness of reality. To imagine anything is to imagine, but not to judge, it to be real. If then the real is that which is connected with the one space and time, anything which is imagined as real must be so connected by the imagination. Such a view of imagination and its relation to the form of intuition seems accordingly to be not only possible, but to have good reasons in its favour. It has, moreover, at least the advantage that we need not multiply entities, but can say that the space in which we apprehend some real objects and some imaginary and the space in which we apprehend only imaginary objects, are all one and the same space.[25]

The importance of the idea of one common objective or public space for a metaphysician of experience cannot be overestimated. Quinton's story of two spatially unconnected objective spaces raises the question how the supposedly real occurrences in those two worlds are to be correlated as elements within a single unified framework of experience. It raises the question how the distinction between the real and the imaginary is to be intelligibly and clearly drawn by the common experient of those two worlds.

To return to the narrower context of Kant's theory of pure intuition : Kemp Smith, while criticizing Kant's argument in question, remarks that Kant's view to the effect that space is an intuition 'amounts merely to the statement, which no one need challenge, that space is not a generic class concept'.[26] This criticism is unjust. In this argument Kant recognizes the distinction between space and spatiality, and maintains, as has been explained, that the idea of space in not the idea of an extensional whole reached through the general concept of spatiality (or, as he says, 'the general concept of spaces'). His conclusion that space is an intuition amounts to the statement that space is a non-conceptually apprehended individual and not a conceptually represented class of spaces. This surely serves to reject a view which was held by Leibniz, as we saw.[27] It is not the case therefore that Kant's conclusion is trivial, as Kemp Smith suggests.

Kemp Smith criticizes Kant's argument further by saying that Kant has not succeeded in showing that space is 'radically distinct from the categories, i.e. from the relational forms of understanding'.[28] In reply to this, it may be said that since Kant has shown that our original idea of space is that of an individual, he has by that means already shown by implication that space is not a category. Space contains what we usually call spaces *within* itself, whereas the category of causality (to consider this one only) contains the particular causes not *within,* but rather *under,* itself. The distinction between 'contained *within*' and 'contained *under*' is clearly pressed into service by Kant in his fourth space argument (in the second edition), which falls to be considered in the next chapter.

NOTES :

1. Kemp Smith, *Commentary,* 1918, p. 105; John Watson, *The Philosophy of Kant Explained,* 1908, p. 87. Kemp Smith has only followed Vaihinger. For comments on Vaihinger's account, see Paton, *Kant's Metaphysic of Experience,* 1951, vol. I, p. 116 n.5 (continued on p. 117).
2. Kemp Smith, *loc. cit.*
3. *Critique,* A 32.
4. A 438 = B 466.
5. B 48.
6. See, e.g. A 320 = B 377; A 323ff = B 379ff.
7. § 3, Note 2; Hartman and Schwarz trans., p. 98. Cf. also Paton, *op. cit.,* pp. 118-119.
8. As Robert Paul Wolff in his *Kant's Theory of Mental Activity* (Harvard University Press, Cambridge, 1963) puts it : '. . . the proof of the principle [of the Axioms of Intuition] is a flat contradiction of one of the proofs employed in the Aesthetic'. (p. 228) 'This proof [of the principle of the Axioms of Intuition] should come as something of a shock to the reader who has mastered the Aesthetic, for it is the direct contradictory of an argument offered there to prove that space and time are intuitions rather than concepts'. (p. 229).
9. *Critique,* B 203.
10. B 202-203.
11. We think that much confusion can be avoided by making this distinction between the limited whole space and the infinite whole

space; but this distinction seldom occurs in the expositions of Kant's critics.

12. T. D. Weldon, *Introduction to Kant's Critique of Pure Reason,* 1945, p. 187.
13. Kemp Smith, *op. cit.,* p. 94.
14. See above, pp. 322-323, 327ff.
15. Edward Caird, *The Critical Philosophy of Immanuel Kant,* 1909, vol. I, pp. 271-272.
16. Mark the word 'original' in the last sentence of Kant's fourth space argument in the second edition.
17. Garnett, *The Kantian Philosophy of Space,* 1939, p. 223.
18. *Ibid.* p. 229. It may be noted that something like this is maintained by Paton, who says : 'It should, however, be noted that if the whole precedes the parts logically (or objectively) and the parts precede the whole temporally (or subjectively) there is no contradiction. The whole makes possible the parts in a sense different from that in which the parts make possible the whole'.–*Kant's Metaphysic of Experience,* vol. II, p. 122 n. 3.
19. Garnett, *loc. cit.*
20. Cf. *ibidem.*
21. By 'constituent parts' Garnett means the parts prior to the whole; see *ibid.,* pp. 221-222.
22. *Ibid.,* pp. 222-223.
23. Mark his statement (*ibid.,* p. 223) : '*If we begin with the synthesis of parts,* the contention that they are not constituent parts can never be established; while if the contention is established, the whole is given and we do not *begin with the parts.*' [our emphases].
24. For other attempts at coordinating Kant's views in the Aesthetic and the Analytic, see G. G. Brittan, Jr., *Kant's Theory of Science,* 1978, pp. 90ff.; F. Grayeff, *Kant's Theoretical Philosophy,* trans. D. Walford, 1970, pp. 74-75.
25. A. H. Smith, *A Treatise on Knowledge,* Clarendon Press, Oxford, 1943, p. 83.
26. Kemp Smith, *op. cit.,* p. 107.
27. In 9.2.1.
28. Kemp Smith, *loc. cit.*

CHAPTER TWELVE

KANT'S FOURTH SPACE ARGUMENT

Kant's fourth space argument in the second edition of the *Critique* is substituted for his fifth space argument in the first edition. These are his two versions of what may be called 'his argument from the infinity of space'. The argument is mainly concerned, like the one that immediately precedes it, with showing that the original idea of space is intuitive and not conceptual. It willl be appropriate to consider both the versions of the argument; and, for convenience' sake, the first-edition version of the argument may sometimes be referred to as the first-edition version of Kant's fourth space argument, even although it happens to be his fifth space argument in the first edition.[1]

12.1 The First-edition Version of the Argument

12.1.1 Statement and the usual interpretation of the argument

The argument runs :

> Der Raum wird als eine unendliche Grösse gegeben vorgestellt. Ein allgemeiner Begriff vom Raum (der sowohl einem Fusse, als einer Elle gemein ist), kann in Anschung der Grösse nichts bestimmen. Wäre es nicht die Grenzenlo- sigkeit im Fortgange der Anschauung, so würde kein Begriff von Verhäitnissen ein Principium Unendlichkeit derselben bei sich führen [*Kritik,* A 25.]

In Kemp Smith's translation :

> Space is represented as an infinite given magnitude. A general concept of space, which is found alike in a foot and in an ell, cannot determine anything in regard to magnitude. If there were no limitlessness in the progression of intuition, no concept of relations could yield a principle of their infinitude. [*Critique,* A 25.]

This argument is usually interpreted as follows.[2] The general concept of space (i.e. spatiality) includes what is common to different spaces. The different spaces are of different sizes or magnitudes. Hence the general concept of spatiality, being the concept of what is common to the different spaces, cannot determine anything as regards magnitude or quantity. Now space is represented as an infinite magnitude. Since infinity is a magnitude or quantity, and nothing about magnitude or quantity can be determined by the general concept of spatiality, the idea of the infinity of space cannot be derived from the concept of spatiality (and therefore must be due to the intuition of space).

12.1.2 Remarks on some conjectures about Kant's reason for revision of the argument

Since this argument is replaced by another in the second edition, the presumption is natural that Kant has subsequently detected a defect in it. Paton says : 'In the second edition Kant recognises that a concept can involve infinity, in the sense that it can be present in an infinite number of possible instances as a common characteristic'.[3] Paton here seems to suggest a reason for Kant's revision of the argument.[4] Although Kant maintains in the present argument that the general concept of space can determine nothing about quantity and therefore cannot indicate infinity, he later on recognizes, Paton says, that a concept can involve infinity in the sense of having an infinite number of possible instances. But it is not clear why the recognition of the latter fact should make Kant withdraw the former statement. For the statement that the general concept of space can determine nothing about quantity and therefore cannot indicate infinity remains true in spite of the fact that the concept has an infinite number of possible instances. In the first place, this general concept, no matter how often it may be instantiated, is common to different spaces of different sizes, and as such can determine nothing as regards the magnitude or quantity of the represented spaces. In the second place, the fact that this general concept, like others, has possibly an infinite number of instances signifies only that it has *possibly* an infinite number of instances. But this does not suffice to explain our consciousness that space *is* infinite. To say that space *is* infinite is to say more than that there are *possibly* an infinite number of spaces. Victor Cousin's warning is here worth quoting : '. . . do not here do what is often done, confound *infinite* with *indefinite*'.[5]

It is true, as will be clear later on,[6] that Kant's substituted argument from the infinity of space in the second edition contains an implicit criticism of the view that the idea of the infinity of space can be explained by reference to the infinite possibility of instantiation of the general concept of spatiality. But then the second-edition version of the argument does not contradict, but only serves as a supplement to, the first-edition version, and it is not clear why the latter version is supplanted by the former.

Garnett has given a different account of Kant's reason for revision of the present argument. He thinks that the reason lies in the last sentence of the argument. In this argument Kant intends to conclude that space is represented as a 'given' (i.e. intuited) infinite magnitude; but the last sentence of the argument says that the apprehension of infinite space depends on the 'limitlessness in the progression in intuition'. This theory of a progression is, Garnett says, 'incompatible with the view that space is represented as an infinite magnitude *given*'.[7] He argues that in the progression of intuition the representing mind 'never finds an infinite magnitude of space given immediately but represents it mediately, if at all'[8] and that, therefore, 'the infinitude of space is conceived, and, at least as regards this feature of its nature, space is conceptual'.[9] Since the theory of a progression in intuition threatens the view that space is represented as a *given* infiinite magniude, Kant's present argument is, according to Garnett, obviously defective and, for that matter, recast by Kant in the second edition.

There is no denying that Garnett's suggestion has a good deal of plausibility about it. It may still be observed that if Kant's reason for dissatisfaction with the first-edition version of his argument in question lay merely in its last sentence, he might have either expunged this sentence altogether or substituted for it a more suitable or less misleading sentence, keeping the preceding portion of the argument intact in the second edition. It must be admitted that in so far as the sentence in question may suggest that the idea of the infinity of space is yielded *merely* by the limitlessness in the progression in intuition, it is misleading. One may nevertheless ask whether the doctrine of limitlessness in progression cannot be reconciled at all with the view that the original representation of infinite space is intuitive. Let us reserve this point for subsequent consideration.[10]

12.2 The Second-edition Version of the Argument

12.2.1 Statement and the usual interpretation of the argument

Kant's revised argument is as follows :

> Der Raum wird als eine unendliche *gegebene* Grösse vorgestellt. Nun muss man zwar einen jeden Begriff als eine Vorstellung denken, die in einer unendlichen Menge von verschiedenen möglichen Vorstellungen (als *ihr* gemeinschaftliches Merkmal) enthalten ist, mithin diese *unter sich* enthält, aber kein Begriff, als ein solcher, kann so gedacht werden, als ob er eine unendliche Menge von Vorstellungen *in sich* enthielte. Gleichwohl wird der Raum so gedacht (denn alle Theile des Raumes ins Unendliche sind zugleich). Also ist die ursprüngliche Vorstellung vom Raume *Anschauung* a priori, und nicht *Begriff.* [Kritik, B 39-40.]

In Kemp Smith's translation :

> Space is represented as an infinite *given* magnitude. Now every concept must be thought as a representation which is contained in an infinite number of different possible representations (as their common character), and which therefore contains these *under* itself; but no concept, as such, can be thought as containing an infinite number of representations *within* itself. It is in this latter way, however, that space is thought; for all the parts of space coexist *ad infinitum.* Consequently, the original representation of space is an *a priori* intuition, not a concept. [*Critique,* B 39-40.]

This argument is usually interpreted thus :[11] A general concept has an infinite number of possible instances under it, but cannot have an infinite number of those instances within it, whereas space has an infinite number of spaces within it. The original representation of space therefore cannot be like that of a general concept, and so must be intuitive.

In accordance with this interpretation, Kant's argument can be rendered a little clearer by taking the general concept of spatiality and contrasting it with space. The concept of spatiality is a general concept, since it is a concept of what is common to an infinite number of spaces (which are its instances). Now spatiality, although it has an infinite number of spaces *under* it, cannot be thought of as containing that infinite number of spaces *within* it; but space (which is represented as an infinite magnitude) is thought of as containing an infinite number of spaces *within* it. Space, therefore, unlike spatiality, does not represent a general or common character, and hence unlike the representation of spatiality, the original representation of space must be non-conceptual, that is, intuitive.

12.2.2 A doubt as to the essential point of the argument (Whether it really has anything to do with the infinity of space)

The *exact* point of Kant's argument in the revised form is, however, far from clear. It is often maintained that the essential point of the argument concerns the relation between space and spaces.[12] Space is related to spaces, not as a class-concept to its instances, but as a whole to its parts.[13] Spaces are included in space. The instances of a concept are not included *in*, but subsumed *under*, it : for example, spaces are instances of, and so are subsumed *under*, the concept of spatiality. There is, then, a great difference between the relation of inclusion and that of subsumption, or, between 'being parts of' and 'being instances of'.[14] The relation of inclusion rather than of subsumption between spaces and space shows that space is not a concept; and accordingly Kant concludes that the original representation of space is not conception.

It is noteworthy that in the last paragraph there is no reference to the infinity of space. Indeed, if the essential point of Kant's argument in question be stated as above, the infinity of space has obviously no essential bearing on the argument. In that case, it might be thought that the leading sentence of the argument is quite misleading and that the argument might as well be recast, by omitting all reference to the infinity of space, as follows :

> Every concept must be thought as a representation which is contained in its instances as their common character,[15] and which therefore contains these *under* itself; but no concept, as such, can be thought as containing its instances *within* itself. It is in this latter way, however, that space is thought; for all the parts of space coexist *within* space. Consequently, the original representation of space is an intuition, not a concept.

With respect to the above recasting, the following observations might be considered to be in order :

(i) There are some who have actually interpreted Kant's argument in question without making the least mention of the infinity of space.[16]

(ii) In the Aesthetic as well as in the *Inaugural Dissertation*, there are indications to show that the above recasting is quite in conformity to Kant's actual practice :

(a) Thus in the third space argument (in the second edition) of the Aesthetic, Kant says, as was noticed before, that the parts of space are not, as it were, constituents out of which it can be composed, but 'can be thought only as *in* it'. Here also, then, he points out the relation of inclusion of spaces *in* space. But in the third space argument he connects this fact of the inclusion of spaces *in* space, not with the infinity, but with the unity or singularity, of space. This suggests that the fact of the inclusion of spaces in space is the all-important point on which Kant relies both in the third and in the fourth space argument for the intuitivity of the idea of space. That fact brings out the unity or singularity of space, which is emphasized in the third space argument. The unity of space is maintained in spite of multiplicity in it. There is a great difference in respect of the relation of multiplicity to unity between intuition and conception. In intuition the multiplicity is already involved *in* the one object of intuition;[17] whereas in conception the multiplicity is only brought *under* a unity (i.e. a common character).[18] It is this contrast between intuition and conception which is brought into prominence in the fourth space argument under consideration. And the recasting of this argument attempted above serves only to emphasize this point.

(b) No doubt, in the present argument Kant has explicitly mentioned the *infinity* of space. But, then, substantially the same argument has been previously connected by him, not with the infinity, but with the singularity, of space in the *Inaugural Dissertation,* where he says :

> *The concept of space is a singular representation,* including all spaces *in* itself, not an abstract common notion containing them *under* itself. For what we call 'many spaces' are only parts of the same boundless space . . . *The concept of space is thus a pure intuition,* since it is a singular concept.[19]

In the above exposition Kant no doubt calls the one space 'boundless', and similarly he speaks of 'the one all-embracing space' in the third space argument of the Aesthetic. And yet both the arguments are connected with the singularity rather than with the infinity of space.

But though the *Dissertation* argument quoted above has been, like the third space argument of the Aesthetic, connected with the singularity of space, it has nevertheless been substantially reproduced in the present fourth space argument of the Aesthetic, only now replacing its connexion with the singularity of space by a connexion with the infinity of space. But this fact that virtually the same argument is once connected with the singularity, and once with the infinity, of space shows that its present connexion with the infinity of space is perhaps not as fundamental as its insistence on the relation of inclusion rather than that of subsumption between spaces and space.

[The reason why Kant insists on the infinity of space in the present argument might be this. In the first edition Kant tried to base on the infinity of space an argument for the intuitivity of the idea of space. But, for some reason or other, he felt called upon to revise that argument. And the revision is attempted in the present argument of the second edition; indeed this seems to be the reason why the arguments of both the editions have the same leading sentence. But what is supplied in the present argument does not look like a revision proper of the old argument. It seems that instead of emending the old argument he has rather replaced it by an altogether different argument.[20] The present argument of the second edition has nothing in common with that of the first edition except the leading sentence, that is, the claim that it is based on consideration of the infinity of space. The argument of the first edition, whether defective or not, was nevertheless novel. But the argument substituted in the second edition appears to be an elucidation of part of the third space argument.]

(iii) As regards the advantage of the interpretation that frees Kant's argument in question from all reference to the infinity of space in the way suggested above, it might be said that the interpretation precludes all such objections as relate to the infinity of space. These objections are of two types :[21] (1) that space is in fact not infinite, but finite, though unbounded, and (2) that, supposing space to be infinite, the representation of it cannot be intuitive for the simple reason that the infinite space is no *given* object of intuition.

It is now time to come to a decision with regard to the above interpretation. What is called an advantage of that interpretation will be reckoned rather as its defect by some, who may insist that Kant's argument should be taken as it is and that the objections mentioned above should not be dodged, but faced. This is certainly a quite reasonable attitude, and we cannot help sharing it.

The next task, then, is to consider Kant's argument in the light of such other interpretations as make it primarily dependent on the alleged infinity of space. One such interpretation is adopted by Prichard, and since he is not alone in accepting it, it is worthy of some examination.

12.2.3 An examination of Prichard's interpretation

Prichard's interpretation is this :[22] Although a concept has an infinity of (possible) individuals coming under it, it does not consist of an infinite number of elements; thus, e.g. the elements that go to make up the concept of triangularity or redness are not infinite. But space consists of an infinite number of elements, and therefore space is not a concept (that is, the representation of space is not a concept but an intuition).

This interpretation is not without its difficulties. The word 'representations' occurring in the following two contrasted statements of Kant's is expected to have the same sense : (i) 'Every concept contains an infinite number of different possible representations . . . *under* itself', but (ii) 'no concept, as such, can be thought as containing an infinite number of representations *within* itself'. But on Prichard's interpretation, the word is taken in two different senses in the two cases : in the sense of 'instances' (or, as he says, 'individuals') in the first case, and in the sense of 'partial representations' or 'marks' (or, as he says, 'elements') in the second.[23]

Moreover, it is doubtful whether the view here ascribed to Kant by Prichard (and others)[24] – namely, that a concept, unlike space, is not analysable into an infinite number of elements – is really Kant's. In any case, the view is contradicted by what Kant says in the following passage of the *Critique* :

> . . . if we limit our attention to the sphere of the concept which marks out a genus, we can no more determine how far it is possible to proceed in the [logical] division of it, than we can judge merely from the space which a body occupies how far it is possible to proceed in the [physical] division of its parts. Consequently, every genus requires diversity of species, and these in turn diversity of subspecies; and since no one of these subspecies is ever itself without a sphere (extent as *conceptus communis*), reason, in being carried to completion, demands that no species be regarded as being in itself the lowest. For since the species is always a concept, containing only what is common to different things, it is not completely determined. It cannot, therefore, be directly related to an individual, and other concepts, that is, subspecies, must always be contained under it.[25]

[A view similar to the one expressed in the above passage is presented in Kant's *Logic* (§ 11).][26]

As regards Prichard's interpretation, it has to be considered, then, to be somewhat suspect.

Since Prichard's interpretation is discarded, the issue whether a (general) concept must consist of a definite number of marks or is in principle analysable *ad infinitum* is irrelevant and need not be discussed.

12.2.4 The preferred interpretation

We think Kant's argument under examination is best interpreted in terms of the following two points :

A general concept has an infinite number of possible instances *under* itself, but it does not contain them *within* itself. Since a concept does not contain its instances *within* itself, the concept by itself does not enable us to pronounce on the number of its instances. The most that can be said is that it *possibly* contains – or, in other words, that it purports to refer to – an infinite number of instances. So the general concept of spaces (i.e. of spatiality) cannot be regarded as the source of our consciousness that there are, and are all at once, an infinite number of spaces. We are in possession of the idea (according to Kant) that spaces 'coexist *ad infinitum*', that is, that they are all at once to infinity.[27] This idea, which cannot be explained in terms of any mere discursive concept, must have a non-conceptual source.

Secondly, (as Kant's clause 'all the parts of space coexist *ad infinitum*' implies) we represent the spaces as 'parts of space', that is, as being not only infinite in number, but also the parts of space, which is why our representation of space is that of an infinite whole. Now, spaces, in order that they may be instances of the general concept of spaces, must be distinguishable factors; but they cannot be distinguished except *within* space. As Kuno Fischer puts it, the general concept of space 'must be abstracted from various spaces, as the concept man is from various men', and then this concept

> must contain all the attributes which are common to all spaces, and *only* these. There should then, evidently, be further attributes by which the various spaces are distinguished, and these distinguishing attributes must be here, as in all other cases, *not* the common ones. Can any one tell us a single conceivable attribute to distinguish one space from another –

> a single attribute, *not* spatial and spatial *only*? All spaces, however they may differ, only differ in space . . .[28]

(It may be added that spaces are not originally distinguished even by reference to the objects occupying them, because, as was noticed in connexion with Kant's first space argument, objects, which may be qualitatively and quantitatively quite alike, can be distinguished, ultimately, by reference to their difference of locations.)[29] Space *within* which spaces are distinguishable spatially somehow (that is, in a manner that cannot be conceptually spelled out) thus provides the very instances of the general concept of spaces, and accordingly Kant says that 'the original representation of space is an *a priori* intuition, not a concept'.

The two objections, already mentioned, to Kant's fourth space argument with reference to the alleged infinity of space are considered in the next chapter.

NOTES :

1. Cf. above, p. 27.
2. See, e.g. Kemp Smith, *Commentary,* 1918, p. 108; Paton, *Kant's Metaphysic of Experience,* 1951, vol. I, p. 120; F. Grayeff, *Kant's Theoretical Philosophy,* trans. D. Walford, 1970, p. 42.

   Garnett, however, does not accept the usual interpretation, and has in this connexion criticized Vaihinger; see his *The Kantian Philosophy of Space,* 1939, pp. 191-194. Garnett's own interpretation does not appeal to us.
3. Paton, *op. cit.,* p. 120.
4. The word 'recognises' in Paton's clause 'In the second edition Kant recognises' makes us suppose that he is suggesting a reason for Kant's revision of the argument in question.
5. Victor Cousin; *The Philosophy of Kant,* trans. A. G. Henderson, Chapman's Quarterly Series, No. V, John Chapman, London, 1854, p. 48.
6. In 12.2.4.
7. Garnett, *op. cit.,* p. 195.
8. *Ibid.,* p. 194.
9. *Ibid.,* p. 195.

10. Below, pp. 414, 429-430.
11. See, e.g. Kemp Smith, *op. cit.,* pp. 108f.; Paton, *op. cit.,* p. 120; C. D. Broad, *Kant : An Introduction,* ed. C. Lewy, 1979, p. 35.
12. See, e.g. S. Körner, *Kant,* 1960, p. 34.
13. W. Windelband, *A History of Philosophy,* trans. J. H. Tufts, 1959, p. 539.
14. J. Hartnack (*Kant's Theory of Knowledge,* 1968, p. 20) regards the difference between 'a part of' and 'an instance of' as the fundamental point on which Kant's argument in question is based.
15. On the question whether a concept, for Kant, is contained in its *instances* (which are objects) or in the *representations* of those instances (i.e. objects); cf. Hartman and Schwarz, *Immanuel Kant : Logic,* p. 96 n. 2. [Strictly speaking, the content of a concept is contained in our intuitions of objects, which are its instances; cf. Paton, *op. cit.,* p. 194]
16. See Körner, *loc. cit.*
17. 'Every intuition contains in itself a manifold . . .'; *Critique,* A 99; cf. also B 136a.
18. Concepts, for Kant, 'rest on functions', and by 'function' he means the unitary act of 'bringing various representations under one common representation'. See A 68 = B 93.
19. § 15, B, C; Handyside trans., pp. 59-60.
20. Cf. Kemp Smith, *op. cit.,* p. 108 (last para, second sentence).
21. See below, 13.1 and 13.2.
22. Prichard, *Kant's Theory of Knowledge,* 1909, p. 48. [Prichard writes 'conception' instead of 'concept', and 'perception' instead of 'intuition'.]
23. Paton takes the word 'representations' (or, as he translates it, 'ideas') to stand for 'instances' in both of its occurrences here. Cf. Paton, *op. cit.,* p. 120 (third para), and notes 2 and 3 to that page.
24. J. Watson, *Kant and His English Critics,* James Maclehose, Glasgow, 1881, p. 45; Caird, *The Critical Philosophy of Immanuel Kant,* 1909, vol. I, p. 270. Caird, however, points out that Kant only 'provisionally' assumes the view that a 'conception' is 'the combination of a certain definite number of marks' in order to refute the Leibnizian view that space is an 'obscure conception'.
25. A 655f. = B 683f.

26. *Logic,* § 11, Note; Hartman and Schwarz trans., pp. 103-104 : . . . there is no lowest concept (*conceptus infimus*) or lowest species in the series of species and genera under which not yet another would be contained, because it is impossible to determine such a concept . . . Only *relative to use* are there lowest concepts which have received this meaning, as it were, by convention, to the extent that one has agreed to go no further down'. Cf. also M. Thompson, 'Singular Terms and Intuitions in Kant's Epistemology', *Review of Metaphysics* 26 (1972), p. 330.
27. Or, in the translation used by Prichard, *loc. cit.,* spaces '*ad infinitum* exist simultaneously'.
28. Kuno Fischer, *A Commentary on Kant's Critick of the Pure Reason,* trans. J. P. Mahaffy, Longmans, Green & Co., London, 1866, pp. 41-42.
29. Above, 4.1.2.3 and 4.1.2.3.1.

CHAPTER THIRTEEN

KANT'S FOURTH SPACE ARGUMENT (Continued)

13.1 On the Infinity of Space

The first and foremost objection to Kant's fourth space argument is that space is as a matter of fact not infinite, but finite, though unbounded.[1] Bennett accordingly says that 'its sole premiss is false'.[2]

Criticism of this sort cannot, however, be regarded as just. One need hardly point out that Kant's model of space is different from that of the relativistic physicists, for whom space (or, what is for *them* the same, the universe)[3] is finite-though-unbounded. But the models being different, the question of contradiction does not arise here. Accordingly, what can in the end be justly maintained is not that the premise of Kant's argument is to be rejected as *false,* but that it has to be set aside as being *irrelevant* to the contemporary context. This is the worst that can be said against Kant.

The situation, however, really is not even as bad as that, for the following two reasons :

In the first place, the relativistic theory of the finitude of space has not gained universal acceptance among the contemporary physicists. There are distinguished scientists who, without abandoning the theory of relativity, nevertheless advocate a cosmological theory which upholds the infinity of space and time. Reference is being made here to what has been called the 'steady-state' theory maintained by Sciama, Bondi, and Hoyle. For the relativity theory as also for another theory (held by Alpher, Bethe, and Gamow) differing from the former in detail, the universe is finite both in size and in age, and 'its history is one of continuous evolution from an assignable beginning when all matter was concentrated in a single dense mass, to the present far-flung distribution of a multitude of galaxies';[4] while the steady-state theory, 'in opposition to evolutionary views, alleges the spontaneous and continuous creation of matter in space'[5] and describes the process in a way that involves the denial of finite space and time.[6] Naturally, varieties of objections have been urged against this last theory; but Hoyle maintains that all these objections can be met.[7] It is not for us to judge which of these currently advocated cosmological theories is the best; it can only be noted that 'at this stage of scientific knowledge decision between the alternatives still hangs in the balance'.[8] Such being the situation, it is clear that if the only reason for rejecting a philosophical argument based on a premise that appeals to the infinity of space be the conflict of the premise with the scientist view, then no such reason can be unambiguously adduced with confidence.

In the second place (although this second point is not altogether different from the first), as regards the relativistic theory of finite-though-unbounded space itself, one may well raise the question how much of it is scientist and how much speculative. Russell, though he is no less critical of Kant's premise under consideration than Bennett, has thought fit in a different context to discriminate between two parts of Einstein's theory :

> Einstein's substitution of space-time for space and time represents a change of language for which there are the same sort of grounds of simplicity as there were for the Copernican change of language. This part of Einstein's theory may be accepted with considerable confidence. But the view that the universe is a three-dimensional sphere of finite diameter remains speculative; no one would be surprised if evidence were found which would lead astronomers to give up this way of speaking.[9]

It cannot be said, therefore, that we know, in the strong sense of knowing, that the actual space is finite.

What we want to emphasize is not that Kant's *premiss is* true, but simply that there is no decisive reason for setting it aside as quite unworthy of attention. [This is said because Bennett summarily rejects Kant's argument with the remark : 'The obscurity of this argument does not matter, since its sole premiss is false'.[10]] We cannot lose sight of the possibility that the model of an infinite space may at some time again in future prove, to the satisfaction of all, more adequate. We learn that recent work in astronomy and cosmology dealing with the universe in the large has tended to show that the possibility just mentioned is worth envisaging, and further that, should this possibility be realized, 'the mathematical ideas of set theory will come more prominently into play'.[11]

We are, therefore, forced to conclude that Kant's argument in question cannot be unceremoniously set aside for the one and only reason that its premise has to do with the infinity of space.

[Bennett has taken Kant's premise to be 'that space is necessarily infinite';[12] and that is why perhaps he is so confident that the premise is false. But, in fact, Kant's premise is not that space is *necessarily* represented, but only that it is represented, as an infinite given magnitude. True, his conclusion is not simply that the representation of space is an intuition, but that it is an *a priori* intuition. The occurrence of 'a priori' in his conclusion, however, does not by itself justify Bennett's paraphrase of the premise. Kant may have inserted 'a priori', in his conclusion because he thinks he has already proved before that the representation of space is a priori.[13] Even on the supposition that he has taken the present argument itself to be proving the apriority as well as the intuitivity of the representation of space, one need not ascribe to him the stronger premise such as that stated by Bennett. For there is reason to believe that Kant thinks the representation of an infinite space as such, no matter whether it is necessary or not, is non-empirical.[14]]

13.2 On the Givenness of the One Infinite Space

The second objection to Kant's argument in question to the effect that the infinite whole space is actually not *given* to us falls to be considered next.

This objection, which is urged by Prichard,[15] is virtually the same as his objection to Kant's third space argument on the score that 'space as a whole is not object of perception', and is, accordingly, subject to the comments that we have already made on the latter.[16]

Attention may be called here to what Caird has said by way of anticipating and answering this objection on behalf of Kant.[17] He says that Kant has himself shown in the Analytic and the Dialectic that an infinite whole can no more actually be *given* than any other individual object in the completeness of its determination. According to Kant, the whole space could be determined (that is, determinately known), which is not to say that it is actually ever determined, only through a successive process of synthesis. In this successive process of synthesis, however, the idea of the whole space is presupposed from the start. Now it is the idea of the presupposed whole which appears in the present argument as the representation of space as an infinite given whole. The infinite whole space is not *actually* given in the sense of being given in the completeness of its individual determination; it is nevertheless *potentially* (indeterminately) given, or, as Kant says, *represented* as given, because the idea of it is presupposed in, and does not originally arise from, the successive process of synthesis by which it is sought to be determined. (We may here refer to the discussion made in the second section of Chapter Eleven).

In the rejected first-edition version of the argument from infinity Kant has said that the principle of infinity is *yielded* by the limitlessness in the progression in intuition. This may suggest that the infinite space can in no sense be represented as *given*. There is no such suggestion in any sentence of the substituted argument of the second edition. The limitlessness in the progression in intuition is but a progression from intuition to intuition *ad infinitum;* and even the second-edition argument (although it does not mention the progression in question) leaves this to be understood that it is a progression *within* the infinite space, that is, one that presupposes and is guided by the idea of the infinite space. This presupposed idea of the infinite is, in other words, the representation of the infinite magnitude *given.* (For reasons stated already,[18] the original source of this representation or idea is not the general concept of spaces.)

More will be said on this point in the final section of this chapter.

13.2.1 Garnett's criticism of, and suggestion on, Kant's fourth space argument considered

Garnett, however, thinks that Kant has not succeeded in establishing, even in the second-edition version of the argument in question, that the idea of space, *so far as its infinity is concerned,* is non-conceptual or intuitive. Garnett says that in this argument Kant believes that we have a total or complete apprehension of the infinite whole of space.[19] But the *total* apprehension of the infinite whole space cannot in the nature of the case be immediate and so intuitive, but is bound to be mediate or non-intuitive. Space is, for Kant, represented as an infinite whole in the sense that an infinite number of parts are represented as being *in* space. But, Garnett contends, the mind 'is just as incapable of viewing an infinite number of parts immediately as actually displayed before it as it is of continuing in the progression far enough to reach the infinite whole of space and viewing it directly'.[20] The principle of infinity yielded by the limitlessness in the progression of intuition (which is mentioned in the first-edition version of Kant's argument) is really a conceived principle, but similarly the fact (stressed in the present argument of the second edition) that an infinite number of parts are represented as being *in* space cannot show that the infinite whole space is directly presented to us in its completeness.

Garnett, although he is dissatisfied with Kant's present argument as it stands, suggests a further modification of it by which he thinks the difficulty mentioned above can be avoided.[21] The difficulty of the present argument is for Garnett due to Kant's assumption that the mind has a complete or *total* apprehension of the infinite whole space. This difficulty can be avoided, he thinks, by making a distinction between a *total* or *complete* apprehension of the infinite whole space and a *partial* apprehension of it. For he maintains that although a *complete immediate* apprehension of the infinite space is impossible (at least for man), a *partial immediate* apprehension of it may fairly be admitted. Garnett argues that we should distinguish between object and apprehension. The object may be either infinite or finite; likewise the apprehension of the object may be either total or partial;[22] these two sets of distinction are quite independent of each other; accordingly there may be a partial apprehension of an infinite object. The partial apprehension of an infinite object may, again, be either direct (i.e. immediate) or indirect (i.e. mediate). So we may envisage the possibility of a partial direct apprehension of an infinite object. Kant, however, is prevented from realizing the possibility of a partial direct (or immediate) apprehension of an infinite whole space by his inability to perceive the ambiguity of the term 'representation' – an ambiguity similar to the one pointed out by G. E. Moore in the term 'sensation'.[23] 'Representation' may mean either the act (process) of representing or the object represented. Now the fact that the object represented has a certain character does not entail that the representing or the way of apprehending that object must have a similar character, thus, e.g. the actual infinity of space does not necessarily imply that the apprehension also of the infinite space must be total or complete rather than partial. Kant, however, thinks at one stroke 'both the infinitude of space as the object and the totality or completeness of the act of apprehension as the process',[24] and is thus landed into the mistaken view that the mind has a total or complete immediate apprehension of the infinite whole space. Now, a question arises : Can there really be a partial and immediate apprehension of the infinite whole space ? And is there anything in Kant to suggest the possibility of such an apprehension ? Garnett says that although Kant has not himself realized the possibility of such an apprehension, he has nevertheless provided the basis for an affirmative answer to the question raised above. For, as Garnett puts it,

> the whole purport of Kant's preceding argument has been that the entire connotation of space is given immediately to the mind. The process of apprehension is partial rather than total not because the infinitude of space (as well as its other qualities) is not given immediately, but because other apprehensions of the same object (space) are possible.[25]

A blind man touching a part of the elephant could not have a partial immediate apprehension of the whole elephant, but *inferred* something else from the given datum, because 'the connotation of that datum did not exhaust the connotation of that object (elephant)';[26] but in the case of the infinite space, we

> apprehend it immediately *qua* infinite because this characteristic is as directly displayed to our contemplative gaze as any of its other qualities. The fact that there are several ways of gazing at it would involve a limitation of the qualities presented each time only if the connotation varied with each.

> Since there is no such variation, each partial apprehension yields the entire nature of the object. Infinite space is immediately and partially apprehended.[27]

A critical appraisal of Garnett's account of the partial immediate apprehension of the infinite space will now be in order.

By 'immediate apprehension' Garnett means 'intuition'; his view is that we have a partial, not total, intuition of the infinite space. The difficulty is how exactly the qualification 'partial' is to be understood. The explanation that he himself gives is of no help. He says that 'other apprehensions of the same object (space) are possible', that 'there are several ways of gazing at it [the infinite space]'. But the meaning of these sentences remains obscure. It may be as well to inquire whether or not Garnett's usage of 'partial or total apprehension' is the same as the ordinary usage of it.

In the ordinary usage, the partiality or totality of an apprehension is not its intrinsic property, but is to be understood rather in terms of the partiality or totality of the object to which it relates. 'Partial apprehension' in this sense is 'apprehension of only some qualities, or some part or parts, of an object'. As for Garnett, however, it is his special contention that the partial-total and mediate-immediate distinctions 'refer to the process rather than to the object'.[28] When he says that we have a partial immediate apprehension of the infinite space, he means that it is the infinite *whole* space, not simply a part of it, which is the direct object of this partial apprehension. The partiality of the apprehension here is not taken to reflect on that of the object concerned. Indeed, if Garnett is to be consistent, he cannot use the phrase 'partial immediate apprehension of space' in the sense of 'immediate apprehension of a part of space'. For, according to him, Kant's position in the Aesthetic is that the parts of space are not immediately apprehended at all : these are, he says, not the given features of intuition, but only 'thought of as in' space.[29]

Nor can it be supposed that by 'partial immediate apprehension of space' Garnett means 'immediate apprehension of only some of the qualities of space'; for he has explicitly said, as already noted, that 'the whole purport of Kant's preceding arguments has been that the entire connotation of space is given immediately to the mind'. 'Entire connotation' here means *all* the relevant qualities.

These considerations lead to the conclusion that Garnett's usage of the phrase 'partial apprehension' is not the same as the ordinary usage of it. This conclusion is unavoidable so long as it is assumed that Garnett is consistent.

Adhering still to the assmption regarding Garnett's consistency, it remains to ask, What does he mean by 'other apprehensions of' or 'several ways of gazing at' the infinite space ? What are the occasions for these several apprehensions or gazings ? The question is important because the alleged fact that there are *several* apprehensions or gazings constitutes his reason for calling each of these 'partial' rather than total.[30] Now, since he maintains that Kant in the Aesthetic does not regard the *parts* of space as given objects of intuition, he cannot find the requisite occasions in the apprehensions of the parts of space. Upon his interpretation of the Aesthetic, the one infinite space is intuited *temporally prior* to the distinction of parts in it.[31] The apprehensions (which are for *him* conceptual representations) of the parts of space, being thus temporally posterior to the intuition of the infinite space, cannot be supposed to provide the occasions for the latter. Is the intuition, or immediate apprehension, of the infinite space in its alleged occurrence temporally prior to the distinctions of parts in it to be called partial or total ? This question would not arise if he did not invoke the theory of temporal priority.

We may here stop short and examine the assumption that Garnett's exposition is consistent. It may be noted first that, although he maintains that Kant's view of space in the Aesthetic is inconsistent with his view in the Analytic, he does not say that Kant has held conflicting views within the brief compass of the Metaphysical Exposition of the Concept of Space itself. Should, then, Garnett's account of the arguments of the Metaphysical Exposition be found to reveal any inconsistencies, these must be due to him rather than to Kant. With this principle in mind, we may proceed to consider the following statements quoted from him :

> (1) When by a process of delimitation the mind thinks of parts of space as in space, what really lies back of each such conceived part is the one space.[32]

[This statement is part of Garnett's exposition of Kant's third space argument.]

> (2) Space is represented as an infinite given quantity since the parts are all at once given into infinity. The infinite space is given equally with a foot and with an ell, not because the mind may progress from the one to the other and so on, but because all such parts are simultaneously in the given space.[33]

[This is part of Garnett's exposition of Kant's fourth space argument of the second edition as contrasted with the argument of the first edition.]

It should be clear from these statements that the theory of temporal priority (of the intuition of the whole space to the representations of its parts) is progressively losing its force. This point, however, may be set aside for the time being. The suggestion of the quoted first statement is, at any rate, not so much that we begin by intuiting the one space and end by distinguishing or thinking of its parts as it is that each occasion of conceiving a part of space is *really* an occasion of intuiting the one space. This gives us a clue to the sought-for occasions of the *several immediate apprehensions* of the one space : several immediate apprehensions of the one entire space are possible *in connexion with our several conceptual representations of the parts of space.* The difficulty of this suggestion for the doctrine of *partiality* of the immediate apprehension of the one space does not matter; for what is more noteworthy is the incompatibility of this suggestion with the suggestion of the other statement made by Garnett. According to his second statement, the parts of space are 'given' (that is, not conceived, but immediately apprehended), and the infinite space is *'given equally'* with this part and any other part of space. Here, then, one finds a different explanation of the nature of the occasions for the several immediate apprehensions of the one infinite space; several immediate apprehensions of the entire space are possible *in connexion with our several immediate apprehensions of the parts of space.* [And this latter explanation is adhered to by him in his reply to an anticipated objection to the view that the infinite whole space is directly given to the mind *partially.* The objection is this : '. . . if the apprehension of space is partial, a finite portion is directly apprehended and its infinitude is necessarily inferred . . .'.[34] And his reply is : '. . . the whole purport of Kant's preceding arguments has been that the entire connotation of space is given immediately to the mind'.[35] The implication of the reply is that since the entire connotation of space is given in the given portion of space, it is not that the infinitude (the 'quality' of infinitude)[36] of space is not given so as to be inferred. This reply, good or bad, bears only on the second point of the objector, namely, that infinitude is inferred, but not on his first point, namely, that a finite portion of space is *directly apprehended.* The suggestion is fortified, therefore, that an immediate apprehension of the infinite space occurs on the occasion of *an immediate apprehension of a finite portion of space.*] We are now in a position to make a list of some of the inconsistencies on the part of Garnett :

(i) Within the self-same compass of Kant's Metaphysical Exposition of the Concept of Space, which Garnett himself does not take to be a patchwork of inconsistencies, we are now asked to believe that the parts of space are *not* intuited, and then that these *are* intuited. Alternatively, the occasions for the several intuitions of the one infinite space are now suggested to lie in the *conceptual* representations of the parts of space and then in the *non-conceptual* or immediate representation of those parts.

(ii) The *partial* intuitions ('immediate apprehensions') of the infinite space are suggested to have their occasions on the representations (no matter whether intuitive or conceptual) of *the parts of space.* And nothing has been done by Garnett to preclude the conclusion that it is the *partiality* of the parts of space (that is, of these *objects*) that gets transferred to the intuitions (that is, to these *processes* of intuiting) of the entire space. This tacit encouragement of the conclusion that the partiality here is ultimately of objects rather than of processes is clearly out of keeping with the claim that the partiality in question is rather of processes than of objects.

(iii) It is not quite clear whether the theory of temporal priority of the intuition of the entire space to the representations of its parts is maintained throughout Garnett's discussion of Kant's Metaphysical

Exposition of the Concept of Space. Whatever be the truth, the theory is either surrendered or not. In the former case, the inconsistency of Garnett's account hardly requires mention. But in the latter case also, an inconsistency breaks out, although at a different level. For in the case of temporal priority, at least one of the several occasions of the intuitions of the entire space is such that the entire space is then intuited prior to the representation of any part of it, any limited portion of it. But this intuition of the entire space cannot be called *partial*; for the limiting situations have not yet emerged. Thus, on Garnett's interpretation, Kant might at least once admit, and admit *without confusion,* that the mind has *total* intuition of the entire space. This cannot be reconciled, however, with Garnett's assertion that Kant's doctrine of the total intuition of the entire space depends on his 'unhappy confusion with reference to the term "representation"',[37] that is, the *confusion* between process and object of representation.

After the above comments on Garnett, we may, in fine, make the following observations :

(1) Garnett's criticism that Kant has adopted an untenable doctrine of the *total* or *complete* intuition of the infinite space may after all be disregarded. Garnett himself is led to maintain that an examination of Kant's fourth space argument (in the second-edition version) in the light of his 'preceding arguments' shows that Kant's real view is rather that we have a *partial* intuition of the infinite space.[38]

(2) As concerns Garnett's own account of the partial intuition (or intuitions) of the whole space on behalf of Kant, it is not satisfactory : it only makes difficulties, as has been found.

(3) In so far as Garnett (sometimes) suggests that the intuition of the whole space is occasioned by the intuitions of the parts of space, this suggestion, considered *in itself,* is not contradictory of the interpretation we ourselves have previously put upon Kant's doctrine of the intuition of the whole space. Garnett's reason for this suggestion of his is not, however, acceptable. His reason is that the intuition of the whole space is occasioned by the intuitions of the particular spaces, because 'the entire connotation' of the whole space is given in the given portions of space. But the entire connotation of the whole space admittedly includes the characteristic of unlimitedness, and it is hard to

believe that the given portions of space are in the same sense unlimited : these are just *limited* portions of space. [In the Kantian language, these arise through *limitation* of the one space.] As for the account we have previously given, it is (it may be recalled) rather that the intuition (in the minimum negative sense of non-mediated non-general representation)[39] of the whole space is presupposed in the intuitions of the parts of space, because the intuitions of these parts of space *qua limited* presuppose the representation of the unlimited whole, and this presupposed representation is not in its turn conceptually mediated.[40] [Our knowledge that the whole space is presupposed in the intuitions of the limited spaces is no doubt discursive; but it does not follow that the presupposed representation is itself discursive.][41]

13.3 Concluding Remarks on Kant's Fourth Space Argument

In this argument, Kant has highlighted the inexhaustible individuality of space. One can go on determining space *ad infinitum;* one may add part to part *ad infinitum* without exhausting space; one can enlarge one's intuitive consciousness of it without limit. Space provides from *within* itself the very instances, infinite in number, of the general concept of spatiality, which derives from representations of some of them, and so the representation of space is not mediated by this concept.

If, however, one thinks of space as the extendedness or spatiality of objects, the perspective changes. The representation of space then ceases to be looked upon as 'original' in the sense of being prior to the concept of spatiality. The concept of spatiality then comes to be viewed as a concept that is derived from the representation of the common feature of extended (spatial) empirical objects. In that case it is the spatial objects of sense which provide the instances of the concept of spatiality. Obviously, on this view the original representation of space is conceptual and empirical. To this view Kant, in the Metaphysical Exposition of the Concept of Space, is systematically opposed. In his first space argument, he has indicated that the original representation of space is not that of extendedness or spatiality, but of a framework in which objects are located outside us and as themselves outside and beside one another and accordingly as not only different, but in different places. He suggests there the priority of space over the objects in the sense that it is *ultimately* in virtue of locations in space that objects get individuated. In his second space argument, he carries further this view of the priority of space by maintaining that we can in some sense imagine empty space, which suggests that space is not to be reduced to any determination of objects. Space, according to Kant, is not to be construed as the spatiality or extendedness of objects. [It hardly needs pointing out that Descartes, for example, sought to reduce space to the extendedness of objects.][42]

For Kant, space, *even independently of the objects of the senses,* can provide the instances of the concept of spatiality. This point needs to be clarified and substantiated if the full force of his concluding sentence in the fourth space argument–'Consequently, the original representation of space is an *a priori* intuition, not a concept' – is to be manifest. In this connexion the following extract from the introductory section of the Transcendental Aesthetic is particularly noteworthy :

> Thus, if I take away from the representation of a body that which the understanding thinks in regard to it, substance, force, divisibility, etc., and likewise what belongs to sensation, impenetrability, hardness, colour, etc., something still remains over from this empirical intuition, namely, extension and figure. These belong to pure intuition, . . . *even without any actual object of the senses or of sensation* . . . [Italics not in the text.][43]

The import of this passage is well brought out by A. H. Smith as follows : 'What was the object is now [i.e. after the elimination of the purely empirical and the conceptual] . . . a particular area or volume of space, which is itself a determinate part of the totality of space'.[44] One can now see that the parts of space (areas or volumes), which are still instances of spatiality, are what space provides from *within* itself. The following observation made by A. H. Smith (although couched in words some of which are not, from the fastidious point of view, quite appropriate to our context) throws some further light on this point :

> We have noticed generally that the form of space itself includes . . . the instances of spatiality. In the same way it includes the instances of particularized geometrical concepts. If we think, for example, of the concepts of a circle or a triangle their proper instances are at once infinite and present anywhere in the form of space; for the form of space is such that instances of a circle or a triangle can be anywhere in it. So far from it being true that instances can only be found in objects, the qualities other than geometrical which constitute an object are altogether irrelevant as regards the instantiation of any geometrical concept. Here again we see . . . that the instances are provided by the form of space itself.[45]

Thus the representation of space, in so far as it is the a priori foundation of the concept of spatiality, which is infinitely instantiable, is 'an *a priori* intuition'.

The main difficulty of Kant's fourth space argument concerns, however, his statement that the infinite whole space is represented as *given*. But the difficulty persists owing largely to the persistence of such a notion of 'given' as that the given is so situated in relation to the percipient that he has a synoptic view of it at a glance.[46] In the case in question, however, the given is to be understood only in terms of *immediacy* of awareness, where 'immediacy' in turn is to be understood in the sense of 'not mediated by any process of conception or intellection'.[47] It may be permissible to spell out, as if the previous observations had not been enough, the persistent objection to the suggestion that the *original* idea of the infinite whole space is not mediate, and then see how it errs. The objection, then, is this :

> It is true that when in the perceptual situation we represent to ourselves a particular space, we are immediately aware of it as limited and connected with surrounding spaces, and that when we come to make these surrounding spaces themselves into clear objects of representation in turn, we are equally immediately aware of them as limited and connected with still surrounding spaces, and so on continuously. All this shows only that we can successively go on intuiting particular spaces

> as limited parts of wider and wider wholes. Now, recognising no limit in this progression in intuition of particular spaces,[48] we ultimately, by some sort of imaginative synthesis or intellectual construction, come to form the idea of the one unlimited infinite whole space. This idea, being thus dependent on some sort of intellectual construction, is after all *mediate.*

To this objection the reply is that the idea in question is not dependent on, but is rather presupposed in, the sort of intellectual construction mentioned. For such intellectual construction admittedly awaits the recognition of *limitlessness* in the progression in intuitions, and the question is as to the ground of this recognition. If we intuited simply a great many limited spaces successively, then no amount of imaginative or intellectual synthesis of these convenient-sized bits could give us the idea of an unlimited infinite whole : it could at most give us the idea of a *vast* totality. In addition to our many successive limited intuitions, something is therefore necessary, namely, the recognition of *limitlessness* in the progression in intuitions. But this recognition presupposes that we are already in possession of the idea of the unlimited infinite whole.

Kant does not distinguish between the unlimited and the infinite.[49] As to the idea of the unlimited space, the way in which it serves as a presuppositional factor in experience demands a special notice : it is presupposed not merely in our *advances* to further intuitions of spaces, but also (as Kant suggests in his third space argument) in *each* of our intuitions of limited spaces *qua* limited.[50] It is not the case, then, that this idea has just a regulative significance.[51]

NOTES :

1. See, e.g. Bertrand Russell, *History of Western Philosophy,* London, 1962, p. 688; and Bennett, *Kant's Analytic*, 1966, pp. 66f.
2. *Ibid.,* p. 66.
3. Cf., e.g. Errol E. Harris, *The Foundations of Metaphysics in Science,* George Allen and Unwin, London, 1965, p. 83; D. P. Dryer, *Kant's Solution for Verification in Metaphysics,* 1966, p. 166.
4. Harris, *op. cit.,* p. 92.

5. *Ibid.*, pp. 92f.
6. *Ibidem.*
7. *Ibid.*, pp. 93-95.
8. *Ibid.*, p. 95.
9. Bertrand Russell, *Human Knowledge : Its Scope and Limits,* Sixth Paperback Printing, p. 198.
10. Bennett, *op. cit.*, p. 66.
11. Mark Kac and Stanislaw Ulam, *Mathematics and Logic : Retrospect and Prospects,* a Pelican Book, 1971, p. 191.
12. Bennett, *loc. cit.*
13. Paton, *Kant's Metaphysic of Experience,* 1951, vol. I, p. 117 n. 1.
14. Cf. *Reflexionen Kants zur kritischen Philosophie,* ed. Erdmann, 1884, Bd. II, No. 403. [The Reflexion in question is translated and cited by Kemp Smith also; see his *Commentary,* 1918, p. 106.] Cf. also Broad, *Kant,* 1979, p. 35 (second para).
15. Prichard, *Kant's Theory of Knowledge,* 1909, p. 48 (second para). See also B. Russell, *Our Knowledge of the External World,* London, 1952, p. 118. [Russell's view is examined in the next chapter].
16. In 9.3 [pp. 323ff.].
17. See Caird, *The Critical Philosophy of Immanuel Kant,* 1909, vol. I, pp. 268-272.
18. In 12.2.4.
19. Garnett, *The Kantian Philosophy of Space,* 1939, p. 196.
20. *Ibidem.*
21. *Ibid.*, p. 199.
22. *Ibid.*, p. 197.
23. *Ibid.*, p. 198.
24. *Ibidem.*
25. *Ibid.*, p. 200.
26. *Ibidem.*
27. *Ibidem.*
28. *Ibid.*, p. 198.
29. Cf. above, 9.5.

30. See the quotation as referred to by note 25.
31. This temporal interpretation has been considered more than once in this work.
32. Garnett, *op. cit.*, p. 187.
33. *Ibid.*, p. 196.
34. *Ibid.*, p. 199.
35. *Ibid.*, p. 200. Also quoted before.
36. Cf. his expression 'the infinitude of space (as well as its other qualities)' in the already quoted passage as indicated by note 25. He also observes about space (*Ibid.*, p. 192) : 'Its infinitude is [for Kant] given to us as a quality, and also . . . as a quantity . . .'.
37. *Ibid.*, p. 198.
38. Cf. the quotation indicated by note 25.
39. Cf. above, 1.4.
40. See above, pp. 321f., 327-329.
41. See above, pp. 322-323.
42. As Descartes says : '. . . we never indeed distinguish space from extension in length, breadth, and depth . . .'. See his 'The Principles of Philosophy', pt. II, § xv, in *A Discourse on Method, etc.*, trans. Veitch, 'Everyman's Library, No. 570', 1949, p. 206.
43. *Critique*, A 20-21 = B 35.
44. A. H. Smith, *A Treatise on Knowledge*, 1943, p. 78.
45. *Ibid.*, pp. 81-82.
46. On the point that this notion of 'given' is not relevant to the Kantian view of pure intuition of infinite space, cf. Schulze's reply to Eberhard, in H. E. Allison, *The Kant-Eberhard Controversy*, 1973, Appendix B, p. 173 (11.11-14).
47. For a critique of Parsons' view that the immediacy of an intuition 'means that the object of an intuition is in some way directly present to the mind, as in perception . . .', see above, pp. 19ff.
48. Cf. A. E. Taylor, *Elements of Metaphysics*, University Paperbacks, 1961, p. 247 (11.4-5).
49. Cf. his fifth argument on time at A 32 = B 47-48; Cf. also his words (at A 418 = B 445) : 'is without limits or beginnings, i.e. is infinite'.

50. See above, pp. 321-322.

51. This may be treated as a passing comment on the suggestion that the idea of infinite space is for Kant an Idea of Reason. (The sources of this suggestion are : Kant, *The Critique of Judgement* [§ 26] trans. J. C. Meredith, 1980, pp. 102f. [V, 254f.]; Kant, *Metaphysical Foundations of Natural Science*, trans. E. B. Bax, George Bell and Sons, London, 1883, 'General Observation on Phenomenology'; in the fourth division, pp. 238-239.)

CHAPTER FOURTEEN

A FINAL ESTIMATE

14.1 Some Post-Kantian Alternatives to Kant's Theory Considered

Kant's theory that the original idea of space is an a priori intuition had its repercussions on subsequent researches concerning the nature of the idea of space.[1] Accordingly a number of alternatives to this theory have developed. A critical examination of some of these alternatives has to be undertaken lest this Study should remain formally incomplete. We propose to consider three prominent theories which are among these alternatives.

A probable objection to at least the first two of the theories to be considered is that they are just psychological accounts of the genesis of the idea of space and are as such not proper objects of consideration for this Study. But it must be emphasized that, concerned as they are with the genesis of the idea of space, they yet claim to have a bearing on the epistemological question of the *status* of this idea : they claim to establish the conclusion, contradictory of Kant's, that this idea is empirical, not a priori. Moreover, an eminent Kantian scholar[2] does refer *inter alia* to these theories in the context of a criticism of Kant's theory itself and even prefers one of these to Kant's theory.

Since a detailed discussion of the theories in view is not feasible in this work, a uniform general principle of evaluation is needed. It has been found, while studying Kant's first space argument, that his main contention against the empirical account of the idea of space is that such an account errs by already presupposing this idea in the attempted explanation of it.[3] If he is right – if, that is to say, the idea of space is a priori –, then an empirical account of this idea must involve a *petitio principii.* This yields the requisite principle of evaluation for the theories to be considered, which is to analyse each of them only so far as is necessary to make it plain that it involves a *petitio principii.*

14.1.1 Critique of the Brown-Bain-Mill theory of the idea of space

The first theory to be considered is the one advocated by Brown, Bain, and Mill. The theory is called 'the psychological theory' of 'the idea of extension'[4] by Mill, who has sought to defend it against objections urged on behalf of Kant by Mahaffy.

The main point of the theory is, as Mill succinctly puts it, 'that the idea of Space is, at bottom, one of time – and that the notion of extension or distance, is that of a motion of the muscles continued for a longer or a shorter duration'.[5]

According to Bain,[6] the muscular sense yields two modes of feeling, or unique discriminative sensibility : sensibility to the *amount or intensity or degree* of muscular effort involved in the contraction of a muscle, and sensibility to the *duration* (i.e. a shorter or longer continuance) of the muscular effort in question. The former is the empirical source of the idea of *resistance* and the latter that of the idea of *extension or space.* It is argued that the idea of the *succession* of muscular feelings becomes the idea of a certain kind of *length* which transforms itself into the idea of linear extension (or, in Brown's phraseology, longitudinal extension).[7]

It seems that the idea of extension which is the point to be explained is already presupposed in the above account. As Hamilton observes :

> Length is an ambiguous term; and it is length in space, extensive length, and not length in time, protensive length, whose notion it is the problem to evolve. To convert, therefore, the notion of a certain kind of length (and that certain kind of length being also confessedly only length in time) into the notion of a length in space, is at best an idle begging of the question . . .[8]

Mill, however, argues that this criticism is unfair, because it is the deliberate contention of the theory in question that the idea of the one kind of length, namely, extensive length, is a product of the idea of the other kind, namely, protensive length.[9] Nevertheless the question arises : How can the idea of the mere *succession* of muscular feelings engender the idea of *extension,* of which the essence is *coexistence* ?

In answer to this question Mill says that when Brown and Bain speak of the succession of muscular sensations, there is no reason to think that they mean *mere* succession, because the idea of time being already supposed to be given, besides muscular feelings, the idea of *simultaneity* cannot be considered to be lacking. Hence there is no absurdity in maintaining that the idea of simultaneous existence, or extension, evolves from the idea of succession of muscular feelings in combination with the already acquired idea of simultaneity.[10]

Mill has accordingly restated the muscle-and-time theory of the idea of space as follows :

> Suppose two small bodies, A and B, sufficiently near together to admit of their being touched simultaneously, one with the right hand, the other with the left. Here are two tactual sensations which are simultaneous, just as a sensation of colour and one of odour might be; and this makes us cognise the two objects of touch as both existing at once. The question then is, what have we in our minds when we represent to ourselves the relation between these two objects already known to be simultaneous, in the form of Extension, or intervening Space – a relation which we do not suppose to exist between the colour and the odour. Now those who agree with Brown, say that whatever the notion of Extension may be, we *acquire* it by passing our hand or some other organ of touch in a longitudinal direction from A to B : that this process, as far as we are conscious of it, consists of a series of varied muscular sensations, differing according to the amount of muscular effort, and, the effort being given, differing in length of time. When we say that there is a space between A and B, we mean that some amount of these muscular sensations must intervene; and when we say that the space is greater or less, we mean that the series of sensations (amount of muscular effort being given) is longer or shorter . . .[11]

In the above exposition the expression to be noticed particularly is 'longitudinal direction from A to B'. Here Mahaffy's criticism is quite natural, namely, that any 'mention or postulating of *direction* cannot be for a moment allowed', because direction has no possible meaning except in space.[12] To such a criticism, however, Mill's reply is as follows :

First, to postulate direction is 'to postulate, not space, but the element which the notion of space is made of'.[13] For the notion of space is that of 'the aggregate of directions', just as the notion of time is that of the aggregate of successions, so that one should say more properly that space means direction than that direction means space.

Secondly, what is postulated is not direction, but 'the distinctive sensations which, from the first, accompany the motions of a limb in what we, with our acquired perceptions, call variety of directions'.[14] That there are such distinctive sensations cannot be denied, because then 'we should not . . . know, when our eyes are shut, in what direction our arm is moving'.[15]

The above reply made by Mill may now be examined. It is elear from the first point in his reply, where he says that space and time are respectively the aggregate of directions and the aggregate of successions, that for him direction is no element in the notion of time. This is indeed a reasonable view, because when we ordinarily speak of time as moving in one direction we already spatialize time by representing it in a straight line. One may also concede to the second point of Mill's reply, where he says that the different kinds of muscular sensation which arise from the movements of limbs are the only intended point to be attended to, in distinction from the movements of limbs in different directions. According to Mill, then, the muscular sensations of themselves do not involve the notion of direction, nor is this notion involved in that of time as such. The problem now arises : How can the notion of direction, an admittedly spatial determination, arise from the muscular sensations and the notion of time ? The only road open is to maintain that although neither muscular sensations in themselves nor the idea of time in itself contains the notion of direction, the *combination* of the two former results in the latter. Indeed, this is rather admitted by Mill and others in their expositions. But, then, as Höffding points out, a transformation is here admitted, 'a psychical synthesis, analogous to chemical synthesis, out of which arise compound substances with properties not possessed by the elements'.[16] Here we are provided with a doctrine of 'mental chemistry', of which Mill is an advocate, though not a consistent one, as William James has observed.[17] This inevitable recourse in the end to the doctrine of mental chemistry is, as James rightly maintains, a virtual surrender to the Kantian apriorism; for this practically amounts to the confession that the idea of space or of anything spatial (e.g. direction) has ultimately a 'super-sensational' source.[18] In other words, Mill has not succeeded in explaining the idea of space empirically without already presupposing in a way this idea.

14.1.2 Critique of James's theory of extensity

William James is also severely critical of the Kantian view of the idea of space, about which he says : 'I call this view mythological, because I am conscious of no such Kantian machine-shop in my mind, and feel no call to disparage the powers of poor sensation . . .'.[19] [James has also rejected the theories put forward by Lotze,[20] Wundt, Helmholtz, Lipps, and others.][21]

Even a Kantian scholar like Kemp Smith is of the opinion that Kant's theory of the apriority of the idea of space is based on a faulty assumption about the nature of sensations, which is 'first effectively called in question by William James'.[22] The word 'effectively' here clearly indicates Kemp Smith's approval of James's theory of extensity of sensations.

James's theory is well known. The essence of the theory is, in his own words, that 'there is an *extensive* quality given immediately in certain particular sensations'[23] and that this quality, *'discernible in each and every sensation', 'is the original sensation of space,* out of which all the exact knowledge about space that we afterwards come to have is woven by processes of discrimination, association, and selection'.[24] This quality he calls, after James Ward, 'extensity'.[25]

William James has given a number of illustrations and used a number of alternative terms to indicate what is meant by 'extensity'. Yet the meaning of this crucial word remains obscure. He says that extensity is 'the element of voluminousness' in our sensations,[26] 'a certain enormousness of feeling',[27] and so on.[28] But such words as 'voluminousness' and 'enormousness', if not used in Pickwickian senses, are apt to be taken in their ordinary senses. In the ordinary usage they are applied to material objects and mean 'occupying a large volume of space', 'filling a large portion of space', and the like. Evidently, if they are applied to sensations or sensa, they should mean that the sensa in question occupy a certain considerable portion of space. Not that it will be absurd to say of sensa that they occupy space. Moore in his 1910-11 lectures on sense-data explains the view that takes sense-data to be parts of a material object as the view which means that the sense-data, e.g. colours, occupy parts of 'the volume in space occupied by the whole [material] object'.[29] James also has said, at least in one place, that extensity or enormousness of feeling carries the awareness of the filling of a considerable portion of space : 'Loud sounds have a certain enormousness of feeling. It is impossible to conceive of the explosion of a cannon as filling a small space. In general, sounds seem to occupy all the room between us and their source; . . .'.[30] The pertinent question here is whether 'extensity' or 'enormousness of feeling' means, according to him, the same as 'filling or occupying a large space'. On referring to another passage in his book, one finds him saying : '. . . although a feeling of absolute bigness may, *a feeling of place cannot,* possibly *form an immanent element in any single isolated sensation'.*[31] In this passage 'a feeling of absolute bigness' means, as the context shows, the feeling (that is, sensation)[32] of extensity or the feeling of enormousness : such phrases as 'feeling of enormousness' and 'enormousness of feeling' are used interchangeably by him. The passage, oviously, suggests a *negative* answer to the question asked above. It means that although the felt extensity is, the felt occupation of place is not, an immanent quality of sensa, or as he says, sensations. This contradicts his earlier observation that 'a centain enormousness of feeling' (that is, felt extensity) with respect to sounds involves their 'seeming to occupy all the room between us and their source' (that is, their felt occupation of a very considerable portion of space, the word 'seem' here signifying 'sense-feeling'[33]). These discordant notes in James's account suggest only that he has not succeeded in rendering clear the meaning of 'extensity'.

Bradley says :

> What has been called 'extensity' appears to me (as offered) to involve a confusion. When you know what you mean by it, it seems to turn to be either spatial at once and downright, or else not spatial at all. It seems useful, in part, only as long as you allow it to be obscure.[34]

Bradley's alternative 'or else it is not spatial at all' would not be acceptable to James, who explicitly calls extensity a 'spatial quality'[35] or an original 'spatial feeling'.[36] And this is easily understandable, because, should extensity be itself non-spatial, James's account of the idea of space in terms of it would be open to his own criticisms of the associationists' attempt to build up this idea out of non-spatial elements.[37] Extensity is, then, for him *spatial*; but, surely, he cannot admit that it is 'spatial at once and downright'. His view, at least in intention, is rather that it is a felt quality in sensation from which our idea of space develops. But Joseph argues :

> If . . . there is a wide interval between an initial apprehension of . . . extensity and our developed apprehension of a systematic spatial order, then extensity and spatial order should be one and the same thing, which we apprehend at first confusedly and afterwards clearly, since apprehension of one thing cannot develop into apprehension of another.[38]

The implication of this criticism is that James cannot both eat the pudding and have it, or in other words, cannot escape from the dilemma that extensity is either non-spatial or spatial in the exclusive sense of 'or'.

Indeed, there is no satisfactory answer, from James's side, to the question, in what sense is extensity 'spatial' ? To call it 'spatial', as he does, for no better reason than that 'all the exact knowledge about space that we afterwards come to have'[39] is derived from it is to beg the issue against the advocates of alternative theories. To say that it is spatial because subsequent analytic attention discriminates in it spatial characteristics is useless for two reasons : first, unless extensity in its primordial givenness itself offered, however vaguely, spatiality to our awareness, the subsequent employment of it as the relevant object of analytic attention would be preposterous, and, secondly, how to decide that what subsequent analytic attention is supposed to reveal has not been rather read into it (extensity) under the influence of some a priori representation ?

It may be argued that James's inability to have provided a satisfactory *analysis* of the nature of extensity matters little, because, on his view, extensity is, though not clearly analysable, yet discernible in sensation. He says : 'In calling the quality in question a *sensational* quality, our own account equally disclaimed ability to analyze it, but said . . . that it was a *first* psychical thing. This is merely a question of probable fact, which the reader may decide'.[40] Here, however, the following observations may be made :

First, if extensity be a *given 'sensational quality'*, it cannot be a mere matter of 'probable fact'.

Secondly, even as acute a psychological observer as Bradley (to refer to him again) reports :

> And my experience is this. Whenever I observe I either get something which seems to imply space right out, or else I get something which seems not to have even extensity. I can find volume everywhere – that I do not doubt – but not all volume appears to me to come possessed of side-by-sideness, or even to have features joined and divided by any fixed order of relations. When on the other hand I dwell on my perception, it tends to become distinct spatially, without, so far as I can see, becoming merely extensive.[41]

Thirdly, James, in speaking of sensation in the case of extensity, cannot mean 'pure sensation'; for he says : *'Pure sensations can only be realized in the earliest days of life.* They are all but impossible to adults with memories and stores of associations acquired'.[42] Again, he says, no two sensations are 'exactly the same'.[43] Obviously, the sensations to which he refers in the case of extensity are adult sensations, and he says, 'Sensation in turn never takes place in adult life without Perception'.[44]

What evidence is, then, there to guarantee that in extensity there is *'the original sensation of space'* ? May not this so-called sensation be rather a *perception* than just a sensation ? At any rate, James has rendered himself incapable of denying confidently that the so-called sensation of extensity is rather an *empirical intuition* (in the wider sense of this Kantian expression)[45] in which the idea of space is already presupposed.[46]

14.1.3 Critique of Russell's perspective hypothesis

Russell is one of the staunchest critics of the Kantian account of the idea of space. In his *Our Knowledge of the External World* he accuses Kant of unusual ignorance of psychology,[47] and of consequent failure to appreciate that 'different senses have different spaces'[48] and that the one physical space is ultimately the product of 'logical construction'.[49] This theory that 'much mental labour has gone into the construction of the one all-embracing space'[50] out of the given private spaces is examined below.

Russell's doctrine of private spaces has been referred to approvingly by some critics of Kant's theory of the pure intuition of space. We have seen that Quinton is one such critic.[51] The doctrine of private spaces has for its natural complement the doctrine that the one public space is the outcome of logical construction.[52]

Russell presents his theory initially in the form of a hypothesis.[53] He assumes 'that each mind looks out upon the world, as in Leibniz's monadology, from a point of view peculiar to itself'.[54] The view of the world obtained by one percipient is accordingly different, though the difference may be very slight, from that obtained by any other. From points not occupied by any percipient, there also exist views of the world which are unperceived, but would be perceived if the points were occupied by percipients. Since a view perceived from a point is conditioned by the sense-organs, nerves, and brain of the percipient concerned, it cannot be exactly the same as an unperceived view from that point; 'but we can reasonably suppose that *some* aspect of the universe existed from that point of view, though no one was perceiving it'.[55] The system consisting of the views of the world, perceived and unperceived, is called by Russell the system of 'perspectives', and a perceived perspective, that is, a view of the world as actually perceived, is called a 'private world'.[56] The sensed contents of a private world are called 'sense-data', and the contents that would be sensed in a perspective if there were a percipient are called 'sensibilia'.[57]

It is possible, Russell says, 'to establish a correlation by similarity' between the data occurring in one perceived perspective (private world) and those occurring in another.[58] If the similarity is great, we say that they are 'near together in space', but this space is totally different from the spaces inside the private worlds and is not perceived, but is constituted by the relations between the perspectives. It is the physical space to be called 'perspective space'. Between two similar perceived perspectives, a whole series of other perspectives, of which at least some are unperceived, can be imagined; and between any two perspectives, however similar, still others more similar can be imagined. In this way the perspective space constituted of relations between perspectives can be rendered continuous and even three-dimensional.[59]

Sense-data occurring in one private world can be correlated on the basis of similarity with those occurring in the neighbouring private world; and the total system of these data along with the sensibilia that might be sensed in the perspectives continuous with the neighbouring worlds in question constitutes what is commonly called a 'thing'. The constituent sense-data and sensibilia are its aspects or appearances. A common-sense 'thing' is thus a logical construction.[60]

As to perspective space, it is 'the system of the private spaces themselves'.[61] The perceived spaces will each count as one point or element in perspective space; and they are ordered on the basis of their similarities. Suppose, certain aspects of a thing in different private worlds are selected on the basis of their similarity in a certain respect, e.g. the visual appearances of a penny which are circular, not elliptic, and arranged in a graduated series of circular appearances of increasing sizes : what is required for this purpose is a movement towards the penny.[62] In this way a whole series of perspectives is formed that describes a straight line in perspective (or, as we say, physical) space; and the penny is to be located at some place along this place : 'the perspectives in which the penny looks big will be said to be nearer to the penny than those in which it looks small'.[63] Now another straight line of perspectives in which the penny is seen end-on may be formed. The place (in perspective, i.e. physical, space) in which the two straight lines meet is 'the place (in perspective space) where the penny is'.[64] As to the correlation between a private space and the part of the all-embracing perspective or physical space, it may now be explained as follows : 'If there is an aspect of a given thing in a certain private space, then we correlate the place where this aspect is in the private space with the place where the thing is in perspective space'.[65]

Some further details in Russell's account may be omitted; for the above will suffice for purposes of a critical appraisal.

It is essential to Russell's account that the sense-data occurring in different private worlds are to be correlated *by similarity.* But in order that such correlation may be effected, it is necessary for a percipient to move in space, and to appeal to the testimony of others. Now the space in which he is supposed to move is clearly and admittedly not his private space, but the common physical space, which is called by Russell 'perspective space'. Evidently, the whole question is here begged, since perspective space is *ex hypothesi* logically constructed, and the construction pre-supposes the correlation in question, which in turn depends for its possibility upon the percipient's movement. As to the testimony of others ; it is not available unless the others are identifiable, and so locatable in the common physical or perspective space, which is for Russell yet to be constructed.

> 'The truth is', as E. E. Harris puts it,
>
> that Russell first assumes the existence and position of things in physical space, including human organisms inhabited by minds; he imagines the lines joining percipients with the things, and their intersection at the place where the things exist, and then, in imagination, he arranges his sense-data along these lines. But none of this elaborate construction could be made without the initial assumption and solely from the hard data of

> one or of any number of percipient minds. Nor has Russell shown that it is possible, from our own hard data, to infer the existence of anything else, unless that existence and its relation to our data are, in the first place, assumed. This method . . . is, therefore, an immense indulgence in *petitio principii.*[66]

The foregoing discussion of some post-Kantian accounts of the idea of space has done something to confirm the contention that this idea cannot be explained in terms of experience without already presupposing the idea.

14.2 Observations of Popper's Objection to Kant's Theory of Pure Intuition

Before bringing this Study to a close, an objection of a quite new kind to Kant's theory of pure intuition as such may be considered. The objection has been urged by Karl Popper, and is as follows :

> . . . Kant's sharp distinction between intuition and discursive thought cannot be upheld. 'Intuition', whatever it may be, is largely the product of our cultural development, and of our efforts in discursive thinking. Kant's idea of one standard type of pure intuition shared by us all (perhaps not by animals in spite of a similar perceptual outfit) can hardly be accepted. For after having trained ourselves in discursive thought, our intuitive grasp becomes utterly different from what it was before.[67]

Popper's objection draws its inspiration from Benjamin Lee Whorp's report on the Hopi Indians.[68] In the Hopi language there are no words or other devices such as grammatical forms or constructions that refer to tenses, or to the enduring or the lasting. 'After long and careful study and analysis' of this language,[69] Whorf concludes : 'In this Hopi view, time disappears and space is altered, so that it is no longer the homogeneous and instantaneous timeless space of our supposed intuition . . .'.[70] On the basis of this report, Popper criticizes Kant's theory of the pure intuition of time by saying that if the report be incorrect (which he thinks 'unlikely'), it at least shows possibilities that Kant has never considered, and that if the report be correct, 'then our intuitive grasp of time – the way in which we "see" temporal relations – would partly depend on our language and the theories and myths incorporated in it . . .'.[71] This criticism would presumably be extended to Kant's theory of the pure intuition of space also,[72] because, as noted above, Whorf reports that in the Hopi view our picture of space also 'is altered'.

Now, in so far as Popper's criticism is based on an appeal to the Hopi language, it hardly proves anything. *What* the Hopi Indians do or can perceive and conceive is to be distinguished from *how* they express themselves in language (unless, however, one is prepared to accept the view that intuition and conception are the same as language). It is true that language is partly an index to what one perceives and conceives; but there are also 'non-linguistic behavioral criteria' for ascribing to a person a certain conceptual ability and perceptual capacity.[73] To depend entirely upon language in this matter, particularly when the language is not also ours, is surely unwarranted.

It has to be asked, moreover, whether *our* ideas (intuitions and thoughts) are expressible in the Hopi language too, or more precisely, whether there is anything in Whorf's report to rule out the possibility that Indo-European ideas relating to space and time are translatable into the Hopi language and whether there are corresponding Hopian ideas translatable into Indo-European languages. The following extract from Whorf's report is worth examining in this connexion :

> It may now be seen how the Hopi do not need to use terms that refer to space or time as such. Such terms in our language are recast into expressions of extension, operation, and cyclic process provided they refer to the solid objective realm. They are recast into expressions of subjectivity if they refer to the subjective realm – the future, the psychic-mental, the mythical period, and the invisibly distant and conjectural generally.[74]

What this passage goes to show is only the peculiarity of the Hopi language : it at any rate does not rule out intertranslatability. But if so, then one is required to be careful before drawing the conclusion that the unique style of expression debars the Hopi Indians from 'sharing' our intuitions and thoughts.

14.3 Concluding Remarks on the Study as a Whole

The arguments contained in Kant's Metaphysical Exposition of the Concept of Space have been analysed, and it has become clear that although they are brief, they have a sufficient inherent strength to absolve them from the charge that they are not arguments at all.[75] The standard objections to them have also been examined, and it has been found that the objections are not such as to justify the view widely prevalent nowadays that the Kantian arguments have been refuted beyond redemption. Some of the prominent theories that purport to provide alternatives to the Kantian account of the idea of space have been taken seriously and examined critically; the examination has shown that they are not free from what Kant regards as the fundamental error of space-empiricism, namely, the error of presupposing the very idea to be explained.

These considerations make it plain that Kant's argument and conclusion in his Metaphysical Exposition in question retain their importance to this day. The difficulties associated with the arguments have not been concealed in the present Study. Although some difficulties have been, we trust, overcome, some others (namely, those which centre round the alleged unity and infinity of space) have been only mitigated in varying degrees. Upon further reflection, the latter may reappear in more serious forms, and some fresh difficulties may crop up. But, then, this shows that the need for further reflection remains. Accordingly, Kant's arguments and conclusion in question may well be accepted at least as a reminder of the need for carrying on still further research on the nature of the consciousness of space.

NOTES :

1. Cf. M. Jammer, *Concepts of Space,* Harvard University Press, Cambridge, 1954, chap. v.
2. Kemp Smith; see note 22 (below).

3. Cf. Chapter 3.
4. John Stuart Mill, *An Examination of Sir William Hamilton's Philosophy,* Longmans, Green, and Co., London, 1889, sixth edition, p. 283.
5. *Ibidem.*
6. For a detailed extract from Bain's 'The Senses and the Intellect', original edition, pp. 113-117, see *ibid.,* pp. 273-278.
7. Cf. *ibid.,* p. 278.
8. Cited from Hamilton's 'Dissertations on Reid', p. 869, by Mill; see *ibid.,* pp. 278-279. Hamilton's objection is actually directed against Thomas Brown, but also applies, by implication, to Bain.
9. *Ibid.,* p. 279.
10. *Ibid.,* pp. 279-280.
11. *Ibid.,* p. 280.
12. Cited by Mill; see *ibid.,* p. 306. [J. P. Mahaffy's criticism is contained in the Introduction to his translation of Kuno Fischer's *Commentary on Kant's Critick of the Pure Reason,* 1866.]
13. Mill, *op. cit.,* p. 307.
14. *Ibidem.*
15. *Ibid.,* pp. 307-308.
16. H. Höffding, *Outlines of Psychology,* trans. Mary E. Lowndes, Macmillan, London, 1904, p. 202.
17. William James, *The Principles of Psychology,* authorized edition, Dover, 1950, p. 272.
18. *Ibid.,* p. 273.
19. *Ibid.,* p. 275.
20. Since great importance is sometimes attached to Lotze's local sign theory, some further references to critiques of this theory may be in order; thus, see L. T. Hobhouse, *The Theory of Knowledge,* Methuen, London, 1921, pp. 49f.; S. Alexander, *Space, Time, and Deity,* vol. II (reissued 1966), p. 169; B. Blanshard, *The Nature of Thought,* 1955, vol. I., p. 60.
21. James, *op. cit.,* pp. 276-281.
22. Kemp Smith, *Commentary,* 1918, p. 86. n.3.

23. James, *op. cit.,* p. 272.
24. *Ibid.,* p. 135.
25. *Ibidem.*
26. *Ibid.,* p. 134.
27. *Ibid.,* p. 136.
28. Still other expressions used by him are 'massive feeling', 'element of varying vastness' [*ibid.,* p. 134], and 'a feeling of absolute bigness'; *ibid.,* p. 154.
29. G. E. Moore, *Some Main Problems of Philosophy,* 1965, p. 34. [Moore's 1910-11 lectures are printed in this book.]
30. James, *op. cit.,* p. 136.
31. *Ibid.,* p. 154. (Emphasis added by James himself.)
32. To be accurate, the word 'feeling' is used by James in his book under reference (cf. vol. I, p. 186) in the wider sense of consciousness in general. In the present case, the word stands for 'sensation', as is clear from the fact that he speaks of extensity indifferently as 'sensation', (II. 135) and as 'feeling' (II. 136). [It may be pointed out incidentally that Kant assigns to the words 'sensation' (*Empfindung)* and 'feeling' (Gefühl) distinct meanings; cf. his *The Critique of Judgements,* § 3, and also Kemp Smith, *op. cit.,* pp. 82-83 and the relevant notes.]
33. Cf. G. E. Moore's use of the word 'seem' in : 'The patch of colour seemed to occupy a certain area . . . This area was also a sense-datum'. Moore, *op. cit.,* pp. 38-39.
34. F. H. Bradley, *Appearance and Reality,* paperback 1969, p. 30 n.1.
35. James, *op. cit.,* p. 136.
36. Cf. *ibid.,* p. 151.
37. For his criticism of the associationists' attempt, see *ibid.*, pp. 270-272.
38. H. W. B. Joseph, 'The Psychological Explanation of the Development of the Perception of External Objects (1.)', *Mind* N. S. 19 (1910), p. 311. Joseph's criticism is directed against the theory of extensity as defended by Stout.
39. Already quoted before; see the third para of 14.1.2.
40. James, *op. cit.,* p. 278; cf. also *ibid.,* p. 136.
41. Bradley, 'In What Sense Are Psychical States Extended ?' *Mind* N. S. 4 (1895), p. 232.
42. James, *op. cit.,* p. 7.

43. Cf. *ibid.*, p. 8.

44. *Ibid.*, p. 1.

45. On the wider sense of the Kantian expression 'empirical intuition', cf. note 62 to Chapter 2 (p. 70).

46. For a defence of Kant's *'a priori* theory of Space' against James's attack, cf. also H. W. Carr, 'Is the Knowledge of Space *A Priori* ?' (a symposium article), *Proceedings of the Aristotelian Society* 3 (1895), pp. 119-122.

47. B. Russell, *Our Knowledge of the External World,* 1952, p. 118.

48. *Ibidem.*

49. *Ibid.*, p. 119.

50. *Ibid.*, p. 118.

51. See above, 10.1.1.1.

52. Cf. above, 10.1.2.1

53. Russell, *op. cit.*, p. 94 (cf. his expression 'Let us imagine' in the third para of the page referred to).

54. *Ibidem.*

55. *Ibid.*, p. 95.

56. *Ibidem.*

57. Russell, *Mysticism and Logic,* George Allen and Unwin, London, 1919, pp. 148ff.

58. Russell, *Our Knowledge of the External World,* p. 96.

59. *Ibidem.*

60. *Ibidem.*

61. *Ibid.*, p. 97.

62. *Ibidem.*

63. *Ibid.*, p. 98.

64. *Ibidem.*

65. *Ibid.*, p. 99.

66. Errol E. Harris, *Nature, Mind and Modern Science,* George Allen and Unwin, London, 1968, pp. 291-292.

67. Karl R. Popper, *Objective Knowledge : An Evolutionary Approach,* Clarendon Press, Oxford, 1973, p. 135 (first para).

    [Popper's objection to Kant's theory of pure intuition is made *from the evolutionary standpoint.* An objection *from the same standpoint* to Kant's apriorism regarding the idea of space is, as is well known, that this idea is a priori to the individual, but a posteriori to the race; see Herbert Spencer, *The Principles of Psychology,* Williams and Norgate, London, 1899, 4th ed., vol. II, p. 195. For an incisive criticism of Spencer's view in question, see Höffding, *op. cit.,* pp. 354-356.]

68. Cf. Popper, *op. cit.,* p. 135 (second para).
69. Benjamin L. Whorf, 'An American Indian Model of the Universe', in Richard M. Gale, ed., *The Philosophy of Time : A Collection of Essays,* Macmillan, London, 1968, p. 378.
70. *Ibid.,* p. 379.
71. Popper, *loc., cit.*
72. Cf. Popper's expression 'Intuition in general, and the theory of time in particular'; *ibid.,* p. 134.
73. Gale, *op. cit.,* p. 302.
74. Whorf, *op. cit.,* p. 386.
75. See Preface, second paragraph.

BIBLIOGRAPHY

1. Alexander, S., *Space, Time, and Deity,* 2 vols., Humanities Press, New York, reprinted, 1950 by special arrangement with the Macmillan Company; reissued, Macmillan, London, 1966.
2. Allison, H. E., *The Kant-Eberhard Controversy : An English translation together with supplementary materials and a historico-analytic introduction to Immanuel Kant's On a Discovery According to which Any New Critique of Pure Reason Has Been Made Superfluous by an Earlier One : Uber eine Entdeckung nach der alle neue Kritik der reinen Vernunft durch eine altere entbehrliche gemacht werden soll,* Johns Hopkins, Baltimore, 1973.
3. Aristotle, 'de Anima', in *Aristotle's de Anima in the Version of William of Moerbeke and the Commentary of St. Thomas Aquinas,* trans. K. Foster and S. Humphries, Yale University Press, New Haven, 1959.
4. Ayer, Sir A. J., *The Problem of Knowledge,* Penguin, Harmondsworth, 1977.
5. Baker, J. T., 'Henry More and Kant : A Note to the Second Argument on Space in the Transcendental Aesthetic', *Philosophical Review* 46 (1937), pp. 298-306.
6. Beck, L. W., *Studies in the Philosophy of Kant,* Bobbs-Merrill, Indianapolis, 1965.
7. Beck, L. W., *Early German Philosophy : Kant and His Predecessors,* Belknap, Cambridge, Mass., 1969.
8. Beck, L. W., (ed.) *Proceedings of the Third International Kant Congress* (held at the University of Rochester, March 30–April 4, 1970), D. Reidel, Dordrecht-Holland, 1972.
9. Beck, L. W., 'Lovejoy as a Critic of Kant', *Journal of the History of Ideas* 33 (1972), pp. 471-484.
10. Beck, L. W., (ed.) *Kant's Theory of Knowledge,* D. Reidel, Dordrecht-Holland, 1974, Preface, vii.
11. Bennett, J. F., *Kant's Analytic,* Cambridge University Press, London, 1966.
12. Bird, G., *Kant's Theory of Knowledge,* Routledge & Kegan Paul, London, 1962.

13. Blanshard, B., *The Nature of Thought,* 2 vols., George Allen & Unwin, London, 1955.

14. Bradley, F. H., 'In What Sense Are Psychical States Extended ?' *Mind* N. S. 4. (1895), pp. 225-235.

15. Bradley, F. H., *Appearance and Realityl,* 2nd ed., Oxford University Press, London, 1969.

16. Brittan, G. G., Jr., *Kant's Theory of Science,* Princeton University Press, Princeton, New Jersey, 1978.

17. Broad, C. D., *Scientific Thought,* Routledge & Kegan Paul, London, 1952.

18. Broad, C. D., 'Hume's Doctrine of Space', *Proceedings of the British Academy* 47 (1961), pp. 161-176.

19. Broad, C. D., *Kant : An Introduction,* ed. C. Lewy, Cambridge University Press, Cambridge, London, 1979.

20. Broad, C. D., *Leibniz : An Introduction,* ed. C. Lewy, Cambridge University Press, London, reprinted, 1979.

21. Buchdahl, G., *Metaphysics and the Philosophy of Science : The Classical Origins : Descartes to Kant,* Basil Blackwell, Oxford, 1969.

22. Buchdahl, G., 'The Conception of Lawlikeness in Kant's Philosophy of Science', in Beck, (ed.) *Proceedings of the Third International Kant Congress,* 1972 (see above), pp. 149-171.

23. Caird, E., *The Critical Philosophy of Immanuel Kant,* 2. vols., 2nd ed., James Maclehose & Sons, Glasgow, 1909.

24. Calkins, Mary Whiton, *The Persistent Problems of Philosophy,* 4th revised ed., Macmillan, London, 1923.

25. Carr, H. W., 'Is the Knowledge of Space *A Priori ?' Proceedings of the Aristotelian Society* 3 (1895), pp. 119-122.

26. Cassirer, E., *Substance and Function* and *Einstein's Theory of Relativity* (both books bound as one), trans. W. C. Swabey and Marie Collins Swabey, Dover, New York, 1953.

27. Cassirer, H. W. *Kant's First Critique : An Appraisal of the Permanent Significance of Kant's Critique of Pure Reason,* George Allen & Unwin, London, 1978; Humanities Press, New York, 1978.

28. Cousin, V., *The Philosophy of Kant,* trans. A. G. Henderson, Chapman's Quarterly Series, No. V, John Chapman, London, 1854.

29. Descartes, R., 'The Principles of Philosophy [1644], in *A Discourse on Method, etc.*, pp. 145-228; trans. J. Veitch, 'Everyman's Library, No. 570', J. M. Dent and Sons, London, 1949.

30. Dryer, D. P., *Kant's Solution for Verification in Metaphysics*, George Allen & Unwin, London, 1966.

31. Economos, J. J., 'Kant's Theory of Concepts. The A-Priori-Empirical Distinction Reconstituted', *Kant-Studien* 64 (1973), pp. 63-70.

32. Eddington, Sir A. S., *The Nature of the Physical World*, Cambridge University Press, 1944.

33. Ewing, A. C., *A Short Commentary on Kant's Critique of Pure Reason*, Methuen, London, 1938.

34. Fischer, Kuno, *A Commentary on Kant's Critick of the Pure Reason*, trans. J. P. Mahaffy, Longmans, Green & Co., London, 1866.

35. Fullerton, G. S., 'The Doctrine of Space and Time', *Philosophical Review* 10 (1901), pp. 113-123.

36. Gale, R. M., (ed.) *The Philosophy of Time*, Macmillan, London, 1968.

37. Garnett, C. B., Jr., *The Kantian Philosophy of Space*, Columbia University Press, New York, 1939.

38. Gram, M. S., *Kant : Disputed Questions*, Quadrangle, Chicago, 1967.

39. Gram, M. S., *Kant, Ontology, and the A Priori*, Evanston, 1968.

40. Grayeff, F., *Kant's Theoretical Philosophy : A Commentary to the Central Part of the 'Critique of Pure Reason'*, trans. D. Walford, Manchester University Press, Barnes & Noble Inc., New York, 1970.

41. Groos, K., 'Hat Kant Hume Treatise gelesen ?' *Kant-Studien* 5 (1900), pp. 177-181.

42. Handyside, J., (trans.) *Kant's Inaugural Dissertation and Early Writings on Space*, Open Court, Chicago, 1929.

43. Harris, E. E., *The Foundations of Metaphysics in Science*, George Allen & Unwin, London, 1965.

44. Harris, E. E., *Nature, Mind and Modern Science*, George Allen & Unwin, London, 1968.

45. Hartnack, J., *Kant's Theory of Knowledge*, trans. M. H. Hartshorne, Macmillan, London, 1968.

46. Hintikka, J., 'On Kant's Notion of Intuition (Anschauung)', in Penelhum and MacIntosh, (eds.), *The First Critique*, etc., 1969 (see below), pp. 38-53.

47. Hintikka, J., 'Kantian Intuitio', *Inquiry* 15 (1972), pp. 341-345.

48. Hintikka, J., *Logic, Language-Games, and Information : Kantian Themes in the Philosophy of Logic,* Clarendon, Oxford, 1973.

49. Hobhouse, L. T., *The Theory of Knowledge : A Contribution to Some Problems of Logic and Metaphysics,* 3rd ed., Methuen, London, 1921.

50. Höffding, H., *Outlines of Psychology,* trans. Mary E. Lowndes, Macmillan, London, 1904.

51. Howell, R., 'Intuition, Synthesis, and Individuation in the *Critique of Pure Reason',* Nous 7 (1973), pp. 207-232.

52. Hughes, G. E. and Cresswell, M. J., *An Introduction to Modal Logic,* Methuen, London, 1972.

53. Hume, D., *A Treatise of Human Nature,* London, 1739-40; ed. L. A. Selby-Bigge, Clarendon, Oxford, 1967.

54. James, W., *The Principles of Psychology,* 2 vols., Dover Publications Inc., 1950.

55. Jammer, M., *Concepts of Space,* Harvard University Press, Cambridge, Mass., 1954.

56. Johnson, W. E., *Logic,* in Three Parts, Dover, New York, 1964.

57. Joseph, H. W. B., 'The Psychological Explanation of the Development of the Perception of External Objects', *Mind* N. S. 19 (1910), pp. 305-321.

58. Joseph, H. W. B., *An Introduction to Logic,* 2nd ed., revised, Clarendon, Oxford, 1967.

59. Juchem, H.-G., 'On the Development of the Term "Intuition" in the Pre-Critical Writings of Kant', in Beck (ed.) *Proceedings of the Third International Kant Congress,* 1972 (see above), pp. 685-692.

60. Kac M. and Ulam S., *Mathematics and Logic : Retrospect and Prospects,* Penguin, Harmondsworth, 1971.

61. Kant, I., : Nova dilucidatio' [1755], trans. F. E. England, in *Kant's Conception of God : A Critical Exposition of Its Metaphysical Development Together with a Translation of the Nova Dilucidatio,* pp. 211-253, George Allen & Unwin, London, 1929. (Referred to in this work as the *Nova Dilucidatio.)*

62. Kant, I., 'The Mistaken Subtility of the Four Syllogistic Figures' [1762], trans. T. K. Abbott, in *Kant's Introduction to Logic and his Essay on the Mistaken Subtility of the Four Figures,* pp. 79-95, Vision Press, London, 1963.

63. Kant, I., 'Enquiry Concerning the Clarity of the Principles of Natural Theology and Morals' [Prize Essay, written 1762, published 1764], trans. G. B. Kerferd and D. E. Walford, in *Kant : Selected Pre-Critical Writings and Correspondence with Beck,* pp. 3-35, Manchester University Press, New York, 1968; also trans. L.W. Beck, in *Kant's Critique of Practical Reason and Other Writings in Moral Philosophy,* University of Chicago Press, Chicago, 1949.

64. Kant, I., 'On the First Ground of the Distinction of Regions in Space' [1768], trans. Handyside, in *Kant's Inaugural Dissertation and Early Writings on Space,* 1929 (see above), pp. 19-29. (Sometimes referred to in this work as Kant's essay of 1768.)

65. Kant, I., 'Dissertation on the Form and Principles of the Sensible and Intelligible World' [1770], *ibid.,* pp. 35-85. (Referred to in this work as *Inaugural Dissertation.)*

66. Kant, I., *Kritik der reinen Vernunft* [1781 and 1787], hg. v. T. Valentiner, DER PHILOSOPHISCHEN BIBLIOTHEK BAND 37, Felix Meiner, Leipzig, 1922. (Referred to in this work as *Kritik.)*

67. Kant, I., *Critique of Pure Reason, trans. :*

(i) J. M. D. Meiklejohn, Colonial Press, New York, 1900;

(ii) F. Max Müller, Macmillan, New York, 1902;

(iii) N. Kemp Smith, Macmillan, London, 1963.

(Referred to in this work as *Critique.)*

68. Kant, I., *Prolegomena zu* einer jeden künftigen Metaphysik, die als Wissenschaft wird auftreten konnen [1783], hg. v. K. Vorlander, DER PHILOSOPHISCHEN BIBLIOTHEK BAND 40, Felix Meiner, Leipzig, 1920. (Referred to as *Prolegomena.)*

69. Kant, I., *Prolegomena to Any Future Metaphysics,* a revision of the Carus translation with an introduction by L. W. Beck, Bobbs-Merrill, Indianapolis, 1976. (Referred to as *Prolegomena.)*

70. Kant, I., 'Metaphysical Foundations of Natural Science' [1786], trans. E. B. Bax, in *Kant's Prolegomena and Metaphysical Foundations of Natural Science,* pp. 135-245, George Bell and Sons, London, 1883, (Referred to as *Metaphysical Foundations of Natural Science.)*

71. Kant, I., *The Critique of Judgement* [1790], trans. J. C. Meredith, Clarendon, Oxford, 1980.

72. Kant, I., 'On a Discovery According to which Any New Critique of Pure Reason Has Been Made Superfluous by an Earlier One' [1790],

trans. Allison, in *The Kant-Eberhard Controversy,* 1973 (see above), pp. 105-160. (Referred to in this work as *On a Discovery.*)

73. Kant, I., *Anthropology from a Pragmatic Point of View* [1798], trans. Mary J. Gregor, Nijhoff, The Hague, 1974.

74. Kant, I., *Logic* [first published in 1800 in an edition by G. B. Jasche], trans. R. S. Hartman and W. Schwarz, Bobbs-Merrill, Indianapolis and New York, 1974.

75. Kant, I., 'Reflexionen', in B. Erdmann, (ed.) *Reflexionen Kants zur kritischen Philosophie,* 2 Bande, Leipzig, Bd. I, 1882; Bd. II, 1884.

76. Kant, I., 'Correspondence', in *Kant : Philosophical Correspondence 1759-99,* ed. and trans. A. Zweig, University of Chicago Press, Chicago & London, 1967.

77. Kemp, J., *The Philosophy of Kant,* Oxford University Press, London, 1968.

78. Kemp Smith, N., *A Commentary to Kant's 'Critique of Pure Reason',* Macmillan, London, 1918.

79. Kemp Smith, N., *The Philosophy of David Hume,* Macmillan, London, 1960.

80. Korner, S., *Kant,* Penguin, Harmondsworth, 1960.

81. Koyré, A., *From the Closed World to the Infinite Universe,* Johns Hopkins, Baltimore, 1968.

82. Koyré, A., *Newtonian Studies,* Phoenix ed., University of Chicago Press, Chicago, 1968.

83. Laird, J., *Hume's Philosophy of Human Nature,* Methuen, London, 1932.

84. Latta, R., *Leibniz : The Monadololgy and Other Philosophical Writings,* Clarendon, Oxford, 1898.

85. Lectere, I., 'The Meaning of "Space" in Kant', in Beck, (ed.) Proceedings of the Third International Kant Congress, *1972* (see above), pp. 393-400.

86. Leibniz, G. W., 'On Analysis Situs' [1679], in Loemker, (trans. and ed.) *Gottfried Wilhelm Leibniz : Philosophical Papers and Letters,* 1956 (see below), I, pp. 390-396.

87. Leibniz, G. W., 'First Truths' [*ca.* 1680-84], *ibid.,* I. pp. 411-417.

88. Leibniz, G. W., 'On the Elements of Natural Science' [*ca.* 1682-84], *ibid.,* I, pp. 426-447.

89. Leibniz, G. W., 'Discourse on Metaphysics' [1686], *ibid.,* I, pp. 464-506.

90. Leibniz, G. W., 'Correspondence with Arnauld' [1686-87], *ibid.,* I, pp. 507-537.

91. Leibniz, G. W., 'On What Is Independent of Sense and of Matter' ['Letter to Queen Sophia Charlotte of Prussia, 1702'], *ibid.,* II, pp. 888-898.

92. Leibniz, G. W., 'The Controversy between Leibniz and Clarke' [1715-16], *ibid.,* II, pp. 1095-1169.

93. Leibniz, G. W., *New Essays Concerning Human Understanding* [Written in the 1690's, but first published in 1765], trans. A. G. Langley, 2nd ed., Open Court, Chicago and London, 1916; also partially translated by Latta (see above), pp. 355-404.

94. Locke, D., 'Strawson's Auditory Universe', *Philosophical Review* 70 (1961), pp. 518-532.

95. Locke, D., *Perception and Our Knowledge of the External World,* George Allen & Unwin, London, 1967.

96. Loemker, L. E., (trans. and ed.) *Gottfried Wilhelm Leibniz : Philosophical Papers and Letters,* 2 vols., University of Chicago Press, Chicago and Illinois, 1956.

97. Lotze, H., Metaphysics (in Three Books, Ontology, Cosmology, and Psychology), Eng. trans. ed. Bernard Bosanquet, Clarendon, Oxford, 1884.

98. Lovejoy, A. O., 'Kant's Antithesis of Dogmatism and Criticism', in Gram, (ed.) *Kant : Disputed Question,* 1967 (see above), pp. 105-130.

99. Malpas, R. M. P., 'The Location of Sound', in R. J. Butler, (ed.) *Analytical Philosophy, Second Series,* 131ff., Basil Blackwell, Oxford, 1965.

100. Martin, G., *Kant's Metaphysics and Theory of Science,* trans. P. G. Lucas, Manchester University Press, Printed in Great Britain by Butler and Tanner Ltd, 1955.

101. Mathews, H. E., 'Strawson on Transcendental Idealism', in Walker, (ed.) *Kant on Pure Reason,* 1982 (see below), pp. 132-149.

102. Moore, G. E., *Philosophical Papers,* George Allen & Unwin, London, 1959.

103. Moore, G. E., *Some Main Problems of Philosophy,* George Allen & Unwin, London, 1965 (fourth impression).

104. Mill, J. S., *An Examination of Sir William Hamilton's Philosophy,* 6th ed., Longmans, Green, and Co., London, 1889.

105. Pap, A., *Elements of Analytic Philosophy,* Macmillan, New York, 1949.

106. Parkinson, G. H. R., *Logic and Reality in Leibniz's Metaphysics,* Clarendon, Oxford, 1965.

107. Persons, C., 'Kant's Philosophy of Arithmetic', in Morgenbesser, Suppes and White, (eds.), *Philosophy, Science and Method : Essays in Honour of Ernest Nagel,* St. Martin's Press, New York, 1969, pp. 568-594; also in Walker, (ed.) *Kant on Pure Reason,* 1982 (see below), pp. 13-40.

108. Paton, H. J., *Kant's Metaphysic of Experience : A Commentary on the First Half of the 'Kritik der reinen Vernunft',* 2 vols., George Allen & Unwin, London, 1951.

109. Paton, H. J., 'The Key to Kant's Deduction of the Categories', in Gram, (ed.) *Kant : Disputed Questions,* 1967 (see above), pp. 247-268.

110. Penelhum, T. and MacIntosh, J. J., (eds.) *The First Critique : Reflections on Kant's 'Critique of Pure Reason',* Wadsworth, Belmont, 1969.

111. Popper, K. R., *Objective Knowledge : An Evolutionary Approach,* Clarendon, Oxford, reprinted, 1973.

112. Popper, K. R., *The Logic of Scientific Discovery,* Hutchinson of London, 8th impression, Oct. 1975.

113. Prichard, H. A., *Kant's Theory of Knowledge,* Clarendon, Oxford, 1909.

114. Quinton, A., 'Spaces and Times' *Philosophy* 37 (1962), pp. 130-147.

115. Reichenbach, H., *The Philosophy of Space and Time,* trans. Maria Reichenbach and J. Freund, with introductory remarks by R. Carnap, Dover, New York, 1957, copyright © 1958 by Maria Reichenbach.

116. Remnant, P., 'Incongruent Counterparts and Absolute Space', *Mind* N. S. 72 (1963), pp. 393-399.

117. Riehl, A., *Der philosophische Kritizismus : Geschichte und System,* 2 Bande, Bd. I : 'Geschichte des philosophischen Kritizismus', 3. Aufl., Alfred Kroner Verlag in Leipzig, 1924.

118. Rotenstreich, N., *Experience and Its Systematization : Studies in Kant,* Nijhoff, The Hague, 1965.

119. Russell, B., *Mysticism and Logic,* George Allen & Unwin, London, 1919.

120. Russell, B., *Human Knowledge : Its Scope and Limits,* 6th paperback printing, Simon and Schuster, New York, 1948.

121. Russell, B., *A Critical Exposition of the Philosophy of Leibniz,* George Allen & Unwin, London, 1949.

122. Russell, B., *Our Knowledge of the External World,* George Allen & Unwin, London, 1952.

123. Russell, B., *The Principles of Mathematics,* George Allen & Unwin, London, 1956.

124. Russell, B., *Logic and Knowledge, Essays 1901-1950,* ed. R. C. Marsh, George Allen & Unwin, London, 1956.

125. Russell, B., *History of Western Philosophy,* George Allen & Unwin, London, 1962.

126. Russell, B., *An Inquiry into Meaning and Truth,* the William James Lectures for 1940 delivered at Harvard University, Penguin, Harmondsworth, 1965.

127. Russell, B., *The Problems of Philosophy,* Oxford University Press, London, 1968.

128. Schlick, M., 'On the Relation Between Psychological and Physical Concepts', in H. Feigl and W. Sellars (eds.) *Readings in Philosophical Analysis,* pp. 393-407, Appleton-Century-Crofts, New York, 1949.

129. Schrader, G., 'Kant's Theory of Concepts', in Wolff, (ed.) *Kant : A Collection of Critical Essays,* 1968 (see below), pp. 134-155.

130. Sellars, W., *Science and Metaphysics : Variations on Kantian Themes,* Routledge & Kegan Paul, London, 1968.

131. Sidgwick, H., *Lectures on the Philosophy of Kant and Other Philosophical Lectures and Essays,* Macmillan, London, 1905.

132. Smith, A. H., *A Treatise on Knowledge,* Clarendon, Oxford, 1943.

133. Smith, A. H., *Kantian Studies,* Clarendon, Oxford, 1947.

134. Spencer, H., *The Principles of Psychology,* vols. 2, 4th ed., Williams and Norgate, London, 1899.

135. Stadler, I., 'Perception and Perfection in Kant's Aesthetics', in Wolff,

(ed.) *Kant : A Collection of Critical Essays,* 1968 (see below) pp. 339-384.

136. Stout, G. F., 'Is the Knowledge of Space *A Priori ?' Proceedings of the Aristotelian Society* 3 (1895), pp. 130-133.

137. Strawson, Sir P. F., *The Bounds of Sense : An Essay on Kant's 'Critique of Pure Reason',* Methuen, London, 1966.

138. Strawson, Sir P. F., 'Bennett on Kant's Analytic', *Philosophical Review* 77 (1968), pp. 332-339.

139. Strawson, Sir P. F., *Individuals : An Essay in Descriptive Metaphysics,* U. P. 81. Methuen, London, 1969.

140. Swinburne, R., *Space and Time,* Macmillan, London, 1968.

141. Taylor, A. E., *Elements of Metaphysics,* U. P. 25, Methuen, London, 1961.

142. Thompson, M., 'Singular Terms and Intuitions in Kant's Epistemology', *Review of Metaphysics* 26 (1972), pp. 314-343.

143. Vaihinger, H., *Kommentar zu Kants Kritik der reinen Vernunft,* 2 Bande, Spemann, Stuttgart, 1881-1892.

144. de Vleeschauwer, H.-J., *The Development of Kantian Thought – The History of a Doctrine,* trans. A. R. C. Duncan, Nelson, Edinburgh, 1962.

145. Walker, R. C. S., *Kant,* Routledge & Kegan Paul, London, 1978.

146. Walker, R. C. S., (ed.) *Kant on Pure Reason,* Oxford University Press, Oxford, 1982.

147. Walsh, W. H., *Reason and Experience,* Clarendon, Oxford, 1963.

148. Ward, K., 'The Unity of Space and Time', *Philosophy* 42 (1967), pp. 68-74.

149. Watson, J., *Kant and His English Critics : A Comparison of Critical and Empirical Philosophy,* James Maclehose, Glasgow, 1881.

150. Watson, J., *The Philosophy of Kant Explained,* James Maclehose and Sons, Glasgow, 1908.

151. Weldon, T. D., *Introduction to Kant's 'Critique of Pure Reason',* Clarendon, Oxford, 1945.

152. Weldon, T. D., 'Kant's Perceptual Vocabulary', in Penelhum and MacIntosh, (eds.), *The First Critique,* etc. 1969 (see above), pp. 34-37. [Title supplied by editors.]